Bloom's Modern Critical Interpretations

Bloom's Modern Critical Interpretations

The Tale of Genji

Edited and with an introduction by
Harold Bloom
Sterling Professor of the Humanities
Yale University

CHELSEA HOUSE
PUBLISHERS
A Haights Cross Communications ✔ Company

Philadelphia

©2004 by Chelsea House Publishers, a subsidiary of
Haights Cross Communications.

A Haights Cross Communications ✛ Company

Introduction © 2004 by Harold Bloom.

Printed and bound in the United States of America

10 9 8 7 6 5 4 3 2 1

Library of Congress Cataloging-in-Publication applied for.

The Tale of Genji / edited and with an introduction by Harold Bloom.
    p. cm. — (Bloom's modern critical interpretations)
Includes bibliographical references and index.
  ISBN 0-7910-7584-2
 1. Murasaki Shikibu, b. 978? Genji monogatari. I. Bloom, Harold. II.
Series.
        PL788.4.G43 T33 2003
        895.6'314—dc22

                                        2003019987

Contributing editor: Amy Sickels

Cover design by Terry Mallon

Cover: "Scene fifty-four of *Tale of Genji*," Library of Congress, LC-USZC4-10706

Layout by EJB Publishing Services

Chelsea House Publishers
1974 Sproul Road, Suite 400
Broomall, PA 19008-0914

www.chelseahouse.com

Contents

Editor's Note

My Introduction ponders the fusion of irony and self-destructive erotic longing in Lady Murasaki's enigmatic masterwork.

Donald Keene, eminent historian of Japanese literature, gives an overview of *The Tale of Genji*, stressing its ongoing centrality in Japanese literature.

Proust is invoked by Doris G. Bargen as an apt analogue to *The Tale of Genji*, after which Richard Bowring notes Murasaki's use of poetry to characterize the essential nature of crucial relationships.

Norma Field, charting the splendors of longing in the saga, allows us to see how his erotic disasters mold the hero, while Amy Vladeck Heinrich returns us to the function of poetry in this novel.

The question of narrative voice is investigated by Amanda Mayer Stinchecum, after which the distinguished scholar Ivan Morris explores the intricacies of court existence.

Substitution, whether through erotic or narrator surrogates, is seen as an informing principle of *The Tale* by H. Richard Okada, while Esperanza Ramirez-Christensen appreciates Murasaki's lyricism.

Royall Tyler illuminates the complex agon between Genji and his tragic love, Murasaki, after which Haruo Shirane meditates upon kingship in *The Tale*.

In this volume's final essay, John R. Wallace compares Lady Murasaki's aesthetic stance with that of the modern novelist Mishima Yukio, finding in him a violent negation that may share more with European eroticism.

HAROLD BLOOM

Introduction

And when I play my *koto* rather badly to myself in the cool breeze of the evening, I worry lest someone might hear me and recognize how I am just "adding to the sadness of it all"; how vain and sad of me. So now both my instruments, the one with thirteen strings and the one with six, stand in a miserable, sooty little closet still ready-strung. Through neglect—I forgot, for example, to ask that the bridges be removed on rainy days—they have accumulated dust and lean between the cupboard and a pillar.

There is also a pair of larger cupboards crammed to bursting point. One is full of old poems and tales that have become the home for countless insects which scatter in such an unpleasant manner that no one cares to look at them any more; the other is full of Chinese books that have lain unattended ever since he who carefully collected them passed away. Whenever my loneliness threatens to overwhelm me, I take out one or two of them to look at; but my women gather together behind my back. "It's because she goes on like this that she is so miserable. What kind of lady is it who reads Chinese books?" they whisper. "In the past it was not even the done thing to read sutras!" "Yes," I feel like replying, "but I've never met anyone who lived longer just because they believed in superstitions!" But that would be thoughtless of me. There is some truth in what they say.

(translated by Richard Bowring)

Lady Murasaki, in her *Diary* as in *The Tale of Genji*, conducts an almost Proustian search for lost time, which is appropriate in a writer who truly was the genius of longing. The splendid Genji paradoxically is destroyed by his own incessant longing for the renewed experience of falling in love. When the significantly named Murasaki, the authentic love of his life, wastes away as an involuntary reaction to having been replaced, Genji does nor survive her for more than a decent interval.

The Tale of Genji is eons away from Proust, yet I wonder whether Lady Murasaki's incessant longing is not a valid analogue for Proust's search. In Proust, love dies but jealousy is eternal; the narrator still quests for every possible detail of Albertine's lesbian attachments even though his memories of his dead beloved have become very tenuous. Jealousy is subdued in Lady Murasaki, as exclusive female possession of the male is not possible.

I would hesitate to affirm that the perspective of *The Tale of Genji* is entirely female, so firmly does Lady Murasaki identify herself with "the shining Genji." And yet the exaltation of longing over fulfillment throughout the novel may be an indication that the male vision of sexual love is essentially secondary.

Lady Murasaki's own splendor, like Proust's, is her gathering wisdom, in which a mingled spiritual and aesthetic nostalgia takes the place of a waning social order. To be a genius of longing, you must excel in narrative patience, and it is astonishing how well she varies her stories. (...)

Lady Murasaki's vast romance narrative has been part of literary culture in English since Arthur Waley completed his version in 1933. I read Waley's *Genji* a half-century ago, and retained vivid impressions of it, but have only now read Edward G. Seidensticker's very different translation, though it has been available since 1976. Rereading Waley alongside Seidensticker is instructive: *Genji* is so nuanced and splendid a work that one hopes for many more versions. The German translation by Oscar Bent (1966) provides yet another reflection of Murasaki's immense tale, and enriches a reader who knows neither medieval nor modern Japanese. One gathers that Murasaki's language, in relation to our Japanese contemporaries, is somewhere between Old English and Middle English in regard to us. She is not as distant as *Beowulf,* nor so close as Chaucer; modern Japanese translations therefore are essential for current readers.

Doubtless *The Tale of Genji* is more culturally remote from us than Waley, Seidensticker, and Benl make it seem, but literary genius is uniquely capable of universality, and I have the strong illusion, as I read, that Lady Murasaki is as available to my understanding as Jane Austen is, or Marcel Proust, or Virginia Woolf. Austen is a secular novelist, and so is Murasaki: her romance, as it develops, seems more and more a novel, except that it has a bewildering plethora of protagonists. There are almost fifty principal characters, and keeping clear who has been married and when, or had a sexual relationship, or is secretly someone's father or daughter, can be rather difficult. In reading through Seidensticker's version of nearly eleven hundred pages (it is more faithful and less condensed than Waley's), one never loses interest, but it is difficult not to get lost. Genji, an imperial prince sent into internal exile as a commoner, is an exuberantly passionate personage, whose longings are perpetual, mutable, and impatient when thwarted. It may be more accurate to speak of "longing" than "longings." He *is* a state of longing, and evidently irresistible to the extraordinary (and extraordinarily varied) women of the court and of the provinces.

We are not to consider Genji to be a Don Juan, though he certainly manifests what Lord Byron called "mobility." Lady Murasaki herself, through her narrator, clearly finds Genji more than sympathetic; he is a figure who radiates light, and who ought to be emperor. Eros, in Murasaki and her major contemporary woman writers, is not exactly what we think we mean by "romantic love," but in obsessiveness, self-destructiveness, and overdetermination or apparent inevitability there is little pragmatic difference. Though everyone in *The Tale of Genji* is a Buddhist, and so warned by doctrine against desire, just about all of them are very susceptible indeed, Genji most of all. Renunciation, that "piercing virtue," as Emily Dickinson termed it, is resorted to only after disaster by each lady in turn, and only after many turns by the perpetually passionate Genji.

Genji, who will never be emperor, is particularly liable to sudden (and then lasting) attachments to ladies not of the first rank, thus repeating his imperial father's passion for Genji's mother, forced out of the court by the malice of more aristocratic consorts. Broken by the experience, Genji's mother dies while he is still a baby, and his eagerness for intimacy clearly has a link to this early loss. But Lady Murasaki, who, before her *Tale* is done, will have anticipated Cervantes as the first novelist, is also an accomplished ironist. Her delicious second chapter, "The Broom Tree," gives us a pragmatic symposium on love conducted by Genji and three other courtiers:

> At this point two young courtiers, a guards officer and a functionary in the ministry of rites, appeared on the scene, to

attend the emperor in his retreat. Both were devotees of the way of love and both were good talkers. To no Chujo, as if he had been waiting for them, invited their views on the question that had just been asked. The discussion progressed, and included a number of rather unconvincing points.

"Those who have just arrived at high position," said one of the newcomers, "do not attract the same sort of notice as those who were born to it. And those who were born to the highest rank but somehow do not have the right backing—in spirit they may be as proud and noble as ever, but they cannot hide their deficiencies. And so I think that they should both be put in your middle rank.

"There are those whose families are not quite of the highest rank but who go off and work hard in the provinces. They have their place in the world, though there are all sorts of little differences among them. Some of them would belong on anyone's list. So it is these days. Myself, I would take a woman from a middling family over one who has rank and nothing else. Let us say someone whose father is almost but not quite a councillor. Someone who has a decent enough reputation and comes from a decent enough family and can live in some luxury. Such people can be very pleasant. There is nothing wrong with the household arrangements, and indeed a daughter can sometimes be set out in a way that dazzles vote. I can think of several such women it would he hard to find fault with. When they go into court service, they are the ones the unexpected favors have a way of falling on. I have seen cases enough of it, I can tell you."

Lady Murasaki's irony makes us wonder as to just which are the "rather unconvincing points." In what may be the *Tale*'s ultimate irony. Genji encounters the major relationship of his life in a ten-year-old girl he calls Murasaki, whom he adopts and brings up. Her name (and the author's) refers to the aromatic lavender plant, and Genji's relationship to her is outrageous from the start:

> She thought little of her father. They had lived apart and she scarcely knew him. She was by now extremely fond of her new father. She would be the first to run out and greet him when he came home, and she would climb on his lap, and they would talk happily together, without the least constraint or embarrassment.

He was delighted with her. A clever and watchful woman can create all manner of difficulties. A man must always be on his guard, and jealousy can have the most unwelcome consequences. Murasaki was the perfect companion, a toy for him to play with. He could not have been so free and uninhibited with a daughter of his own. There are restraints upon paternal intimacy. Yes, he had come upon a remarkable little treasure.

Again we are given an ironic pathos, which seems to me Lady Murasaki's most characteristic tonality. She herself came from the second level of court aristocrats, her family having fallen gradually from much higher rank. When we first meet the child who will be renamed Murasaki by the infatuated Genji, her nurse is called Shonagon, which seems to me an irony aimed at Sei Shonagon, whose *The Pillow Book of Sei Shonagon* is the chief rival to *The Tale of Genji*, and who is deprecated in Lady Murasaki's *Diary* as being "dreadfully conceited" in her supposed display of false erudition in the use of Chinese characters, almost as if she were the Ezra Pound of her day.

Lady Murasaki, more than nine hundred years before Freud, understood that all erotic transferences were substitute-formations for earlier attachments. Plato, even earlier, thought the same, though for him the archetypal relationship was to the Idea, rather than to the parental image. When the child Murasaki is fourteen, Genji takes her:

It was a tedious time. He no longer had any enthusiasm for the careless night wanderings that had once kept him busy. Murasaki was much on his mind. She seemed peerless, the nearest he could imagine to his ideal. Thinking that she was no longer too young for marriage, he had occasionally made amorous overtures; but she had not seemed to understand. They had passed their time in games of Go and *hentsugi*. She was clever and she had many delicate ways of pleasing him in the most trivial diversions. He had not seriously thought of her as a wife. Now he could not restrain himself. It would be a shock, of course.

What had happened? Her women had no way of knowing when the line had been crossed. One morning Genji was up early and Murasaki stayed on and on in bed. It was not at all like her to sleep so late. Might she be unwell? As he left for his own rooms, Genji pushed an inkstone inside her bed curtains.

At length, when no one else was near, she raised herself from

her pillow and saw beside it a tightly folded bit of paper. Listlessly
she opened it. There was only this verse, in a casual hand:
  "Many have been the nights we have spent together
  Purposelessly, these coverlets between us."

As her foster father, Genji has brought a figurative stigma of incest to
Murasaki, and she herself will never become a mother. The narrator, as
always, makes no judgments, and the violated fourteen-year-old makes the
transition into a phase of happiness with Genji, but such a phase is purely
ironic. Genji, perpetually questing for what is not to be found, goes on to
other consorts, while holding Murasaki in place. But she is a remarkable
consciousness, who will not abide with him, and she turns to Buddhist
devotion as the path back to herself, and to her own childhood. Since Genji
will not permit her to become a Buddhist nun, she arranges a ceremony in
honor of the Lotus Sutra, which allows women their part in salvation. And
after that, she lapses into a long day's dying to ease her pain, as John Milton
might have termed it. With her beauty as a child returned to her, she dies,
leaving Genji properly bereft.

Lady Murasaki no more blames Genji than she would chide one season
for replacing another. And yet, after this, he is on the path that must lead
finally to life's triumph over him. After another year, he begins to make ready
to depart, and dies between chapters 41 and 42, as though Lady Murasaki
herself were too attached to her creation to represent his dying. Chapter 42
begins, "The shining Genji was dead, and there was no one quite like him."
The novel will go on for another three hundred and fifty pages, and the
genius of an ironic pathos continues to manifest itself, but it becomes
another tale.

The book became, and still is, a kind of secular Bible for Japanese
culture. What *Don Quixote* almost uniquely was to Miguel de Unamuno, *The
Tale of Genji* has been for a myriad of Japanese men and women of aesthetic
sensibility. As a secular scripture, Lady Murasaki's huge romance-novel takes
on a very ambiguous status, because it is almost impossible to define the
book's relationship to Buddhism. Desire, the longing for another person, is
almost the primal fault in most versions of Buddhism. Longing destroys
Genji, and the best among his women. But it is the essence of Genji, and as
readers we are captured by him, and by the answering passion that he evokes.
The best book I have found on Lady Murasaki's masterwork, by Norma
Field, accurately and eloquently is titled *The Splendor of Longing in the "Tale
of Genji"* (1987). And there, I think, is where Murasaki's genius must be
located, in that oxymoronic "splendor of longing." A longing is a yearning

that never can be fulfilled, a desire never to be appeased. After reading Lady Murasaki, you never feel the same again about loving, or falling in love. She is the genius of longing, and we are her students even before we come to her.

DONALD KEENE

The Tale of Genji

Genji *Monogatari* (The Tale of Genji) is considered to be the supreme masterpiece of Japanese literature. The author, Murasaki Shikibu, borrowed much from earlier monogatari and collections of waka, and especially from the diaries of court ladies, but her novel rises in solitary grandeur like a great mountain over lesser hills. In every age since *The Tale of Genji* was first written and circulated at the court it has been accorded special respect, and it would not be possible to list all the other works of Japanese literature it has inspired. During the centuries after the completion of *The Tale of Genji* the court life it so superbly evoked was overshadowed by the rise to power of the samurai class, and at times its very existence seemed to be imperiled; but the fierce warriors who threatened the way of life at the court generally did not long remain immune to its charms, and they turned with respect and a kind of nostalgia to *The Tale of Genji*. Kawabata Yasunari once wrote that it was impossible to understand the culture of the Muromachi period (though it is often discussed by historians in terms of turbulent forces from below overthrowing the traditional authorities) without a knowledge of the extraordinary influence this supreme product of the aristocratic culture continued to exert.[1] Even today its magnetic attraction persists, as we know from the many translations and adaptations into modern Japanese made by writers who felt they needed to replenish their writings through their

From *Seeds in the Heart*. © 1999 by Donald Keene.

culture's central work of literature. And, at the time of the greatest crisis of modern Japan, the wartime bombings and the defeat, Kawabata turned to *The Tale of Genji* for reassurance and comfort. He related that reading it, at a time when the thought of death never left him, persuaded him that he must go on living "along with these traditions that flowed within me."[2] *The Tale of Genji* is not only the quintessence of the aristocratic culture of Heian Japan, but has affected the aesthetic and emotional life of the entire Japanese people for a millennium.

AUTHORSHIP OF THE WORK

Our best source of information concerning the authorship of the novel[3] is the diary kept by the author, Murasaki Shikibu, herself. An entry for the eleventh month of 1008 mentions the existence of a rough draft of part (or perhaps all) of the work. It has been conjectured from other evidence that Murasaki Shikibu began writing *The Tale of Genji* sometime between 1001, the year her husband Fujiwara no Nobutaka died, and 1005, when she entered the service of the Empress Shōshi (Akiko). Dates ranging from 1005 to after 1013 have been suggested for the completion.[4] We know from mention in *The Sarashina Diary*, written about 1021, that all of *The Tale of Genji* must have been completed by that date.[5]

Murasaki Shikibu's diary reveals unusual gifts of expression, but neither the diary nor any of the earlier monogatari prepares us for the achievement of *The Tale of Genji*. In the past (especially during the Muromachi period) some, reluctant to believe that a woman could have written so grand a work, insisted that it must have been composed by Murasaki Shikibu's father, Fujiwara no Tametoki, who merely left details for his daughter to fill in.[6] No one now denies that Murasaki Shikibu wrote all, or at any rate most, of *The Tale of Genji*, though differences of style, vocabulary, and the manner of waka composition have led critics to question the authorship of some chapters.[7]

The ten chapters at the end were also at one time attributed to another hand, most often to Murasaki Shikibu's daughter, the waka poet Daini no Sammi. This theory[8] is no longer taken seriously, though these chapters have an unquestionably darker, more oppressive tone than the earlier ones. Others have argued that some additional chapters existed before the present text in fifty-four chapters became standard, but little evidence supports such a hypothesis. One missing chapter, entitled "Kumogakure" (Disappearance in the Clouds), is said to have related the death of Genji, not described in any current text; but opinions in the old commentaries are divided between the view that it was so painful for the author to contemplate Genji's death that she could not bring herself to write this chapter (even though she gave it a name), and the contrary assertion that although Murasaki Shikibu wrote the chapter it was destroyed by imperial command because this example of the evanescence of human life had induced an excessive number of readers to "flee the world" and take refuge in Buddhist monasteries.[9] Modifications of the text unquestionably occurred, as we can infer from the numerous variants, but for most purposes it can be assumed that Murasaki Shikibu wrote the entire work.

MURASAKI SHIKIBU (973 – 1013)

The dates of the birth and death of Murasaki Shikibu have not been established, but 973 is now accepted by many scholars as the year of her birth, and her death occurred sometime after 1013, when she was mentioned for the last time in a contemporary document.

We know from Murasaki Shikibu's own writings as well as other sources that she was the daughter of Fujiwara no Tametoki, an official who, though of highly distinguished ancestry, enjoyed only a mediocre career as a provincial governor. An office he held early in his career, Shikibu no Daijō, accounted for the title *shikibu* (secretariat) in the name by which Murasaki Shikibu is known; it was common for women to be called by the names of the offices held by their fathers or husbands. Murasaki was a nickname, probably derived from the character of the same name in her novel; she seems to have been known, before she acquired her nickname, as Tō (for Fujiwara) Shikibu."[10]

Tametoki was a fourth-generation descendant of Fujiwara no Fuyutsugu, the founder of the "flowering fortune" of the Fujiwara family, and his wife (Murasaki's mother) was a fifth-generation descendant of the same man. By Tametoki's time, however, the glory of this particular branch of the Fujiwara family had been dimmed, and its members belonged to the zuryō class.[11] The most distinguished literary figure among Murasaki's ancestors was her great-grandfather, Fujiwara no Kanesuke, one of the chief *Gosenshū* poets. Later generations of Murasaki's ancestors had been honored by the inclusion of poems in imperial anthologies of waka, but this literary distinction had not brought them political power.

Tametoki was not only an accomplished waka poet but excelled at kanshi composition.[12] Many of his kanshi were included in such collections as the *Honchō* Reisō (c. 1010).[13] In 996, after ten years without office, Tametoki was appointed governor of Awaji, an inferior post. Disappointed, he composed a kanshi describing his grief and presented it to the Emperor Ichijō The kanshi so impressed the emperor that he directed Fujiwara no Michinaga, who had already appointed a relative governor of Echizen, to cancel this appointment and give the post to Tametoki instead.[14] The anecdote indicates the recognition accorded to Tametoki's kanshi, but it must have been galling for a man of his ancestry to have to depend on a poem for preferment.

Murasaki Shikibu apparently lost her mother when she was a small child. She grew up in her father's house, where she was educated together with a brother, as we know from a passage in her diary, in which she described how much more quickly than her brother she (from her place on the other side of a screen) absorbed the lessons in Chinese given by their father. She recalled, too, that her father regretted that she had not been born a boy: if she had been a man, she might well have developed into a capable, perhaps even brilliant, writer of kanshi and excelled otherwise at the kinds of learning that brought recognition from the court. This, however, would have deprived Japanese literature of its greatest glory, for men scorned to write fiction, and the composition of waka was virtually the only exception to their refusal to use Japanese for literary purposes.

We know little else about Murasaki's early years, though her poems suggest that she fell in love at least once. In 996 she violated custom by accompanying her father to his post in Echizen, apparently in order to avoid marriage with a second cousin, the governor of Chikuzen. The suitor, Fujiwara no Nobutaka, was in his middle forties, had several wives and concubines, and a number of children, the oldest a son of twenty-six. The difference in age and these family circumstances, more than the personality of the man, may have occasioned Murasaki Shikibu's reluctance to marry him; however, life in the unfamiliar, depressing surroundings of Echizen seems to have changed her mind: in the spring of 998, before her father completed his term of office, she returned alone to the capital, and that autumn she and Nobutaka were married.

In the following year the daughter later known as Daini no Sammi was born. Judging from the poems she and Nobutaka exchanged, Murasaki's married life was happy, but in 1001, less than three years after their marriage, Nobutaka died, perhaps a victim of the epidemic that had raged since the previous year. His death deeply affected Murasaki, as we can infer from poems she composed at the time:

"Remembering how I had grieved over my fate and then gradually returned to normal, I wrote:"

kazu naranu	Helpless as I am,
kokoro ni mi wo ba	I cannot lead my life as
makasenedo	My heart desires;

mi ni shitagau wa	I have learned how to submit
kokoro narikeri[15]	My desires to my fate.
kokoro ni wa	I wonder what place
ika naru mi ni ka	In the world could satisfy
kanauran	Such desires as mine?
omoishiredomo	Although I know to hope is vain,
omoishirarezu[16]	I cannot keep from hoping.

It has been conjectured that Murasaki Shikibu began writing *The Tale of Genji* before 1005–1006, when she was appointed lady-in-waiting (*nyōbō*) to Shōshi, the consort of the Emperor Ichijō. A brilliant group of court ladies had been assembled around Shōshi by her father, Michinaga, and Murasaki Shikibu may have been invited to join this group because parts of *The Tale of Genji* had already been circulated and admired. Murasaki Shikibu's activities at Shōshi's court are described in the diary in which she recorded events between the autumn of 1008 and the beginning of 1010. Perhaps Murasaki Shikibu kept the diary at the suggestion of Michinaga, as an "answer" to *The Pillow Book of Sei Shōnagon*, written at the rival court of the Empress Teishi (Sadako).[17]

COMPOSITION OF THE WORK

Murasaki wrote little in her diary about the composition of *The Tale of Genji*, but passing references make it clear that the work was already well known, perhaps from having been read aloud before the Emperor Ichijō and Shōshi. Men at the court normally did not read fiction, considering even the best examples to be no more than diversions for women, but perhaps Ichijō, hearing praise of the work from the ladies around him, was curious about the contents. It is recorded that he praised the knowledge of Chinese revealed by allusions in the text, expressing the belief that Murasaki must have read the *Nihon Shoki*. He probably meant that she wrote in a far more coherent and organized manner than earlier writers of fiction, more like a historian than a romancer. Its high reputation among men of the court is also attested by mention of Michinaga's generosity in providing fine paper, ink, and brushes for the scribes who made the copy, though it is unlikely that Michinaga himself read the novel; his readings seem to have been confined to the Chinese classics.

It has been speculated that the first germs of *The Tale of Genji* were probably tales of court life of the past related by some lady to the empress and her entourage. Although this lady may have been guided by a "scenario" written in kambun[18] that gave the essential facts of the tales, she extemporized in "free" sections that were not part of the frame story.[19] Murasaki's act of writing down the text ended the possibility of significantly modifying the story in retelling; but the word *monogatari* (telling of things) itself continued to be used, as if it were still being orally related. Many passages in the present text of *The Tale of Genji* suggest the typical manner of speech of court ladies, though at times Chinese literary influence also seems to be present.[20]

It is difficult to establish sources for *The Tale of Genji*, and equally difficult to determine how Murasaki Shikibu set about writing her book. It would be natural to assume that she began with the first chapter, "Kiritsubo," but there have long been theories to the contrary. One persistent tradition is that Murasaki, gazing from the Ishiyama Temple at the moon reflected in the waters of Lake Biwa, was inspired to write about her hero, Genji, during the period when he was exiled to Suma, a place with a somewhat similar landscape. The title of the best-known text of the work, *Kogetsu-shō*, meaning "lake moon collection," alludes to this legend, and visitors today to the Ishiyama Temple are shown the room (known as *Genji no ma*) where Murasaki Shikibu began writing *The Tale of Genji*, and even the inkstone she used.[21] Another recurrent theory is that Murasaki Shikibu began by writing the chapter "Waka-Murasaki" (Young Murasaki), perhaps by way of imagining in Genji an ideal husband for her own daughter.[22]

Scholars who accept "Kiritsubo" as the first chapter in order of composition are divided between those who express boundless admiration for the skill with which Murasaki adumbrated in this chapter the major themes of the entire work, and those who ask that it be read with indulgence, making allowance for her inexperience.[23]

The order of composition of the chapters is complicated by the fact that some relate events that occur simultaneously to those in earlier chapters instead of advancing the narrative in chronological sequence. These chapters are known as *narabi, or parallel chapters,* as contrasted with the *hon no maki*, or basic chapters.[24] The existence of these "parallel" chapters has suggested that the work was not written in the present order, but that some chapters were inserted into an existing text, even though there was no room for them chronologically.

Basic doubts about the order of composition of the chapters were convincingly expressed by Takeda Munetoshi in 1954.[25] He postulated the existence of an "Ur-text" of *The Tale of Genji* consisting of seventeen chapters in which Murasaki was the principal character. Sixteen chapters in which Tamakazura was the principal character were subsequently inserted at appropriate places to make up the thirty-three chapters of the First Part of the work. The original seventeen chapters ended with Genji acclaimed by all as the foremost man of the land. His son, the Emperor Reizei, whom everyone supposes to be the son of the old emperor, Genji's father, has learned the secret of his birth, and he bestows on Genji a rank second only to a retired emperor. He further insists that Genji sit by his side, sharing with him the place of honor, an unprecedented mark of respect."[26]

The main female characters in the Ur-text, or "Murasaki line" of chapters, apart from Murasaki herself, are Kiritsubo (Genji's mother) and Fujitsubo (the romantic obsession of Genji's life). The "Tamakazura line," named after the daughter of Genji's friend Tō no Chūjō, includes such memorable women as Yūgao and Suetsumuhana. The characters of the "Tamakazura line" are not mentioned in the chapters of the "Murasaki line" because, following Takeda, they had not yet been created; but characters of the "Murasaki line" do appear in the "Tamakazura line" because they already existed. Takeda reinforced this theory with objective evidence, such as the different titles and other appellations used for the characters in the two lines.[27] The characters who first appear in the "Tamakazura line" are more complex, in Takeda's view, than those of the "Murasaki line" and are sometimes treated with a humor not present earlier, suggesting an evolution in the author's manner.[28] Takeda's thesis has not been universally accepted, but it is the most plausible explanation yet offered of the parallel chapters and the many discrepancies of style.

Takeda believed that after Murasaki Shikibu had written the first thirty-three chapters she was persuaded to continue the story. However, her outlook on the world had for some reason changed, and the glory of Genji described in the First Part was much diminished. The chief incident of the Second Part is Genji's marriage to the third daughter of the Retired Emperor Suzaku, who has taken Buddhist orders. Suzaku, worried about the future of his favorite daughter, induces Genji to marry her. Genji accepts, in part because the princess is also a niece of his beloved Fujitsubo.

The marriage has unfortunate consequences for everyone concerned. First of all, it creates a rift between Genji and Murasaki, who is understandably upset over his marriage to a royal princess. Genji assures Murasaki of his unchanging love, and explains why he felt obliged to marry Suzaku's daughter. But Murasaki falls ill and is tormented by the jealous spirit of the late Lady Rokujō, a lover of Genji who has never forgiven Murasaki for having taken Genji from her. Murasaki begs to be allowed to become a nun, but Genji cannot bear to let her go. Before long, she dies. Genji is so distraught over Murasaki's illness and death that he neglects the Third Princess, a childlike creature who, hardly realizing what is happening, has a secret affair with Kashiwagi, the son of Genji's best friend. Genji, like his father before him, is obliged to take in his arms and recognize as his own the child of his wife and another man. His glory no longer seems so radiant.

The Third Part (once again following Takeda) describes events that take place after Genji's death. The characters in this part of the novel are remarkably beautiful and gifted, but their failings are also conspicuous. They are presumably closer to the real people of Murasaki Shikibu's day than those of the First or Second parts, and their lives are colored by griefs and passions that would have been immediately familiar to the people mentioned in her diary. The novel ends in a manner that may strike readers as inconclusive, but it has never occurred to Japanese scholars that the novel may be unfinished. Murasaki Shikibu took leave of her world in the manner of the painters of horizontal scrolls who, after depicting scenes crowded with people, show at the end one last haunting figure disappearing into the dark.

STYLE OF THE WORK

The Tale of Genji is famous not only because of its beauty but because of the difficulty of its style. In the past, when there were few detailed commentaries and no satisfactory translation into modern Japanese, even highly educated Japanese were not embarrassed to confess that it was easier for them to read Waley's English translation than the original. The main problem is the poetic ambiguity of many sentences that may leave in doubt the subject or the nature of the action performed. The difficulty cannot be explained merely in terms of the antiquity of the text; some works (like *The Tale of the Bamboo Cutter*) which antedate *The Tale of Genji* are far easier for modern readers to understand. The style was unique to Murasaki Shikibu, and she employed it because she felt confident that her anticipated readers at the court would be able to follow even very complicated sentences without difficulty. Any passage would do almost equally well to suggest the complexities, which tend to disappear in fluent translations that eliminate run-on sentences or augment the original with explanations. The following passage occurs near the beginning of the "Yūgao" chapter:

> *Mikuruma irubeki kado wa sashitarikereba, hito shite Koremitsu mesasete, matasetamaikeru hodo, mutsukashige naru ōji no sama wo miwatase shitamaeru ni, kono ie no katawara ni, higaki to iu mono wo atarashū shite, kami wa, hajitomi shigoken bakari agewatashite, sudare nado mo ito shirō suzushige naru ni, okashiki hitaitsuki no sukikage, amata miete nozoku. Tachisamayouran shimotsukata omoiyaru ni, anagachi ni taketakaki kokochi zo suru.*

It is not possible to make an absolutely literal rendering, but the meaning is approximately: "Because the gate through which carriages were admitted was locked, he sent a man for Koremitsu, and while he waited, he ran his eyes along the disreputable-looking street [and noticed] that [someone] in the house next door had newly [put up] what they call a cypress-bark fence, above which [someone] had lifted the row of four or five shutters; the blinds looked very white and cool, and he could dimly see through them many charming foreheads peeping [at him]. When he tried imagining the lower parts [of the figures] that seemed to be wandering around, he had a feeling that they must be very tall."

The translation by Arthur Waley renders this passage:

[H]e managed to find the house; but the front gate was locked and he could not drive in. He sent one of his servants for Koremitsu, his foster-nurse's son, and while he was waiting began to examine the rather wretched-looking by-street. The house next door was fenced with a new paling, above which at one place were four or five panels of open trellis-work, screened by blinds which were very white and bare. Through chinks in the blinds a number of foreheads could be seen. They seemed to belong to a group of ladies who must be peeping with interest into the street below. At first he thought that they had merely peeped out as they passed; but he soon realized that if they were standing on the floor they must be giants. No, evidently they had taken the trouble to climb on to some table or bed; which was surely rather odd![29]

Edward Seidensticker's translation is closer to the original:

The carriage entrance was closed. He sent for Koremitsu and while he was waiting looked up and down the dirty, cluttered street. Beside the nurse's house was a new fence of plaited cypress. The four or five narrow shutters above had been raised, and new blinds, white and clean, hung in the apertures. He caught outlines of pretty foreheads beyond. He would have judged, as they moved about, that they belonged to rather tall women.[30]

Waley's amplification of the text—especially his placing the women on "some table or bed," though it is hard to imagine a Heian room containing either—was undoubtedly inspired by his desire to make the text as immediately intelligible as possible to the European reader. Murasaki Shikibu does not explain why the women looked tall, and Waley felt obliged to insert an explanation.[31] Seidensticker evidently preferred not to mention the peeping of the women nor their lower parts (*shimotsukata*), nor did he attempt to explain the tallness of the women. Waley is perhaps closer to the original than Seidensticker in the leisurely pace of the sentences. But probably no translator could be completely faithful both to the original and to the English language.

An even more striking aspect of the style is the presence in the text of almost eight hundred poems. Quickly read in translation, they seem to add little to the narrative, and one is likely to be left merely with an impression that people of the Heian period were able to talk in poetry, and that they beautified their language as they beautified every other aspect of their lives. Closer reading of the poems, however, makes it evident that they contribute not only to the beauty of the style but also to the creation of a lyrical mode of narration.[32]

The style of the prose of *The Tale of Genji*, despite its difficulty, would affect writings in the courtly tradition over the centuries. Passages were incorporated almost word for word in the Nō plays,[33] and certain incidents would be alluded to innumerable times, in poetry as well as prose.[34] The descriptions of nature, whether observed in a palace garden or at some lonelier spot, are without exception lovely, all but poems in themselves. The expressive genius of the Yamato language—Japanese before it was greatly affected by Chinese influence—is nowhere better displayed than in the prose and poetry of *The Tale of Genji*.

HISTORICAL BACKGROUND

The Tale of Genji covers a period of about seventy years. It opens, as we can tell from various clues in the text, during the reign of the Emperor Daigo (897-930), an age that would be recalled as the high point of Heian civilization, and continues up to a time close to Murasaki Shikibu's own day. It has convincingly been suggested that the model for Genji was Minamoto no Takaakira, the tenth son of the Emperor Daigo; not only was he (like Genji) made a commoner with the surname of Minamoto (or Genji)[35] but he too was exiled (in 969) and later recalled to the capital.[36] It is likely that, regardless of whether or not Murasaki Shikibu had Takaakira in mind when she created the character of Genji, her readers, noting the resemblances, associated Genji with the historical figure. Other references within the novel to historical events confirmed the impression that the story had actually occurred. The work is nevertheless fiction, not a literary retelling of history.

The world of the "Shining Prince" may well have been Murasaki Shikibu's refuge from the world in which she actually found herself, a transmutation of the prose of daily life at the court to the poetry of her imagination. We know from her diary that the men of the court were by no means flawlessly decorous. Even the most distinguished among them not uncommonly got drunk and behaved boorishly. She undoubtedly romanticized, attributing to the past a beauty and elegance often missing from the world she observed, but she did not venture into fantasy; the people she described, though incomparably more gifted and beautiful than those she knew at court, were motivated by the unmistakable passions of human beings.

The occasions when supernatural events occur in the novel, notably the appearances of the baleful spirit of Lady Rokujō, have been explained by some modern commentators in terms of the power of hate or jealousy to harm and even to kill, but Murasaki Shikibu, like other Japanese of her time, believed in the literal existence of such spirits.[37] On the other hand, she dismissed as old-fashioned the kind of unreality present in *The Tale of the Bamboo Cutter*—the birth of a little girl inside a stalk of bamboo, or Kaguya-hime's ability to vanish at will—and she looked down on other early works that relied on the supernatural for their plots. The world of *The Tale of Genji* was a sublimation of Murasaki Shikibu's world, not a never-never land.

SOURCES OF *THE TALE OF GENJI*

The Tale of Genji is likely to seem modern, especially if read in a translation, whether one in contemporary Japanese or a foreign language. We believe in the characters of this work in a way not possible in the case of earlier monogatari such as *The Tale of the Hollow Tree* or, for that matter, much Japanese fiction written before the twentieth century. The characters are so distinctly drawn that we could not confuse the utterances of, say, Murasaki and Aoi or Rokujō and Tamakazura, and in the course of the novel the characters develop as they grow older and have new experiences. Indeed, the internal life of the characters, rather than their actions, is the subject of *The Tale of Genji*. In this sense its ancestor is not the early fiction, noticeably lacking in such qualities, but the diaries, especially *The Gossamer Years*. It is hard to imagine Murasaki Shikibu having created *The Tale of Genji* if there had not existed a tradition of women writing down their private thoughts.

With respect to specific literary influences, it is a commonplace of Japanese criticism of *The Tale of Genji* to mention its indebtedness to *Chang-hen-ko* ("A Song of Unending Sorrow"), the long poem by the great Chinese poet Po Chü-i that was much admired in Heian Japan. The poem concerns the love of the Emperor Hsüan Tsung for Yang Kuei-fei, a beautiful woman who, in the old phrase, "overturned the country." Murasaki Shikibu was certainly familiar with this poem, and alludes to it at the opening of her novel, where she wrote,

His court looked with very great misgiving upon what seemed a reckless infatuation. In China just such an unreasoning passion had been the undoing of an emperor and had spread turmoil throughout the land. As the resentment grew, the example of Yang Kuei-fei was the one most frequently cited against the lady.[38]

Although Murasaki was thinking of "A Song of Unending Sorrow" when she wrote the opening of *The Tale of Genji*, it is an overstatement to suggest that Po Chü-i's poem inspired the novel. The poem relates how the Chinese emperor's passionate love for the incomparably beautiful Yang Kuei-fei endangered the state and caused a rebellion during which she was executed by soldiers. It also describes how a priest, by command of the emperor, searched the afterworld for Yang Kuei-fei until he found her. She nostalgically recalled her love and gave the priest keepsakes to take back to the emperor. The poem concludes: "Earth endures, heaven endures; some time both shall end, / While this unending sorrow goes on and on for ever."[39]

The love of the emperor for Kiritsubo occasioned the jealousy of other palace ladies, and she died untimely, her hold on life weakened by unhappiness, but there was never any danger of rebellion, and she was certainly not cut down by soldiers. The most memorable keepsake of her union with the emperor was Genji, and the emperor's sorrow was mitigated by this child. Later he found solace in Fujitsubo, a woman who much resembled Kiritsubo.

The search for literary sources has been inspired largely by the difficulty scholars have experienced in imagining that a work of the magnitude of *The Tale of Genji* could have been created without models. The early commentators found sources in the Tendai Buddhist scriptures, the *Records of the Historian* of Ssu-ma Ch'ien, the *Spring and Autumn Annals*, and other Chinese sources. Other commentators, concerned less with literary sources than with the moral intent of the work, provided a simplistic Buddhist explanation that persists to this day: *The Tale of Genji* is the story of a man who was punished for his affair with his stepmother when his own wife betrayed him with another man.

The best-known and most persuasive interpretation, however, was that of Motoori Norinaga, who denied Buddhist and Confucian intent behind the novel and treated *The Tale of Genji* as a work embodying the principle of mono no aware, a sensitivity to things. Motoori wrote in *Tama no Ogushi* (The Jeweled Comb):

There have been many interpretations over the years of the purpose of this tale. But all of these interpretations have been based not on a consideration of the novel itself but rather on the novel as seen from the point of view of Confucian and Buddhist works, and thus they do not represent the true purpose of the author.... Good and evil as found in this tale do not correspond to good and evil as found in Confucian and Buddhist writings.... Generally speaking, those who know the meaning of the sorrow of human existence, i.e., those who are in sympathy and in harmony with human sentiments are regarded as good; and those who are not aware of the poignance of human existence, i.e., those who are not in harmony with human sentiments are regarded as bad.... Since novels have as their object the teaching of the meaning of the nature of human existence, there are in their plots many points contrary to Confucian and Buddhist teachings. This is because among the varied feelings of man's reactions to things—whether good, bad, right, or wrong—there are feelings contrary to reason, however improper they may be.... In the instance of Prince Genji, his interest in and rendezvous with Utsusemi, Oborotsukiyo, and the Consort Fujitsubo are acts of extraordinary iniquity and immorality according to the Confucian and Buddhist points of view.... But *The Tale of Genji* does not dwell on his iniquitous and immoral acts, but rather recites over and over again his awareness of the sorrow of existence, and represents him as a good man who combines in himself all good things in men.[40]

Motoori, later in the same essay, declared that the purpose of the author of *The Tale of Genji* was similar to that of a man who collects muddy water in order to have lotuses bloom: "The impure mud of illicit love affairs described in *The Tale of Genji* is there not for the purpose of being admired but for the purpose of nurturing the flower of the awareness of the sorrow of human existence."[41]

If Motoori's explanation is correct, Murasaki Shikibu was inspired by a literary rather than a didactic purpose, and similarities between *The Tale of Genji* and Buddhist or Confucian writings are therefore coincidences or of only minor significance. Other scholars have pointed out the political overtones of the novel; for example, the fact that the hero belongs to the Minamoto clan (Genji), though the Fujiwara family was supreme at the time, surely had importance for her first readers,[42] and may have suggested even that Murasaki disapproved of Fujiwara hegemony. Some critics, especially during the 1950s, insisted that *The Tale of Genji* was an exposé of the contradictions and corruption in the upper aristocracy, written by an embittered member of its lower ranks, but this is hardly the impression received from the novel itself.

It is not clear to what degree Murasaki Shikibu intended her work to convey religious or political meaning. In describing the world around her hero she no doubt drew on the assumptions of her class and particularly of the women at Shōshi's court. At an even more unconscious level, she may have drawn on folklore. For example, Genji's exile to Suma was perhaps derived from the story of the exiled young noble, known in many parts of Asia.[43] This is the story of a young prince who is slandered and forced to go into exile; but eventually, after proving his worth, he returns in triumph to the capital. A knowledge of this tale may have guided Murasaki Shikibu as she wrote about Genji's time of trial at Suma and return, but the historical instance of Minamoto no Takaakira's exile was closer at hand; and Genji's exile at Suma, though a time of trial, was not the occasion for proving his mettle and winning a glorious reputation.

The relations between Genji and his enemy Kokiden, the consort of his father, the old emperor, have also been traced to folkloristic sources, in this case the widely known tales about cruel stepmothers.[44] If Murasaki Shikibu had these tales in mind when she wrote about Genji and Kokiden, she confused the issue by giving contrasting examples of step-mother–stepson relations. Genji's love for his stepmother Fujitsubo is of vastly greater importance to the novel than his suffering at the hands of Kokiden; and the pains Genji takes to ensure that his son Yūgiri will never see Murasaki are occasioned not by fear that Murasaki will mistreat her stepson but by a premonition that one glimpse of Murasaki will be all that Yūgiri needs to fall in love with her. Yūgiri in fact does get a glimpse of Murasaki when storm winds blow down the screens that normally conceal her, and his astonishment over her beauty proves that Genji's fears were well grounded. If one had to judge from these examples, one could only conclude that Murasaki Shikibu, far from intending to write a story in the manner of *The Tale of Ochikubo*, about a cruel stepmother, was warning of the danger that beautiful stepmothers are likely to inspire improper sentiments in their stepsons.

Murasaki's clearest statement on why she wrote *The Tale of Genji* is found in the celebrated account of the "art of fiction" found in chapter 25, "Hotaru" (Fireflies). Genji, going to Tamakazura's room on a summer's day, finds her reading a pile of books, to pass the boredom of the rainy season. At first he teases her over the credulity of women, who are willing to be deceived by the fabricators of romances. But, on second thought, he continues in this vein:

> If it weren't for old romances like this, how on earth would you get through these long tedious days when time moves so slowly? And besides, I realize that many of these works, full of fabrications though they are, do succeed in evoking the emotions of things in a most realistic way. One event follows plausibly on another, and in the end we cannot help being moved by the story, even though we know what foolishness it all really is....

He moves from this somewhat grudging recognition of the value of fiction to a more positive statement:

> It was rather churlish of me to speak badly about these books as I did just now, for the fact is that works of fiction set down things that have happened in this world ever since the days of the gods. Writings like *The Chronicles of Japan* really give only one side of the picture, whereas these romances must be full of just the right sort of details.... The author certainly does not write about specific people, recording all the actual circumstances of their lives. Rather it is a matter of his being so moved by things, both good and bad, which he has heard and seen happening to men and women that he cannot keep it all to himself but wants to commit it to writing and make it known to other people—even to those of later generations. This, I feel sure, is the origin of fiction.[45]

Genji goes on to suggest that fiction may correspond to the "accommodated truths" of Buddhism which, though not strictly the truth, have the same end as the teachings of Buddha: the enlightenment of mankind. Medieval scholars interpreted *The Tale of Genji* as a *hōben*, an expedient for gaining truth painlessly. But Murasaki Shikibu indicates that, quite apart from the possible value her work (or any other example of fiction) may have in enlightening people, it results from the compulsion that authors feel to record events that have so deeply moved them that they cannot bear to think that a time might come when they would be forgotten.

THE STORY

The novel opens with an account of the birth of its hero, Prince Genji, together with the circumstances preceding his birth. Genji's mother,

Kiritsubo, though much loved by the emperor, is of inferior birth and lacks backing at the court. She is accordingly slandered and maltreated by other palace ladies who are jealous of the attentions the emperor showers on her. She dies when Genji is only three years old. A few years later, a Korean physiognomist, asked to tell the boy's fortune, predicts that if Genji should ascend the throne, as his birth (he is the son of the reigning emperor), his intelligence, and his extraordinary beauty seem to prescribe, there will be disaster. On the other hand, Genji's face does not reveal the traits of a minister who can order affairs of state on behalf of the emperor.[46] The emperor, disturbed by the prediction, which seems to rule out the boy's ever occupying a position of importance, decides to preserve the boy from harm by making him a commoner and giving him the surname of Minamoto, or Genji.[47]

After the death of Kiritsubo, apparently a victim of mental torment, the emperor is inconsolable until he hears rumors of the daughter of a former emperor who is said to look exactly like the dead lady. This is the first example of a leitmotiv that runs through the novel: a man will fall in love again and again with the same woman, though her identity may be different. Genji falls in love with Fujitsubo after learning how much she resembles his mother, and later with Murasaki who resembles her aunt Fujitsubo, now a nun and inaccessible. His interest in Yūgao and her daughter Tamakazura stems from a single love. Late in the novel, Genji's supposed son Kaoru loves Ukifune because she resembles Ōigimi.

When the emperor chooses Fujitsubo as his official consort, the women of the palace cannot complain, for she is of the highest birth. Genji, on whom his father dotes so much that he can scarcely bear to let the boy out of his sight, is allowed to play in the presence of his youthful stepmother, and she soon becomes his ideal of beauty. Even after his initiation into manhood at the age of twelve and his marriage to Aoi, six years older than himself, Genji remains under Fujitsubo's spell, which is one reason why his marriage fails. His wife Aoi, ironically, is the only woman in the book who remains impervious to Genji's charm, and Genji first appreciates Aoi's beauty only when she is on her deathbed. Murasaki Shikibu does not attribute this coldness of husband and wife to any specific cause, but leads us to believe that they are incompatible, and that nothing can change this fact.

Genji has a son by Aoi, the intelligent but charmless Yūgiri. He also has a son as the result of his brief, poignant relationship with Fujitsubo. This son, whom the world supposes to be the emperor's, eventually ascends the throne as the Emperor Reizei.[48] Genji is far from exultant over having a son on the throne; he is tormented by the fear that the unusual resemblance between Reizei and himself will be noticed, and filled with shame that he has betrayed his father. After Reizei becomes emperor he discovers the secret of his birth and is appalled to think that he has failed to pay his real father the appropriate homage. The honors he bestows on Genji represent the apogee of Genji's glory and a fulfillment of the prophecy of the Korean physiognomist. (He is neither an emperor nor a surrogate of the emperor but has been given a rank equivalent to that of a retired emperor.) Many scholars believe that the chapter "Fuji no Uraba" (Wisteria Leaves) marked the end of the First Part of the work; Murasaki Shikibu seems originally to have intended to conclude her story of Genji at this point.

At the opening of the Second Part, the Retired Emperor Suzaku, who has taken Buddhist orders, asks Genji to marry his third daughter. For all his many affairs with different women over the years, he unquestionably loves Murasaki best, but she was of insufficiently exalted birth to be designated as his official consort. Genji accedes to Suzaku's request, though without enthusiasm. This marriage upsets the harmony that has hitherto reigned over his Rokujō Palace, where each of Genji's principal ladies occupies a wing with a garden whose flowers reveal her choice of season. The childless Murasaki, though resentful of Genji's alliance with the Lady of Akashi during his exile, never seriously fears this retiring lady as a rival, and (another example of a model stepmother!) gladly rears the lady's child as if it were her own. But the status of the Third Princess makes Murasaki apprehensive, despite Genji's assurances, that she will be supplanted in his affections. The Third Princess's position becomes even more exalted when Reizei abdicates in favor of her brother. The distraught Murasaki expresses the desire to become a nun and "leave the world," but Genji restrains her. She falls ill, and the distressed Genji completely neglects the Third Princess. Kashiwagi, the son of Genji's friend Tō no Chūjō, has fallen desperately in love with the Third Princess after a single glimpse of her. The two have a brief, guilt-ridden affair. Soon afterward Murasaki dies. Genji seriously considers taking vows as a Buddhist priest, but his sense of responsibility to those who depend on him obliges him to postpone this decision. The Second Part ends with a description of Genji, who is appearing in public for the first time after the death of Murasaki. We are told that he seemed more beautiful than ever.

The chapter entitled "Niou," at the beginning of the Third Part, opens with the bleak statement, "Genji was dead, and there was no one to take his place."[49] The last third of *The Tale of Genji* has for its heroes two young princes, Niou, a grandson of Genji, and Kaoru, the son of Kashiwagi and the Third Princess. Both are uncommonly attractive, but each is only a part of Genji: Niou combines Genji's beauty with an impetuous ardor that generally wins any woman, but he lacks Genji's sensitivity; Kaoru has more than his share of Genji's sensitivity, but he lacks self-assurance and fails to win the heart of either of the two women he loves. The flaws in these young men suggest the diminution that has occurred in the world since Genji's death. The absence of a hero who is described only in superlatives has the effect of making the last part of the novel seem more realistic; it may have been for this reason that future readers tended to identify themselves with the characters of this part. Niou and Kaoru are rivals for Ukifune, whose despair at being forced to choose between them induces her to attempt suicide, a development in the plot that would have been inconceivable in earlier sections of the novel.

CHARACTERS IN THE NOVEL

We tend to remember, even more than the plot of *The Tale of Genji*, the characters created by Murasaki Shikibu. This in itself was an extraordinary achievement: nothing in any of the earlier monogatari prepares us for these characters. Only in the diaries does one come across people with the complexity of real human beings and who can be conceived of as having an existence apart from the book. Genji himself is not especially complex, but on almost every page devoted to him there is some little touch that makes us believe in him. The opening of the chapter "Young Murasaki," where Genji sees Murasaki (then a girl of ten) for the first time, presents numerous effective details that enable us to see Genji with particular clarity. Although he has gone to the hermitage in the mountains hoping to obtain a miraculous cure from the ague that has been bothering him, he is by no means so overcome by fever that he is oblivious to his usual pleasures. A companion tells him about a beautiful spot in the west country where an old man, a former governor, lives with his wife and daughter. At the mention of a daughter Genji's interest is at once aroused and he wants to know more about her. The passage is brief and not especially striking, but it is a first sounding of a theme that will eventually acquire major importance, Genji's exile to the very spot his companion had described, and his romance with the former governor's daughter, the Lady of Akashi.

That evening, though still suffering from his illness ("possessed by a hostile power," according to the holy man who is attempting to cure him), he ventures out to a nearby house and goes up to the fence in order to peep through a crack and get a look at the people inside. Peeping through cracks in fences or hedges was an almost inevitable feature of courtship in a world where young men of the upper classes had few opportunities to see women of their class; there is a special verb, *kaimamiru*, to describe this action. Genji's curiosity is rewarded: he sees inside a little girl who reminds him of "a certain person," another reference to events that have not yet been revealed to the reader, in this case Genji's love for Fujitsubo. Soon afterward

Genji is invited to visit a learned cleric who lives nearby. The man, as Buddhist priests are apt to do, speaks of the unreliability of this world and the supreme importance of the world to come, stirring in Genji thoughts of his own sins, though once again the reader does not know what specifically is meant. Genji turns the conversation to the subject of the little girl, and to the priest's great surprise, asks to be allowed to take charge of the girl's education. He alludes briefly to his unhappy marriage with Aoi, saying that he is now living alone.[50] The priest imagines that Genji does not realize the girl is much too young for romance, but Genji waves off this objection: he is not proposing anything improper, but (for reasons he does not disclose) he wants the girl near him. Although he insists that he is not being frivolous, we are inclined to doubt the veracity of his words, remembering his earlier escapades, but he manages to persuade the nun who is Murasaki's guardian that he is earnest, and the girl comes to live with him.

Was Genji sincere in his professions of disinterested concern for the young Murasaki's welfare? Probably he does not himself know, but he clearly is entranced by the girl despite her extreme youth. He behaves toward Murasaki like a tender father or older brother. One day, for example, he asks her if she misses him when he is away. She nods, and he tells her, "You are still a child, and there is a jealous and difficult lady whom I would rather not offend. I must go on visiting her, but when you are grown up I will not leave you ever. It is because I am thinking of all the years we will be together that I want to be on good terms with her."[51] The jealous and difficult lady mentioned by Genji is, of course, Rokujō, but we do not understand just how terrible her jealousy is for several more chapters, when we learn that Rokujō's "living ghost" kills Aoi.

Genji promises to marry Murasaki when she is grown up, but he never suggests when this might be. The scene where he finally decides the moment has arrived is surprisingly brutal. We are given no details, but the implications are unmistakable:

> She was clever and she had many delicate ways of pleasing him in the most trivial diversions. He had not seriously thought of her as a wife. Now he could not restrain himself. It would be a shock, of course.
>
> What had happened? Her women had no way of knowing when the line had been crossed. One morning Genji was up early and Murasaki stayed on and on in bed....
>
> She had not dreamed he had anything of the sort on his mind. What a fool she had been, to repose her whole confidence in so gross and unscrupulous a man.[52]

Murasaki's shock and disillusion are likely to be shared by the reader. For a moment at least Genji's charm is tarnished. Sooner or later this would have had to happen, Genji thought, and perhaps he was right; but even after Murasaki has come to accept this aspect of Genji's love and perhaps to desire it, that day when she thought of him as gross and unscrupulous surely could not have been forgotten. The scene, it may be noted, occurs not long after the death of his wife Aoi at the hands of a malignant spirit even as she is giving birth to Genji's child. After the harrowing experience of seeing his wife being tormented by a vengeful spirit so powerful that exorcism was futile, Genji may well have needed comfort: his violation of Murasaki at this particular time is psychologically true, but not endearing.

That Genji can be discussed in these terms is evidence that he is no cardboard Prince Charming. But it would be wrong to infer from this incident that he was a great lover in the European mold, a Don Giovanni whose conquests were to be recorded in Leporello's catalogue by numbers rather than by names. Once Don Giovanni had conquered a woman he lost all interest in her, and if (like Donna Elvira) she failed to realize that their affair had ended and that it was futile to appeal to his love, he humiliated her openly by asking his servant to make love to her. Genji never forgets any woman he has loved, and even when he discovers to his horror that he has made a dreadful mistake, as when he woos the princess with the red nose, he does not drop her, but sees to it that her needs are taken care of and even continues the pretense of still being her suitor. With each woman he courts he is different, not simply in the manner of Don Giovanni's wooing a peasant girl in a way she can understand, but in satisfying each woman's dreams of a perfect lover.

Genji's most disastrous love affair was with the proud and aristocratic Lady Rokujō He was attracted to her initially by the very difficulty of approaching such a woman, the widow of a former crown prince. Early in the novel Genji and several friends discuss the ideal wife and they agree that women of the highest rank are to be avoided, but Genji was drawn to Rokujō, who undoubtedly belongs to this class. Once he succeeded in making her his lover, his passion cooled: "He could not deny that the blind intoxicating passion which possessed him while she was still unattainable had almost disappeared. To begin with, she was far too sensitive; then there was the disparity of their ages, and the constant dread of discovery which haunted him during those painful partings at small hours of the morning."[53]

Rokujō falls far more deeply in love with Genji than he with her. Realizing that his love has waned, she decides to accompany her daughter, who has just been named the high priestess, to the Great Shrine of Ise; she hopes that leaving the capital may help her to forget Genji. Before her departure she attends the festival of the Kamo Shrine, supposing that it would prove a distraction, only to suffer the indignity of having her carriage pushed rudely out of the way by the attendants of the carriage belonging to Genji's wife Aoi. The proud Rokujō feels so humiliated that perhaps at that moment she unconsciously wishes Aoi dead. Soon afterward, unbeknownst to Rokujō herself, her "living spirit" goes to torment Aoi. At first the cause of Aoi's sickness baffles the doctors, but diviners eventually succeed in compelling the spirit that possesses Aoi to speak. The words that issue from Aoi's mouth are not in her own voice but, as Genji realizes to his horror, Lady Rokujō's. Moments later Aoi gives birth to a son, and dies soon afterward.

Rokujō receives the news with mixed feelings. Perhaps she feels secretly pleased that a rival for Genji's affection is now out of the way, but for some time she has noticed a strange scent of incense, the kind used when exorcising demons, clinging to her clothes and hair, no matter how often she bathes, and she has gradually come to realize that she herself has been responsible for Aoi's death.[54]

Rokujō is the most interesting of the many women who figure in *The Tale of Genji*. Not only does her "living ghost" have the power to kill, but after her death her "dead ghost" torments Murasaki; however, she herself is by no means hateful, and Genji, though he realizes she has killed his wife, cannot face leaving her: "And yet, after all, he did not wish to make a final break. He told himself that if she could put up with him as he had been over the years, they might be of comfort to each other."[55] When Genji fails to get in touch with Rokujō after the death of Aoi, she surmises that it is because he blames her, and she is all the more determined to leave the capital and accompany her daughter to Ise. Genji, alarmed at the thought of losing her, visits her at the Shrine in the Fields, a lonely place on the outskirts of the capital. The description of the meeting of Genji and Rokujō contains some of the most beautiful writing of the entire work:

> The autumn flowers were fading; along the reeds by the river the shrill voices of many insects blended with the mournful fluting of the wind in the pines. Scarcely distinguishable from these somewhere in the distance rose and fell a faint, enticing sound of human music.... They came at last to a group of very temporary-looking wooden huts surrounded by a flimsy brushwood fence. The archways, built of unstripped wood, stood out black and solemn against the sky. Within the enclosure a number of priests were walking up and down with a preoccupied air. There was something portentous in their manner of addressing one another

and in their way of loudly clearing their throats before they spoke. In the Hall of Offering there was a dim flicker of firelight, but elsewhere no single sign of life. So this was the place where he had left one who was from the start in great distress of mind, to shift for herself week after week, month after month! Suddenly he realized with a terrible force all that she must have suffered.[56]

The meeting of the lovers is tender. They exchange poems. Then, "suddenly he realized with astonishment that though after that unhappy incident he had imagined it to be impossible for them to meet and had so avoided all risk of his former affection being roused to new life, yet from the first moment of this strange confrontation he had immediately found himself feeling towards her precisely as he had before their estrangement."[57] They spend the night together: "At last the night ended in such a dawn as seemed to have been fashioned for their especial delight. 'Sad is any parting at the red of dawn; but never since the world began, gleamed day so tragically in the autumn sky,' and as he recited these verses, aghast to leave her, he stood hesitating and laid her hand tenderly in his."[58]

At this moment it would be impossible to think of Rokujō as the fierce incarnation of jealousy who killed Genji's wife. We sense her beauty, her grief, and, above all, her love for Genji, given special poignance because she is much older than he; she knows that before long she must lose him. That is how she is depicted in the Nō play *Nonomiya*, one of the most moving of the entire repertory. Rokujō's suffering prevents us from passing judgment on her; this, too, is evidence of how much more complex she is than any character of earlier Japanese literature.

For most readers, however, Murasaki is the "heroine" of *The Tale of Genji*. From Genji's first glimpse of her as a little girl, angry because a playmate has released her pet sparrow, until her death, she is never far from his mind, and again and again he reminds himself of her perfection. But we seldom see her except when she is unhappy—first when Genji unexpectedly takes her, later when she resigns herself to never being able to bear a child, and often when she fears that Genji's love has strayed to another woman. Genji, for all his philandering, always insists that Murasaki occupies a unique place in his heart; but when he meets Fujitsubo again after the death of the old emperor he is astonished by her beauty, and he realizes afresh how closely she resembles Murasaki:

> For years Murasaki had served to keep Lady Fujitsubo, to some extent at any rate, out of his thoughts. But now that he saw how astonishingly the one resembled the other he fancied that all the

while Murasaki had but served as a substitute or eidolon of the lady who denied him her love. Both had the same pride, the same reticence. For a moment he wondered whether, if they were side by side, he should be able to tell them apart.[59]

How wretched Murasaki would have been if she had thought that perhaps she was no more than a substitute for Fujitsubo! The other ladies in Genji's life expect much less than Murasaki. The Lady of Akashi, for example, is too self-effacing ever to make any demands on Genji, and she even surrenders her daughter to Murasaki to raise as her own. The most striking female characters are those who appear in what Takeda called the "Tamakazura line" of chapters, especially Yūgao, Suetsumuhana, the Lady of Ōmi, and Tamakazura.

Yūgao is terrified of Genji. When he promises to take her "somewhere very nice where no one will disturb us," she cries out, "No, no, your ways are so strange, I should be frightened to go with you."[60] Indeed, he behaves like the hero of some Gothic romance, never revealing his identity or showing his face before the frightened young woman. Yūgao dies after Rokujō has appeared to her in a nightmare she has in the abandoned old house where Genji has taken her. Suetsumuhana, the princess with the red nose, lives in a deserted palace. Genji makes his way through the underbrush, sure that some sleeping beauty must be hidden there, only to find a fantastic creature, living in another world, too shy to appear before others, though she does not suspect how ridiculous she appears. The last thing Genji wishes is to have this fright as his mistress, but he gravely courts her in old-fashioned language, exactly as she most desires, and she responds with musty gifts. The Lady of Ōmi, a minor character, is memorable because of her foolish pretensions; she displays a rather appealing vulgarity, a lone exception to the good taste that rules the court. (She is an unrecognized daughter of Genji's friend Tō no Chūjō) Tamakazura, the daughter Yūgao bore Tō no Chūjō, is memorable too, if only because it is to her that Genji, speaking for Murasaki Shikibu, gives the famous explanation of the value of fiction.

Genji responds perfectly to each woman. He is a genius at lovemaking, and if he had lived in a society where monogamy was strictly enforced or if, deciding that Murasaki was an ideal wife, he had never looked at another woman, the world would have been the poorer. Unlike Don Giovanni, he not only woos and wins each lady but he makes each feel sure of his love, and each is content with her small part of his life. When Genji lays out the plans for his Rokujō Palace, there are apartments not only for the women he still loves but for Suetsumuhana and even for the Lady from the Village of Falling Flowers, a woman much older than himself who was one of the less important concubines of his father.

Only one woman in the book is intentionally unkind to Genji, his father's consort Kokiden. On learning of Genji's affair with her younger sister Oborozukiyo, she is outraged. She had earlier become Genji's enemy because she feared that the emperor would name the peerless Genji, rather than her own son, as his successor. Even after Suzaku safely ascended the throne, her anger was not appeased, and Genji's scandalous behavior afforded her a perfect opportunity to demonstrate that she wielded greater power than Genji at court, despite his beauty and talent. She creates so unfriendly an atmosphere that Genji finds life at the court intolerable, and he leaves for exile in Suma. Kokiden's unkindness recalls the proverbial cruelty of the stepmother, anxious for the success of her own children, but unlike most stepmothers of fiction, she has real cause for complaint: Genji, after all, has seduced her sister.

The only woman who refuses Genji when he makes advances is the wife of a provincial governor.[61] They accidentally meet again years later at the barrier house on the road to the east as she is returning from the provinces with her aged husband. She and Genji exchange poems referring to the irony of being at the Ausaka Barrier, whose name contains the verb *au*, "to meet," though they are destined never to meet again. Soon afterward the lady's husband dies, and rather than yield to the advances of another man, she becomes a nun. It is hard to think that she does not regret her coldness to Genji years before.

Genji remains an important character in the Second Part, but he does not dominate the action as earlier on. The most memorable figure is Kashiwagi, the son of Tō no Chūjō, who has the affair with Genji's consort, the Third Princess. The overmastering passion that drives him to violate the wife of the man he most admires brings him no joy or even relief. He falls ill, and when he sees Genji he is tormented by the fear that Genji knows his secret. The chapter entitled "Kashiwagi" (The Oak Tree) opens:

> The New Year came and Kashiwagi's condition had not improved. He knew how troubled his parents were and he knew that suicide was no solution, for he would be guilty of the grievous sin of having left them behind. He had no wish to live on.[62]

After the Third Princess has given birth to Kaoru, Kashiwagi's child, she falls into a wasting illness, and in a desperate attempt to save her life the Buddhist rites of ordination as a nun are administered. The next morning the malignant spirit who has afflicted the Third Princess reveals herself, seemingly Rokujō once again, jealous even of so spiritless a creature as this princess.

Soon afterward Kashiwagi dies. The next chapter, devoted to Yūgiri, describes his wooing of Kashiwagi's widow, Ochiba, the second daughter of the Emperor Suzaku. Yūgiri's wife, Kumoinokari, had been his childhood sweetheart, and he married her only after overcoming the opposition of their parents to the match, but Yūgiri's great devotion to Kumoinokari (that had won him praise as a model husband) seems to have made her into something of a termagant. Turning elsewhere to escape from his overbearing wife, he decides to court Ochiba, though she is still in mourning for Kashiwagi. This princess stubbornly refuses to yield to Yūgiri's wooing, her resolve strengthened by the words of her dying mother, who warned her never to take a second husband. Kumoinokari, aware that her husband is spending his nights elsewhere (she does not realize, of course, that Yūgiri has been unsuccessful), becomes obsessively jealous. Yūgiri, puzzled and enraged by his failure to win the princess, pursues her all the more frantically. Ochiba's women urge her not to be so cold to a splendid gentleman, and finally conspire to admit Yūgiri to her chamber. Not until the next morning does he get his first good look at the woman for whom he has risked his reputation as a serious and dignified member of the court.[63] Kumoinokari returns to her father's house, taking her daughters. When Yūgiri appears and demands that she return home, she refuses to listen to him. We are told:

> Lying down among the children, he surveyed the confusion he had managed to create in both houses. The Second Princess must be utterly bewildered. What man in his right mind could think these affairs interesting or amusing? He had had enough of them.[64]

Yūgiri's self-analysis is exact. Although his appearance is described with the usual superlatives, he is a much reduced version of his father, and his pursuit of the reluctant princess is not only undignified but, in the end, ludicrous. It is as if he decided that, being the son of a great lover, he must demonstrate on occasion that he, too, can win a desirable woman. He chooses Ochiba without ever having seen her and knowing nothing about her qualities, a mechanical display of lust devoid of affection. And once he has succeeded by sordid means in having his way with the princess, he realizes that it has given him no pleasure. He comes to his senses, a smaller man even in his own eyes.

Genji allows Yūgiri to see Murasaki's face only after she has died. Yūgiri wept that such beauty was lost to the world, but for Genji the shock was so severe that, as many times before (but much more earnestly), he considered "leaving the world" to become a Buddhist priest. There had always been a good reason for postponing the step, but at the end of the chapter "Minori" (The Law) Genji seems at last to have made up his mind. In the following chapter, "Maboroshi" (Mirage), he destroys old letters (except those from Murasaki), plays with his grandson Niou, visits the uncomplaining Lady of Akashi after a long absence, and reminisces about the two women he loved most, Fujitsubo and Murasaki. One day succeeds another and Genji has still not carried out his resolve. The chapter concludes with Genji's watching Niou scampering around to scare off the devils before New Year and reflecting sadly that soon he would have to say goodbye to this child, too. This is the last we see of Genji.

Chapters 42, 43, and 44 are invariably included in editions of *The Tale of Genji*, but many scholars have expressed doubts concerning their authenticity. Chapter 42, "Niou," is germane to the narration, even though it is literarily inferior to preceding chapters; but chapters 43 and 44, describing respectively a younger son of Tō no Chūjō and a son of Tamakazura and Prince Higekuro, are scarcely more than digressions. Chapter 44, "Takegawa" (Bamboo River) opens in this unpromising fashion:

> The story I am about to tell wanders rather far from Genji and his family. I had it unsolicited from certain obscure women who lived out their years in Higekuro's house. It may not seem entirely in keeping with the story of Murasaki, but the women themselves say that there are numerous inaccuracies in the accounts we have had of Genji's descendants, and put the blame on women so old that they have become forgetful. I would not presume to say who is right.[65]

It is possible that some scribe or commentator, intending to make the story easier to read, added materials in the hope of tying up loose ends; or it may be that a quite independent story was woven into the text of *The Tale of Genji* by someone who thought that the work would profit by expansion.[66] In any case, it is with relief that we reach the last ten chapters; indeed, many people believe that they constitute the finest part of the entire work.

The last ten chapters are known as the Uji chapters. Uji is today a short way from Kyoto, but at the time it seemed distant and was reached with difficulty, as we know from descriptions of the journey such as: "As he came into the mountains the mist was so heavy and the underbrush so thick that he could hardly make out the path; and as he pushed his way through thickets the rough wind would throw showers of dew upon him from a turmoil of falling leaves."[67] There was also a danger of encountering bandits on the deserted trails to Uji. Even the name Uji was depressing: puns were often made on Uji and *ushi*, meaning "sad."[68] The dismal sound of the Uji River is heard again and again in these chapters, and it is associated especially with the unhappiness of the girl Ukifune, torn between two lovers, Niou and Kaoru.

Ukifune is the half-sister of the two princesses who are introduced to us at the opening of the Uji chapters, Ōigimi and Nakanokimi. They are the daughters of a prince, a younger brother of Genji, who was living in retirement as a sage and hermit at Uji. The constant noise of the river was a hindrance to meditation, but he devoted himself to his religious studies with such diligence that he was revered as a saint. Kaoru, who has grown up into a bookish young man much attracted to religion, hears of the prince and visits him. At the prince's house Kaoru encounters an old woman called Bennokimi who hints that she knows something of the secret of his birth. Kaoru has long been tormented by uneasiness about the identity of his real father, and this uncertainty contributes to his inability to act decisively. He eagerly listens as Bennokimi reveals that Kaoru is the son not of Genji but of Kashiwagi, and shows him letters Kashiwagi had received from the Third Princess.

Kaoru returns again and again to Uji, despite the hardship of the journey. His friend and rival Niou suspects that Kaoru's frequent visits to Uji are inspired by a romance, and his suspicions are confirmed when he learns of the two princesses. However, Kaoru is in fact not interested in the princesses, and it is only after their father's death that, more by way of expressing condolences than as a would-be lover, he addresses letters to the sisters. He gradually is attracted to the older sister, Ōigimi. Niou also writes her, but she spurns to answer his letters, aware of his reputation, but Kaoru's letters are so serious that she responds without fear. Kaoru before long shows greater affection, but Ōigimi has resolved never to marry, and she rarely vouchsafes more than a few words or a poem.

Kaoru, attracted by Ōigimi's seriousness, a fair match for his own, hits on the idea of shifting Niou's attention to the younger sister, Nakanokimi, though he is aware of Niou's promiscuity. Ōigimi for her part tries to divert Kaoru's affection for herself to her sister. Bennokimi, sympathizing with Kaoru, admits him to Ōigimi's bedroom, but she senses his approach and flees, leaving her sister alone. When Kaoru discovers Nakanokimi, he feels sorry for her and angry at Ōigimi.

Kaoru's plan is successful. Niou marries Nakanokimi; but this does not alter Ōigimi's resolution not to marry. Worry causes her to lose weight, and she examines with satisfaction her face in the mirror, sure that no man will now be attracted to her. When it becomes clear that Niou is unfaithful to her sister, Ōigimi feels disillusion with Kaoru, who had assured her of Niou's steadfastness. She had trusted Kaoru, but this is no longer possible, and she begins to think of death as the only release from her trials. When she dies not long afterward, Kaoru regrets he did not follow her suggestion and marry Nakanokimi, rather than bring unhappiness both to himself and Ōigimi.

Kaoru learns from Nakanokimi about her half-sister Ukifune, and when he is told that she resembles Ōigimi, his interest is aroused. One day he returns to Uji, where he catches sight of Ukifune through a crack in a door. The resemblance to Ōigimi is indeed astonishing (one recalls Murasaki's resemblance to Fujitsubo), and he is drawn back again and again.

Kaoru is by no means infatuated with Ukifune—even after they have become lovers he cannot help contrasting her unfavorably with Ōigimi—but he is attentive and always behaves correctly. Niou, once again getting wind of a romance, goes to Ukifune's room one night and, mimicking Kaoru's voice, gains admission. He spends the night with her, and pleases her more than the forbidding Kaoru. But she is under no illusions about him.

One snowy day Niou makes his way to Uji and carries Ukifune off to a house on the other side of the river where they spend two days together. Ukifune is torn by mixed feelings—love for Niou, whom she knows she cannot trust, and fear that Kaoru, whom she does not love, will learn of her affair with Niou and abandon her. Kaoru in fact discovers that Niou has been visiting Ukifune and is outraged. He stops writing, and she thinks of suicide.

> The girl felt as if she were being cut to shreds. She wanted to die....
>
> And outside the river roared. "There are gentler rivers," said her mother, somewhat absentmindedly. "I'm sure the general [Kaoru] feels guilty about leaving her all this time in this godforsaken place."
>
> Yes, it was a terrible river, swift and treacherous, said one of the women. "Why, just the other day the ferryman's little grandson slipped on his oar and fell in. Any number of people have drowned in it."
>
> If she herself were to disappear, thought Ukifune, people would grieve for a while, but only for a time; and if she were to live on, an object of ridicule, there would be no end to her woes. Death would cancel out the accounts, nothing seemed to stand in the way.[69]

Ukifune's depression is more profound than any described earlier in the novel, and toward the end she resolves to throw herself into the terrible river. She makes preparations for death: "Unobtrusively, she began tearing up suggestive papers, burning them in her lamp and sending the ashes down the river."[70] She disappears soon afterward. Everyone supposes she is dead, but she has not drowned, recalling ironically the meaning of her nickname, "floating (or drifting) boat." This name was derived from the poem she composed and gave to Niou: "Immutable may be / the color of the orange tree / on this small island; / and yet this drifting boat / cannot know where it is bound."[71]

Kaoru's reactions to the news of Ukifune's death are surprisingly cold. His calm seems rather out of character, but perhaps he is deceiving himself: long after Niou has shifted his attentions to other women, Kaoru, though he cannot forgive Ukifune for deceiving him, still searches for her.

Ukifune is found by some priests near the river, incapable of speech, and is nursed back to health. In response to her entreaties, she is admitted to holy orders, and goes to live with some nuns. Kaoru accidentally learns where Ukifune is and asks a boy, one of her brothers, to beg her to see him; but she sends the boy away without an answer. This is where the novel ends.

The Uji chapters are literally the best part of *The Tale of Genji*. There are not many characters, and each is carefully drawn. Genji is so marvelously beautiful and accomplished that it is hard for readers to identify with him. This problem does not arise in the case of Kaoru or Niou, whose beauty is fully described but whose flaws are equally obvious. Both *kaoru* and *niou* are verbs meaning "to be fragrant," and these nicknames suggest their courtliness; but whereas Kaoru's mysterious scent is a natural part of him over which he has no control, Niou resorts to blending perfumes in order to keep up with his rival. Niou is the less attractive of the two men, even though we are told that he is handsomer than Kaoru and can gather from Ukifune's preference that he possesses greater charm; but it is hard to forgive his ruthlessness in pursuing the few women whom Kaoru has loved. There is a bitterness in the relations between the two men absent from Genji's with his rival, Tō no Chūjō, another sign perhaps that they belong to a world in decline in which friendship is unhesitatingly discarded for personal advantage.

The doctrine of mappō, the latter days of the Buddhist Law,[72] may have colored Murasaki Shikibu's portrayal of times closer to her own than those of the peerless Genji, times when the sorrow of human existence was no mere phrase. The persons of the Uji chapters live in a world much darker than Genji's. The unhappy Ōigimi has resolved never to marry; her sister Nakanokimi is persuaded by his beauty to trust Niou, only to discover his heartlessness; Ukifune, an unsophisticated girl, finds being courted by two desirable young men so oppressive that she attempts suicide; and the two men, so superlatively gifted, are both frustrated in their desires. The story of these unforgettable persons develops systematically and even inevitably; there is no question here of chapters having been written out of order or later inserted.

CONTEMPORARY APPEAL OF THE WORK

Murasaki Shikibu devoted her greatest attention to the elements in human life that have changed least over the centuries. Because the emotions of her characters are so easily intelligible, we sometimes obtain a startling impression of modernity, and it is easy to overlook even the aspects of life in Heian Japan that differ most conspicuously from our own. Although we are repeatedly informed that court ladies were normally invisible to men, hidden behind curtains and intervening screens, it is difficult to believe that these people whom we feel we know so intimately could have fallen passionately in love without once getting a proper look at each other, and we may therefore suppress the reality of the curtains and screens, regardless of what Murasaki Shikibu says. It is hard even to keep in mind what the faces of the women must have looked like: women customarily blackened their teeth and shaved their eyebrows (painting false eyebrows on their foreheads); but when we attempt to visualize the women of *The Tale of Genji* we are more likely to think of Japanese women we have actually seen than the lookalikes of the old illustrations.

Arthur Waley, writing in 1933, discussed the resemblances that reviewers had found between *The Tale of Genji* and the works of Proust, Jane Austen, Boccaccio, and Shakespeare, commenting, "Her book indeed is like those caves, common in a certain part of Spain, in which as one climbs from chamber to chamber the natural formation of the rock seems in succession to assume a semblance to every known form of sculpture—here a figure from Chartres, there a Buddha from Yun-Kang, a Persian conqueror, a Byzantine ivory."[73] Waley did not deny the resemblances that reviewers had found between the writings of Murasaki Shikibu and modern writers: "Murasaki, like the novelist of to-day, is not principally interested in the events of the story, but rather in the effect which these events may have upon the minds of her characters. Such books as hers it is convenient, I think, to call 'novels,' while reserving for other works of fiction the name 'story' or 'romance.'"[74]

Critics have questioned the appropriateness of referring to *The Tale of*

Genji as a "novel." The lowly reputation of fiction as a whole in the Heian period contrasts with the prestige that novels enjoy today; but Tamagami Takuya, who disliked referring to any monogatari as a novel, conceded that The Tale *of Genji* was read and discussed by men as well as women,[75] suggesting that, whether or not modern in any other sense, the work was treated with the respect due a work of high literary value. This contemporary evaluation has not wavered. *The Tale of Genji* is the central work of Japanese literature. It was read and imitated by generations of court writers, and was adapted for use in different forms of drama, not only the aristocratic Nō[76] but the plebeian Bunraku and Kabuki theaters. It was the model (though considerably distorted) for Saikaku's *Life of an Amorous* Man (1682), the work that is considered to mark the birth of the characteristic form of fiction of the premodern period. It furnished the advocates of the Shintō revival of the eighteenth century (notably Motoori Norinaga) with the supreme example of distinctively Japanese expression. In the twentieth century it has been translated into modern Japanese by Tanizaki Jun'ichirō and other important writers, and through these translations has reached an infinitely greater number of readers than ever before. It has been beautifully translated into English, French, and German, bringing it world renown.[77] It occupies in Japanese literature the place of Shakespeare in English literature, of Dante in Italian literature, or of Cervantes in Spanish literature. It is also a monument of world literature, the first novel of magnitude composed anywhere, a work that is at once distinctively Japanese and universally affecting.

NOTES

1. *Kawabata Yasunari Zenshū*, XXIII, p. 319
2. See *Dawn to the West*, I, p. 824.
3. The appropriateness of the term "novel" has been much discussed. I use it as a convenience, rather than "monogatari," "tale," or "romance."
4. *Nihon Koten Bungaku Daijiten*, II, p. 408.
5. See Ivan Morris, *As I Crossed a Bridge of Dreams*, p. 55. The diarist wrote that an aunt presented her with "fifty-odd volumes of *The Tale of Genji*." She did not date this entry, but it follows close after mention of the death in 1021 of her nurse.
6. See *Nihon Koten Bungaku Daijiten*, II, p. 406.
7. It has been suggested that some other person who was close to Murasaki Shikibu wrote the chapters "Niou," "Kōbai," and "Takegawa."
8. It was advanced by Ichijō Kaneyoshi in his book of *Genji* criticism entitled *Kachō Yōjō* (1492).
9. See *Nihon Koten Bungaku Daijiten*, II, p. 400.
10. See Ii Haruki, *Genji Monogatari no Nazo*, p. 137
11. See Akiyama Ken, *Genji Monogatari*, p. 99.
12. Tametoki's waka were included in imperial collections, notably the *Goshūishū* in which there are three. Poem 147 in this collection is of the *jukkai* variety, a complaint, using the imagery of flowers, over his failure to gain advancement.

13. Akiyama, *Genji*, p. 100.

14. *Ibid.*, p. 100. The story is given in *Tales of Times Now Past* and elsewhere.

15. See Yamamoto Ritatsu, *Murasaki Shikibu Nikki, Murasaki Shikibu Shū*, p. 136. The poem is included in the *Senzaishū*.

16. *Ibid.*

17. Akiyama, *Genji*, p. 108.

18. In kambun, rather than in kana, because of its greater concision, and possibly also on the analogy of *Nihon Ryōiki*, which was composed in kambun as the basic material for sermons to be delivered in Japanese.

19. Tamagami Takuya, *Genji Monogatari Kenkyū*, pp. 147, 150.

20. *Ibid.*, pp. 150–51.

21. Unfortunately for this charming legend, the temple burned to the ground after the time of Murasaki's supposed visit.

22. See Ii, *Genji*, p. 45. Abe Akio, a noted specialist of *The Tale of Genji*, also believed that Murasaki Shikibu began her work with the "Waka-Murasaki" chapter. See Aileen Gatten, "The Order of the Early Chapters in the *Genji monogatari*," pp. 30–33.

23. See Arthur Waley's translation of *The Tale of Genji*, p. 7, note 1, where he stated, "Murasaki, still under the influence of her somewhat childish predecessors, writes in a manner which is a blend of the court chronicle with the conventional fairy-tale." However, the "Kiritsubo" chapter is singled out for special praise in *Mumyō Zōshi* (Story Without a Name) and in many later works.

24. See *Nihon Koten Bungaku Daijiten*, II, p. 410.

25. Takeda Munetoshi, *Genji Monogatari no Kenkyū*. Gatten, in her absorbing article "The Order," discussed problems in the narration when the work is read in the accepted order. She drew on the theory of Abe Akio, who postulated two lines of composition, the "Wakamurasaki Group" and the "Hahakigi Group." These two lines correspond very closely to Takeda's theory. Abe believed that the "Kiritsubo" chapter was written perhaps at the time of the twenty-first chapter, "Otome," but Gatten decided that the "Kiritsubo" chapter was indispensable to the narration of the early chapters and must *in some form* have existed before the "Wakamurasaki" chapter was written. (Gatten, "The Order," p. 39.)

26. Takeda, *Genji*, p. 34–35.

27. *Ibid.*, pp. 17ff.

28. *Ibid.*, pp. 64–65.

29. Waley. *Genji*, p. 92.

30. Edward Seidensticker, *The Tale of Genji*, I, p. 57.

31. Waley was not the only one to believe that the women must be standing on something. Ikeda Kikan in his edition of *Genji Monogatari* (in Nihon Koten Zensho series), I, p. 234, had the women on *fumidai*, a kind of platform. This is more plausible than Waley's table or bed, but it also requires an explanation of why they were on a fumidai. Other commentators have suggested that the floor level was higher than Genji would have expected, and for this reason the women seemed taller than they actually were.

32. Esperanza Ramirez-Christensen wrote, in "The Operation of the Lyrical Mode in the *Genji Monogatari*," p. 39, "What happens in the passages under consideration is that the poetic function is being superimposed upon the narrative progression, slowing it down and transforming its constitutive elements (plot-character-setting) into paradigmatic transparencies of meaning. The paradigm, by reiterating the same message in various reifications, endows the narrative with a certain permanence, and at the same time a certain ambiguity and richness." Her essay is specifically concerned with the first three of the ten Uji chapters, but her illuminating observations are valid for the entire work.

Another essay in the same book (*Ukifune: Love in The Tale of Genji*, edited by Andrew Pekarik) by Amy Vladeck Heinrich, "*Blown in Flurries*: The Role of the Poetry in

'Ukifune,'" gives further proof of the vital function played by the poems, though they are often overlooked by those who write about *The Tale of Genji*.

33. This is the subject of Janet Goff's *Noh Drama and The Tale of Genji*. See below, pp. 1022–24, for an example of how a passage from the "Suma" chapter of *Genji* was used in the Nō play *Matsukaze*.

34. I am thinking, for example, of the passage in Part One of the "Wakana" chapter in which a cat on a leash upsets the screen protecting the Third Princess from the gaze of outsiders. Kashiwagi gets only a glimpse of the princess, but it is enough to make him fall desperately in love, the commencement of their tragic affair. See Seidensticker, *Genji*, II, pp. 592–93; Waley, *Genji*, pp. 642–43.

35. Akiyama, *Genji*, p. 8.

36. Takaakira's rebellion figures in *The Gossamer Years*, and the Mother of Michitsuna sent a poem to Aimiya, Takaakira's wife, when he was exiled to Kyūshū Aimiya was the sister of the Tōnomine Captain. See chapter 9, notes 17 and 36 (pages 403–4).

37. The role of ghosts in the work is exhaustively discussed by Mitoma Kōsuke in *Genji Monogatari no Minzokugakuteki Kenkyū*. See also Norma Field, *The Splendor of Longing in the Tale of Genji*, pp. 51–63, where spirit possession is discussed.

38. Translation in Seidensticker, *Genji*, I, p. 3.

39. Translation by Witter Bynner in Cyril Birch, *Anthology of Chinese Literature*, I, pp. 266–69.

40. Translation in Ryusaku Tsunoda, Wm. Theodore de Bary, and Donald Keene, *Sources of Japanese Tradition*, pp. 532–34.

41. *Ibid.*, p. 534.

42. See Haruo Shirane, *The Bridge of Dreams: a Poetics of "The Tale of Genji,"* pp. 10–11, for a discussion of this aspect of the work.

43. Shirane, *The Bridge*, pp. 3–4 considers this theme, and cites (p. 228) the article by the folklore scholar Origuchi Shinobu, "Shōsetsu gokyoku bungaku ni okeru monogatari yōso," in which it is discussed. Field (in *The Splendor*, pp. 33–35) quotes Origuchi and considers the same theme in *Tales of Ise* and similar works. See also Mitani Kuniaki, *Genji Monogatari Shitsukeito*, pp. 24–31.

44. Field (in *The Splendor*, pp. 97–103) considers the stepmother (and stepdaughter) theme in Heian literature with reference to *The Tale of Genji*.

45. Translated by Ivan Morris in *The World of the Shining Prince*, pp. 308–9.

46. Translation in Seidensticker, *Genji*, I, p. 14.

47. Minamoto was one of the two most powerful noble families of the time, the other being the Fujiwara. The Sino-Japanese reading of Minamoto is Gen; hence, the name Genji, or "he of the Minamoto clan." The character Genji is not given a personal name anywhere in the work.

48. The irregularity in the succession was responsible for the action of the prewar militarists in banning publication of the offending chapters of Tanizaki's modern-language translation of *The Tale of Genji*.

49. Arthur Waley, *The Lady of the Boat*, p. 15. The passage occurs in the Seidensticker translation in *Genji*, II, p. 735.

50. See Waley, *Genji*, p. 146. Seidensticker, who was evidently using a different text, omitted this passage.

51. Seidensticker, *Genji*, I, p. 142. See also Waley, *Genji*, p. 227.

52. Seidensticker, *Genji*, I, p. 180.

53. Waley, *Genji*, p. 100. See also Seidensticker, *Genji*, I, p. 63.

54. See Waley, *Genji*, pp. 262–78; also Seidensticker, *Genji*, I, pp. 165–74.

55. Seidensticker, *Genji*, I, p. 183; Waley renders the passage, "He thought with great tenderness and concern of Lady Rokujō's distress; but it was clear to him that he must

beware of ever again allowing her to regard him as her true haven of refuge. If however she would renew their friendship in quite new terms, permitting him to enjoy her company and conversation at such times as he could conveniently arrange to do so, he saw no reason why they should not sometimes meet." (*Genji*, p. 294.)

56. Arthur Waley, *The Sacred Tree*, p. 41. See also Seidensticker, *Genji*, I, p. 186.

57. Waley, *The Sacred Tree*, p. 43.

58. *Ibid.*, p. 44.

59. *Ibid.*, p. 61.

60. Waley, *Genji*, p. 106.

61. Waley refers to the lady as Utsusemi, Seidensticker by the translation of this name, the Lady of the Locust Shell. Her rejection of Genji occurs in chapter 2.

62. Seidensticker, *Genji*, II, p. 636. See also Arthur Waley, *Blue Trousers*, p. 230.

63. See Seidensticker, *Genji*, II, p. 708.

64. *Ibid.*, p. 710.

65. *Ibid.*, p. 751. See also Waley, *The Lady*, p. 41.

66. In the absence of firm information about the transmission of the text during the two centuries between Murasaki Shikibu's manuscript and the oldest surviving manuscript, it is impossible to be sure whether or not these three chapters were in the original version. For a brief history of the texts of *The Tale of Genji*, see Aileen Gatten, "Three Problems in the Text of 'Ukifune,'" pp. 87–89. The earliest surviving recension of the entire text with variants was completed by Minamoto Chikayuki in 1255. Four chapters in Fujiwara Teika's handwriting, made early in the thirteenth century, survive, and later manuscripts purport to be copies of his text.

67. Seidensticker, *Genji*, II, p. 772.

68. *Ibid.*, p. 781.

69. *Ibid.*, p. 999.

70. *Ibid.*, p. 1006.

71. Translation by Amy Vladeck Heinrich in Pekarik, *Ukifune*, p. 156.

72. According to the doctrine of mappō, after the death of Shakyamuni Buddha there would be three great periods affecting his teachings: during the first, of five hundred years, they would flourish; during the second, of one thousand years, they would decline; and in the third period, of ten thousand years, they would gradually disappear. In Japan it was widely believed that the third period, that of mappō, would begin in 1052. Once the world entered this phase, it would be impossible for individuals to save themselves; they would have to depend on the saving grace of Amida for salvation.

73. Arthur Waley, *The Bridge of Dreams*, p. 23.

74. Waley, *The Sacred Tree*, pp. 30–31.

75. Tamagami, *Genji Monogatari Kenkyū*, p. 144.

76. See Goff, *Noh Drama*, for an account of how the dramatists borrowed from *The Tale of Genji*.

77. The earliest English and French (partial) translations, made in the nineteenth century, did little to promote the reputation of *The Tale of Genji* abroad, but the translations into English of Arthur Waley (1926–33) and Edward Seidensticker (1976), into French by Rene Sieffert (1978–85), and into German by Oscar Benl (1966) have been widely read and admired.

DORIS G. BARGEN

The Search for Things Past in the Genji monogatari

Marcel Proust has become the spectre haunting *Genji* studies. There have been many provocative references and a few general observations, but, despite agreement on the importance of the comparison, there has been no critical work specifically devoted to the task of comparing and contrasting Murasaki Shikibu and Marcel Proust. The absence of analysis is surprising because a sustained comparison illuminates both the *Genji monogatari* and *A la recherche du temps perdu*.[1] In these two classic works sexual preoccupation is, to a remarkable degree, symbolically incestuous,[2] grounded in excessive love, and determined by intricate family histories. As in the story of Phaidra and Hippolytos,[3] both Murasaki's and Proust's heroes suffer wounds from the past. These wounds motivate sexual behavior marked by image transference and compulsive regressive shifts from loved one to primary substitute to secondary substitute. Finally, frustrated love stimulates a search for the past which is a major theme of Murasaki's book and the title of Proust's.

MYTH MAKERS

The Tale of Genji begins with the fateful passion of the Old Emperor for his favorite, but low-ranking consort, Kiritsubo. From this excessive love,

From *Harvard Journal of Asiatic Studies* 51, no. 1 (June 1991). © 1991 by Harvard Journal of Asiatic Studies.

Genji is born. Genji's sexual orientation[4] is imprinted into his infant's consciousness by his parents' passion. His pursuit of a mother figure in his love affairs is motivated by the loss, at the age of two, of his mother, whom his father continues to venerate. The ominous exclusiveness of the Old Emperor's love for Kiritsubo is widely perceived as the mirror image of the Chinese Emperor Hsüan Tsung's love for Yang Kuei-fei at the peak (718–756) of the T'ang Dynasty. This love, symbolic of a period of growing political chaos and discontent, led to a historic uprising in An Lu-shan's rebellion (755), the flight of the Emperor, and the death of his concubine. By Murasaki Shikibu's time (?973–?1014), the historic events were transformed into myth and well known through Po Chü-i's "Song of Unending Sorrow" or *Ch'ang hen ko*.[5] Murasaki's monogatari, however, goes far beyond an isolated instance of love's excess and its political consequences. In her fictional portrait of an age, the theme of excessive love, introduced in the brief episode of the Kiritsubo Emperor's archetypal variant on the Chinese legend, is repeated over three generations, beginning with Genji's. With each generation, the theme grows in psychological complexity and tragic implications.

The beginning of the *Genji*, as established by literary tradition,[6] is indeed deceptively matter-of-fact about events of grave impact. Genji and his stepmother Fujitsubo commit symbolic incest.[7] Since it is said that the Emperor Hsüan Tsung had originally intended Yang Kuei-fei for one of his sons,[8] Genji's incestuous love is an even closer analogy to the Chinese legend than his parents' excessive but otherwise legitimate passion. With this form of illicit love, Genji does more than break a moral taboo; he violates a social religious taboo.[9] To the pursuit of a mother figure is added the cuckolding of the father on the one hand and the blasphemous offense against the sun goddess Amaterasu-ōmikami on the other. The child born from the incestuous union, namely, the future Reizei Emperor, becomes the living memento of Genji's triple offense. What saves Genji from public disgrace— and Fujitsubo with him—is his ability to keep secret his passion and its illicit fruit.

In a society with a complex marital structure in constant flux,[10] Genji practices polygyny more than did his father. While his love demonstrates image transference (attraction facilitated by physical resemblance), he avoids the monomaniacal fixation on one person at a time which had caused his father so much distress. Instead, whenever he anticipates the loss of one beloved person, he prepares for the possession of the next.

Despite some discontent with and criticism of his behavior, his promiscuity (but not his ventures into incest) was the norm in the judgment of Murasaki Shikibu's contemporaries. Whether or not criticism of Genji by some important female characters can be taken as the author's indirect criticism of her male-dominated society is difficult to ascertain. It can be shown, however, that the psychologically more complex heroes of the second and third generations have lost Genji's capacity for easy image transference. In this respect, Kashiwagi and Kaoru are the most sombre, tragically inclined heroes, especially when compared to the pedestrian Yūgiri and the frivolous Niou, respectively.

One existential condition in particular stimulates the need for image transference and substitution: orphanhood. Although orphanhood does not bear traumatic consequences for Genji, who does not remember his mother, he nonetheless seems motivated by the memory of its hardships when he seeks custody of the child Murasaki. Genji asks Murasaki's grandmother for custody of the child whose mother bore her "just before she died" (90; 1:288).[11]

> "I have heard the sad story, and wonder if I might offer myself as a substitute for your late daughter. I was very young when I lost the one who was dearest to me, and all through the years since I have had strange feelings of aimlessness and futility. We share the same fate, and I wonder if I might not ask that we be companions in it." (92; 1:292)

Since Genji is struck by the ten-year-old Murasaki's physical resemblance to both his stepmother and mother, the question arises whether he is motivated by pity or self-pity, by their shared fate or by incestuous image transference, or by a combination thereof.

In order to retain the pose of the Shining Prince after the cuckolding of his imperial father, Genji needs the shrewdness of a politician. Conversely, Genji's sense of political responsibility provides him with a reason to keep the secret of his son, the future Reizei Emperor's incestuous illegitimacy. Because of these immediate concerns, Genji cannot afford to probe into the mysteries of the past. When the secret of paternity is revealed to the Reizei Emperor, without Genji's knowledge, it is the troubled son rather than the father who, at least momentarily, becomes obsessed with the past. While the innocent Reizei Emperor may hope to reason his way through the moral maze, Genji prefers not to think about the matter. He in fact continues to believe that the concealment of the Reizei Emperor's identity was successful: "Genji's worries had passed and his great sin had gone undetected" (592; 4:157). However, Genji does do penance at Suma for his love affair with Oborozukiyo, the wife of his half-brother, the then reigning Suzaku Emperor. In Suma a tempest inspires in him fears about "the end of the world" (248; 2:215). The storm also inspires a curious dream in which his deceased father summons him back to court and deters him from suicide, thus releasing him from "brief punishment for certain sins" (250; 2:219). It is as if Genji, repenting a similar but comparatively minor lapse, had miraculously been forgiven for the greatest sin of all, ironically, by his own father. At any event, Genji's boundless happiness and gratitude in response to the dream suggest that he received forgiveness for more than the venal sins for which he originally went into exile.

In *The Tale of Genji*, the discovery, the exploration, and the re-creation of myth are divided, with some overlapping, among the myth-maker Genji, the explorer Kaoru, and the re-creator Ukifune. Since Genji abstains from a conscious investigation of the past in order to avoid confrontation with taboos of incest and the equally unthinkable sin against the imperial line, since the middle generation of Yūgiri and Kashiwagi is preoccupied by the unheroic task of trying to extricate itself from the thickets sown by Genji and his contemporaries, it is only in the Uji chapters that Murasaki allows two members of the third generation a Proustian search for the past. Kaoru and Ukifune in particular are detached enough in time and space to contemplate past generations and to begin to understand the implications of excessive and incestuous love. In Proust's *A sort recherche du temps perdu*,[12] however, discovery, exploration, and re-creation of Marcel's private mythology fall to the single figure of the narrator-hero.

Both Marcel and Genji respond in their childhood and youth to external models of excessive love. The myth of Hippolytos in *Phèdre* colors Marcel's childhood, while the Swanns provide the model of excessive love. For Genji, the myth is that of Yang Kuei-fei, and the excessive love that of his father for his mother. The responses of Genji and Marcel to these influences determine their mature behavior and, in Genji's case, the behavior of generations to come.

MYTHS BECOME HISTORY:
THE DECLINE OF AN AGE

Sexual transgressions and violated taboos can precipitate not only the fall of a family, as in *Phèdre*; they can signal the decline of a whole society and culture. Both Murasaki and Proust portray the social and cultural decline of the times in which they wrote. In particular, the works abound in political antagonisms that split society in two camps and suggest imminent turn-overs of power. In Heian-kyō marital and political intrigues plague rival clans; in Proust's France the Dreyfus affair serves as a lengthy prologue to the chauvinistic hysteria of World War I.

The Shining Prince himself is a symbol of the coming decline. He is in a precarious position as the son of an emperor and an imperial consort of a not very impressive social position [*ito yamugoto naki kiwa ni wa aranu* , *NKBZ* 1:93] who suffers from intrigues of higher ranking consorts. Genji's transgression has become "socialized" by his defilement of the imperial line so that the Reizei Emperor becomes aware that "things are wrong, out of joint" (342) [*monogokorobosoku rei naranu kokochi namu suru, NKBZ* 2:443]. The heroes of the following two generations feel the problem of birth even more drastically. They must suffer the consequences of their progenitors' excessive love end seek relief from emotional disturbance in an obsessive quest for the significance of the past. The Eighth Prince in particular complicates the quest by misguiding and confusing the heroes of the Uji chapters.

Although he is Genji's half-brother, the Eighth Prince does not possess the radiance, discretion, or sensitivity that encourage a condoning of Genji's "sin." The Eighth Prince's excessive love for the mother of the two older Uji sisters takes a spiteful turn when, after the death of his beloved wife, he has an affair with her niece, a high-ranking lady-in-waiting, the *chūjō no kimi*, and fathers Ukifune. His "self-loathing" (920) [*ai naku sono koto ni oboshi korite, NKBZ* 5:448] for the betrayal of his principal wife and her idolized daughters as well as his lingering attachment to them hinders the pure pursuit of such Buddhist ideals as the detachment from all desire. While in the case of Genji symbolic incest leads to conflicts that are solved within a secular context, with the Eighth Prince the same phenomenon leads to conflicts of this world that prevent religious fulfillment. In other words, in the case of the latter, secular conflicts are hidden by religious ambitions that hinder the pure pursuit of eros.

The Eighth Prince's continuing plight and dogmatic confusion have upsetting effects upon Kaoru and Ukifune. While neither Genji's radiance is without blemish nor the Eighth Prince's heart totally dark, the latter has been perceived sympathetically because of his pathetic nature and religious calling. Scholars have ignored his destructive influence on others in the service of his personal salvation.[13] It is, however, important to recognize that the Eighth Prince becomes an unfortunate role model for the disoriented third generation. While continuing to be fascinated by the priest whose hidden personal history contains a series of disasters from orphanhood to political frustrations, the younger Uji characters are oppressed rather than inspired by his formidable authority. Especially in the Uji chapters the appropriate image of "drifting" occurs frequently in connection with images of the Uji river, which contains a whirlpool of meanings, such as the flow of time, memory, Lethe, and death.

In *A la recherche du temps perdu*, too, social origins and status frequently stand in an inverse relation. The aristocracy must give way to "the rising tide of democracy" (II, 10; II, 15). No wonder, then, that the aristocracy's obsession with pedigrees seems anachronistic. Here as in the Uji chapters, where the focus moves away from the high nobility in the capital to a fallen prince and fallen princesses in the Uji "wilderness," the high nobility may officially still be in possession of its heroic stature, but for the literary imagination heroes have been replaced by anti-heroes,[14] as it were, whether they are social upstarts or members of the fallen aristocracy. Even outsiders like Mme Verdurin become prominent in a society whose class barriers have been knocked askew. Marcel himself comes from a well-to-do bourgeois family. His ambition to join the *haute volée* of the Faubourg Saint-Germain leads him down the "Guermantes Way," which is the symbolic as well as geographic antipode of "Swann's Way."

PSYCHOLOGICAL RESPONSES TO A DIMINISHED WORLD, AND THE MYTH OF LOVE

In the *Recherche* as in the *Genji* social and political ambitions are woven into an intricate network with the psychological need for substitutions and image transferences. When Marcel's grandmother dies, he too dies symbolically. When he is "born again" (II, 358; II, 345), the world has changed as much for him as for Murasaki's characters after the death of the Shining Prince. The deaths of these two important figures (Genji and Marcel's grandmother) help to mythologize them and to strip the aura of myth from their depraved counterparts (the Eighth Prince and Mme de Guermantes). It is no coincidence that Marcel's love for Mme de Guermantes does not long survive his grandmother. Instead, Marcel returns to the type suggested by the dead body of his grandmother, which is, curiously, "the form of a young girl" (II, 357; II, 345). Thus Marcel's fixation on his grandmother, from which he temporarily escaped in his pursuit of Mme de Guermantes, is again evoked in his renewed courtship of Albertine and, ultimately, of Mlle de Saint-Loup, a girl who is at once Saint-Loup's daughter, Swann's granddaughter, and almost as an illustration of the intricate network of interrelated characters—Mme de Guermantes' great-niece.

Deprivations by separation or death result in an intense feeling of loneliness. To compensate for traumatic loss, the afflicted—most prominently, Marcel, Genji, Kaoru—feel the desire for excessive love which is also symbolically incestuous.[15] *Repeated* deprivation—such as Genji's loss of his mother and then Fujitsubo, Kaoru's loss of three father figures (Genji,

Kashiwagi, and the Eighth Prince), Marcel's separation from his mother and then his grandmother—lead to an intensified loneliness, estrangement from society, and, finally, the desire to replace family, group, or clan affiliations by the focus on a single individual. Image transferences may still occur, but they will be less determined by intimate family connections; e.g., Kaoru's specific attachment to Ukifune (the last of the Uji sisters), and Marcel's pursuit of Albertine.[16] All these particular bonds are solipsistic if not narcissistic in so far as the partners not only withdraw from larger social issues but also seek to share the same introverted sexual inclination, a concern for the past, and an indifference to physical reproduction.

For Genji, the trauma of parental death nearly coincides with the traumatic circumstances of his birth. Other characters make the traumatic connection between birth and death more consciously, later in life, as, for instance, Marcel, Kaoru, and Ukifune. None of the above, with the exception of Genji, has children, and Genji is puzzled by the fact that his progeny are so few. In his relationship with Murasaki he precludes the dangers of excessive love by dispersing his affections among several women, as was common in Heian times. His amorous diversification appears almost designed to avoid future "sins" and to avert the downfall of an age, which Chinese legend has shown obsessions can cause. As *Genji* had been fortunate in keeping his "sin" a secret from the general public, he may have unconsciously felt compelled to divert to others a portion of his boundless love for Murasaki—in the interest of society and to atone for his "sin." Can it be merely a coincidence that he dreams at Suma of his father's forgiveness and is inspired to father the future Akashi Empress, far away from court and near the place of repentance? It is as if Murasaki waited at home as a living reminder of the past.

Kaoru seeks also to comprehend the past and to atone for parental sins rather than to devote himself to promiscuity and procreation, which is what society expects of him: "longing to know the facts of his birth, Kaoru had prayed that he might one day have a clear explanation" (795; 5:151). A clear causal connection is established between "the old doubts" concerning his birth and his sexual "reserve," his "strain of melancholy that kept him from losing himself in romantic dalliance" (740; 5:23–4). Known and ridiculed as "Lord Proper" for his prudishness and long-lasting bachelorhood, Kaoru surrenders to social pressures[17] and marries only when he feels abandoned by his male companion, Niou, who reluctantly succumbs to princely duties and produces an heir for the throne. Niou's wife, Nakanokimi, the middle of the Uji sisters, devotes herself to maternity and restricts her spiritual intimacy with Kaoru. Not surprisingly, there are no children from Kaoru's own formalistic marriage to the Second Princess.[18] Even more than in the case of Murasaki's regretted childlessness, Kaoru's voluntary abstinence demonstrates that his obsessions are with the past rather than the future.

Kaoru's compulsion to solve the riddle of the past is reinforced by his growing awareness of a society in decline. His resistance to the degenerate standards of the age is reflected in his role as "the fragrant captain" (740; 5:22). Competitions in scents are only one indication of the state of Heian arts. While Niou's blend of perfumes consists of a highly exaggerated concoction which stirs allegations of "a certain preciosity" (740; 5:22), Kaoru is known for his natural fragrance.[19] Moreover, the telling fragrance metaphorically expresses Kaoru's inability—if not his refusal—to play a social role: "He could not hide. Let him step behind something in hopes of going unobserved, and that scent would announce his presence" (739; 5:21).

There is, therefore, tragic irony in his idolization of the Eighth Prince as his chosen father because this confounded figure is responsible for Kaoru's dangerously self-defeating obsession with the past.[20] Kaoru's implied homoerotic inclinations[21] are the result of an almost hysterical desire not to repeat the sins of the fathers. Namely, what Kaoru's three father figures share in their most passionate affairs is the responsibility for their offspring's confused sense of identity. Thus the Reizei Emperor must silently bear the psychological weight of Genji's incestuous affair with Fujitsubo; Kaoru's identity problem is rooted in Kashiwagi's adulterous passion for the Third Princess, and, finally, it is Ukifune who most poignantly mirrors the plight of an illegitimate and unacknowledged child and who suffers from being the fruit of an affair that symbolizes the Eighth Prince's betrayal of his idolized *kita no kata*.

Kaoru breaks with the common pattern of arranged marriages and adulterous love by image fixation through family resemblance. Originally, his attraction (incestuous and homoerotic) to the Eighth Prince constituted an image transference of the traditional kind, in this specific case, from his assumed father Genji to Genji's half-brother. When Kaoru learns that Kashiwagi was his real father, he nonetheless continues to venerate the memory of a wholly imaginary father figure at Uji as the key to an understanding of the past. Curiously, the problems embedded in Kaoru's origins are foreshadowed by the experience of the Reizei Emperor, his guardian. Reizei is bound by his high office to neglect his filial duties and to pretend, by keeping the "secret" of his illegitimacy, that the imperial line is pure. Kaoru might have venerated his father's memory but chooses instead to honor thus the late Eighth Prince, his self-chosen father figure.

When the Eighth Prince dies, Ōigimi becomes his first substitute, because she resembles him more than does Nakanokimi. It is important to note that Kaoru, upon Ōigimi's death, is first drawn to her younger sister, but, since she resembles her mother, the attraction consists of friendship rather than passion. Through Nakanokimi's mediation, Kaoru learns of Ukifune, who is said to bear a striking resemblance to her father and, by inference, to Ōigimi. If in chronological terms Ōigimi is the Eighth Prince's first substitute, Ukifune becomes his second. In other words, the general assumption that Kaoru selected Ukifune to be the late Ōigimi's substitute suffers from an important oversight, namely, that Ōigimi is not Kaoru's original choice for his affections. It is precisely this unexplored complexity of Ōigimi's role as substitute for her late father that had inhibited her and Kaoru from entering into a conventional love relationship.[22]

Furthermore, it is no accident that the narrative is interspersed with timely resurgences of the memory of Kaoru's original point of reference, the Eighth Prince, just as he hears tantalizing bits of news about Ukifune. And, while it has been pointed out that Ukifune's first appearance on the scene is intimately connected with Ōigimi through the imagery of the Uji Bridge,[23] it is equally significant that Kaoru is moved by the fact that Ukifune is just returning from a pilgrimage to Hatsuse where she prayed for her father (cf. 921, 932, 935). In short, Ukifune is not merely Ōigimi's substitute, but, less obviously, her father's double. Conversely, Kaoru, being the Prince's disciple and having adopted his manners if not his mannerisms, represents a "return" of the father for Ukifune (on a literally subconscious level, as she never knew the Eighth Prince). Although Kaoru's pursuit of these two Uji sisters is founded on their family resemblance to his male paragon, the Eighth Prince, it is a doomed and delusory effort because he cannot possibly find a father substitute in them. Nonetheless, by his obsession with Uji, Kaoru gradually overcomes the conflict between sexual abstinence preached by the Eighth Prince and his personal need for "kindred spirits" (834) [*itodo waga kokoro kayoite oboyureba*, NKBZ 5:241] in an otherwise unbearably lonely quest for the truth.

By warning Kaoru as well as his two favorite daughters, Ōigimi and Nakanokimi, against carnal desire (cf. 805; 5:172; 806; 5:176–7), the Eighth Prince unwittingly stimulated awareness of their sexual dilemma.[24] Yet awareness is not enough to effect sexual fulfillment. Ōigimi is dominated by her father and dies a virgin, grieving for him and worrying over her younger sister Nakanokimi's involvement with the faithless Niou. By contrast, Nakanokimi resembles her mother, who designated the infant as a "keepsake" or *katami* (776; 5:111) just before she died in childbirth. Under the influence and protection of her mother's last will, Nakanokimi alone among the Uji sisters has enough distance from her father to escape from his possessive sphere.[25] Thus her departure from Uji and her marriage may violate her father's wishes, but they actually do no more than throw her notion of the "past and future [...] into a meaningless jumble" (898; 5:392).

While Nakanokimi's drama is played low key, Ōigimi's and Ukifune's stories reach tragic proportions. Despite the fact that Ukifune is unrecognized by her father and deemed unworthy of indoctrination against the other sex, she provokes his resentful spirit by loving the two men (Niou and Kaoru) who have been intimately involved with his legitimate daughters.[26] A male possessing spirit has to be accounted for in Ukifune's possession case, a rare phenomenon in the *Genji*. If Kaoru's infatuation with Ukifune is confined to the idea that she is Ōigimi's sole substitute, and if Fujii's thesis that Ōigimi, metaphorically speaking, desired Ukifune's flesh ["*Oigimi wa Ukifune no niku o hoshita*"][27] holds, then one should expect Ōigimi to have possessed Ukifune. However, spirit possession typically does not follow the path of logic but of "oblique aggressive strategy."[28] Instead of being haunted by her half-sister," Ukifune, obsessed as she is with longing for her real father, becomes vulnerable to his wandering spirit. However, Ukifune survives the crisis brought on by her excessive love and exemplifies a radical way to cope with the past, namely, by artistic withdrawal.[29]

If the traumata of birth and death evoke two incompatible forces, namely, an excessive desire for love and an obsession with the past that makes conventional love all but impossible and tends to exclude procreation, the conflict of forces can be mediated by a third factor. Through the imagination psychological conflicts can be transcended. However, the imagination, depending on the character in question, has various uses ranging from self-delusion to artistic creation.

Like Genji and Kaoru, Proust's Marcel is exposed to repeated deprivations which challenge his imaginative resources. Prevarication in order to obtain his mother's good-night kiss is soon replaced by more refined imaginative techniques, such as image substitution. To prevent procreation, which is betrayal of the past, Marcel like Kaoru in particular, loves the inaccessible.

Inaccessibility is often ensured by the presence of a rival. While amorous rivals are ordinarily undesirable, here they are welcomed and needed. With his self-defeating strategy, Kaoru practically incites Niou to whisk away from him one Uji sister after another. When he finally wants Ukifune for himself alone, it is because he can be safe from the threat of excessive love. She is in a trance and it is only via the allegorical Bridge of Dreams, i.e., in the realm of the imagination, that he can join her.

Both Proust and Murasaki depict triangular love relationships with a specific psychological complexity and creative aftermath. These love affairs are dramatized in a unique way. In Proust's novel, Marcel's male role models are men who pursue inaccessible or inappropriate women. Swann is bewitched by Odette, Saint-Loup by Rachel. When Marcel falls in love, it is with Albertine, the leader of the androgynous band at Balbec, a girl whom Marcel suspects of lesbianism. Baron Charlus' homosexual affair with Morel is another *mésalliance*. In the *Recherche*, therefore, as in the *Genji*, love's inaccessibility is ensured not in the conventional way—by political animosities, marriage politics, or social intrigues—but by the fact that the lovers choose partners not of the same but of different sexual proclivities so that heterosexuals love homosexuals or bisexuals, and vice versa. This peculiarity of the protagonists' sexual orientation is deeply rooted in traumata of birth and death which in turn cause their obsession with the past through image substitution.

As with Marcel and Albertine, the association of disturbed sexuality and inaccessibility appears in *The Tale of Genji* as well, especially in the Uji chapters. Here it is the homosexually inclined male protagonist, Kaoru, who is drawn to Ukifune because she, among the daughters of the Eighth Prince, most resembles her father. So great is the resemblance that Kaoru identifies the two—directly, via the *tertium comparationis* of Ōigimi. His emphasis is not the living woman in front of him but on the deceased idol: "He wanted to go in immediately and say to her: 'So you were deceiving us. You are still alive'" (934) [*yo no naka ni owashikeru mono o, to iinagusamemahoshi* NKBZ 5:481].[30] To assume the deceased idol to be Ōigimi is the standard interpretation which seriously detracts from the complexities surrounding Kaoru's and Ōigimi's Platonic love relationship. It appears that especially in the Uji chapters various levels of analogous relationships need to be explored, even across generational lines, to reach to the depths of character motivation. Thus, in so far as Kaoru seeks in Ukifune, "this last sad foundling" (1023; 6:219), either a father or a brother, his love bears incestuous and homosexual features.

However, there is a possibility that Kaoru for once is drawn into the ways of the world, sexually, at Ukifune's Eastern Cottage which seems "a house apart from this gloomy world" (963; 6:77). Indeed it is a safe place from the haunts of the past.[31] Here Kaoru's intentions of making Ukifune a substitute for Ōigimi are overturned with "a new experience" (967; 6:85) of physical lovemaking that he and Ōigimi had denied themselves out of veneration for the past. Here, amidst the everyday world of ordinary life, yet "unfamiliar" in the vulgarity of "the sleepy voices of peddlers" and women workers as strong as "veritable demons" (967; 6:85),[32] Kaoru momentarily takes Ukifune for who she really is, in isolation from memories of the past. When Kaoru takes Ukifune back to Uji, to repeat the past, as it were, memories return, and Ukifune again seems in danger of neglect. Yet the events at the cottage are not easily reversible. To Kaoru's great astonishment, Ukifune now assumes priority for Ōigimi. Whatever happened at the Eastern

Cottage is startling, different from Kaoru's innocent night with Ōigimi. Then, at the anniversary of the Eighth Prince's death, memories of the past and "the smell of holy incense" (828; 5:226) dominated the love scene and did not permit a consecration of the present through the physical consummation of love. Instead, Kaoru and Ōigimi made a pact to be "curiosities" (828; 5:228) because of their sexual abstinence. Having successfully struggled for so long to remain faithful to the late Ōigimi (and the Eighth Prince, by inference), Kaoru now almost unawares makes the image transference to Ukifune.

The objects of image transference, Murasaki's Ukifune and Proust's Albertine, seek to escape from the complications of love relationships characterized by disharmonies in sexual orientation and the obsession with the past. By breaking away from their lovers, both Ukifune and Albertine liberate themselves from the phantoms of the past for whom they were forced to substitute. Ukifune's attempt at suicide fails, but, until her survival is discovered, her lovers must come to terms with her "death." This they do by increasingly absurd image transferences even as they continue to investigate the circumstances of her disappearance.

By contrast, Marcel must come to terms with Albertine's genuine suicide. Like Ukifune, Albertine had been a catalyst for the evocation of the past, for "the perpetual resurgence, at the bidding of identical moments, of moments from the past" (III, 488; III, 478). Significantly, Marcel's courtship of Albertine ends as it began, with references to Balbec and to Racine's *Phèdre*. When a telegram informs him that Albertine "was thrown by her horse against a tree while she was out riding" (III, 485; III, 476), he interprets her death suicide and acknowledges his complicity: "from my prison she had escaped to go and kill herself on a horse which but for me she would not have owned" (III, 510; III, 500). Previous reflections on *Phèdre* now assume prophetic character.[33]

Despite Proust's allusions to the myth of Phaidra and Hippolytos, his own narrative dispenses with supernatural effects in favor of a modern psychological approach. Murasaki Shikibu retains some elements from folk mythology and popular superstitions, but she too achieves a remarkably high degree of psychological characterization in the *Genji*, especially in the Uji chapters. Ukifune's possession by a demonic spirit owes something to the world of the supernatural, but the author's treatment of the scene (cf. 1044–6; VI, 269–71), in which a bewildered public clumsily tries to come to grips with the transfixed figure under the tree by identifying her, or her possessor with a fox or wood spirit, is apparently meant to be grotesque, while the possession, its cause and its aftermath are not. More importantly, the exorcism of the spirit of her father[34] and Ukifune's survival represent a triumph of rationality which is further explored in the psychological analysis of Ukifune's difficult recovery from her dramatic confrontation with the past."[35]

MYTH RE-CREATORS

After making several generations of fictional characters, or individuals in the different phases of their lives, relive and repeat a mythic pattern drawn from Po Chü-i or Racine, Murasaki and Proust select one of the characters to carry on the tradition of mythopoeia[36] in a forgetful age and a society in decline.[37] Both Murasaki and Proust employ repetition as a structural element "to suggest a fresh truth" (I, 955; I, 894).[38]

Repetitious events occur at different times and in different social contexts and never affect the same person in the same way. For example: Kaoru's loss of his three father figures affects him differently from his literal and symbolical losses of the three Uji sisters; Marcel loses both his grandmother and Albertine twice, first literally and then symbolically (and, one is tempted to anticipate, a third time in "the self-construed third dimension of his fiction). In this way successive analogous events are reminders of the past, hence the frequency of regressions toward childhood and adolescence.[39] These reworkings are, in fact, a literary analogue to the psychoanalytic method.[40]

Winding his way through a complex system of image transferences or substitutions, Kaoru seeks in Ukifune his last chance for fatherly love; and Marcel's pursuit of Albertine recalls his anxious need to possess his mother and grandmother. In addition, repetitions occur as cross references. For instance, Murasaki and Ukifune are both rejected by their fathers, and their alleged deaths are associated with possession by evil spirits, even if that is where the analogy ends. In Proust's novel, Albertine's violent death foreshadows Saint-Loup's death in World War I, both deaths suspected to be suicides.

Albertine's death, twice experienced, inspires Marcel to becomes a writer and to explore this "faint allegory of countless other separations" (III, 516; III, 506) with new means, in seclusion from the world. When choosing his reclusive vocation, Marcel withdraws from society. When Ukifune survives her attempt at suicide and turns to art for an understanding of the mysterious crises of her birth, "death," and "rebirth," she conforms to one of the strongest cultural imperatives of Heian times. For both Ukifune and Marcel the survival of their own symbolical deaths may, as one critic says about Proust's hero, signify "both the loss of self and the creation of a new, stronger identity (the artist)" and constitute "an elaborate attempt to reverse the authority of the past over the present, to overcome past anxieties by 'replaying' them under new ground rules."[41]

In both Murasaki and Proust, the agony and relief of remembering and forgetting traumatic events begins anew, with one difference: for the "reborn" Ukifune and for Marcel the survivor art becomes the alternative to love. The phase of experience is followed by a phase of seclusion and artistic creation. Despite the seclusion Ukifune seeks at the nunnery and Marcel in the sanatorium, there are occasional voluntary or involuntary exposures to the declining society around them. Ukifune falls prey to matchmaking as those who waked her from her suicide trance reveal their selfishness. The bishop's sister abuses Ukifune by coercing her into the role of her late daughter, and the bishop's mother shocks the nuns by her impious frivolities that seem to support the Buddhist notion of the law in its deteriorating phase (mappō). Similarly, Marcel's arrival at his last Guermantes party sounds the depressing death-knell of an era. However, for both melancholy protagonists, there is the hopeful possibility of recapturing lost values through creativity and, simultaneously, of atoning for the unknown sins of the fathers.

Ukifune's inspiration is Kaoru and she is "touched [...] to know that she had not been forgotten" (1077; 6:348). Her traumatic experiences have in fact turned her into an ally and kindred spirit of Kaoru, not only in the sense that she has become more preoccupied with "Memories of the past" (1075; 6:343) than before but also in her newly acquired sexual indifference: "Those disastrous events had so turned her against men, it seemed, that she meant to end her days as little a part of the world as a decaying stump" (1074; 6:342). Although news of Kaoru's arrival is accompanied by an acute sense of depersonalization, that is, a dramatic confrontation with her former self and "the strangeness of it all" (1077; 6:348), the encounter with him is psychoanalytically a positive déjà-vu experience[42] and promises to open up the mysteries of the past. "Kaoru's superiority" (1077; 6:347) helps to free Ukifune spiritually from her possession by the malevolent spirit of her father in whom excessive love had taken its most vengeful form.

Kaoru himself becomes subject to depersonalization when he, "haunted" by Ukifune's "mystery," takes her half-brother along to Uji as a mediator for "an encounter that might otherwise seem unreal" (1080; 6:356). Since Ukifune has become "one of the wanderers" (1073; 6:337) and Kaoru "like a sleepwalker" (1083; 6:364), they are both literally and metaphorically "adrift," searching for the past and for each other, recognizing through déjà vu that the fate of the one is mirrored in that of the other. A temporary depersonalization, like Keats's famous "negative capability," seems for Murasaki as for Proust to be a prerequisite for the recovery of the past through art. Inasmuch as Ukifune is one step further removed from society than the more outgoing, but nonetheless introverted, Kaoru, she may also be that much closer to the realm of the imagination, to the first intimations of creativity to which the chapter "At Writing Practice" [*Tenarai*] testifies, The almost involuntary, spontaneous composition of poems[43] is now Ukifune's "chief pleasure" (1075; 6:342). In view of her previous restlessness and wanderings this new pleasure can hardly be overrated as a source of personal satisfaction and as the adoption of a socially acceptable role.

Like Marcel's difficult pilgrimage from love to art, Ukifune's movement also includes sexual complications, the experience of death, loneliness, depersonalization, and disillusionment with a society in decline. Her fate echoes that of previous generations, most notably Murasaki's. Like Marcel, although more intuitively so, she is receptive to seasonal impressions and sensual reminders of the past. What the famous memory-evoking madeleine in the tea is to Marcel, namely, the peace and contentedness of childhood, the "first spring shoots" (1075; 6:343) are to her. The bracken sprouts: or *sawarabi* (cf. 872–3; 5:335–6) formerly sent to Uji, without her knowledge, in remembrance of the Eighth Prince, now evoke her memories of Kaoru and Niou, the lovers she found in lieu of the unkind father she never really knew. These harbingers of spring also become harbingers of the past as personified in the arrival of Kaoru.

Before Marcel comes to a creative halt at the Guermantes doorstep, he is a nautical wanderer: "I set off, trailing my shadow behind me, like a boat gliding across enchanted waters" (III, 709; I, 691). At a critical time in their relationship, Kaoru and Ukifune together contemplate the Uji river which is of mythic complexity, like Marcel's Sea. The river is not only a symbol of the passage of time (cf. 989; 6:136) but also of the quest for the past itself. When Kaoru repeatedly sits by the water to watch for the reflections of the images of his lost loves—first the Eighth Prince and Ōigimi (963; 4:78), then Ukifune (cf. 1077; 6:346)—it is nothing but his lonely narcissistic self that he can see. For the crowd fearful of the Buddhist Latter Days of the Law (*mappō*), the Uji river contains the time's apocalyptic aspects—imminent decline, death, lustration—and Ukifune experiences them all in her thwarted attempt at suicide in the river. Deep in his thoughts over Ukifune's disappearance, Kaoru blames himself for having fallen prey to the attractions that first drew him to Uji and for selfishly keeping Ukifune in his old romantic haunts:

> here was the river, beckoning, and she had given in to it. If he had not left her in this wilderness, she might have found life difficult, but she would hardly have sought a "bottomless chasm." How sinister his ties had been with this river, how deep its hostility

flowed! Drawn by the Eighth Prince's daughters, he had come the
steep mountain road all these years, and now he could scarcely
endure the sound of these two syllables "Uji." There had been
bad omens, he now saw, from the start: in the "image," for
instance, of which Nakanokimi had first spoken, an image to Boat
down a river. (1025-6; 6:225)

With her crisis Ukifune has become associated with an image derived
from the *nademono* purification ceremony in which paper dolls are soiled and
cast into the river.[44] Thus she has become vulnerable to her father's
vengeance. After the exorcism of the Eighth Prince's evil spirit, she still
occasionally considers her "soul [...] on driftwood" (1070; 6:330), especially
when she feels under pressure from society to reveal her identity and once
again to be like the rest of the world. But having escaped annihilation
through her miraculous extrication from the river, she has become an "extra-
temporal being," like Marcel. She at last seems aloof from contemporary
affairs and raises herself through her imagination like a bridge over troubled
waters.

THE RECOVERY OF THE PAST

Of all of Murasaki's characters, Ukifune in particular proves that the
search for human substitutes is illusory. On the other hand, the awareness of
futility—a prerequisite for a more spiritual, artistic quest—grows out of
precisely these frustrations with substitutes, and, in the heroine's peculiar
case, the repetition of the trauma itself in her possession by the demonic
spirit. The apparently cruel bewitchment is steeped in ambiguity,[45] for while
in its nightmarishness it radically destroys illusions, it also forestalls suicide
and opens up possibilities for a wholly imaginative, literary approach to the
past.

With Ukifune, the *leitmotif* of excessive love receives a new variant.
According to the established pattern, excessive love is highly conducive to
psychological conflicts because its roots lie hidden in the trauma of parental
death, deprivation, or neglect. Since Ukifune's mother views the Eighth
Prince critically for his abandonment of her and their child—a typical fate of
high ranking ladies-in-waiting and their children[46]—it is not surprising that
Ukifune's stance toward her lost parent is more ambivalent than that of other
characters' whole-hearted idolization. While in the past the shift from
excessive love to substitute love correlated with a shift from a predominantly
physical to a predominantly spiritual relationship, Ukifune experiences the
two forms of love simultaneously, in her affairs with Niou and Kaoru.

Although both forms of love contain the same features of excess and substitution after traumatic loss, they are distinguishable on the basis of the usual sequence of events in which trauma is followed by a series of substitutions. As lost love is repeatedly replaced, the protagonists' awareness of moving away from the original object of love increases and, together with the inevitability of the substitutes' shortcomings, causes a growing tendency toward the spiritualization of substitute love relationships. Substitutes can thus be categorized as *primary* (or predominantly physical) and *secondary* (or predominantly spiritual) substitutes. Yet unlike the slow transitions between primary and secondary substitutes made by other characters in the *Genji*, time and the repetitive process are dramatically condensed in Ukifune's double affair.

Guilt further complicates matters. Before Ukifune, the shift between primary and secondary substitution had occurred with varying degrees of guilt about betraying the memory of lost love. The burden was painful but bearable for the Kiritsubo Emperor and the Eighth Prince because they did not seek secondary substitutes until after the death of their primary substitutes. Genji's case is somewhat different. Not only does the specific taboo nature of his primary substitute love allow him to justify the search for a new substitute, but the tacit consent of the withdrawn Fujitsubo actually encourages him to do so, last but not least in the interest of keeping the illicit union a secret. Thus Genji's love for Murasaki functions to appease his conscience. While primary and secondary substitute love were chronologically separate for the Kiritsubo Emperor and the Eighth Prince, Genji's transition is less clear cut. As a result, Genji's substitution of Murasaki for Fujitsubo produces neither the continuing sadness of his father nor the self-loathing of his half-brother, but relief.

By contrast Ukifune's tortures originate in the simultaneity of her two affairs and the concomitant duplicity she cannot conceal—in the face of much gossip she must suspect that Niou and Kaoru know of each other. Her triangular love relationship with the two men turns the formerly allegorical conflict about lost love into a literal one. In Ukifune's double affair the mutually exclusive and incompatible primary and secondary forms of substitute love appear not sequentially, as with Genji and others, but simultaneously. Consequently, the dynamics of love are changed and the emotional entanglement increased to the extent that Ukifune wants to put an end to her life.[47]

With Niou and Kaoru, Ukifune is in a double bind. Her love for Niou involves her in the betrayal of her benefactor and half-sister Nakanokimi. More severe still is the symbolic entanglement in the taboo of incest. At the Eastern Cottage, a place apart from the world and its moral code, Ukifune and Kaoru both pursue their symbolically incestuous needs. Here Ukifune's longing for a father seems at least momentarily satisfied in the image of the caring, reliable Kaoru, the former disciple of the Eighth Prince. Conversely, Kaoru's identification of Ukifune with his idolized substitute father allows him to suspend the image of a previous substitute (Ōigimi). Due to the near synchronization of the affairs Kaoru is not called upon to substitute for an intermediary object of excessive or primary love (Niou) but directly satisfies a parental fixation (Eighth Prince).

In his role as the Eighth Prince's former disciple, Kaoru demonstrates a spiritual rather than a merely physical resemblance to the male paragon. Kaoru's presence has the effect of a father figure and disturbs the triangular constellation; in Freudian terms, Kaoru represents a "return of the repressed."[48] At the Eastern Cottage Kaoru tempts Ukifune with incestuous desires. When Ukifune resolves to part ways with society and to throw herself into the Uji river, her death wish is intercepted by a supernatural event which is synonymous with an incestuous phantasy. The last Uji sister is possessed by the demonic spirit of her father,[49] who, according to folkloristic stereotyping by some passers-by, comes to her in the shape of a fox.[50] The fox involves Ukifune not only in a confrontation with the past through the experience of symbolic death, but also constitutes a tragic cure for lost love. In symbolically becoming one with an animal, Ukifune furthermore reverts to an atavistic state helping to relieve her from social obligations, specifically, the pressure to decide whom to wed.[51] Paradoxically, the heroine's withdrawal through possession and trance is recognized by her society as a radical exposure to severe conflicts, and the exorcism that is provided by that society is believed to constitute part of the conflict-solving process.[52]

While Genji's love for his stepmother is depicted like any secretive love affair—apart from the specifically subversive consequences of incest and adultery—Ukifune's possession by her father's demonic spirit appears as a theriomorphic myth.[53] Differences in literary form reflect the differences in degree of taboo violation (son–stepmother as opposed to daughter–father) and also the protagonists' voluntary or involuntary participation in incest. What began with Genji and Fujitsubo as a conscious violation of the taboo, and was henceforth banned to the sphere of the unconscious, emerged in the Uji chapters in the struggle of the main characters to lift desires hidden in the unconscious to the level of the conscious.[54] Genji's delegation of consciously committed incest to the unconscious—the realm of dream—is reversed by Ukifune whose "Writing Practice" is an attempt to understand what possessed her and what led to her desire for self-destruction, questions which initiate a Proustian "recherche" of the past. In the Uji chapters the theme of incest is brought full circle, and a link to the past is established which appears as a reconciliation between the past, present, and future.

The mature Marcel believes that involuntary memory is the sole catalyst for recapturing the past. Ukifune arrives at an analogous belief after her possession and her trance are followed by her creative, spiritual link to the past, her construction of a Bridge of Dreams. Marcel's reflections bear a curious affinity to Ukifune's response to her possession and its aftermath:

> I feel that there is much to be said for the Celtic belief that the souls of those whom we have lost are held captive in some inferior being, in an animal, in a plant, in some inanimate object, and thus affectively lost to us until the day (which to many never comes) when we happen to pass by the tree or to obtain possession of the object which forms their prison. Then they start and tremble, they call us by our name, and as soon as we have recognised their voice the spell is broken. Delivered by us, they have overcome death and return to share our life.
>
> And so it is with our own past. (I, 47; I, 44)

The character constellation at the end of *The Tale of Genji* is more substantial in terms of the delineation of personalities than that of *A la recherche du temps perdu*. The Uji chapters show Kaoru painfully carrying the burden of the past. In spite of the fact that he is present only as a representative of the last of three generations, his concerns span the whole of the *Genji*. Through his quest for Genji (his fictional father), Kashiwagi (his real father), and the Eighth Prince (his chosen father), Kaoru is intricately woven into the total fabric of Murasaki's dramatization of three generations.

Regardless of the fact that secondary substitutes are usually further removed in time, genealogy, or some other factor from the original object of love than the excessively loved primary substitute, the protagonists' encounter with them enhances the awareness of repetitious events, especially when the trauma itself is evoked. Then secondary substitutes function as mediate links to the past. Not surprisingly, therefore, more emphasis is placed on the depiction of secondary substitutes and their psychological complexities and significance than on the primary substitute of excessive love itself. Thus, Murasaki's problems with Genji are given greater attention than those of Fujitsubo; for Kaoru, the Uji sisters, especially Ukifune, gain priority over the Eighth Prince; and for Ukifune, Kaoru outlasts Niou. Albertine, who is Marcel's chief substitute, poses so many riddles for the hero that he feels compelled to probe further and further into the mysteries of the past.

While by sheer physical intensity primary substitute love compensates more or less successfully for traumatic loss, secondary substitute love is inevitably unsuccessful because it cannot replace both cause (original loss) and effect (excessive primary substitute love). The emotional failure of the second type of love has important psychological results. In the primary substitution, pretraumatic (or archetypal) harmony is reconstituted, at least as an illusion. In the secondary substitution, however, the traumatic incident itself—the parent's sudden inaccessibility—is repeated. From a sense of confusion and frustration the needy tend to exchange roles with the needed. The victim twice deprived, of archetypal and of primary love, now becomes the victimizer. Assuming the role of the inaccessible lover, he simultaneously seeks and rejects the substitute.

Some secondary love relationships, as, e.g., Kaoru–Ukifune or Marcel–Albertine, are further complicated because the lovers' roles are interchangeable to the extent that the fate of the one mirrors that of the other. Emotional fulfillment is hopelessly impossible because each seeks in the other what the other, because of social status or sexual orientation, cannot possibly provide. Mutual inaccessibility guarantees "frustration" in the very love relationship that, conventionally, provides reciprocal emotional fulfillment. Genji and Murasaki experience a milder version of the conflict; they are troubled because they have no children of their own. But the intensity of the Kaoru–Ukifune and Marcel–Albertine relationships draws the lovers towards self-destruction.

Sometimes self-destruction actually occurs. In the *Genji*, Ōigimi seeks death by starvation. Her de facto suicide foreshadows Ukifune's death wish. The older and the younger sisters, unlike the middle one, remain in the Prince's sphere of influence. Since Nakanokimi is protected by her mother's will, she suffers comparatively little from having disobeyed her father by leaving Uji to marry the unreliable Niou. Ironically, it is Ōigimi, the most obedient of the daughters, who rejects—as suitor—the guardian of her father's choice and dies.[55] Her unwillingness to accept another (Kaoru) as substitute (for her beloved father), combined with her refusal to serve (Kaoru) as substitute (for the lost parent), lead to a novel variant on the idea of substitution: as she can neither serve as, nor accept another as, a substitute, she conceives of offering a substitute *for herself*. The traditional search for a substitute is radically replaced by the substitution of self. Yet Ōigimi's strategy is, ironically, obstructed by those for whose benefit it is apparently designed—Kaoru and Nakanokimi believe Ōigimi to be irreplaceable.[56] Ōigimi's categorical refusal to conform to the established pattern of substitution contributes to her sense of guilt over the betrayal of Nakanokimi and the rejection of Kaoru.

Her despair mounts when she recognizes that the failure of her strategy also threatens her bond with the Eighth Prince. She finds herself incapable of dreaming of her father as one way of remaining attached to him.[57] Ōigimi's romantic *Liebestod* is the symbolically incestuous variant of Kashiwagi's self-starvation. Furthermore, her straightforward fixation may explain why she is never possessed and why her unsuccessful attempt to achieve consolation in dreams leads her to resort to a strategy directly aimed at following her possessive father into death.[58] Unlike Ōigimi, who idolizes her father much as he idolized her (as well as her younger sister), Ukifune alone confronts the dark side of the Eighth Prince in spirit possession.[59] Her unhappiness brings to the fore the malevolent spirit of her dead father.[60] When the demon is exorcized, suicidal despair is revealed to have invited destructive forces.[61] In the code language of the supernatural the demonic Eighth Prince confesses his fatally possessive claim on his daughters, two of whom he victimized, through indoctrination [Ōigimi] and possession [Ukifune]:

> "You think it is this I have come for?" it [the spirit] shouted. "No, no. I was once a monk myself, and I obeyed all the rules; but I took away a grudge that kept me tied to the world, and I wandered here and I wandered there, and found a house full of beautiful girls. One of them died, and this one wanted to die too. She said so, every day and every night. I saw my chance and took hold of her one dark night when she was alone. But Our Lady of Hatsuse was on her side through it all, and now I have lost out to His Reverence. I shall leave you." (1050; 6:283)

At the end of the *Genji* and the *Recherche*, Ukifune and Marcel, having been touched by death, are preoccupied with the imaginary realm of the Bridge of Dreams. In Greek mythology, Acheron is the river of no return; the Uji river and the Venetian labyrinth of waterways[62] carry a similar meaning. Mythic heroes require artful cunning to escape from the Underworld or from the Minotaur's Labyrinth; Ukifune and Marcel require both artfulness and art.

NOTES

This article is the substantially revised version of a paper presented at the "World of Genji" conference at Indiana University in 1982. I would like to thank William J. Tyler and Janet A. Walker for their advice and encouragement.

1. Among the earliest perceptive, if still cryptic, comparative insights are those by Donald Keene, in his *Japanese Literature: An Introduction for Western Readers* (New York:

Grove Press, 1955), pp. 75–78; and those by Ivan Morris, in his pioneering cultural background study to the *Genji monogatari*, *The World of the Shining Prince: Court Life in Ancient Japan* (1964; rpt. Harmondsworth: Penguin, 1979), passim. Less convincing in the attempt to grapple with the formidable concept of time is Armando Martins Janeira, "The Idea of Time in the Japanese and Western Novel: Proust and Murasaki," *France-Asie/Asia*, No. 197 (1969), pp. 127–34; *Japanese and Western Literature: A Comparative Study* (Rutland, Vt.: Tuttle, 1970). The first book-length literary study in English on the *Genji* mentions the translation of Proust's work into Japanese as an instrument for revitalizing interest in Murasaki Shikibu; see Norma Field, *The Splendor of Longing in the Tale of Genji* (Princeton: Princeton University Press, 1987), p. 8 and p. 309, n. 5. Another important comprehensive study leaves its single bold comparative statement unexplored: "In contrast to Marcel Proust's *A la recherche du temps perdu*, to which the *Genji* has been frequently compared, man is unable to conquer or transcend external time." Haruo Shirane, *The Bridge of Dreams: A Poetics of The Tale of Genji* (Stanford: Stanford University Press, 1987), pp. 130–31. Proust scholars have compared *A la recherche du temps perdu* to works by many writers but not to Murasaki; see Victor E. Graham, *Bibliographie des études sur Marcel Proust et son Oeuvre* (Genéve: Droz, 1976), and the *MLA International Bibliography*. A study of art and nature in the two novels came to my attention too late for consideration; see Shirley Mescher Loui, "Murasaki and Proust: Time and Again—A Comparison of *The Tale of Genji* and *A la recherche du temps perdu*," Diss. Washington University 1987.

2. The definition of incest is a difficult matter as it greatly varies from culture to culture. In addition, historical changes in attitude combined with the subversive nature of incest make it impossible to ascertain its universal laws and to distinguish between degrees of taboo violation, which, except in the case of the very nearest blood relatives, seem to rest on a rather arbitrary basis when compared cross-culturally. The aim of this study cannot be to determine whether incest was practiced widely or how it was judged in Murasaki's and Proust's time; rather, the focus will be on the psychological ramifications of symbolic incest in the fictive world of the authors discussed, that is, on desires that shed light on a universal taboo. For a discussion of "The Incest Problem," cf. Robin Fox, *Kinship and Marriage: An Anthropological Perspective* (Harmondsworth: Penguin, 1967), pp. 54–76.

3. While Racine's Thésée openly accuses his son of adultery and incest (cf. *Phèdre*, IV, 2), it is unclear whether marriage between a woman and her stepson was regarded by the Greeks as incestuous; see Euripides, *Hippolytos*, ed. William Spencer Barrett (Oxford: Clarendon P, 1964), p. 12, n. 1. By virtue of the fact that Proust uses Racine rather than Euripides as a source, the theme of incest gains in emphasis. According to McCullough, carnal relations between stepparents and stepchildren in Heian times were "disapproved [...] considered wrong, but not completely out of the question." William H. McCullough, "Japanese Marriage Institutions in the Heian Period," *HJAS* 27 (1967): 135, 136. Thus step-relationships fall into the shadowy region between the "unthinkable" (McCullough, p. 135) sexual affairs between parents and children or brothers and sisters on the one hand, and all other unrestricted relationships with more distant blood relatives on the other hand. The authors who portray step-affairs make the unthinkable thinkable by hinting at the taboo of incest while keeping a safe distance from it. This is true, at least, of the authors discussed here.

4. This term is used in the general psychoanalytical sense (to refer to the libido's object) and not in the narrow political sense (to distinguish between heterosexuality and homosexuality).

5. Concentrating on purely descriptive comparative moments, Lin Wen-yueh traces elements from the first chapter of *The Tale of Genji* to Po Chü-i's poem; see "The Tale of Genji and The Song of Enduring Woe," trans. Diana Yu, 1973; rpt. *Renditions: A*

Chinese–English Chinese–English Translation Magazine, No. 5 (Autumn 1975), pp. 38–49. For an extended analysis, see David Pollack, "The Informing Image: 'China' in *Genji Monogatari*," *MN* 38.4 (1983): 360–75; rpt. in Pollack, *The Fracture of Meaning: Japan's Synthesis of China from the Eighth through the Eighteenth* (Princeton: Princeton University Press, 1987).

6. For a discussion on "The Order of the Early Chapters in the *Genji monogatari*," see Aileen Gatten, in *HJAS* 41.1 (1981): 5–46; cf. also, Shirane, *The Bridge of Dreams*, pp. 56–62 passim, passim, 120–23.

7. The apparent differences between the son–stepmother–father triangles depicted by Euripides in his tragedy and by Murasaki in her novel are illuminating in respect to the characters' motives for incestuous desire, their attitude toward it, their solution and punishment. In his comparative study of "The Hippolytos Triangle, East and West," Donald Keene rejects the Genji-Fujitsubo affair of the *Genji* as an example of the Hippolytos triangle "because of the entirely different overtones" which put little emphasis, at least overtly, on incest; see Keene, in *Yearbook of Comparative and General Literature*, 11 (1962): esp. 166. However, both the Greek tragedy that Keene has in mind as a foil and the *Genji* arise from the protagonists' concern over parental love and deprivation that lead them to step-relationships and image substitution for a solution. In the *Genji* the strong mother fixation behind the Shining Prince's attraction to his stepmother evokes even more clearly the force of incest than Phaidra's pursuit of her husband's image in Hippolytos. In Euripides it is not the aggressive Phaidra but Hippolytos who is under the spell of strong parental fixation, in his case not compelling but inhibiting him, in *all* matters of heterosexual love. One might say that Racine's triangle is as far apart from Euripides' as Murasaki's. Keene sees the Hippolytos triangle most properly reflected on the stage of the Nō and the Japanese puppet theatre; see ibid., pp. 167–70.

8. Cf. Werner Speiser, *China: Geist und Gesellschaft* (Baden-Baden: Holle, 1959), p. 142; cf. also Masako Nakagawa Graham, "The Consort and the Warrior: *Yōkihi* [] *Monogatari*," *MN* 45.1 (1990): 9, n. 19. Eugene Eoyang discusses the incest motif in a thematically related Chinese legend: "The Wang Chao-chün [] Legend: Configurations of the Classic," *Chinese Literature: Essays, Articles, Reviews* 4 (1982): esp. 8, 9, 20.

9. On the question of taboo-breaking in the *Genji*, see Field, *The Splendor of Longing*, pp 26–27; cf. also Shirane, *The Bridge of Dreams*, pp. 90-96; 100-103.

10. Cf. Haruko Wakita, "Marriage and Property in Premodern Japan: From the Perspective of Women's History," intro. and trans. Suzanne Gay, *JJS* 10.1 (1984): 73–99.

11. Murasaki Shikibu, *The Tale of Genji*, trans. Edward G. Seidensticker (New York: Alfred A. Knopf, 1976), p. 88; cf. p. 90. Quotations from *The Tale of Genji* will be from this translation. Page numbers are included in the text and are followed by volume and page numbers of the edition of Abe Akio , Akiyama Ken , Imai Gen'e , eds. *Genji monogatari*, *NKBZ*, vols. 12–17 [*Genji monogatari*, 6 vols.], (Shōgakukan, 1970-76).

12. Marcel Proust, *Remembrance of Things Past*, trans. C. K. Scott Moncrieff and Terence Kilmartin; vol. III's "Time Regained," trans. Andreas Mayor (New York: Random House, 1981). Quotations will be identified in the text by Roman numerals for volume numbers and Arabic numerals for page numbers. They are followed by references to *A la recherche du temps perdu*, ed. Pierre Clarac and André Ferré, 3 vols., Bibliothèque de la Pléiade (Paris: Gallimard, 1954).

13. According to Edwin A. Cranston, "A genuine religious calling is also depicted, exemplified by Prince Hachi." *Journal of the Association of Teachers of Japanese* 11.2 and 3 (1976): 191. Field cautiously qualifies the Eighth Prince's pious image, underlining the "ironic implications" in his public portrayal as "worldly saint" [*zoku hijiri* , *NKBZ* 5:120]. In an apparent effort not to condemn the prince, the critic reassures us that the "Eighth Prince's ambiguities are paltry compared with Genji's." *The Splendor of Longing*, pp. 225;

241. Shirane hints only indirectly at a flaw in the "devout Eighth Prince" by comparing his total neglect of Ukifune unfavorably to Prince Hyōbu's eventual acknowledgment of Murasaki. The Eighth Prince's so-called "lingering attachments" are seen as prototypical of many an ambitious father's lot in the *Genji*. Shirane does not indicate that the Eighth Prince's "'darkness of heart' (*kokoro no yami*)" is best understood as an excess of the norm. *The Bridge of Dreams*, pp. 155; 153; 184; 185; 186. In fact, Shirane stops short of analyzing the Eighth Prince's evocation of the waka that shows a parent to be possessive of his child to the point of distraction. Why, considering the Shining Prince's notorious "pseudo-incest" (in Shirane's terminology), should not his half-brother, less favored by fate, find himself in limbo due to incestuous phantasies—repressed desires that alone may explain the contradictory nature of his spiritual legacy?

14. Takahashi Tōru, for instance, refers to the Kaoru-Ōigimi love relationship as a "*han-monogatari*", "Ōigimi no kekkon kyohi," in *Kōza Genji monogatari no sekai*, ed. Aklyama Ken, Kimura Masanori , Shimizu Yoshiko, 9 vols. (Yūhikaku, 1983) [hereafter *KGMS*], 8: 143.

15. Often the deceased or otherwise "lost" persons are close relatives or marital partners. Jean Racine's *Phèdre*, for instance, seeks the faithless Thésée's image in Hippolyte; Racine, *Oeuvres Complètes: Théatre, Poésies*, Bibliothèque de la Pléiade (Paris: Gallimard, 1956, I, 3, p. 777: "Mes yeux le retrouvaient dans les traits de son père." (Cf. ibid., II, 5, p. 788.) Francesco Orlando recognizes the importance of image transferences: "The importance Hippolytus' physical resemblance to the young Theseus in Phaedra's eyes may suggest problems with the character's history: problems of age, chronology, psychology." Cf. *Toward a Theory of Literature: With an Analysis of Racine's Phèdre*, trans. Charmaine Lee (1st Italian eds., 1972, 1973; Baltimore: The Johns Hopkins Press, 1978), p. 49; cf. also pp. 50, 69ff. However, only forbidden substitutions through family resemblance affect the passions. In Proust, matrimony excludes passion, as shown in the case of Swann and Odette, but other habitual relationships suffer a loss of passion as well, to the extent that they provide security: "affairs of long standing have something of the sweetness and strength of *family* affection" (I, 505; I, 468–69—my italics).

16. While Ukifune is indeed the daughter of the Eighth Prince and strongly resembles him physically, it must be remembered that the Eighth Prince is no blood relation of Kaoru, as the latter eventually finds out. Yet it is precisely because Kaoru knows that the pursuit of the Eighth Prince and his daughters entails an imaginary search for the past that he clings with special ardor to the last of his Uji loves. Albertine, an orphan with few social connections and support, also carries implications of being the last in the succession of Marcel's loves. She too is made to substitute for various people (Gilberte, grandmother, and mother), and her resistance and elusiveness bind the hero ever more desperately to her.

17. Shirane holds that Kaoru should earlier in the story have been accepted by Ōigimi as "a man who appears to be, by almost all standards, an ideal marriage partner." *The Bridge of Dreams*, p. 142.

18. This Second Princess [Onna ni no miya or Fujitsubo no miya] seems to be as unimportant to Kaoru as the neglected wife [Ochiba no miya] of his father Kashiwagi had been. Aside from being his wife's cousin, Kaoru is set up to marry a "type" like his mother by virtue of the fact that the Kinjō Emperor worries about the Second Princess much as his father (the former Suzaku Emperor) had worried about the Third Princess (Kaoru's mother); cf. 885–87; 5:364–67.

19. For "the role of scent in determining [...] personalities" (p. 40), see Aileen Gatten, "A Wisp of Smoke," *MN* 32.1 (1977): 35–48. The differences between Niou and Kaoru in the art of scents are interpreted by Gatten more to Kaoru's than to Niou's disadvantage. Kaoru's natural fragrance is deplored as "a source of embarrassment. Unable to conduct

love affairs in the secrecy appropriate to the times, Kaoru is forced by his inescapable fragrance to become shy with women, aloof from society, and overly interested in religion" (ibid., p. 41). It is debatable whether Kaoru's fragrance is a "source" of what Gatten apparently considers to be defects of his personality, or whether his superior natural fragrance is linked to a noble quest for the past and thus casts a more positive light on Kaoru's character and social role. Although Gatten's essay indicates that Niou falls short in the proper use of scents, the varying quality of this particular art in *The Tale of Genji* is not seen as a barometer, as it were, for morale of Heian society.

20. Kaoru is not entirely unable to imagine an alternative to his life-style, but such intuition as when he sees Nakanokimi's child and wishes it were his is rare:

> If only it were his, thought Kaoru—not, it would seem having entirely given up thoughts of this world. If the one for whom he longed [i.e., Ōigimi] had followed the way of the world and left behind a child, he might find consolation. And such were the workings of his intractable heart that he had had no thought over the days of the possibility that his well-born wife might have a child. Still, one would not wish to describe him as merely perverse. (928; 5:467)

21. Kaoru seems to have felt an intense longing for the "womanish" (779; 5:116) Eighth Prince whom he visits for three years without noticing his daughters. After the death of the Eighth Prince, Kaoru thinks of Wigbeard, formerly a close associate of the Prince, when visiting the Prince's chapel, and seems to treat Wigbeard as more than a companion in grief (cf. 817; 5:202; 819 and n. ‡; 5:207). During the Prince's lifetime, Kaoru had sent Wigbeard a robe of unmistakable fragrance. There are numerous allusions to the homoerotic attraction between Kaoru and Niou, as the latter suggests, "actually we have been closer than close" (984; 6:127).

22. Takahashi Tōru has argued that the Kaoru–Ōigimi love relationship develops in the context of the Eighth Prince's will, which serves Ōigimi not only as an argument against marriage but also as a way to be reunited with her father in death. See "Ōigimi no "Ōigimi no kekkon kyohi," 8:156–57.

23. Fujii Sadakazu's essay on Ukifune as a substitute begins with the assumption that Kaoru selected her to be the late Ōigimi's substitute: "*Naki Ōigimi o shitau Kaoru ga migawari to shite miidashita Ukifune no koto de aru.*" Fujii, "Katashiro Ukifune," in *KGMS*, 8:276. For Kaoru's first glimpse of Ukifune, see ibid., p. 286. Fujii's argument that Ōigimi must, in order to associate with Kaoru, avail herself of the shape of a sister from a different mother (see ibid., p. 284) indirectly underscores my argument that Ukifune's and Ōigimi's shared resemblance to their father is the main point here.

24. Cf. Hasegawa Masaharu, "Uji jūjō no sekai, Hachinomiya no yuigon no bakusei," *Kokugakuin zasshi* (Oct. 1970), rpt. in *Genji monogatari IV*, Nihon bungaku kenkyū shiryō sōsho series (Yūseidō, 1982), pp. 135–44

25. Cf. ibid., pp. 140, 143.

26. Hasegawa argues that the Uji world is governed by the concept of the last will instead of the resentful spirits who had haunted Genji's world at court: "*Ujijūjō no sekai wa, hikaru Genji no sekai ni miru onryō no juryoku kara kaihō sarete iru ga, kawari ni 'kotoba' ni yoru jubaku no sekai de alto.*" Ibid., pp. 140–41. In fact, in Ukifune's possession the two worlds may be seen to merge when a resentful possessing spirit returns to protest a broken will.

27. Fujii, "Katashiro Ukifune," p. 284.

28. For a detailed explanation of this anthropological definition of spirit possession, see Joan Myrddin Lewis, *Ecstatic Religion: An Anthropological Study of Spirit Possession and Shamanism* (Harmondsworth: Penguin, 1971), pp. 32–33, 86, 117, 133.

29. For the change from applied to non-utilitarian arts, in the Uji chapters, see Earl Miner, "The Living Arts in *The Tale of Genji*," (International Genji Conference, Bloomington: Indiana University, August 1982).

30. Kaoru's imaginary encounter is instantly linked to the Chinese legend, specifically to excessive love after the death of the beloved (who, in Kaoru's case, most immediately points to Ōigimi but originally refers to the Eighth Prince). In this scene, Ukifune is generally seen to recall Ōigimi only, see *NKBZ* 5:481, n. 16. Yet in a concurrent conversation, Bennokimi entices Kaoru into reflections on deeper levels of his quest by telling him of Ukifune's temple visit and her longing for her late father (cf. 935): "*tada suginishi onkehai o tazune kikoyuru yue ni nan habemeru*," *NKBZ* 5:482.

31. For Masuda Shigeo, the Kaoru–Ōigimi love relationship transcends sexual interests and instead expresses the need for guardianship, a concept inspired by the loss of a shared father figure. See Masuda, "Ōigimi no shi," *KGMS* 8:182–83.

32. For experiences similar to those of Kaoru, see Shirane, *The Bridge of Dreams*, p. 137. For Marcel, street cries (cf. III, 121–22; III, 126) symbolically express his fear of Albertine's homosexuality.

33. Marcel's incestuous longing for an Albertine who is inaccessible by virtue of her homosexual proclivities, his jealousies and outbreaks of malevolence resemble Phèdre's passion for the equally inaccessible and unlucky Hippolyte who, like Albertine, is killed by his own horses. For the parallel between Marcel and Phèdre, see René de Chantal, *Marcel Proust: Critique Littéraire* (Montréal: Les Presses de L'Université de Montréal, 1967), pp. 404–8. Furthermore, Albertine's death has been linked to the death of Proust's lover Alfred Agostinelli, who was given an airplane by Proust but was unable to control it, as Proust had feared. J. E. Rivers, *Proust and the Art of Love: The Aesthetics of Sexuality in the Life, Times, and Art of Marcel Proust* (New York: Columbia University Press, 1980), pp. 88–89.

34. Field's identification of Ukifune's possessing spirit oscillates between Niou, Kaoru, a "conflation" of the two, and "a defrocked priest." See Field, *The Splendor of Longing*, pp. 279–83. Shirane is conspicuously silent on the topic. He is more interested in identifying the historic model [the Tendai priest Genshin (942–1017)] for the exorcist [Yokawa no Sōzu] than in the meaning of the possessing spirit for Ukifune. Cf. *The Bridge of Dreams*, pp. 194–99. Mitani Kuniaki , who recognizes the dubious nature of the Bishop of Yokawa and his entourage of self-centered relatives, comes to the ingenious conclusion that the *mono no ke* (revealed to be an apostate) is a projection of the Bishop as exorcist. The problem with this interpretation is that it does not account for Ōigimi's death or Ukifune's obligatory albeit oblique interconnectedness to the possessing spirit. Mitani explains this incoherence by pointing to fragmentation as a characteristic feature of the Uji section. See Mitani, "*Genji monogatari* daisanbu no hōhō—chūshin no sōshitsu aruiwa fuzai no monogatari," *Bungaku* 50 (August 1982): 101–103. In my analysis, the shady character of the Bishop not only evokes the character of the Eighth Prince but also serves as a perfect vehicle for exorcizing his spirit.

35. For the much debated thesis that spirit possession involves an indirect protest against the oppressive forces of society, frequently by women, see Lewis, *Ecstatic Religion*, passim. Cf. also, Bargen, "Yūgao: A Case of Spirit Possession in *The Tale of Genji*," *Mosaic: A Journal for the Interdisciplinary Study of Literature* 19.3 (1986): 15–24; Bargen, "Spirit Possession in the Context of Dramatic Expressions of Gender Conflict: the Aoi Episode of the *Genji monogatari*," *HJAS* 48.1 (1988): 95–130. For a discussion of the case of Murasaki no ue, see Shirane, *The Bridge of Dreams*, pp. 114–16.

36. Murasaki and Proust further set themselves apart from the *tertium comparationis* of Euripides and Racine by a metafictional solution to the problematic of excessive love, sexual disturbances, and a quest for the past. Edmund Wilson points out that André Gide's *Philoctète*, a version of Sophocles' *Philoctetes*, allows the outcast hero who suffers from the

wounds of the past to resort to a similar metafictional solution. Gide's Philoctète becomes "a literary man: at once a moralist and an artist, whose genius becomes purer and deeper in ratio to his isolation and outlawry." Wilson, "*Philoctetes*: The Wound and the Bow," in *The Wound and the Bow: Seven Studies in Literature* (New York: Oxford University Press, 1947), p. 289.

37. The arts in general are depicted to have fallen into decline. In the *Genji*, Niou, who has more respect for Kaoru's artistic talent than for his own, becomes critical and suspicious of the prizes bestowed on him and thinks the assembly overvalues his poetry (cf. 990; 6:139–40). In the *Recherche*, Marcel, always critical of public appreciation of the arts, himself becomes increasingly disappointed in the declining power of artists in their old age and their fame, as, for example, Elstir, Bergotte, and Berma.

38. Cf. Morris, *The World of the Shining Prince*, p. 278. Cf. also Edward W. Said, "On Repetition," in *The Literature of Fact*, ed. Angus Fletcher (New York: Columbia University Press, 1976), pp. 145, 152. [Said quotes from Sören Kierkegaard, *Repetition: An Essay in Experimental Psychology*, trans. Walter Lowrie (1941; rpt. New York: Harper & Row, 1964), p. 135.] One Proust scholar has pointed to the tension produced by the "dialectical movement" in the stylistic trait of repetition which is seen as "homologous to ... binary opposition." Robert W. Greene, "Quotation, Repetition, and Ethical Competence in *Un Amour de Swann*," *Contemporary Literature* 25.2 (1984): 152. Concerning the Uji chapters, see the references to "quotation" in Field, *The Splendor of Longing*, pp. 230, 235, 246.

39. Concerning the connection between the possible development of an artistic sensibility and repeated regression to childhood and adolescence, see W. Bräutigam, "Anthropologie der Neurose (unter Benutzung von Franz Kafkas 'Brief an den Vater')," pp. 114–37; in *Philosophische Anthropologie* 1, ed. Hans-Georg Gadamer and Paul Vogler (Stuttgart/München: Thieme; Deutscher Taschenbuch Verlag, 1975), pp. 133–34.

40. The structural peculiarity of "Remembering, Repeating, and Working-Through" is also that of psychoanalysis; cf. Freud, *Stand. Ed.* 12:145-56; and "Working Through" in J. Laplanche and J. B. Pontalis, *The Language of Psycho-Analysis*, trans. D. Nicholson-Smith (New York: Norton, 1974), pp. 488–89.

41. Cf. Randolph Splitter, "Proust's Myth of Artistic Creation," *American Imago* 37 (1980): 410, 411. In his psychoanalytical analysis, Splitter transforms the Marcel at the end of the *Recherche* into a dying mother figure: "Marcel now adopts [his mother's] magical powers as his own and imagines himself to be this artist-mother who gives birth to a work of art. But in so doing he becomes like a sick, dying mother—like his own self-sacrificing grandmother" (p. 397). By extension of this overwrought argument, Ukifune would, after the exorcism of the evil spirit, be endowed with her father's magical powers over her—for two diametrically opposed purposes: religion (which turns her away from the world) and art (which symbolizes her link with the world through her introspective poetic exercises). While her former religious devotion may be a direct result of her possession and in the spirit of the Eighth Prince who loathed himself and the world more than he emulated the Buddha, art is a result of her conflict with her lovers and the resolution to die. My interpretation of Marcel's and Ukifune's artistic inspirations points not *directly* to the parental figures of whose love they have been deprived but *indirectly*, through the inaccessibility of their lovers (who are, moreover, closely related to the heroes' parental image fixations). Figures like Niou and Kaoru, or Albertine and Mlle de Saint-Loup, are, despite their elusiveness, inspiring mediators between the terrors of the past and the present.

42. "Depersonalization" and "déjà vu" are the negative and positive responses to anxiety or trauma. If Ukifune's spirit possession, on the level of the unconscious, reflects the complex relationship with her father, the appearance of her father's double, Kaoru, recalls the repressed situation of the seizure. Sensing that the new situation is similar but

not identical with the old one may eventually lead the heroine to insight but may first of all "create considerable affect by challenging the individual's sense of reality." Rom Harré and Roger Lamb, eds., *The Encyclopedic Dictionary of Psychology* (Cambridge, MA: MIT Press, 1983), p. 142. For the complementary function of depersonalization and the déjà-vu experience, see Ludwig Eidelberg, ed., *Encyclopedia of Psychoanalysis* (New York: Free Press, 1968), pp. 103, 97–98.

43. Motoori Norinaga (1730-1801) defined the nature of *tenarai* as unpremeditated; see Thomas James Harper, "Motoori Norinaga's Criticism of the *Genji Monogatari*: A Study of the Background and Critical Content of his *Genji Monogatari Tama no Ogushi*" [1793–96] (Ann Arbor, Michigan: University of Michigan Ph.D. diss., 1971), p. 175.

44. Cf. Shirane, *The Bridge of Dreams*, pp. 155–56.

45. The initial speculations of those who discover Ukifune attribute her bewitchment to a fox whose ambiguous nature was (and still is) a part of Japanese folklore; see Greg Gubler, "Kitsune: The Remarkable Japanese Fox," *Southern Folklore Quarterly* 38 (1974): esp. 124–25.

46. Cf. Shirane, *The Bridge of Dreams*, p. 153.

47. To the present day variations on the conflicts inherent in triangular courtship and love affairs abound in Japanese literature. The topos is said to date back to the *Man'yōshū*, first allegorically conceived in the rivalry of two mountains for a third in "The Three Hills" [1:13–15], later in more desperately human terms by Takahashi Mushimaro (fl. ca. 730) and a later anonymous poet. In these tales about the Unai-otome [cf. IX:1809–11; IX:1801–3] and the Cherry-Flower Maid [XVI:3786–87], the young women commit suicide in despair over their lovers' fierce rivalry and their own dilemma of choice. Cf. Robert H. Brower and Earl Miner, *Japanese Court Poetry* (Stanford: Stanford University Press, 1961), p. 92. For an extended prose-poem version of the legend, see episode 147 of *Tales of Yamato: A Tenth-Century Poem-Tale*, trans. Mildred M. Tahara (Honolulu: University Press of Hawaii, 1980), pp. 93–98; for other versions of the legend, see ibid., pp. 186 ff.

48. Orlando, *Toward a Freudian Theory of Literature*, passim. One aspect of Orlando's analysis of Racine's *Phèdre*, namely, Hippolyte's plight between the two women—Aricie and Phèdre—applies to some extent to the Uji chapters as well. Orlando sees Hippolyte's "pardonable transgression [with Aricie as] an alternative to the other, a means of escaping the other [viz., Phèdre]" (ibid., p. 83). In both Racine and Murasaki the "pardonable transgression" (with Aricie and Niou) is subordinated to the treatment of the incest taboo.

49. Carmen Blacker cites a contemporary case of alleged fox possession which the exorcist-medium analyzed as an incestuous phantasy: "It is not a fox who is troubling you. It is your dead father. He died in the house of his concubine and hence has been unable to achieve rest." Blacker, *The Catalpa Bow: A Study of Shamanistic Practices in Japan* (London: George Allen and Unwin Ltd., 1975), p. 239. Numerous other fox possessions in modern Japan, often "undeniably sexual in nature" and dating back to the ancient fox lore of China and Japan, are described in Winston Davis, *Dojo: Magic and Exorcism in Modern Japan* (Stanford: Stanford University Press, 1980), p. 178, et passim.

50. According to a well-known feature of Japanese folk mythology, "Foxes, dressed up as men, were believed to be in the habit of seducing and bewitching human beings." Donald Keene, ed., *Anthology of Japanese Literature: From the Earliest Era to the Mid-Nineteenth Century* (1955; rpt. New York: Grove Press, 1960), p. 116, n. 8. Interestingly, Keene's footnote refers to the seduction scene between Genji and Yūgao, specifically, the lovers' half playful and half fearful allusion to foxes. This seduction not only occurs in the context of a triangular love relationship, the resultant tensions among Tō no Chūjō, Genji, and Yūgao also anticipate those of Ukifune, Niou, and Kaoru. Both women become possessed, and by citing foxes, the popular imagination manages to give a name to the

mysterious. Yet familiarization with the supernatural does not relieve the witness(es) of the task of understanding the possessed "victim's" troubled psyche. The air of mystery that continues to hang over both tragic events, despite the expedient of folk myth, suggests the implication of *human* characters. Cf. Bargen, "Yūgao: A Case of Spirit Possession in *The Tale of Genji*," passim.

51. For the role of animals in atavistic behavior, see Roger Shattuck, *The Forbidden: Experiment: The Story of the Wild Boy of Aveyron* (New York: Farrar Straus Giroux, 1980), p. 181.

52. In a useful definition of "Possession trance," Lenora Greenbaum states that "the phenomenon is accepted within the society as a trance induced by a spirit entering the person possessed, and not as an individual psychological aberration." Greenbaum, "Societal Correlates of Possession Trance in Sub-Saharan Africa," in Erika Bourguignon, ed., *Religion, Altered States of Consciousness and Social Change* (Columbus: Ohio State University Press, pp. 42–43.

53. Aside from numerous examples of Greek mythic stories, such as, e.g., Pasiphae and the bull, or Leda and the swan, theriomorphic relations are common in fairy tales and sagas all over the world. Otto Rank's extensive investigations into this subject furthermore identify this form of sexual deviance as incest in literary disguise. Cf. Rank, *Das Inzest-Motiv in Dichtung und Sage: Grundzüge einer Psychologie des dichterischen Schaffens*, 2nd rev. ed. (Leipzig/Wien: Franz Deuticke, 1926), pp. 337–86, esp. 364–67.

54. In his attempt to explain the differences between the various sections of the Genji *monogatari*, Earl Miner distinguishes the Uji chapters by a similar process of cognitive reversal when he refers to the "etherealizing of Genji's world." Miner, "Some Thematic and Structural Features of the *Genji Monogatari*," *MN* 24 (1969): 18.

55. As one critic has suggestively hinted: "As long as Kaoru behaves as a soulful *castrato*, he appeals to Ōigimi as no other man besides her father." Field, *The Splendor of Longing*, p. 237.

56. The idea of Ōigimi's new twist on the pattern of substitution was inspired by Hirota Osamu, "*Genji monogatari ni okeru 'yukari' kara tasha no hakken e*," *Chūko bungaku* 20 (October 1978): 28–38. Hirota points out that the old concept of substitution begins to erode with Murasaki's crisis over the Third Princess. Murasaki's desire to renounce the world and her confrontation with death provide the seed for the development of the irreplaceable individual in the Uji chapters. Cf. Hirota, ibid., pp. 32, 34–35.

57. Fujimura Kiyoshi interprets Ōigimi's inability to dream of her father as her lack of a bad conscience, while in Nakanokimi's case the Eighth Prince is seen as a source of anxiety. See Fujimura, "Hachi no miya no yuigon," *KGMS* 8:116–17. To put the matter differently, it is Ōigimi who actively desires to dream of her father, but cannot [*usetamaite nochi, ika de yume ni mo mitatematsuramu to omou o, sara ni koso mitatematsurane, NKBZ* 5:302, cf. also 5:301]. On the other hand, Nakanokimi, being less obsessed, dreams of him spontaneously.

58. Ōigimi begins to starve herself under increasing pressure for marriage, growing skepticism about men, and fear of soiling the family name—in her own nutshell: "*nao waga dani, saru mono omoi ni shizumazu, tsumi nado ito fukaranu saki ni, ika de naku nari namu*" [*NKBZ* 5:290]. However, as Field has hinted, Ōigimi's frustrations over Nakanokimi's marriage and her own grim prospects for life in Uji are not enough to explain the "extravagant willfulness of her departure." *The Splendor of Longing*, p. 251.

59. Fujii Sadakazu, who sees Ukifune as Ōigimi's substitute or *katashiro* until her rebirth after the possession scene, claims that it is, in fact, the *mono no ke* that rescues her from suicide and holds that, with the energy derived from the supernatural, Ukifune first arranges to leave the world to become a nun (*shukkesha*) and then reconfirms her religious vows (*saishukke*) intending to save Kaoru. "Tsuku bungaku: *Genji monogatari* ron no tame ni," *Bungaku* (Nov. 1982): 100–16, esp. 109–10, 112–14.

60. In contrast to Ōigimi, Ukifune is possessed by the spirit of the Eighth Prince, but she does not die. Although critics of the *Genji* have attempted to identify all other major possessing spirits in the novel, they have been curiously reluctant to identify Ukifune's, possibly because of the Eighth Prince's apparent sacrosanctity. Their reluctance is all the more baffling, since Ōigimi *has* been identified as the girl whose death Ukifune's possessing spirit refers to. Cf. Earl Miner, "The Heroine: Identity, Recurrence, Destiny," in *Ukifune: Love in The Tale of Genji*, ed. Andrew Pekarik (New York: Columbia University Press, 1982), p. 69. Furthermore, Ukifune's possessing spirit is a former monk with a grudge against the world (like the Eighth Prince), and the haunted girls are of the house that is identified as that of the Eighth Prince. Cf. *NKBZ*, 6:283, n. 19, n. 20 and *Genji monogatari hyōshaku*, ed, Tamagami Takuya, 12 vols. (Kadokawa shoten, 1964–68), 12:375–76. It may be interesting to note the connection between Ukifune's earlier visit to Hasedera in memory of her father (see my note 30), the divine intervention of the Hatsuse Kannon in the possession, and the heroine's subsequent refusal to visit Hasedera [see Shirane, *The Bridge of Dreams*, p. 198].

61. Anthropologists and psychologists have linked incestuous to suicidal dispositions, see Herbert Maisch, *Inzest* (1968; rpt. Hamburg: Rowohlt, n. d.), p. 26 [*Incest*, trans. Colin Bearne (New York: Stein and Day, 1972)].

62. Cf. Anne-Lisa Amadou, "The Theme of Water in *A la recherche du temps perdu*," *Modern Language Review* 72.2 (1977): 310–21. Amadou sees in Venice "a rare example in Proust of water as a symbol of destruction" (p. 319).

RICHARD BOWRING

Language and style

THE NARRATOR'S PRESENCE

Izure no ōntoki ni ka, nyōgo kōi amata saburaitamaikeru naka ni, sugurete tokimekitamau arikeri. Hajime yori ware wa to omoiagaritamaeru ōnkatagata, mezamashiki mono ni otoshisonemitamau.

In what reign was it, among the many lesser consorts and ladies of the wardrobe serving the Emperor is one who, though she is not of the highest rank, is favoured above the rest. The other ladies, each of whom have from the outset thought proudly 'I am the one', are scornful and jealous of this presumptuous upstart.

Here, at the very beginning of the tale, we encounter a definite narratorial presence at work, although this may not be immediately clear from the English translation. It is a covert presence, but a presence nevertheless. Firstly, there is the fact that the story begins with a question, which immediately establishes a connection between narrator and audience. There is, in the first five lines, an implication that true historical time is to be involved, and an invitation to the reader to guess, to allow himself to be drawn into the work. The narrative marker '–keri' in 'arikeri', which signifies

From *Murasaki Shikibu: "The Tale of Genji."* © 1988 by Cambridge University Press.

something like 'now then there is/was', is presentational in tone and draws attention to the fact that someone is explaining something. It is often used to establish a story-telling framework, and can be dispensed with once that framework is settled. In normal Japanese discourse every sentence contains within it certain elements that refer to the relationship between producer/speaker and receiver/audience, what linguists term the pragmatic aspect of language. The production of neutral sentences, sentences of the kind one would expect in a narrative where this kind of explicit or deictic reference to the speech-act is usually reduced to zero, is in normal circumstances rather difficult to achieve. At this early stage of development of the language, written Japanese was very close to the spoken language, and all forms of impersonal discourse were cast in classical Chinese. For the purposes of fiction, ways had to be found whereby this insistent presence of the speaker in the sentence could be reduced, and the technique of creating these '–keri' frames was undoubtedly one way round the problem. Once inside this frame, the unmarked form of verbs can be used, often unmarked for both tense and mood; this has an added side-effect in that the description seems more immediate than if it were continually subject to the control of the presentational suffix. One way to reflect this technique in English is to use the historical present, but it must always be kept in mind that the effect is not nearly so strange in the original Japanese for the simple reason that in Japanese the verb is in an unmarked form, whereas the historical present in English is very definitely marked.

It should not be thought, however, that the presence of a covert narrator can be negated simply by eliminating '–keri' from all but the first sentence; the narrator is also present in the honorific suffix '–tamau', which occurs in this passage no less than four times. The existence of the honorific system complicates Japanese narrative enormously, because it too is related to the speech-act: although the main function of '–tamau' here is to identify the subject as being high-born, it still contains within it something of a narratorial presence. It refers to the relative status of narrator and narratee, or audience-in-the-work, *vis-à-vis* the character in the sentence to which it is applied. We have seen in the case of Yūgiri's attitude to Genji after the typhoon how its lack can have the special effect of reducing a man's perceived eminence. In this case the suffix is used because the women referred to, including the upstart Kiritsubo, are all of a higher status than the narrator and her audience. Because honorifics are used in this work only of characters of a particular court rank and above, we know that the narrator must be below that rank, but high enough to be serving at court; about the same status as Murasaki Shikibu, in fact. Note that we are not talking here about the implied author who is responsible for the whole text and its meaning, nor about any 'real' lady-in-waiting; we are dealing with the question of a narratorial presence as it exists within the work.

There are a number of other verbal suffixes and sentence particles that emerge in the text from time to time to betray the presence of a covert narrator; but in contrast to these elements (which are largely present because of the nature of the Japanese language, and which have to be neutralised in various ways), there are also a number of other places where the narrator emerges in overt form, passages of direct narratorial commentary known as 'sōshiji'.

Chapters 2, 3 and 4, which form a small subset on their own, are introduced as follows:

> The Shining Genji, grandiose in name only: it seems there are numerous misdemeanours that invited censure; yet worse still, these secrets that he has kept hidden, realising that such indiscretions could give him a reputation for frivolity if passed on to later generations, have been passed on by others—what malicious gossip!

And Chapter 4, 'Yūgao', ends with:

> I do feel sorry for the way he went out of his way to hide this kind of troublesome matter from others, so initially I left it all out; but there were those who took it all as a made-up tale: 'We know he is a Prince, but why does even someone who knows him tend to praise him as if he were quite without faults?' I cannot avoid, it seems, this sin of acting the malicious gossip.

Nor is it just at the beginning of the *Genji* that this kind of narrator speaks to us directly; at the end of Chapter 15 she excuses herself from giving any more details 'because of a headache' (S 302), and as late as Chapter 34 we come across: 'The melancholy and moving details were innumerable, but I fear they would clutter my story' (S 549), and a little later on: 'In old stories they considered the details of gifts given to be very important so they were enumerated in detail, but they bore me so; neither am I prepared to list the whole grand company' (S 568).

These passages might well be seen as mere lapses by an author who was more at home with oral presentation, and there is quite an influential body of opinion in Japan that believes the *Genji* was read aloud while the ladies at court looked at illustrations to the text. Certainly we know from Murasaki Shikibu's own diary that Emperor Ichijō had the *Genji* read out to him at one stage, and an illustration of the 'Eastern Cottage' chapter in the *Illustrated Genji Scroll*, dating from the early to mid twelfth century, has a scene that suggests a similar scenario; but there is no reason to suppose that this was the only form of reading: the very complexity of the tale argues against it.

Instead, it is better to see these passages as signs that Murasaki Shikibu felt able to manipulate a series of narrative voices when she needed them for various purposes; the 'sōshiji' passages themselves are a very effective way of jolting the audience out of any complacency. It is perhaps for this reason that she saw no need to have a narrator who was either omniscient or consistent. By virtue of the number of years covered, the narrator in the latter part cannot be the same persona as that in the earlier sections, and in general the narratorial voice is left uncharacterised, except that, as we have already noted, the honorifics betray her as a woman of a particular rank. She is a persona present largely because of the very nature of the Japanese language, but then used by Murasaki Shikibu for her own ends.

Given the exquisite ironic interplay in the 'Fireflies' chapter that deals with the theory of fiction, it is probable that Murasaki Shikibu retained the somewhat raw technique of open narratorial intrusion in order to play with her audience, to remind them that they were not reading gossip and that the *Genji* was not to be seen in the same light as its predecessors. In the covert sections, of course, she is usually at pains to neutralise the narratorial presence as much as possible in case it becomes too obtrusive; this leads to some interesting effects as in the following passage, where the narrator's text and the character's text are allowed to become inextricably intertwined.

KASHIWAGI'S TORTURED MIND

Here is Murasaki Shikibu at the beginning of 'The Oak Tree', presenting us with Kashiwagi's thoughts as he convinces himself that he must die. To help the ensuing discussion, four passages have been numbered and five intertextual references marked with superscript letters. The English is intentionally stretched as far as it will go:

> [1] There was no change in the way Kashiwagi continued to suffer like this as the New Year came round. [2] He saw how the Grand Minister and his First Lady were suffering and yet—a life that one is intent on leaving is of little consequence, and it would be in any case a grievous sin; but then, am I the type to want to hold on at all costs, reluctant to leave this world? From youth there have been particular ambitions, and a proud belief in being special in matters both public and private, striving to be that little

bit better than everyone else no matter what, but then there has been a loss of self-confidence on a couple of occasions, a realisation that such desires are hard to fulfil, and as a result a gradual loss of enthusiasm [a]for the world in general; I gave myself wholeheartedly to preparations for the next life, but sensing my parents' unhappiness, it was clear that this would become a heavy [b]burden on the road that led off [c]into hills and fields, and so one had survived keeping busy here and there; then in the end an anxiety that made it impossible to mix with the world gripped and still grips me from all sides; who is there to blame but me? I have brought it all upon myself! [3]Such thoughts, and indeed no one else to blame; no point in berating the gods either; surely all is preordained; in this world where no man has [d]the thousand years of the pine tree we cannot stay for ever, so while I may thus be mourned a little by others, let me make it a sign that [e]my heart burned passionately to know that there is one who deigns to take a moment's interest in me! If I insist on surviving then undesirable rumours are bound to grow and turmoil is likely to result both for myself and her; rather by far that even in that quarter that now must consider me so ill-advised I may be forgiven despite all; everything, in the final instant, must surely dissolve! And since I have transgressed in no other fashion, it may be that pity will emerge from him who for so many years and on so many occasions has done me the honour of companionship— [4]such thoughts, such disconsolate thoughts, and all such utter hopelessness.

Let us say that there are four sentences in the above quotation, although even this is a matter of some debate, because the concept of 'sentence' is under implicit attack here. Sentence 1 is descriptive, the narrator present but only in a covert sense. Among the signs that reveal this hidden presence are the word 'like this' [kaku] which gestures towards the audience, and the honorific verb suffix '–tamau' which links with Kashiwagi [Emon no kamu no kimi … nayami-wataritamau] to identify him as the subject of the verb. But because honorifics inherently refer to the speech-act as well, attention is drawn to the pragmatic aspect of the statement itself, that is to the status of the producer of the sentence *vis-à-vis* both her audience and the character referred to in the sentence. Convention undoubtedly weakens to some extent this deictic force, but nevertheless the narrator is not wholly absent. This suffix '–tamau' appears here only once in relation to Kashiwagi; it is dispensed with thereafter. Such an absence is essential if Murasaki Shikibu wishes to get inside Kashiwagi's mind. One might well expect, for instance, a '–tamau' added to the next verb 'he saw' [mitatematsuru], but it is no longer necessary or desirable.

The beginning of the next sentence, at point 2, is again narrative discourse. Both father and mother are given their official titles and are also given the honorific verb 'oboshinageku', 'were suffering', which marks them as both his and our superiors. Then the narrative slides into Kashiwagi's thoughts. Because of the lack of a clear morphological distinction between direct and indirect discourse in classical Japanese (often the difference is only marked by a verb of thinking, a 'tag' that lies at the very end of a long sentence); the shift is not nearly as sudden as it seems in English. What is perhaps more important is that it is well-nigh impossible to decide whether this whole huge sentence that runs to the end of the quotation is best rendered in the first person or the third person in English. Seidensticker's version of the first part, for instance, reads: 'He knew how troubled his parents were and he knew that suicide was no solution, for he would be guilty of the grievous sin of having left them behind. He had no wish to live on. Since his early years he had had high standards and ambitions and had striven in private matters and public to outdo his rivals by even a little' (S 636). Clearly, certain effects possible in classical Japanese have been ironed out in the interests of providing a smooth English rendition. The Japanese is something more than simply free indirect discourse, that is, reported speech or thought without any signs that it is reported; the mode of the original is even more difficult to pin down and lies in that indeterminate gap between direct and indirect thought. Murasaki Shikibu uses this indeterminacy of her language to powerful effect, for there is constant doubt in the reader's mind as to whose text he is reading (is it the narrator's or the character's?), a doubt that then infects the reader's attitude to what is being said. This doubt extends to modern editors of the Japanese text, who are often at variance as to where particular 'passages' should begin and end. Some modern editions of the classical text for instance punctuate for breaks at 3 and at 4, but others prefer to allow the prose to drive through these points and sustain the tension to the very end.

This passage happens to be crucial in the process by which Kashiwagi convinces himself that he must die. His willingness to kill himself is forcibly expressed early on, when it is set against the claims of filial piety. From that point on Kashiwagi proceeds to try and unravel the reasons for his decision by looking back to past causes. It turns out of course that there are no reasons, because it is not going to be a reasoned act; but Kashiwagi forces himself to go through the motions of self-justification. Overlaying the narratorial uncertainty that we have mentioned above, there is a constant tension opening up a gap between what is being said and what the implied reader knows to be the case; and it is in this gap that Murasaki Shikibu shows her capacity for the production of irony, imperceptibly guiding the reader's reactions to Kashiwagi's thoughts. By setting this particular passage in the form that she does, the author produces a dual perspective which she then exploits.

As part of the attempt to convince himself that his inability to face his own emotions is the result of an ineluctable fate, Kashiwagi invents for himself a personal history, a new past that is somewhat different from the one that we know. He has had tremendous ambitions, he has been thwarted, hard done by, hence the desire to retire completely from the world. This last aspect will be true of his son Kaoru, but does not sound convincing for Kashiwagi. The number of illogical connections increase as we proceed. His own action of violating the Third Princess brings a sort of involuntary retirement from the world, which then becomes something to which 'blame' must be attached. He convinces himself that he is all alone. This then becomes a further excuse for dying, because he wishes to avoid undesirable rumours, and to regain the respect and forgiveness of both the Third Princess and Genji. Kashiwagi is not here appealing to some sort of warrior's code of honour: the argument we are made to recognise is simply specious, a hopeless attempt to rationalise the irrational. By showing us the working of his fevered mind, the author reveals how Kashiwagi only succeeds in hiding his true emotions from himself.

This passage also contains within it five intertextual references, which are completely hidden from the reader of the translation, but which have their own important function. The first three references (a, b and c) occur at 'for the world in general', 'heavy burden', and 'into hills and fields'. Each of these phrases draws us back to a relatively well-known poem from the classical canon as it existed in Murasaki Shikibu's day.

The first poem is by the poet Ki no Tsurayuki whom we have already had occasion to mention: 'Somehow because I myself felt sad, I bore a grudge for the world in general.' The next is by Mononobe no Yoshina: 'I wish to enter into mountain paths where the sadness of the world cannot be seen, but the one I love has become a heavy burden to me.' The third is by the poet-priest Sosei: 'Where can I live and avoid the world, when my heart seems to wander out into hills and fields?' Reference d takes us back to the poem: 'Sad indeed: is it that things never turn out as one had hoped, for who can have the thousand years of the pine tree?', and the last poem, referred to in e, is: 'Summer insects waste their lives; that too is because they fly into the fire / their hearts burn passionately.'

Although it is doubtful whether Murasaki Shikibu expected her

audience to recognise all these references immediately, except perhaps for
the last two, they combine to create a textual resonance that helps to increase
the seriousness of the prose by tying it to precedent; they also help to
emphasise the degree to which Kashiwagi is inventing his past, using a range
of poetic phrases to fool himself the more. In this particular case, then, this
kind of technique of quoting poems, known in Japanese as 'hikiuta' or
'drawing out poems', gives Kashiwagi the opportunity to create a textual
framework fashioned from the canon within which he can place himself and
from which he can take a measure of comfort. It has even been suggested that
a number of other elements in this passage bring to mind the first section of
the tenth-century *Tale of Heichū*, the story of a man fated to fail in his
numerous love affairs.

EQUIVOCAL NARRATION

A further example of the subtle use of narratorial presence and of how texts
can intermingle is to be seen in the following passage from 'Trefoil Knots',
where Kaoru is about to subject himself to a sexually frustrating night with
Ōigimi. Both asterisks and numbers refer to points that will be taken up in
the discussion that follows; again the English is intentional:

> Intending to stay* the night and have a quiet talk, he whiles away*
> the time. It is not that obvious, but his attitude of seeming[1]
> resentment is gradually getting so out of hand that it becomes
> uncomfortable and increasingly difficult to talk freely; but then
> he is usually such an extraordinarily sympathetic man that she
> receives* him, unable to treat him too brusquely. She has* the
> inner door to the altar open, the lamps turned up, and sits*
> behind both blinds and a screen. Lamps are placed outside as well
> but: they are unsettling, I'm in such disarray, too bright, he orders
> them away and lies down* close by. She has* fruits and other food
> brought out, although without much ceremony. For his men she
> has* splendid food and drink. They are gathered in what seems
> like a corridor, so these two, left alone apart from the others, are
> engaged* in intimate conversation. Although it seems[2] she will
> never relax, such is the way she talks*, so alluring, so attractive,
> that he is obsessed and frets; how absurd![3] The ridiculousness of
> lying here in such uncertainty, separated by no more than a flimsy
> screen; it really is too foolish![4] he thinks over and over again, but
> outwardly calm they talk* on and on in generalities about this and
> that moving or interesting event. Inside she has ordered* her

women to stay close, but apparently they feel he should not be kept* so much at arm's length, so they do not look too closely but retire and lie down, leaving no one even to trim the lamps.

The perspective here is constantly changing between Kaoru, Ōigimi, the servants inside and the narrator, whose presence is betrayed by virtue of the honorific suffixes applied to the character's actions at the asterisked points. There are a number of places where a verb or adjective of 'seeming' introduces a dual perspective: at 1 for instance, 'his attitude of seeming resentment' [monouramigachi noru], the point of view is Ōigimi's, but because the statement occurs within a sentence that is marked for a narratorial presence by virtue of the honorifics, there is a certain amount of interference as the narrator moves like a shadow behind Ōigimi. The same kind of thing occurs at 2, where the viewpoint is now Kaoru's, but again one finds the shadow of a narrator; this in turn is suddenly strengthened at the end of the sentence at 3 by 'how absurd!' [omoiiraruru mo hakanashi], which can be taken either as a narratorial interjection or a thought by Kaoru himself. This in turn is echoed at 4, until we realise by reading on that this particular interjection is meant to belong to Kaoru.

The net effect of this kind of narratorial presence which allows itself to shadow more than one character's point of view is to deliberately destabilise the reader, undercutting any decision on his or her part as to who may or may not be in the right at any particular point. This is a technique at which Murasaki Shikibu is particularly adroit. Equivocal narration reinforces the impression that both Kaoru and Ōigimi have their own legitimate view of the relationship between them, and that these views are fated never to coincide. As we are swung first one way and then the next, we come to appreciate the subjectivity of all vision; and that is one major message of the latter part of the whole tale.

POETRY IN PROSE

The *Genji* contains 795 poems interwoven with the prose at almost every turn, poems which present a problem for translator and interpreter alike. What are they doing here? How do they function, and why are they so necessary? But first: what do we mean by the term 'poetry' in Japanese? We are used to seeing poetry as a special language with special rules and constraints that give it its very identity. What are these rules in the Japanese context?

In simple terms a Japanese poem is a statement thirty-one syllables long. With no rhyme and no word stress, the Japanese language created its special version in a direction that is surprising and somewhat difficult to grasp. Rhythm is provided by an alternating current of 5/7 or 7/5 syllables, and the form that we find in the *Genji*, so-called 'short poems', are made up of just five such measures: 5/7/5/7/7. There is often a caesura before the final 7/7. What the Western reader must realise is that there is no clear concept of more than one line of poetry here: a Japanese poem is essentially a single line. This point is especially important because English translations usually present these poems in five lines; to quote a formulation by Mark Morris that makes this clear to specialist and layman alike:

> To make a poem was to attempt the transformation, or deformation, of a single Japanese sentence. A good [poem] was the successful outcome of a struggle with a virtual line of prose. The early ... poets embraced what has to seem an unusual technical and formal challenge: to accept as the fundamental terms of their engagement with language the syntactic patterning of the Japanese sentence, and then to work to break its forward flow, curtailing here and pruning there, resisting the pull towards final predication. They took up the chain of words and wove cat's-cradles along and through it.

It will be seen that as there is no concept of more than one line, there can be no paratactic techniques, no rhyme and little if any conscious parallelism. What we are given instead is a complex of wordplay, inversion, and linked images that create a whole series of complications along one line. This was mirrored in the shape of the poem on the page. It always had to be marked off from the prose in some way in order to be identified for what it was, but this was usually little more than an extra indent at the beginning. Occasionally the calligraphic spacing could become playful and idiosyncratic, but by and large it was written as one or two lines, depending on the size of the paper and the size of the hand. A poem was therefore *physically* easy to incorporate into the prose structure; in many cases, if the typographical sign of indentation were not present it would be easy to miss the poem qua poem altogether in some parts of the text.

It will be obvious why Japanese poetry does not translate well, and why translators of the *Genji* have had such problems with this form. Modern Japanese versions by and large leave the original poems standing, because although they are usually difficult enough to need some form of interpretation, it is impossible to translate them into the modern language without utterly destroying them. Translators into other languages are not in a position to present the originals and so must try their best. Waley by and large simply resorts to quotation marks and usually feels no compunction in glossing over the distinction between poem and dialogue; often, indeed, he ignores the form altogether and simply paraphrases. Seidensticker uses the couplet form which unfortunately sets up expectations of techniques and rhyme that are not fulfilled, so his versions occasionally appear unnecessarily flat. Two recent Chinese versions have had extreme difficulty with this same problem, and in one case the translator has had to invent an entirely new poetic form for the purpose.

The ubiquitous presence of poetry in the *Genji* is largely explicable in terms of the development of a prose style in the Heian period, a development which is in many ways the story of a battle for dominance between poetry and prose. As we have already pointed out, Japanese poetry had been flourishing for some centuries, but at the beginning of the Heian period prose still meant Chinese prose, and so it continued until well after the demise of Emperor Saga in 842. Japanese prose emerged against a background of poetry, and always had to face the fact that it was considered of inferior status; hence the struggle that we can see being actually played out in a number of crucial early and mid-tenth-century texts.

In the *Kokinshū* (c. 905), the anthology dedicated to inventing and defining a poetic canon as part of a general attempt to secure cultural hegemony, prose was merely a means of giving a poem a context. By 'context' here we are referring literally to the habit of introducing each poem with a short description of the circumstances of its composition and the name of the poet. Being a 'deformed' statement, a Japanese poem can only rarely stand on its own; it demands either prose to contextualise it or another poem with which it can interact. In this sense it is always in need of being supplemented. In *The Tales of Ise*, produced some thirty or forty years later, we already find prose emerging from its supporting role and actually achieving parity with what it was designed to interpret. The chief concern of the *Ise* was the exploration of the process of poetic creation, the investigation of how and why poems are engendered; hence the prose has a life of its own and in places actually threatens to burst its bounds, to become too powerful and expand into narrative. It is always frustrated in this attempt by the presence of poetry which brings it to a halt, but in the best sections there is a miraculous balance of the two.

In *The Tales of Yamato*, a similar but later text of mixed poetry and prose which is usually dated between 951 and 970, the question of contexts is approached from a different angle. Here the interest is not in the act of creation as a cultural phenomenon but as a social and historical phenomenon; it is designed to invent a tradition of poetic composition, a 'lore'. Thus it names poets, identifies occasions, and makes the private public. Poems are recorded in such a fashion that the circumstances of their production as history become part of cultural memory, as much cultural fact as the poems themselves; and in the process of creating a lore, poetry itself becomes subordinate to prose. There is in fact a moment in *The Tales of Yamato* where we can see this shift in hierarchy occurring before our very eyes: as we read into the later sections, we find poetry yielding ground to its own context as the desire to legitimise poetry leads to its eventual displacement. The prose that was initially introduced to explain the provenance of the poem becomes of greater interest and importance. By the middle of the tenth century the way was open for further developments in prose; but as the *Genji* testifies, the poets who created the *Kokinshū* had done their job well. Poetry was to continue to be the major repository of the metaphors by which the culture was to express itself. Prose still needed such resources, so that it was a natural gesture for Murasaki Shikibu to choose to enrich her prose with the constant presence of poetic lines and poetic allusions.

The functions of poetry in the *Genji* are many and varied, but there is one aspect that is constant: the link with love and sexual attraction. We have already touched on Section 1 of *The Tales of Ise*, where poetic creation was tied to the onset of sexuality, and where the poem was seen as a means, at times the only means, of bridging the erotic gap between self and other. Poetry had from its beginnings been equated with divine speech, having the potential to bring into being that of which it spoke, and by this time it is clearly marked as belonging to the realm of erotic possession/obsession. The talented poet was at one and the same time the talented lover, and despite the attempt to legitimise Japanese poetry in the *Kokinshū*, this link with sexual licence remained strong. This is in turn connected with another of those rules of poetry which mark it off as being special language: Japanese poetry contains no honorifics. It is, to paraphrase Mark Morris once again, a type of anti-honorific. This means that the language of poetry is the one form of Japanese that is free of the more normal pragmatic elements that reinforce the concept of hierarchy and status. Barring Chinese, which was in any case marked exclusively 'male' and 'public', Japanese poetry was in fact the only form of non-hierarchical language available; it allowed contact between two people who might not otherwise have been able to communicate. And as two lovers were normally in precisely such a situation, it became the language of love *par excellence*.

This lack of honorifics also helps to explain the prevalence of poetic composition at court. This is sometimes seen as a puzzle: to what extent does the poetry in the *Genji* and works like it actually reflect literary habits in Heian court society? It is of course quite inconceivable that anything but a small minority of courtiers were good poets, capable of rolling off a gem whenever the occasion demanded, but there can be little doubt that the ability to toss off a mediocre poem that showed one knew the basics of the canon was indeed seen as a tremendous social asset. It unlocked precisely those doors that the honorific system kept shut, so that everyone had a vested interest in being able to perform at least on a merely ceremonial level.

When we turn to look at the role of poetry in a specific work, then of course social factors give way to aesthetic ones; poetry and poetic vocabulary in the *Genji* play a major part in Murasaki Shikibu's attempt to create her own particular world. We have already seen in the case of Kashiwagi how the use of poetic allusion can increase the resonance of a passage, so that a character or a scene can take on aspects of broader cultural significance. This is done by using the kind of poetic language established by the *Kokinshū* and subsequent anthologies to provide a convenient shorthand. A sudden increase in such vocabulary signals the creation of a special environment, something that we have already seen occurring within the 'Suma' chapter, and which can be found at many interludes in the work; the scene early on in Chapter 1, for example, where the Emperor sends Yugei as a messenger to Genji's grandmother, is a good example of a high concentration of specifically 'poetic' images, particularly in the description of the dilapidated garden belonging to Genji's mother.

In certain cases, especially in those chapters, such as 'Suma', 'The Rites', and 'The Wizard', that themselves mark time and allow the plot to settle for a while before moving off in another direction, one finds that poetry usurps the function of prose: it takes upon itself the role of expanding the narrative, so that the reader progresses from one poem to another with the prose acting as little more than a link in a chain. This type of writing clearly stems from the style of *The Tales of Ise* and kindred texts. As one might expect, it is the seasonal subject matter that predominates in such situations, fitting for the description of a kind of eddy or cycle in the narrative flow.

Poetry can also be used to connect events or scenes far removed from each other in time and space, linking across whole stretches of the work. Perhaps the best examples of this are the two 'maboroshi' or 'wizard' poems. When Yugei returns from her visit to Genji's grandmother, the Emperor gazes at the gifts, mementoes of Kiritsubo, which include a comb. This creates another reference to Po Chü-i's poem about Yang Kuei-fei, where a comb becomes an icon of the woman for whom he yearns. Then the Emperor whispers a poem: 'Oh that I had a wizard to search her out! Then might I know where her soul might be, even if merely through a messenger.' This word 'wizard' occurs only once more in the whole work, when Genji is in mourning for Murasaki in the chapter of that name: 'Oh wizard, you who traverse the skies, search out where her soul has gone, a soul that does not appear to me even in my dreams.' Genji, in the hands of his author, unwittingly echoes the words and images used by his father long ago, and so reinforces that sense of repetition that governs the whole work. This link is first noticeable when one comes across the second poem referring back to the first, but a second reading of the *Genji* then reverses this process of recognition, so that the first poem is seen to echo the second. Links such as these are common and provide a subtle network of textual connections that underline the complicated series of relationships that exist between characters, and between scenes.

There is one use of poetry in the *Genji*, however, which dominates all others: Murasaki Shikibu uses it to crystallise the essence of a particular relationship or situation. This is connected to the matter of chapter titles and character names which will be discussed in the next section. When Genji finally manages to sleep with Fujitsubo (although there is controversy as to whether this is actually the first occurrence), the scene is treated with extreme indirection; but they exchange a set of poems in dialogue form that immediately reveals their differing attitudes. Poems in the form of dialogue make up three-quarters of all poetry in the *Genji* and act as the norm, a ritual that is an integral element of the tie between poetry and sexuality on which we have already commented. The night is so short, feels Genji: 'Though I meet you, such nights / worlds are rare; oh that I could disappear now within this dream.' 'Mite mo mata au yo mare naru yume no uchi ni yagate magiruru waga mi to mogana.' To this Fujitsubo replies: 'Will they not noise it abroad as a tale to be told / a tale of the night? my dreadful fate, though I might make it a dream from which I would not awake.' 'Yogatari ni hito ya tsutaenu tagui naku ukimi o samenu yume ni nashite mo.' This is more than simple dialogue; the choice of poetry makes it special, so that these statements become important expressions of the character's emotional states: the very fact that they are in poetry makes them significant. Genji is ashamed and hurt but little else at this point. To both it is a dream, but whereas Genji's reaction is self-indulgent as he hopes the moment can be prolonged for ever, for Fujitsubo it is a nightmare into which she might wish to disappear, but which is bound to reveal the truth, come what may. Here there is self-knowledge and irony.

In many ways this is a typical exchange, for the reply takes up the theme and the vocabulary of the first poem and deftly turns it in a completely different direction. The wordplay on *yo* as meaning both 'world' and 'night' is reflected in the reply, as is the image of a dream. The pair of poems can stand as a sign not only of the present relationship of Genji and Fujitsubo, but also of the way that relationship will progress, for the tale that Fujitsubo fears is *The Tale of Genji* itself.

A second example of how poetry operates can be seen in Chapter 27 'Flares', a very short chapter which lies between the practical but rather sordid business of marrying off Tamakazura and the typhoon that finally comes to wreck Genji's garden. Genji has already made it plain that he has designs on Tamakazura herself, and the author takes the opportunity of a short interlude to drive home the point. Tamakazura feels that she has been lucky in having Genji rather than her real father Tō no Chūjō look after her affairs, despite Genji's waywardness:

> The new moon was quick to set. The sky had clouded delicately over and the murmur of the rushes was sadder. They lay down side by side with their heads pillowed against the koto. He stayed very late, sighing and asking whether anywhere else in the world there were attachments quite like this one. Reluctantly, fearful of gossip, he was about to leave. Noticing that the flares in the garden were low, he sent a guards officer to stir and refuel them ... 'You should always have flares,' he said. 'An unlighted garden on a moonless summer night can be almost frightening.' "They burn, these flares and my heart, and send off smoke. The smoke from my heart refuses to be dispersed." 'For how long?' Very strange, she was thinking. "If from your heart and the flares the smoke is the same, then one might expect it to find a place in the heavens." 'I am sure we are the subject of much curious comment.' (S 455–6)

This scene is a perfect example of how Murasaki Shikibu uses a landscape to reflect the emotional state of the characters. The scene exists for no other reason than to act as an illustration of Genji's fading hopes. The flares in the garden are low and he makes one last attempt to bring them to life, because 'an unlighted garden ... can be almost frightening'. And there in the prose ('for how long?') lies a hidden reference to the first poem of the love sequences in the *Kokinshū*.

So important is the dialogic nature of poetry in the *Genji* that poems produced in isolation, known as 'dokueika', stand out with great intensity; because the norm is a dialogue, these poems have the effect of emphasising the loneliness of the character who produces them, as if only half the expected amount of poetry had been produced. It is a situation where 'the other' has been reduced to zero, and the reader of the *Genji* in translation should be prepared to place more weight on the isolation of the poems than he might expect. Of a total of 111 examples of these single poems, fifty-two are produced by Genji, nineteen by Kaoru and eleven by Ukifune, the characters who are most alone and most tormented by their own emotions.

TRANSLATIONS

The interesting task of comparing the two English versions of the *Genji* by Waley and Seidensticker has been done in detail by Cranston, Ury and others elsewhere; here all that will be attempted is a treatment of some of the major ways in which the versions differ, together with a discussion of some important problems that face the translator.

It is thought that most, if not all, the chapter titles in the original were produced not by the author, but by readers as a necessary convenience. Many of these titles are words and images that stem from a poem or a passage that was clearly considered to be emblematic of the chapter as a whole. So, for instance, Chapter 27 is named after a word, 'flares', that appears twice in the exchange of poetry between Genji and Tamakazura that forms the centre of this short episode. Seidensticker has written that the translation of these titles took him an inordinate amount of time and effort, because many of them contain wordplays difficult to transpose into English.

The matter of titles is connected with the other vexing matter of the names of the characters. It seems incredible but nonetheless true that almost no-one of any importance in the *Genji* has anything remotely approaching what we would consider to be a personal name: characters are usually referred to by a title or a rank. Tō no Chūjō, for instance, actually means Head of the Imperial Secretariat and Middle Captain. The male ranks change constantly in the course of such a long work, and the women are referred to by various locutions such as 'the woman of the west wing' or 'the main wife', references which tend to change according to the immediate context. Clearly none of these titles or phrases is adequate for identifying these people as characters throughout the whole work.

Readers of the *Genji* soon found this situation intolerable and devised a series of names that everyone now uses as a universal shorthand, but which do not actually occur in the text. By and large these names appear in the English translations. This is best seen as the only solution to an intractable problem, but a problem it remains. As Seidensticker notes in his introduction, the names for some characters stem from a similar source as many of the titles, namely crucial poems which can appear well after the initial mention of the character in question. Yūgiri, for instance, who is never once identified in this manner in the text itself, takes this name, which means 'evening mist', from a poem in Chapter 39, a poem that he produces when visiting Kashiwagi's widow at Ono; Yūgiri himself of course appears much earlier on in the book in Chapter 9. Similarly both Aoi, 'The Lady of the "Aoi" Chapter' and Kashiwagi, 'The Oak Tree', are named after passages that occur in the chapters in which they die. In Aoi's case she takes her name from the title of Chapter 9, which in turn is taken from a poetry exchange with which she has no connection (S 164); in Kashiwagi's case he is referred to as an oak because that tree was a symbol of the Palace Guards in which he held rank (S 654).

It will be seen what a fundamental change the work undergoes when the translator is forced to use these appellations at an early stage; not only does it seem that the author was, in some respects, even more subtle with her planning than she actually was, creating a link where none exists, but it gives an entirely different feel to the characters. In the original they are sometimes hard to identify immediately, and their shifting sobriquets make them and their reactions unusually dependent upon context. It always comes as something of a shock to find that the most important woman in the book, Murasaki herself, is never directly referred to by that name in the Japanese: the name is a label taken from a poetry exchange in Chapter 5. Murasaki is a plant (a species of gromwell), the root of which is used to produce a purple dye; it has connotations of affinity and intimacy that probably come from a wordplay on the word *ne* which can mean both 'root' and 'to sleep with'. There is a further hidden connotation for Genji himself in that the colour is linked to the colour of the wisteria, and Fujitsubo means Wisteria Court.

One must set against all the above, however, the fact that the author's name stemmed from the name of her heroine, and we know from her diary that this nickname was already current among her contemporaries. This suggests that although in strict textual terms these names did not exist, it is possible that her readers had already started the process of naming her characters for their own convenience quite early on, and that there was an unwritten tradition of naming from the very beginning.

There are a number of other aspects that cause extreme difficulty for the translator. Does he, for instance, translate these names that refer to plants and flowers, or does he leave them in the original? The pitfalls here can be seen with 'murasaki': Seidensticker uses the word 'lavender', which is quite wrong and takes some getting used to, but it is infinitely preferable to 'gromwell'. He does not go to the extent of calling the heroine herself Lavender, but in a pre-Waley translation of 1882 the Japanese Suematsu Kenchō did feel impelled to call her Violet, which brings in an additional complication through connotations that suggest prim Victorian ladies and which are out of place in such a work.

Then there is the crucial problem of architecture. One of the aspects of Waley's translation that stands out today is that he transposed his story into a non-Japanese setting. Heian houses and mansions had few solid walls, the buildings were on low stilts, and rooms were divided off from the outside by blinds and a veranda. Inside there was little more than a series of screens and flimsy partitions. When inside, everyone spent most of the time at floor level and women in particular had to take care they were not seen standing when men were present. There is certainly a problem of how accurately such a world could have been portrayed in English, given that few in Waley's day had ever seen a Japanese room. Waley uses a small catalogue of words and phrases that eventually transposes us into a semi-Western, semi-Mediterranean setting: there are 'porticos', 'terraces', a 'loggia', and 'borders' and 'moats' in the garden; people sit on 'chairs', look through 'windows', recline on 'couches' and retire into their 'chambers'. 'Genji flung himself onto a divan' (W 37); 'He descended the long stairs' (W 19); 'there was a clatter of hoofs in the courtyard' (W 419); and whenever someone writes anything, a desk with drawers invariably materialises: 'He was sitting by the lamp, looking at various books and papers. Suddenly he began pulling some letters out of the drawers of a desk which stood near by' (W 21). All this is important because the cumulative effect is to naturalise what is actually an entirely foreign and strange environment. Perhaps Waley could not have done anything more, but the comparison with Seidensticker is striking. The physical world depicted in the two translations is entirely different. In Waley we tend to be placed at the wrong eye level, and it is difficult to imagine from his translation that when a man stood outside by the veranda, his eyes would have been level with the skirts of the lady kneeling on the floor of her room some four feet off the ground, with no 'wall' between them.

This inevitably brings us to a more general comparison of both versions. The first thing to note is that Seidensticker's version was very much needed: it is in general far closer to the original, is far more accurate, and gives us a better picture of the ironies of which Murasaki Shikibu was capable. It is undoubtedly less romanticised and should be accepted henceforth as the standard translation. Waley, of course, was himself a genius with words, English words, and his version not only made Japanese literature famous, but is a work of art in its own right. But the degree to which he plays fast and loose with the text is astounding. There are savage cuts in the middle 'Tamakazura' sections and in chapters 33 and 36, cuts which show that he had begun to lose patience with the large number of static scenes. He omitted the whole of Chapter 38, 'Suzumushi', without warning the reader, and made cuts in other places that turn out to be crucial. Murasaki's death scene, for example, is curtailed, omitting those parts that are vital for an understanding of Yūgiri's relationship with both Murasaki and Genji. Yūgiri in general emerges as a lesser figure in Waley than he should. The 'art of fiction' section in Chapter 25 'Fireflies' is also notorious for the degree to which Waley was prepared to help his authoress write an apologia for a modern novelist. The list of hidden delinquencies is in fact endless.

Waley did not often reveal himself, but on occasions he let drop some surprising pronouncements:

> Murasaki has an inordinate fondness for death-scenes, coupled with a curious incapacity to portray grief. Her alertness suddenly leaves her. Usually she is interested in the different reactions of her characters towards a common situation. But in the presence of death the people in *The Tale of Genji* all behave alike ... she is compelled, whenever she handles the subject, to descend to mere conventionalism ... some peculiarity of Murasaki's psychology makes her death-scenes banal and feelingless.

Such an attitude explains why Waley felt it necessary to hurry over these passages, but it is difficult to accept when one encounters the power of Murasaki's death in Seidensticker's rendition. Even more baffling is the following statement where, after giving the *Genji* honorary status as a novel, Waley writes: 'If we go on to compare it with Stendhal, with Tolstoy, with Proust, the *Tale of Genji* appears by contrast to possess little more psychological complication than a Grimm's fairy tale.' There is more than a hint here of Virginia Woolf's attitude to the work: in a review of Waley's first volume written in 1925 she wrote that, despite her admiration, 'the lady Murasaki is not going to prove herself the peer of Tolstoi and Cervantes or those other great storytellers of the Western world'. Admittedly Waley had at this stage only got as far as Chapter 18 or thereabouts, but such an attitude common to both Waley and his famous contemporary alerts us to the interesting possibility that he might have actually *underrated* the work with which he was dealing. But when all is said and done, who would in fact be prepared to say more than Seidensticker himself, who in a generous preface to his new version points out the boldness of Waley's cutting but also paid tribute to his wonderful rhythms? To read the newer version after Waley is to receive an object lesson in the possibilities of different translations, and to marvel anew at the potential inherent in the original to support and engender—even by default—such a richness of response.

NORMA FIELD

Three Heroines and the
Making of the Hero

DICHOTOMIES AND SUBSTITUTION: FUJITSUBO

Most of the characters of the *Tale of Genji* are known to its readers by
suggestive sobriquets such as "Evening Face" (Yūgao), "Village of the Falling
Flowers" (Hana Chiru Sato), or "Evening Mist" (Yūgiri), which are culled
from key poems associated with the characters within the text. Many of these
names also serve as evocative chapter titles. It is not known to what extent
the author or her earlier readers were responsible for these acts of naming,
but convention now assigns the preponderance to the latter. The common
designation of the characters within the novel is a version of official rank or
place of residence, the particular choice being strategic to emphasis of tone
or information.[1] In certain situations however, the characters are starkly
identified as "the man" or the woman," or, with honorific suffix, "the
gentleman" or "the lady." The situations are erotic, and these words signal
that a climactic moment may be at hand. Of all the women pursued by the
hero Genji, there are two who are never referred to in this fashion: they are
Fujitsubo and Princess Asagao, the hero's stepmother and cousin,
respectively.[2] The first is the object of Genji's lifelong attachment; the
second, his staunchest resister. For reasons that are either not provided or
have become invisible over the centuries, Princess Asagao never permits
herself a moment when the narrator could justifiably dub her a "woman." It

From *The Splendor of Longing in 'The Tale of Genji.'* © 1987 by Princeton University Press.

93

is otherwise with Fujitsubo. During the one episode in which she incontrovertibly yields to the reckless young Genji, she is steadily referred to as "Her highness" (1:305; S 98; W 95). Fujitsubo is never divested of her majesty.

The circumstances of this heroine's entry into the work are promisingly complex. She replaces the Kiritsubo Lady, Genji's poor dead mother, who, though but the daughter of a late major counsellor, had dominated the Emperor's affections and was consequently hounded to death by the jealous members of his household. It had been a mistake, reflects the Lady's grief-stricken mother, to have permitted her to enter court service in accordance with her late husband's immoderate ambitions. Some years later, the Emperor, who had remained inconsolable, hears of a young lady bearing a remarkable resemblance to Genji's mother. This is Fujitsubo, daughter of a figure known only as "the former Emperor." Her mother, mindful of her predecessor's fate, is reluctant to expose her daughter to such trials even though her higher station might shield her to some degree. Like so many mothers of literary heroines, however, this one dies at a critical point in her daughter's life. Sixteen-year-old Fujitsubo has no choice but to accede to her brother Prince Hyōbu's view that unprotected though she was, she would be better off at court than elsewhere.[3]

Fujitsubo is an instant success. Her uncanny resemblance to the dead lady wins the Emperor's undivided affection, which fortunately she can receive without fear of reprisal because of her own high birth. The problem, of course, is that she also attracts her stepson Genji, but five years her junior. The Kiritsubo Emperor, the most genial of cuckolds, personally attests to the new wife's resemblance to his young son's late mother and encourages their friendship. Of course, there are limits to their intimacy: once Genji is initiated and married, he is no longer permitted within Fujitsubo's curtains of state. Henceforth, their thoughts are conveyed in the notes of her koto and his flute.[4]

For some time Fujitsubo makes but fleeting appearances, and then only in Genji's thoughts, as he listens to his fellow young men discuss the ideal woman, or overhears gossip about his carryings-on ("The Broom Tree"), or sits through a terrifying night with the corpse of a lover ("Evening Faces"). It is not until the fifth chapter ("Lavender") that Fujitsubo speaks in person, on the occasion of an unexpected and, as will be seen, fateful meeting with Genji. Sometime thereafter, the narrator, in a moment of unusual freedom with intimate detail, observes that Fujitsubo's ladies have been troubled when attending her at her bath. This leads ineluctably to the day when Fujitsubo is compelled to witness the Emperor's joy over the birth of a son he had not fathered and over this new son's resemblance to an older favorite, Genji.

With the Emperor's passing in the tenth chapter ("The Sacred Tree"), Fujitsubo is exposed to the vindictive passion of another lady of the court, Kokiden, the principal victim of the dead Emperor's devotion first to Genji's mother and then to herself. Not that Kokiden has been entirely robbed of her due, for the Kiritsubo Emperor, in one of his more prudent moments, had demoted Genji to commoner status and designated as heir Suzaku, his son by Kokiden. Now it is Kokiden's season, for she is the daughter of the supremely powerful Minister of the Right as well as mother of the new Suzaku Emperor. There is still a thorn in her side, however, for the late Emperor, in recompense for having demoted his favorite son Genji, had decreed his supposed son by Fujitsubo (Reizei) crown prince at the time of Suzaku's ascension; moreover, he had promoted Fujitsubo to the status of empress, which, of course, made her superior to Kokiden.

Even after the Emperor's death, the secret of her fleeting affair with Genji weighs heavily upon Fujitsubo, and she finds but slender protection in her title. To make matters worse, Genji continues to prey upon her, thus increasing the risk of disastrous exposure for their young son Reizei as well as themselves. Dark thoughts invade her mind: "Even if I am spared Lady Chi's fate, I will surely become the laughing stock of the court" (2:106; S 198; W 206–207). Lady Ch'i was a favorite consort of the Han Emperor Kao-tsu, who had thought to put his son by her on the throne after his death. Instead, his Empress captured Lady Ch'i, cut off her hands and feet, gouged out her eyes, burnt her ears, and forced down a burning potion that left her unable to speak.[5] Fujitsubo decides to relinquish her rank as empress and take religious vows. It is none too soon, for some of Genji's sins come home to roost, and, in a parallel gesture, he chooses retreat before exile is forced upon him.

Like everyone else in Genji's faction, Fujitsubo lies low during the years of Genji's seclusion in Suma and Akashi. Prosperity, though not tranquillity, comes with Genji's return to the capital and Suzaku's abdication. Now Fujitsubo, as the mother of the new Reizei Emperor, is granted the emoluments due to a retired emperor.[6] She uses her newfound power to scheme with Genji to secure Akikonomu, the late Rokujō Lady's daughter, as their son's consort even though she was coveted by the retired Suzaku Emperor. Then, having done everything in her means to assure the stability of her son Reizei's reign, she languishes to die at the age of thirty-seven ("A Rack of Cloud"). She returns once, wraith-like, to haunt Genji in chapter twenty ("The Morning Glory").

This is the explicit extent of Fujitsubo's role in the novel. It is surprisingly limited—as if, trapped in a secret relationship with Genji, she must be shrouded from our prying eyes, as if, being the incarnation of every ideal, she must be used sparingly. Even her poetry output is modest—twelve poems, of which ten are addressed to Genji.[7] Obviously, Fujitsubo's importance to the tale far exceeds her visible activity. It would not be hyperbolic to suggest that she embodies the principal dynamic forces of the work. They constitute dichotomies whose interrelationships and transformations are the source of abiding interest in the novel, a testimony to its author's passionately intellectual imagination. Let us begin with a description of Fujitsubo's manner during that fateful night with Genji in the "Lavender" chapter. She thinks of their previous (unrecounted) meetings.[8] Despite her resolve that there be no more, Genji had stolen in again: "she was so wretched, she looked as if she could endure no more, yet she was sensitive and sweet, though as reserved as ever, reflective, even intimidating ..." (1:305; S 98; W 95). This is one of the most generous descriptions ever given of Fujitsubo. It comes embedded in a moderately long "sentence" beginning in Fujitsubo's mind and ending in Genji's, and it serves to illustrate the complexity of the author's mode of apprehending her characters as well as her penchant for piling one qualifying phrase upon another, with the result, in this instance, of producing a concrete representation of Fujitsubo's contradictory aspects.[9]

The dichotomies embodied by Fujitsubo may be variously generalized as sacred and profane, identical and similar, original and substitute, erotic and political, natural and cultural, arbitrary and motivated, mythic and fictive, otherworldly and this-worldly. Let us provisionally take "the sacred and the profane" to stand for the series (which, not being sacred, is of course expandable). These sets overlap, contradict, and undergo trans-formations in the course of the Genji. The complex relationship prevailing between the sets of terms may be described as one of "complementary bipolarity" with the precaution suggested by Andrew Plaks in his use of the term to describe the relation of "yin and yang" to other paired opposites:

> When we use the terms "yin" and "yang" as a shorthand for referring to this entire range of polar conceptualizations, we must be careful not to assume that all these paired concepts can theoretically be lined up in parallel fashion such that the two sets of poles form two logical categories of experience. In fact, the many sets of conceptual polarities, which serve as frames of reference for the perception of reality, are overlapping schemes not reducible to a final two-term analysis.[10]

Complementarity, however, is but one mode of relationship, and we ought to consider the choice of "sacred and profane" (or yin and yang) as the "shorthand" term for the series even, or especially, if it is one of convenience—that is, convention, tradition. We must, of course, also keep in mind the relation of the terms *within* each set.

Now, what is the function that "sacred and profane" is serving here as the representative polarity? I am of course borrowing from Mircea Eliade, for whom "the sacred and the profane" describe "two modes of being in the world."[11] The (former) is associated with origins, essences, timelessness, rituals, revelations, and the inexplicable and therefore represents otherworldliness within this world; the (latter) on the other hand, is bound to the quotidian, the changing, and the rational and consequently is the very essence of this-worldliness.

To turn to the example at hand, the logic of Japanese imperial rule is that mythic reality is embodied by the emperor, who represents a continuity from that time in the beginning when heaven and earth were linked and divine rule was established in the Middle Land of the Reed Plains, as Japan is called in the early (eighth-century) chronicles. Through his participation in court ritual, the emperor regularly interrupts the profane time of ordinary mortals (who grow old and die) to restore the sacred moment of creation. Naturally, it is his son who must succeed him; necessarily, his women are exclusively his.[12] Of course, this son and these women are at the heart of the problem: for the emperor's sacred vitality is manifested in his multiple sexual relations, with the consequence that there is frequently, if not predictably, more than one son. The ready (and apparently dignified) solution of designating the eldest as heir is all too susceptible to being undermined by the rivalry of the sons and their respective backers. The damning taint of manipulated variation is not easily eradicated. The issue of succession, implicated in the political machinations revolving around women (i.e., potential mothers), forever betrays the presence of the profane at the heart of divine rule.

Now, even from this schematic description, it should be possible to extract certain tensions in the relation within oppositional pairs. On the one hand, "sacred" and "profane" may be said to stand in an oppositional complementarity; that is, it is virtually commonsensical that without the profane, the sacred could not be discerned, just as order requires chaos, or figure ground. Now it is also apparent that much as figure needs ground, ground is not on the same footing, so to speak, as figure. Figure, in order to be figure, must constitute (and thereby demote) its surroundings as ground; ground offers itself as mere matter for the composition of figure.[13] *Within* the set "sacred and profane" (and in the others as well) we can distinguish both a symmetric, horizontal (complementary) opposition and an asymmetric, vertical (supplementary) one. The former often masks the latter but cannot displace it, just as, conversely, depending upon our analytical desires, the latter may be made to subsume the former.

By this analogy, women as the bearers of future emperors serve as the incidental ground for the sacred (natural) phenomenon of the imperial succession. For the appearance of the sacred to be maintained, the manipulation of the women by their ambitious kinsfolk must be suppressed, that is to say, dissimulated as the education and cultivation of beloved daughters or sisters. When such daughters or sisters become the mothers of crown princes, then men who are by birth (by nature) excluded from the sacred realm of the emperor acquire a foothold therein—a metonymic link that may, perhaps, be made to serve as a metaphoric one. The distinctiveness of Fujitsubo is that she does not need to be transformed by "marriage" to an emperor or by delivery of an heir in order to partake of the sacred since she is born to that order. There is a certain redundancy, in other words, to her becoming an imperial consort. (Historically, of course, the choice of a princess of the blood as empress was inimical to the mechanism of the Fujiwara regency, which depended on the entry of a ministerial, commoner daughter into the emperor's household.) Countering this redundancy, however, is the lack implicit in Fujitsubo's entering the novel as a substitute.

Let us now shift our attention to the pair, "original and substitute." Both Genji and his father are initially drawn to Fujitsubo because of her resemblance to another. She stands at the head of an important list of heroines who recreate the image of another, original woman in the eyes of a male character. Of all such heroines Fujitsubo alone may have some inkling of this role because the Kiritsubo Emperor encouraged her to treat Genji kindly on account of her resemblance to his dead mother. I am tempted to call her an "original substitute," not only because she is the first, but also because, as the daughter of an emperor, she cannot realistically be said to be replacing Genji's mother who was merely the daughter of an ambitious major counsellor. Still, since the *Genji* never wastes such juxtapositions, we should hold this link in reserve.

As for the resemblance: to be like another is clearly not the same as being identical to that other. Indeed, it is the logic of resemblance that allows fiction to distinguish itself from myth, which is governed by the logic of identity whereby, for example, a deity known for destructive furor in one region turns out to be the same as a beneficent deity in another.[14] Now it is true that resemblance in the *Genji* is usually based on blood tie, which is purportedly natural and beyond human control and therefore a mythic element. Physical resemblance based on blood tie, however, is found not to guarantee moral similarity, let alone identity, as Genji learns in the case of the Third Princess, a hoped-for Fujitsubo substitute. What the tale shows repeatedly is that the confusion, created by desire, of resemblance and identity is a fertile one for fiction. It is crucial in the process of claiming—indeed, in inventing—the terrain of human psychology for literary exploration.

For our purposes, it is time to rephrase Eliade's description of the sacred and the profane as "two modes of being in fiction." Substitution, implying human agency, is a fictional mode par excellence. And fiction, at the same time that it is a term in that series of bipolarities within which it is locally opposed as falsehood to mythic (or, in a different perspective, historical) truth, also strives to transcend the series as a global mode of cognition. It is this property of fiction that operates to make of the *Genji* a novel. In this scheme, "sacred" and "profane" become whatever is interesting or banal according to the values of fiction, which may or may not coincide with those of "being in the world." Thus, a certain mythic yearning within fiction is indicated in the basing of resemblance on blood tie. And of course, the emperor, or rather the idea of the emperor, marks an ontological center, a point of origin in the *Genji*. A mother, on the other hand, is a personal point of origin, and Fujitsubo, being the daughter and consort of emperors, touches on both centers. Genji himself was driven from both, by his mother's death not long after his birth, and by his father's decision to remove him from the succession. The affair with Fujitsubo suggests a desire to recover lost centers of the self, a hunger for mythic dimensions of the self that is paradoxically expressed insofar as its object is a substitute figure. I should emphasize that it is the longing for mythic identity, not that identity itself, that is fictionally valuable. The ineffaceable distance between the actuality of Genji and the desired center is the territory of fiction.

When the boy Genji learns of Fujitsubo's unearthly resemblance to his dead mother, "his young heart is deeply moved" (1:120; S 16; W 17). Should their relationship be deemed to have been incestuous "in fact"? The question has been posed and answered variously, according to available concepts and prevailing ideology. Among modern readers, the late Oka Kazuo did not hesitate to write of Genji's "mother complex" (Oedipus is not honored in the Japanese phrasing). Fujii Sadakazu has undertaken a painstaking study of Heian marriage codes to show that the incest taboo is respected throughout the tale.[15] Surveying the complex of associations surrounding the word *tsumi* ("crime," "guilt," "pollution," "sin," etc.), which appears no fewer than 198 times in the course of the *Genji*, Nomura Seiichi casts doubt on the appropriateness of interpreting Fujitsubo as a tragic, guilty heroine.[16] One current tendency in Japanese scholarship is to transfer the guilt from the erotic to the political sphere, an odd mirroring of the shift in Fujitsubo's characterization within the tale itself. Thus, Genji and Fujitsubo are guilty not of violating the incest taboo but of disrupting the imperial succession.

Although scholarly efforts to provide a socio-historical context to incest are indisputably useful, the findings cannot be transported directly back into the novel to resolve its ambiguities. Such findings tend to be most helpful in providing a field that can set off the distinctiveness of the literary phenomenon in question. Political and erotic guilt, rather than being mutually exclusive, are mutually metaphoric, just as political and erotic concerns are shown to be interdependent throughout the tale. Indeed, incest provides an ideal ground for the play of the mutuality of the political and the erotic, as well as of the sacred and the profane, the mythic and the fictional.

To pursue this oscillating dynamic, we should return to the moment of the young Genji's demotion to commoner status. In arriving at this decision, his father relies on Indian and Korean as well as domestic modes of physiognomy. Only the Korean examination (which the Emperor cannot witness in person because of a decree against receiving foreigners) is recounted. Genji's mien is pronounced to be that of one who "should become the father of his nation and ascend to the peerless rank of monarch," but this accolade is balanced by a warning of dire consequences should he in fact attain such heights (1:116; S 14; W 15–16). This is the first of three prophecies about Genji's fate. The second, coming when Genji learns of Fujitsubo's pregnancy, elusively refers to an inconceivably extraordinary future along with the possibility of misfortune (1:308; S 100; W 96). The third, disclosed at the time of the birth of Genji's daughter, the future Akashi Empress, had predicted that of his three children, one would become emperor, another empress, and the least of them chancellor (2:275; S 273; W 287).

Now prophecies represent another, sacred world of transcendental knowledge potent enough to govern human relativity. But in the world of fiction it would be uninteresting for a prophecy to be merely, straightforwardly fulfilled. (It makes heroic action tedious, if not altogether superfluous.) This is where incest as transgressive love becomes indispensable. Genji takes the wife of his father the Emperor and fathers a son who will succeed to the throne. Through this private appropriation of the public, that which is profane in the historical ideology of the imperial system becomes a new fictional sacred. (The emperor, literarily speaking, is profane: he does not generate stories. The four emperors appearing in the *Genji* are granted few interesting moments.)

Violating the imperial succession is of course a political act, but it is also a sexual transgression as well, given the nature of emperorhood. Now for Genji to qualify as a fictional hero, he must be free of the taint of political desire, and there is no more powerful antidote for this than erotic desire.

The pursuit of power is instantly transformed if it is the consequence, and not the cause, of passion, for we are accustomed to thinking of passion as irrational, irresistible, and therefore (God–) given. If the object of the passion is forbidden, so much the better (one who would risk everything for love cannot be charged with mundane ambition). Fujitsubo as empress and as his father's wife, a step-mother, a metaphoric mother, is doubly forbidden to Genji.

I should pause over this description of Fujitsubo as doubly forbidden. The first source of taboo, that she is the wife of an emperor, is unproblematic, both as a fact within the tale and as a matter of fictional value. The second, that she is the wife of the hero's father, is more complicated. The study on marriage taboos referred to earlier mentions an apparent prohibition against relations with one's stepmother, but Fujii dismisses it as inconsequential and accordingly concludes that the Genji–Fujitsubo affair only violates the purity of the imperial line. He does, however, detect a "taboo-like atmosphere" or "taboo as metaphor."[17] Now the *Tale of Genji* abounds in examples of metaphoric incest; where it is not actualized, it is, certainly, flirted with. In "New Herbs, Part Two," Kashiwagi, the son of Tō no Chūjō, Genji's closest companion and foil, violates the Third Princess, daughter of a retired emperor and Genji's wife. At the time, Genji is the father of the reigning emperor and is receiving the emoluments due to an ex-emperor. Kashiwagi is, accordingly, violating the pseudo-empress-wife of his pseudo-emperor-father. Mirroring this is Genji's biological son Yūgiri's visual violation of his stepmother Murasaki. Genji's own relationship with Murasaki begins as one of father and daughter; their backgrounds contain enough parallels to make them sibling-like as well. Genji poses as a father to two other women to whom he is erotically drawn, Akikonomu and Tamakazura, who are also the daughters of former lovers (the Rokujō Lady and Yūgao). It seems reasonable to conclude that Murasaki Shikibu was interested in exploring attachments that are problematic at least in part because of excessive proximity. Beyond offering the generic interest of forbidden love, the motif overlaps with the pursuit of origins/originals and substitutes: repossessing a dead lover through her daughter, or recovering one's own beginnings through union with a mother/sister. The pursuit is all the more tantalizing if there are fathers and brothers, actual or equivalent, lurking in the wings.[18]

It should be admitted that political ambition, even though unbecoming to heroes, can provide a fictional interest different from that of erotic anguish. And Genji is ambitious, as we shall see, but his political manipulations are usually masked, at times transparently, by erotic tension. Prophecy also contributes to this dissimulation. For instance, it is possible

that Genji's violation of the imperial succession does not ultimately
constitute a transgression, for according to a higher principle, he was born to
rule, if not directly, then through his enthroned children. The aura of fate
cleanses and sanctifies Genji's actions so that it seems indecent (if it should
even occur to us) to regard them as calculated. So, as Genji works to
consolidate his gains and ensure their transmission, it seems but the simple
and satisfying fulfillment of fate. At the same time, the hint of the illicit as
well as of political scheming precludes the sense of a naive realization of
prophecy. Prophecy and action stand in a peculiar relation: each has the
potential of rendering the other superfluous, yet each can legitimate the
other. We will have further occasion to consider these matters, but for the
moment, let us say that in the *Genji* prophecy can sanction but not predict.

We have been neglecting Fujitsubo. In the affair with Genji, Fujitsubo
slips from the public, official realm into a private, erotic one. She struggles
to abolish this private realm with Genji and more or less succeeds when she
takes vows after the death of the Kiritsubo Emperor. Her object is to see her
son safe on the throne. To this end, she must prevent Genji from repeating
his follies, without, at the same time, making him so dejected as to take the
tonsure himself, thus leaving their young son altogether unprotected. Once
girded by her vows, Fujitsubo becomes more generous with her attentions,
even speaking to him on occasion without intermediaries as was customary
for high-born women. In time, upon Genji's return from his self-imposed
exile, the two become political allies, acting in bold unison to establish the
Reizei Emperor's reign on a secure footing. A marvelous economy develops
in which the hidden, pent-up energy of erotic longing is converted into
visible political performance. The reticent Fujitsubo turns verbose and even
ruthless on occasion. When Genji reports to her of the retired Suzaku
Emperor's desire to have the orphaned Akikonomu come to him, Fujitsubo
coolly responds:

> Indeed, we are humbled by His Majesty's interest, and we must
> feel sorry for hum, but let us make the Rokujō Lady's will our
> excuse and have her daughter enter [Reizei's] Court. We can
> pretend to know nothing of his interest. In any case, he will no
> longer be concerned with such matters [i.e., women], now that he
> is devoting himself to his prayers, and I do not believe he will be
> deeply reproachful if you inform him of your plans. (2:310; S 289;
> W 305)

Working by plan for a desired end is secular and unheroic, again
because it is the absence of visible process that is associated with the divine.

The program of action even for earthly heroes and heroines must be free of self-interest and calculation. (Here the values of fiction and "the world" coincide because both mimic myth, the principal source of heroic paradigms.) To place a daughter in an emperor's service and to bolster her position with cultural display (as in the Picture Contest in chapter seventeen) are appropriate forms of behavior for the scions of ministerial families (the northern branch of the Fujiwara clan being the prime historical example), but they are ironic both in Genji, son of an emperor and a fictional hero, and Fujitsubo, daughter of one emperor, wife of another, and a fictional heroine. But of course, Fujitsubo was introduced to the tale as a substitute for the daughter of an ambitious major counsellor who, like other aspiring men, put his daughter to the service of his dreams. While the Kiritsubo Lady was sacrificed to her dead father's ambitions, Fujitsubo is compelled to become politically ambitious herself—hardly the sense in which she was intended to substitute. In this sense Fujitsubo does indeed replace Genji's mother, and the absolute opposition between divine royalty and secular commoner is overcome. Yet, at the same time, when Fujitsubo and Genji effectively control the court upon the latter's return to the capital, there is an aura of archaic brother–sister rule, an impression retrospectively reinforced by the sororal aspect of the relationship of Murasaki (Fujitsubo's niece and surrogate) to Genji.[19]

If the figure of Fujitsubo contains powerful dichotomies in itself, it also serves to generate what might be called centripetal and centrifugal movements within the novel. Inasmuch as she is forbidden to him, Genji is driven to seeking substitutes elsewhere, and widely. There is of course Murasaki, and far in the future the unsatisfactory Third Princess. They are substitutes by direct descent and high pedigree, who belong to the central narrative, but there are others, the heroines of the subsidiary chapters that readers for centuries have been encouraged to read "adjacently" to the appropriate primary chapters. Utsusemi, Yūgao, and Suetsumuhana, coming from lower social backgrounds (except for Suetsumuhana, the destitute daughter of a long-dead prince), and lacking the sacred attributes that cloak Fujitsubo's story in secrecy, are the heroines of stories that are vividly, even realistically, detailed. Yet, even though these stories are open where Fujitsubo's is closed, they are not without elements of transgression or guilt, almost as if they were the intaglio versions of the Fujitsubo story.

Take the Yūgao episode. Genji falls in love with a nameless young woman of apparently modest circumstance and takes her away to a remote villa, where she dies suddenly and mysteriously. The conditions of Genji's guilt are ambiguous. As with his attachment to Fujitsubo, he is in the grips of an irresistible passion. Whereas the Fujitsubo affair produces a problematic birth, the Yūgao episode ends in death. Reizei's birth is accompanied by a mysterious dream (containing the second of the three prophecies) for Genji; Yūgao's death is evidently caused by a spirit visible to Genji alone. The secret of Reizei's conception is initially confined to Genji, Fujitsubo, and a lady-in-waiting, Ōmyōbu, who may have been the Empress's wet nurse's daughter, a sort of surrogate sister.[20] Similarly, Yūgao's corpse is secretly disposed of by Koremitsu, Genji's wet nurse's son.

One of the surrogate episodes generated by Fujitsubo's rejection of Genji deserves separate attention. Strictly speaking, neither Oborozukiyo nor her story can be described as "surrogate," since the lady is antithetical to Fujitsubo and her story constitutes an important development of the principal narrative. Genji comes upon her accidentally after festivities at court one night when he prowls about in frustration from his inability to gain access to Fujitsubo's quarters. As luck would have it, Oborozukiyo is the daughter of the Minister of the Right and a sister of Kokiden. Genji, young enough to brave what should have been daunting risks, becomes a carefree hero, whose adventures are pleasurable rather in the fashion of an Erroll Flynn movie—something that can hardly be said of the Fujitsubo affair. The Oborozukiyo entanglement is parodic in every way, and the fact that it has such grave consequences is yet another instance of Murasaki Shikibu's skillful wit. Oborozukiyo has been promised to Suzaku, Genji's half brother and Crown Prince, soon to ascend the throne. In other words, Genji is once again usurping imperial property.

The two are discovered in "The Sacred Tree," a beautifully orchestrated chapter featuring the death of the Kiritsubo Emperor and Genji's intrusion into both Fujitsubo's and Oborozukiyo's chambers. The incident with Fujitsubo comes first. Since her husband's death, she has been more strenuous than ever in warding off Genji's attentions, but of course, neither prayer nor barrier can stop him. On this occasion, when Fujitsubo perceives his presence in her apartment, she is so distraught that she falls ill; still Genji refuses to leave, and, as daybreak approaches, the faithful Ōmyōbu and her companion Ben can only bundle him into a closet, shove his clothes in after him, and leave him for an anxious day.[21] Fujitsubo's condition is worrisome enough that her brother Prince Hyōbu is sent for, but by nightfall, she is somewhat improved. Genji cautiously slips out of the closet for one rapturous gaze. Predictably, he wants to be seen as well as to see, and as the lady attempts to flee, he holds her fast by the edge of her cloak and her hair. It is after this encounter that Fujitsubo resolves to take vows.

Genji's meetings with Oborozukiyo are facilitated both by her eager willingness to receive him and her stay at home from court on grounds of indisposal. (Fujitsubo was similarly at her own home when Reizei was conceived.) One night, Genji is unable to make his retreat because of a thunderstorm. For once, he becomes feverish with anxiety lest he be discovered, and sure enough, the Minister of the Right comes in to check on his daughter's safety after the storm. Bits of stray clothing and writing catch the irascible father's eye. Both he and Suzaku had been aware of Oborozukiyo's dalliance and had tried to look the other way, but Genji's flagrancy is too much, especially for the Minister's daughter Kokiden, who brandishes dire threats.[22] It is in the face of this onslaught of hostility that Genji decides to withdraw to Suma (his surprising acumen is masked by the drama and sorrow of the moment). Thus, the great secret remains safe, but a smaller one, mimicking it, is revealed, and Genji submits to the consequences.

NOTES

1. For information on court rank, residences, and many other matters, the reader is advised to consult the *Princeton Companion to Classical Japanese Literature*, by Earl Miner, Hiroko Odagiri, and Robert E. Morrell (Princeton, N.J.: Princeton University Press, 1986).

2. This useful observation is made by Shimizu Yoshiko in her *Genji no Onnagimi* (Hanawa Shobō, 1967), p. 19.

3. All ages are by oriental count, which makes the characters one to two years older than they would be by western count.

4. Koto is the generic name for a group of stringed instruments. The sō no koto has thirteen strings, the kin no koto (often associated with royalty), seven, and the wagon, or Yamatogoto, a native version, six. Each instrument is associated with one or more characters, and music is frequently used to suggest empathy or its absence. Kokiden's music-making during the nights following the Kiritsubo Lady's death is an egregious display of her character. The Suzaku Emperor, wishing to make amends to Genji, proposes music to him upon his return from exile but is rebuffed. On the positive side it is the Akashi Lady's musical interest that attracts Genji and leads to the conception of the Akashi Empress. (Painting, on the other hand, figures in barren relationships: Genji and Murasaki, Reizei and Akikonomu.) A minor nicety about the Genji-Fujitsubo music-making is that although Genji is presumably a consummate performer on all instruments, he is seldom associated with the flute, which is the instrument of Kashiwagi, who will cuckold him many years hence.

5. Gotō Shōko, "Fujitsubo no Eichi," in KGMS 3 (1981): 165. Commentators are fond of this passage (1) as evidence of Fujitsubo's learning and (2) for the plot resemblance of the Chinese example to the *Genji*. The skeletal similarities, however, serve more to emphasize the differences. No matter how shrill or malicious Kokiden can be, it is impossible to imagine such grotesque behavior in the *Genji*. At most, the extravagance of the comparison suggests an unexpectedly melodramatic turn to Fujitsubo's mind.

6. At the time the *Genji* was written, only one woman in history had received such honors. Known as Higashi Sanjōin (961–1000), she was the daughter of Fujiwara no Kaneie (an eminent statesman and the neglectful husband of the author of the *Gossamer Years* and the mother of Emperor Ichijō (r. 986–1011), whose consort Shōshi was Murasaki Shikibu's mistress. Higashi Sanjōin was the older sister of Fujiwara no Michinaga and is thought to have been exceedingly influential with this consummate politician.

7. In this respect she is most similar to the Rokujō Lady with her eleven poems, nine addressed to Genji. The Akashi Lady has twenty-two, thirteen to Genji; Murasaki twenty-three, seventeen to Genji; and Tamakazura twenty, nine to Genji. I am relying on Suzuki Hideo's valuable catalogue of poems listed by character and classified as to *dokuei* (solitary composition), *zōka* or *tōka* (an initiating or responding poem in an exchange between two characters), or *shōwa* (in this case, one of at least three poems composed by as many characters in one setting), to be found in vol. 6 of the Shōgakkan edition of the *Genji*, pp. 517–49. Of the two poems by Fujitsubo not addressed to Genji, one belongs to a *shōwa* composed with other ladies on "her" side in the Picture Contest. The other poem, listed by Suzuki as a *dokuei*, actually harmonizes with a poem in the preceding chapter by Genji.

8. A centuries-old dispute surrounds the question of whether the meeting in which Reizei was conceived was the first for Genji and Fujitsubo. The hypothetical "Her Shining Highness" (Kagayaku Hi no Miya) chapter has been adduced to fill this gap among others. There is, however, only one reference to such a chapter (by the poet Fujiwara no Teika, 1162–1241), which only denies its existence. For a recent evaluation of this once lively topic, see Ikeda Tsutomu's "'Kagayaku Hi no Miya'-ron: Gen-Kiritsubo no Maki no Seiritsu," in KGMS 1 (1980): 85–94. There are fifteenth- and sixteenth-century commentaries that support the view that Genji and Fujitsubo had earlier, unrecounted meetings. See Kitamura Kigin's *Kogetsushō*, 1:275–76. Mitani Kuniaki presents an updated version of this argument in "Fujitsubo Jiken no Hyōgen Kōzō: 'Waka Murasaki' no Hōhō Aruiwa 'Pure-tekisuto' o Shite no *Ise Monogatari*," in (*Imai Takuya Hakushi Koki Kinen*) Monogatari, Nikki Bungaku to Sono Shūhen (Ōfusha, 1980), pp. 288–89.

9. The Shōgakkan text reads as follows: "Miya mo asamashikar*ishi** o omoiizuru dani, yo to tomo no onmonoomoi naru o, [I] *sate dani yaminan*, to fukō oboshitaru ni, ito ukute, imijiki onkeshiki naru [a] *mono kara*, natsukashū rōtage ni, [b] *sari tote* uchitokezu, kokoro fukō hazukashige naru onmotenashi nado no, nao hito ni nisasetamawanu o, [II] *nadoka nanome naru koto dani uchimajiritamawazariken*, to, tsurō sae obosaruru." To describe this as beginning in Fujitsubo's mind and ending in Genji's is to oversimplify, of course: strictly speaking, only [I] and [II] are representations of Fujitsubo's and Genji's thoughts within the narrator's discourse. Phrases such as [a] *mono* kara and [b] *sari tote* are favorite tools in the Shikibu arsenal for producing serial clauses whose contents are not precisely antithetical but are contradictory enough to create a strong tension. The perfective *shi* in asamashikar*ishi** is often used to bolster the argument that there was at least one previous encounter between Genji and Fujitsubo.

10. Andrew Plaks, *Archetype and Allegory in the Dream of the Red Chamber* (Princeton, N.J.: Princeton University Press, 1976), p. 44.

11. Mircea Eliade, *The Sacred and the Profane: The Nature of Religion*, trans. Willard Trask (New York: Harcourt Brace Jovanovich, 1959), p. 14.

12. I am putting aside the important topic of ruling empresses (as distinguished from consorts) as well as the even more problematic subject of near-legendary female rulers such as Himiko. The imperial succession reflected (perhaps promoted) the progressive erosion of the matrilineal tradition even though property continued to be inherited through the mother. See, however, Takamure Itsue's account "Tennō no Katei" in her *Nihon Kon'inshi* (Shibundō, 1963), pp. 57–66, in which she asserts the essentially matrilineal character of the imperial family until the Meiji period.

13. This description is of course greatly indebted to current discussions of the effect of supplementarity stimulated by the work of Jacques Derrida. The topic recurs in various manifestations in his writing, but see, for example, *Of Grammatology*, trans. Gayatri Chakravorty Spivak (Baltimore, Md.: Johns Hopkins University Press, 1976).

14. The point is made by Fujii Sadakazu in the seminal *Genji Monogatari: Shigen to Genzai* (Tōjusha, 1980), pp. 144–45, where he goes on to argue that we must see the logic

of resemblance not as a mere relic of myth in the fictional narratives called *monogatari* but as an active presence, the sign of a stance the fictional narrative assumes toward myth. Of course, the logic of identity survives in fiction as well, in all those plots that involve lost kinship, concealed ethnic origins, and so forth. The attraction of the mystery of birth is perennial, and it can be fairly called the attraction of the mythic, which survives in fiction as in life.

15. Oka's views are contained in his *Genji Monogatari no Kisoteki Kenkyū* (Tōyōdō Shuppan, 1966). Fujii's influential study is contained in the chapter "Tabō to Kekkon" in his *Shigen to Genzai*, pp. 233–51.

16. Nomura Seiichi, "Fujitsubo no 'Tsumi' ni Tsuite," *Genji Monogatari no Sōzo* (Ōfūsha, 1969), pp. 164–80.

17. Fujii Sadakazu, *Shigen to Genzai*, pp. 246–47.

18. For readers who like to trace genealogical tangles: Murasaki is the niece of Fujitsubo, the daughter of her brother Prince Hyōbu; Kashiwagi's violation of the Third Princess is all but absurdly overdetermined, since she, too, is a niece of Fujitsubo, and the daughter of Genji's older brother and weak rival Suzaku. Genji prevents Suzaku from obtaining Akikonomu and presents her to his own son Reizei instead. In the case of Tamakazura, he prevents her from making herself known to her true father, his friend and figurative brother Tō no Chūjō, and dangles her before his own brother, Prince Hotaru, as well as her brother Kashiwagi.

19. One might say that Genji and Fujitsubo represent a mildly parodic version of brother–sister rule (*hikohimesei*) since such ruling sisters were priestesses to the tutelary deities of the clan and Fujitsubo by that time was a Buddhist nun. For a discussion as to whether such ties were incestuous, as well as for numerous examples of such relationships, see Kuratsuka Akiko's *Fujo no Bunka* (Heibonsha, 1979), especially the chapter "Ani to Imōto no Monogatari," pp. 190–221, as well as her article, "Kōtōfu ni Okeru 'Imōto': Kodai Joseishi Josetsu," *Bungaku* 36 (June 1968): 61–73. See also Takamure, *Nihon Kon'inshi*, pp. 58–59.

20. Ōmyōbu's identity is suggested by Saigō Nobutsuna in his *Genji Monogatari o Yomu Tame Ni* (Heibonsha, 1983), pp. 69–76, where he discusses the special relationship between masters and mistresses and their wet nurses' children.

21. The motif of a night spent together unconsummated recurs with several variations. In "Evening Mist," Genji's son loses his head over Ochiba no Miya, his friend Kashiwagi's widow. Despite her obdurate resistance (she is another princess, one of Suzaku's daughters, whose marriage to a commoner brought only misfortune), Yūgiri manages to move her back to the city from her mountain retreat and prepare for nuptials. As a last resort, the princess locks herself into a closet, and Yūgiri is left to spend the night alone outside. In "Trefoil Knots," Kaoru and Ōigimi reenact this scene with intensified refinement.

22. The weak Suzaku continues to be attached to Oborozukiyo even when her preference for his brother is made plain. Is there an unconscious element of revenge in his insistence many years later that Genji marry his immature daughter, the Third Princess?

AMY VLADECK HEINRICH

Blown in Flurries:
The Role of the Poetry in "Ukifune"

There are 795 poems (*waka*) in the fifty-four chapters of *The Tale of Genji*, one indication of the important role such poems played in the daily lives of Heian aristocrats. They are used in the world of the *Genji* in many of the same ways they were used in the society it reflects: as a medium of interpersonal communication, as a means to express individual emotion, and as a social form to acknowledge specific occasions. Nearly 80 percent (624) of these 795 poems are exchanges (*zōtōka*) ("sent and answered poems"); 107 are poems recited in solitude (*dokuei*); and 64 are occasional poems (*kaigō*).[1] But the poems also perform literary functions in the creation of the world of this tale, and are a vital element in its structure. They express intense feeling, and define the personalities of the characters, as well as illuminating their thoughts. They emphasize themes within a narrative progression, and clarify relationships.[2] This essay will explore some of the ways the poems in "Ukifune" contribute to the form and development of the chapter as a whole.

Within the "Ukifune" chapter there are twenty-two poems, divided in a proportion similar to that of Genji as a whole: seventeen are exchanged (one sent poem is left unanswered); two are solitary; one is an occasional poem; and there are two poems which are sent but to which answers are unexpected. Ukifune herself writes thirteen of the twenty-two poems, Niou six, and Kaoru three.

From *Ukifune: Love in the Tale of Genji*. © 1982 by Columbia University Press.

A primary function of the poetry in "Ukifune" is to provide insight into the natures and development of individual characters. Ukifune writes about uncertainty, and emerges in her poetry as one who views the world around her with mistrust, who perceives only insecurity and untrustworthiness. She is unsure of how to respond to her perceptions, although her self-assurance grows as her emotional isolation increases. Niou's poems concern the physical and emotional worlds he inhabits. In general, his reactions are in harmony with those worlds of his perception. Kaoru writes only about the state of affairs in which he finds himself and Ukifune. He makes only fleeting reference to his own feelings, and refers only in tentative and rather generalized ways to Ukifune's; there is no complexity of emotion in his poems.

The poems, especially the exchanges, also indicate the relationships between characters. The personalities which the poems help define both contribute to, and are influenced by, those relationships. Finally, by means of their placement, content, and interrelationships, the poems assist in the development of the prose narrative.

These three functions—to delineate character, to define relationships, and to advance the plot—are of course intertwined within each poem, but for the sake of clarity I shall try to unravel the strands for individual examination. The poems, translated below, are written or recited in the presence of the person to whom they are addressed unless otherwise indicated.[3] I have numbered them for ease of reference, and have noted how they are linked to other poems.

1. Ukifune to Nakanokimi and her son, sent with a New Year's gift of a woven basket and a branch of pine.

mada furinu	This branching pine
mono ni wa aredo	is not yet old, yet know
kimi ga tame	for you as well
fukaki kokoro ni	wholeheartedly I
matsu to shiranamu	anticipate long life

2. Niou to Ukifune, answered by 3.

nagaki yo o	Even while promising
tanomete mo nao	our love will endure,
kanashiki wa	how sad it is!
tada asu shiranu	that in life itself
inochi narikeri	tomorrow is unknown

3. Ukifune to Niou, in response to 2.

kokoro oba	I would not lament
nagekazaramashi	the hearts of men
inochi nomi	could I but think
sadame naki yo to	that it is life alone
omowamashikaba	inconstant in this world

4. Niou to Ukifune, answered by 5.

yo ni shirazu	Surely I shall lose my way
madoubeki kana	in this unfamiliar world!
saki ni tatsu	when even setting forth
namida mo michi o	my rising tears continue
kakikurashitsutsu	darkening the road

5. Ukifune to Niou, in response to 4.

namida o mo	I cannot even stem
hodo naki sode ni	the tears that soak
sekikanete	these narrow sleeves—
ikani wakare o	how might I be the one
todomubeki mi zo	to stay this separation?

6. Kaoru to Ukifune, answered by 7.

Ujibashi no	The enduring bonds
nagaki chigiri wa	of Uji Bridge will not decay.
kuchi seji o	Do not disturb your heart
ayabumu kata ni	with fear that it is
kokoro sawagu na	dangerous to tread upon

7. Ukifune to Kaoru, in response to 6.

taema nomi	Rifts only in this world;
yo ni wa ayoki	the Bridge of Uji
Ujibashi o	is dangerous to tread.
kuchi senu mono to	Yet am I to trust
nao tanome to ya	that it will not give way?

8. Niou to Ukifune, answered by 9.

> toshi futomo
> kawaran mono kawith
> tachibana no
> kojima ga saki ni
> chigiru kokoro wa

> Is it something which
> passing years will change?
> the heart which binds itself
> on this small island
> of the orange tree

9. Ukifune to Niou, in response to 8.

> tachibana no
> kojima wa iro mo
> kawaraji o
> kono ukifune zo
> yukue shirarenu

> Immutable may be
> the color of the orange tree
> on this small island;
> and yet this drifting boat
> cannot know where it is bound

10. Niou to Ukifune, answered by 11.

> mine no yuki
> migiwa no kori
> fumiwakete
> kimi ni zo madou
> michi wa madowazu

> Trampling through
> the snowy peaks
> and the ice at water's edge
> I do not lose my way—
> though I lose myself in you

11. Ukifune to Niou, in response to 10.

> furimidare
> migiwa ni koru
> yuki yori mo
> nakazora nite zo
> ware wa kenubeki

> More surely than the snow
> blown in flurries, frozen
> at the water's edge,
> into the empty sky
> I too shall disappear

12. Niou to Ukifune, with letter; answered by 15.

> nagameyaru
> sonata no kumo mo
> mienu made
> sora sae kururu oh
> koro no wabishisa

> Now even the clouds
> I gaze at, languishing,
> cannot be seen,
> the loneliness!
> when the very sky grows dark

13. Kaoru to Ukifune, with letter; answered by 16.

mizu masaru	In that village of Uji
ochi no satobito	where the waters rise
ika naran	I wonder how you are,
harenu nagame ni	when in unending rain
kakikurasu koro	both heart and sky grow dark

14. Ukifune, recited alone.

sato no na o	Knowing full well
waga mi ni shireba	the bitter meaning of its name,
Yamashiro no	Uji in Yamashiro
Uji no watari zo	is increasingly
itodo sumiuki	a painful place to live

15. Ukifune to Niou, with letter; in response to 12.

kakikurashi	Would that I—
are senu mine no	who pass through life adrift—
amagumo ni	might transform myself,
ukite yo o furu	become a raincloud
mi o mo nasaba ya	on the darkened unlit peak

16. Ukifune to Kaoru, with letter; in response to 13.

tsurezure to	The rain, revealing
mi o shiru ame no	my unhappy state,
oyamaneba	does not let up at all,
sode sae itodo	while the measure in my sleeves
mikasa masarite	increases more and more

17. Kaoru to Ukifune, sent in letter; unanswered.

nami koyuru	I did not even know
koro tomo shirazu	the time the waves crossed over
Sue no Matsu	Sue no Matsu;
matsuran to nomi	I thought only that
omoikeru kana	you would yet wait

18. Niou, recited in the company of Jijū.

izuku ni ka   I know not where
mi oba suten to   to cast aside this life;
shiragumo no   there are no hills
kakaranu yama mo   not overcast with clouds
naku naku zo yuku   as I go weeping, weeping

19. Ukifune, recited alone.

nageki wabi   Though I abandon life—
mi oba sutsutomo   lamenting, desolate—
nakikage ni   that even after death
ukina nagasamu   might bitter rumors spread
koto o koso omoe   preys on my mind

20. Ukifune to Niou, in letter.

kara o dani   If I have left behind
ukiyo no naka ni   not even a body
todomezu wa   in this wretched world,
izuko o haka   to what object then will you
kimi mo uramin   for your resentment find?

21. Ukifune to her mother, in letter.

nochi ni mata   Let us hope that
aimimu koto o   hereafter we shall
omowanan   meet once again,
kono yo no yume ni   our hearts untroubled
kokoro madowade   by this world's dreams

22. Ukifune, addressed to the wind; to be sent to her mother.

kane no oto no   Unite my weeping
tayuru hibiki ni   with the wind-borne echoes
ne o soete   of the silenced bells,
wags yo tsukinu to   and let her know
kimi ni tsutae yo   my life has reached its end

Ukifune, as the central focus of the chapter, has the majority of poems, and the majority of those are responses (*henka*). Indeed, for much of the chapter, she is passive, expressing emotions which result from someone else's suggestion or action. Her inability to assert control is the most prominent attitude of her first several poems.

Her first response, poem 3, concludes with *omowamashikaba* ("could I but think"). The implication is clearly that she cannot; it is not only life which is uncertain, but men's hearts are unsettled as well, and so she must grieve. Her second response, poem 5, states an inability as the premise of the poem: ("I cannot even stem / the tears"). She cannot control herself, much less the development of her relationship with Niou or the demands of the social world which impinge upon it. Ukifune's next two poems, poem 7 (in response to one from Kaoru) and poem 9 (in response to one from Niou), both concern a questioning of perception, especially the disparity between what is presented to her as the condition of the world and what she perceives as her own condition within it. Where Kaoru had posited a stable, enduring bridge, Ukifune sees rifts only. She therefore questions his conclusion that she can rely on its endurance: "yet am I to trust / that it will not give way?" To Niou, who wrote of enduring love within a constant natural world, she questions the applicability of that world to herself: "and yet this drifting boat / cannot know where it is bound." Ukifune sees an unreliable world which is frightening and dangerous; even where she perceives continuity, she does not believe her own life accords with it. She senses that the bridge, in spite of Kaoru's protestations, will give way beneath her feet, and that she is adrift and directionless even in the enduring natural world in which Niou vows his love.

In the eleventh poem in the chapter, Ukifune takes a step in her development, and associates herself with the impermanent aspects of the natural world. The poem is a complex indication of the nature of her relationship with Niou; part of its importance is in her identification with qualities of ice and snow. The snow which she describes as *furimidare* (blown in flurries) exemplifies her perception of her own feelings as tossed by forces outside herself. By uniting herself with the snow and ice, and hypothesizing her own disappearance as well as theirs, she is also removing herself from Niou's more constant world. Ukifune discards this poem, primarily because her mention of *nakazora* ('midair'; empty sky) is too direct a reference to her position between Niou and Kaoru; but also she seems as yet unready to commit herself to the kind of alliance she is beginning to posit between herself and the impermanent qualities of the world.

The fourteenth poem is Ukifune's first solitary poem. She has received letters from both Kaoru and Niou, and must respond to them. For the first time, the presence of one is not vying with the claims of the other: the memories of both are juxtaposed in her mind. Addressing only herself, she is able to state clearly her condition:

sato no na o	Knowing full well
waga mi ni shireba	the bitter meaning of its name,
Yamashiro no	Uji in Yamashiro
Uji no watari zo	is increasingly
itodo sumiuki	a painful place to life.

This blunt expression of unhappiness is pivotal: it balances the two sent poems, one each from Niou and Kaoru, that immediately precede it with the two responses of her own that immediately follow. It is also a turning point in her own poems. Until this, she has expressed distrust of a world in which she finds herself weeping at partings, fearing the future, and rejecting others' perceptions. Now, for the first time, her unhappiness is isolated and totally her own. Having so expressed herself, she begins to seek solutions, as though the sound of her own voice speaking a truth has impelled her to assert herself. The next poem, number 15, clearly articulates a desire to resolve the uncertainties of her own situation by merging herself with the impermanent:

kakikurashi	Would that I—
hare senu mine o	who pass through life adrift—
amagumo ni	might transform myself,
ukite yo o furu	become a raincloud
mi o mo nasaba ya	on the darkened unlit peak

Her passage through the world adrift is the source of her misery; by becoming one with something—here a raincloud, earlier flurries of snow— that is by nature properly floating and unstable, her misery would be relieved.

Ukifune's next poem, number 16, is a break in this development. In writing only of her unrelieved unhappiness, she is hiding her perceptions from Kaoru as she has hidden her actions. He can, and does, interpret her mood as the product of her isolation and his neglect. Her relative openness with Niou is in part, of course, unavoidable, because he is aware of her whole situation and Kaoru is not. But it seems to indicate as well her greater attraction and attachment to Niou.

Her next poem, number 19, is her second solitary poem, and is similar to the first, number 14: it deals only with her own situation, and it follows two poems, one each sent from Niou and Kaoru. Again she responds to the juxtaposition of poems from her two lovers by stepping away from them both and addressing herself. Her exclamation in the earlier solitary poem expressed the bitterness of her life; here she recognizes that the bitterness may very well continue after death. Her own death is now fully established in her mind, and her thoughts proceed beyond it. Once more the clear expression to herself of her own position seems to brace her.

For the most part, Ukifune's previous poems have dealt with her own inability, the world as an untrustworthy place, or her desire to escape from her plight and to disappear into those elements which are naturally unstable. Poem 19 finally begins to question what the results will be of her own action:

nageki wabi	Though I abandon life—
mi oba sutsutomo	lamenting, desolate—
nakikage ni	that even after death
ukina nagasamu	might bitter rumors spread
koto o koso omoe	preys on my mind

Having imagined the results, she moves to control them as much as possible in poem 20. She speaks of her own corpse, and by contemplating the results of her not leaving it behind in the world, she attempts to assert some control over events and feelings after her death. Having, then, resolutely decided to die, and having attempted to influence responses following her death, she is ready to move on. In poem 21, she can anticipate the afterlife as sweet and untroubled, leaving behind the world completely in a way she could not have done even two poems before.

Ukifune's last poem in the chapter is imperative: she is finally giving orders. Her poems are surest when she is alone, as in poems 14 and 19, confronting her condition and not confused by the need to respond to the importunities of the men, or as here, when she has made and accepted her own decision and arranged her affairs. Within this chapter, Ukifune as she appears in her poems has developed from a confused, wavering, and unhappy character to a resolute and resigned one, although still unhappy.

Her first poem in the chapter is the one occasional poem, sent to her half-sister Nakanokimi as a New Year's greeting. It is an interesting gauge for comparison: a simple, unemotional, ordinary poem, dealing with, as the occasion demands, long life. Her final poems are more complex, intense in feeling, and concern her own death. Where the first was undistinguished and seen by other characters as childish and simple, she has come to produce poems that are self-possessed and complex. One function of this initial, conventional greeting poem must be to encourage such a comparison. Another function, of course, is to advance the plot, since the poem, with its letter and gift, becomes the means by which Niou discovers her identity and location.

This consideration of Ukifune's poems also leads to a tentative answer to the question of why Ukifune's general distrust of the uncertainty and unpredictability of life does not lead her to consider the Buddhist path she eventually happens upon. From the evidence in her poems, any path in life seems too unreliable for her to consider as a solution. Her only answer is dissolution and disappearance, a death which will not leave behind even a corpse, like a cloud that passes and leaves only clear sky. It is also possible that she cannot conceive of attaining an appropriate level of detachment. In any event, she does develop to a point where she chooses the finality of death.

There is less development within the poems of Niou and Kaoru; in a sense both characters function in this chapter as foils to Ukifune's changes. Still there are characteristics in their poems which establish a voice for each. Niou's sent poems contain several references to some unknown quality ("that in life itself / tomorrow is unknown"; "never experienced in this world.") However, such perceptions are usually balanced by the stabilizing factor either of love or of Ukifune as a symbol of love. In poem 2, although he sees life as uncertain, he trusts in the love he shares with Ukifune; in poem 4, it is when he leaves her that he fears losing his way; in 10, the physical world is a tangible impediment which he can overcome when Ukifune is his goal; and finally, he writes "I do not lose my way / though I lose myself in you."

The physical world also has a strong presence in Niou's poems; it is more concrete to him than it is to Ukifune. Not only does the world reflect the truth of his feelings, as in poem 8 ("the heart which binds itself / on this small island / of the orange tree"), but his feelings project onto the world and affect his own position in it, as in 4 ("my rising tears continue / darkening the road"). In poem 10, nature in the form of ice and snow has tried to block his way, yet he is able to prevail. In poem 12, the world encloses and traps him as the sky darkens. He is also concerned with process through the world: he refers to roads—*michi wa madowazu; michi o kakikurashitsutsu*—and travels through nature—*fumiwakete*. The real world is substantial for him in a way it is not for Ukifune.

Kaoru's sent poems are more conversational in tone than either Niou's or Ukifune's. They are direct, and say everything they mean to communicate, while Ukifune's and Niou's poems leave vague areas of meaning which must be filled by the recipient of the poem. Kaoru allows less room for varied implications, and composes with fewer subtleties. The result is that little is revealed through his poems. His first, poem 6, states a condition (the bridge and I are firm), and directs a response (don't worry about walking over it). Poem 13 says in effect "it has been raining for a long time; how are you faring?" His last poem, in which he acknowledges Ukifune's infidelity, and his own surprise, is the only poem in the chapter that is incomprehensible without a knowledge of the poem from the *Kokinshū* to which it refers.[4] Still, it is so straightforward that the only way Ukifune can avoid a direct answer is by not responding to it at all. Kaoru's directness is indicative of his exclusion; for much of the chapter he is unaware of the complicated triangle of which he is part.

The exclusion of Kaoru is one aspect of the various relationships revealed by the poems as dialogues within the prose narrative. The lack of mutual understanding in the exchange poems is almost as telling as the communication in them, and accounts for a certain sense of desolation within the chapter. Frequently Ukifune is deliberately hiding her feelings, usually from Kaoru. She systematically conceals not only her feelings, but her actions as well, intentionally allowing him to misinterpret her sadness. A possible explanation of this seems to be that, in addition to her awareness of Kaoru's concern for his reputation, their relationship has been established on an adult–child basis, and however much she has changed and grown, she still responds to him childishly. Sensing where he would disapprove, she hides, for a while at least hoping the problem will resolve itself. There is, in addition, Kaoru's own difficulty in seeing Ukifune as herself, rather than as an image of, or a replacement for, her half-sisters Nakanokimi and Ōigimi, a problem Takahashi Tōru refers to as his "princess complex."[5] It is perhaps easy for Ukifune to mislead him by concealing her individual predicament because it is difficult for him to see her as an individual.

But most important in the dialogue poems is the discrepancy between Ukifune's perceptions of the world and those of the two men. Sometimes when she picks up their images, she draws different conclusions from them; elsewhere, she qualitatively alters their implications in her poems. In poem 6, Kaoru states his belief in the stability of his love and the bridge of Uji, but Ukifune, in her answering poem 7, says that the opposite is true; the bridge and everything else in life is full of gaps. She questions his advising her to rely on such dangerous things.

Niou, in poem 2, creates a contrast between the enduring quality of their love and the unpredictable quality of life. Ukifune responds in poem 3 by negating the contrast, and characterizing both life and love as inconstant and unsettled. Later, in poem 8, Niou compares his love to the constancy of the natural world, by implying that his heart is as unchanging as the ever-green orange tree on Tachibana Island. Ukifune counters that even granting the truth of that constancy, it does not apply to her: "and yet this drifting

boat / cannot know where it is bound." In poem 10, as we have seen, Niou
uses the images of ice and snow to represent the many obstacles he has
overcome to reach her. He places Ukifune at a central point of stability in his
world, and sees her as a compelling goal. Ukifune, however, alters the ice and
snow images into descriptions of a desired state rather than of hindrances.
She would disappear as completely as they do, and so she removes herself
from the central stabilizing position in which Niou has placed her. She aligns
herself with qualities he has seen as obstacles, and would become even more
detached than they. Where Niou is aware of himself as distinct from the
natural world, which allows him to perceive its concreteness more clearly,
Ukifune tries to remove the distinction between self and the physical world,
and so unite those two facts of existence. Each becomes more like the other,
and she has no focal point to steady herself by.

This alteration of images in the two parts of an exchange follows a
similar pattern throughout *The Tale of Genji*.[6] For example, Komachiya
Teruhiko points out that Lady Akashi and Tamakazura similarly altered
images Genji used, so that where his use of images reflected hope for the
future, theirs expressed despair and distrust.[7] Such differing perceptions are
perhaps an inevitable consequence of the position of such women who had
no choice but to rely on their more powerful and privileged lovers and
protectors. Ukifune certainly makes such changes consistently. In poem 12,
Niou writes of the clouds and darkening sky intensifying his loneliness even
as they separate him from Ukifune. She, in her responding poem 15, again
sees those images as emblematic of a desired state. The raincloud, one cause
of their separation, is what she would become, and thus make final that
separation. In Niou's last poem in the chapter, number 18, he is looking for
a place to rest, for a center of calm in a suddenly inhospitable world: "I know
not where / to cast aside this life." Niou's sense of loss is followed by
Ukifune's removing herself still further. As she has tried before to remove her
love from the central force in his world, here she is removing herself entirely,
by speaking of her own corpse as a focal point of Niou's resentment and then
suggesting the absence of that focus:

kara o dani	If I have left behind
ukiyo no naka ni	not even a body
todomezu wa	in this wretched world,
izuko o haka to	what object then will you
kimi mo uramin	for your resentment find?

However, Ukifune does love Niou. If she always withdrew from him
she would not have had such conflict. Their attachment is most apparent in

poems 4 and 5, which are in a sense not a pair composed of a sent poem and a response, but rather two sent poems: Ukifune and Niou are standing together, literally and figuratively, and addressing the same shared experience.[8]

yo ni shirazu	Surely I shall lose my way
madoubeki kana	in this unfamiliar world!
saki ni tatsu	when even setting forth
namida mo michi o	my rising tears continue
kakikurashitsutsu	darkening the road
namida o mo	I cannot even stem
hodo naki sode ni	the tears that soak
sekikanete	these narrow sleeves—
ikani wakare o	how might I be the one
todomubeki mi zo	to stay this separation?

They must part, and their responses to their separation are very much alike. In both, their tears at the prospect of parting are related to the difficulties posed by the world—in his case, the road he must follow in leaving her, and in hers, the despair of preventing a parting the world makes necessary.

This pair of poems is surrounded by references to the necessity of Niou's leaving, and descriptions of the threatening weather. But the exchanges in general are frequently surrounded by the hovering presence of the absent member of the triangle. Ukifune, no matter which man she is addressing, is almost always thinking of the other as well. Kaoru is never aware of this, but when Niou recognizes or suspects that Ukifune is thinking of Kaoru, it excites him, and makes her more attractive. Uji and Ukifune remind Kaoru of Ōigimi and Niou of Nakanokimi.

During Niou's first visit to Ukifune, after he has drawn her the picture of a man and woman together, and recited his poem regretting the uncertainty of life, Ukifune takes up his brush and writes her answer. Its implication that men's hearts are inconstant reminds Niou of her relationship with Kaoru, and he is intrigued by it. Ukifune is all the more charming in his eyes. Before composing poem 4, Niou wonders what Kaoru would think if he knew; and afterward, Niou thinks of his earlier contact with the village of Uji, a contact which involved Nakanokimi, Kaoru, and Ōigimi.

When Kaoru visits Ukifune he finds her changed—she is constantly reminded of Niou. As Kaoru and Ukifune exchange poems, they are thinking of and responding to absent lovers as well as to each other. When Kaoru talks of moving Ukifune to the capital, she bursts into tears, thinking of Niou.

Kaoru, meanwhile, is reminded of Ōigimi. Ukifune's reference to *nakazora* in number 11, with its implication that she is caught between the two men, spurs Niou on to be more captivating than ever, even though Ukifune herself thinks the reference is too blatant and discards the poem.

The most poetically complex interweaving appears in the series of five poems centering around Ukifune's first solitary poem, number 14. She answers, by poem 15, Niou's poem 12, only after she has received Kaoru's poem 13 and recited 14 to herself; her answer to Kaoru in poem 16 completes this set.[9] Although she uses and alters images Niou has used, as we have seen, she uses words directly lifted from Kaoru's poem to respond to Niou: Kaoru's *kakikurasu* is her *kakikurashi*, and his *harenu* is repeated in her *hare senu*, in her poem to Niou.

Finally, Niou's last poem in the chapter is recited in despair when he is denied entrance to Ukifune's house. He is talking with a woman of Ukifune's household, Jijū, instead. Jijū is very much a partisan for Niou in the struggle in Ukifune's mind between the conflicting claims of Niou and Kaoru. Jijū says that rather than send him away like this again, she would even "abandon this life" (*mi o suttete mo*). Niou's poem then begins "where might I abandon this life?" so adopting the image Jijū has just used. His poem ends with the line "as I go weeping, weeping." The scene between them ends with the line "weeping, weeping, she returned [to the house]." It is significant that Niou's last appearance in this chapter is more closely linked to Jijū than to Ukifune. It confirms Nakanokimi's thoughts about him in the beginning of the chapter—that he would go to great lengths in his pursuit even of waiting women—and it anticipates the conversation between Ukifune's mother and the nun Bennokimi when they are discussing Nakanokimi's life and the problems created by Niou's philandering.

The echoes of Jijū's words in Niou's poem serve as a useful reminder that the poems function in relation to the surrounding prose as well as to each other. The ways they are linked to the prose can both expand and limit the meanings of the poems, informing the reader and on occasion misleading the other characters. The poems are both revealing and concealing. In the exchange of poems 8 and 9, Niou assures Ukifune of his love, having in mind her previous expressions of doubt about the durability of love, and remembering as well her attachment to Kaoru. Her response can be read as nervousness about suddenly finding herself in a boat crossing a flowing river, since the adventure of being carried beyond the river could be considered one such unforeseeable event. Surely this is part of Niou's reaction, as he reacts only to her charm. Yet the poem is, at the same time, such a telling expression of Ukifune's view of her own unstable existence that the very name we know her by is taken from it.

The poems 12 through 16, as we have seen, are the first to appear out of paired order, that is, a responding poem does not immediately follow a received poem. Also, they are the first, except for poem 1, which represent the feelings and expressions of people who are not actually present in the same scene. They are consequently in a prose context of rather complicated changes of scene and point of view. Because Ukifune is thinking and dreaming of Niou, we are transferred to his presence, and then by means of his letter and poem we are returned to Ukifune. We find her placed then among her ladies-in-waiting, making comparisons in her mind between Kaoru and Niou. The arrival of Kaoru's letter leads to further comparisons, and to her first direct confrontation with herself. From this bitter sense of her own current lot in life, she looks at Niou's drawing, convinced that desirable as it is their relationship cannot last. This sadness is apparent in her letter to Niou, and so is her mental juxtaposition of the two men, with her poem to Niou containing echoes of Kaoru's words. In this poem then, number 15, the men are not at opposite poles but are close enough to become identified in her mind. The poem has the additional function of transferring the focus to Niou again, who in turn is longing for Ukifune. Her poem to Kaoru, while reflecting her saddened state in the weather and in her own tears, is a dead end to this section. It is a plain statement of unhappiness, and provides another pivot, shifting the focus to Kaoru. His practical response to her sadness is to plan her move to the capital, and he warns his wife of the development.

The interweaving of scenes and characters by means of these poems emphasizes that the plot development is not, as Komachiya says of the Akashi section, a simple melodic development, but is filled with subthemes, merging images, and overlappings which complicate the story.[10] While the weave is most complex in the sections containing poems 12 through 16, it is also apparent elsewhere. Poem 17 shifts the focus of the story from Kaoru, on whom it has been centered, back to Ukifune, who is confronted by his knowledge of her infidelity. Niou's last poem—in addition to its ties to Jijū and to his feeling that he has lost a central, stabilizing force—also, with its repetition of *mi o suten* and the Buddhist implications of that phrase, forms a link connecting it to Ukifune's prayer. This prayer then ties her to her mother: she asks Buddha's forgiveness for dying before her parent. Her following reveries again juxtapose the two men. Her solitary poem 19 arises in part in reaction to Kaoru's admonition "don't make people laugh at me" (*hito ni warawasetamau na*). It leads her again to her mother, whose disapprobation she dreads, and to her younger brothers and sisters, whom she longs to see. While Ukifune's mind is occupied with people she cares for, she is left surrounded by a bustle of people to whom she is indifferent, and among whom she feels isolated.

Ukifune's direct response to Niou's letter, and indirect response to the poem he recited while with Jijū, is poem 20, which makes her death concrete in her own mind. It addition ally makes concrete Niou's *mi o suten*, using *kara o / ... / todomezu* ("not leaving behind a corpse"). Furthermore, as she removed herself from a centralizing position as lover to Niou, she will remove herself from a centralizing position after death. Finally, her own mention of resentment seems to remind her of Kaoru again, and of the feelings she expects him to have. She rationalizes not writing a farewell letter to him by imagining the two men discussing her death and life.

The long letter Ukifune receives from her mother is one of the sources for her two final poems. Her lines "our hearts untroubled / by this world's dreams" refer in part to her mother's nightmares. The image of the prayer bells is a return to a Buddhist thread, prompted by the actual sound of the bells, but also referring to her mother's soon-to-be-unanswered prayers.

The threads of the weave have all narrowed to Ukifune, then, leaving her alone. Her isolation is emphasized by her last poem, which is metaphorically addressed to the wind, and will lie undelivered during the time left to her, and by her status as the reluctant recipient of the activity and solicitousness of both her nurse and Ukon, as they try to feed and console her. But in the end she is left alone, weeping.

NOTES

1. Komachiya Teruhiko, "Uta—dokuei to zōtō: Akashi kimi monogatari ni soku shite," *Kokubungaku kaishaku to kyōzai no kenkyū* (1972), v 17, (15): 113; Imai Takuji, "Genji monogatari no zōtōka" *Kokugo to kokubungaku* (1969), 46, (5): 1, 2.

2. Komachiya, "Uta," pp. 113–14, 119; Komachiya Teruhiko, "Genji monogatari no hyōgen to waka no hassō," *Kokubungaku* (1977), 22 (1): 23; and Suzuki Hideo, "Genji monogatari no waka, hikiuta, kago," *Kōza Nihon bungaku: kaishaku to kanshō bessatsu, Genji monogatari* (May 1978), 1: 149, 159.

3. In preparing these translations, I have relied on the notes and commentary in Tamakami Takuya, *Genji monogatari*, vol. 4, Nihon koten kanshō kōza (Tokyo: Kadokawa shoten, 1957), and Yamagishi Tokuhei, ed., *Genji monogatari*, vol. 5, Nihon koten bungaku taikei vol. 18 (Tokyo: Iwanami shoten, 1963).

4. Kaoru's poem alludes to *Kokinshū* 1093: "kimi ni okite / adashi kokoro o / waga moteba / Sue no Matsuyama / nami mo koenamu." ("When I have a heart / that is faithless / and neglects you, / then will the waves cross over / Sue no Matsuyama.")

5. Takahashi Tōru, "Sonzai kankaku shish—'Ukifune' ni tsuite," *Nihon bungaku*, Nov. 1975, p. 78.

6. Suzuki, "Genji," pp. 150, 159.

7. Komachiya, "Uta," p. 117; "Genji," p. 24.

8. Komachiya refers to a similar pair written by Genji and Murasaki when Genji is in exile. "Uta," p. 114.

9.

Niou	Kaoru	Ukifune	Ukifune	Ukifune
12	13	14	15	16
sent to	sent to	solitary poem	response to	response to
Ukifune	Ukifune		Niou	Kaoru

10. Komachiya, "Uta," p. 121.

AMANDA MAYER STINCHECUM

Who Tells the Tale?
'Ukifune': A Study in Narrative Voice

'The one *who speaks* (in the narrative) is not the one *who writes* (in real life) and the one *who writes* is not the one who is.'

ROLAND BARTHES.[1]

NARRATIVE, NARRATOR, SPEAKER OF THE TEXT

Who tells the tale? Who narrates the narrative? Does narrative by definition require a narrator[2] or are these cognates accidental? Does every text have a narrator, either explicit or implied, or is there a mode of discourse which 'speaks itself'? These questions arise as a matter of course in reading the fiction of James Joyce, Virginia Woolf, William Faulkner, and other twentieth-century novelists, as well as earlier writers such as Jane Austen and Gustave Flaubert. Here the narrator's presence often seems to be replaced, overshadowed by that of the characters themselves. But what about the *Genji Monogatari*? The word *monogatari* literally means 'a telling or recounting of something'; it strongly implies the cognate verb *monogataru* ('to recount something, to tell a tale'), in which the teller, or narrator (*katari-te*) exists a priori. Perhaps we can say that 'narrator' is more clearly contained within the concept of *monogatari* than in the English word 'narrative'.

In early Heian-period narrative tales (*monogatari*) such as the *Ochikubo Monogatari*, the narrator places himself (or herself) between the narrative

From *Monumenta Nipponica* 35, no. 4 (Winter, 1980): 375–403. © 1980 by Sophia University.

and us, the readers, guiding our understanding by means of comments about the characters and the story, and by descriptive narration. In the first two-thirds of the *Genji*, the reader has a strong sense of the narrator's presence, to the extent that the leading scholar in the field, Tamagami Takuya, has interpreted this narrator quite concretely as a lady-in-waiting who records the story as if she were giving an interpretative recital of a text which is itself a record of the telling of the tale by other, earlier ladies-in-waiting who either witnessed the events directly or heard about them from yet other ladies-in-waiting who witnessed them directly.[3] But even within the part of the work dealing with the life of Hikaru Genji, there are many passages in which we seem to see directly into the hearts of the characters, without the intervention of a narrator. These include lines conveying the innermost thoughts of a character which we cannot interpret as the report of a lady-in-waiting who witnessed the situation.[4]

But it is in the last third of the work, in which the events take place mainly in Uji, that we feel the characters' inner world open to us. Particularly in those chapters in which Ukifune's plight reaches a crisis we find the flow of her thoughts (and those of others about her) rendered apparently without any mediation by a narrator. Often the form of this narration is that of direct quotation, concluding with the quotative particles *to*, *tote*, or *nado*, and sometimes a verb such as *omou* ('she thinks'). It also frequently contains exclamatory particles such as *namu*, *zo*, and *ka shi*, which one would expect to find in a direct quotation, expressing the emotion of the speaker. For example, *sonata ni nabiku-beki ni wa arazū ka shi to omou....* (VI, 135–136, 'I certainly must not yield to him, she thinks....'). Thus direct interior monologue is a kind of direct discourse in Japanese and contains a quotative particle.

In other passages the characters' thoughts or feelings do not appear as direct quotation but in a form corresponding to indirect speech. They are marked not by a phrase of direct quotation such as *to omou* but by expressions such as *o omoi-yaru* ('she wonders about'), as in the sentence, *mata kono hito ni mie-tatematsuramu o omoi-yaru namu, imijū kokoro-uki* (VI, 134. 4–5, 'and even wondering how could she meet this one is terrible wretchedness'). A variation of *o omou* is *ni omou*; for example, *ito me-yasuku ureshikaru-beki koto ni omoite* (VI, 148. 10–11, 'she feels it to be a highly proper and pleasing thing'). Long adjectival modifiers form another type of indirect quotation: *kono hito ni ushi to omowarete, wasure-tamainamu kokoro-bososa wa, ito fukō shiminikereba* (VI, 135. 4–5, 'the misery of being thought odious and being rejected by this person sinks into her very deeply'). Here, Ukifune's misery (*kokoro-bososa*) is amplified by the long modifying clause that precedes it. There are elements that identify the voice as Ukifune's (*kono*, 'this', indicates

Ukifune's point of view), while other aspects, for example, the causal construction *shiminikereba* ('because it sank into her'), can only be the result of the narrator's' reasoning. I shall hereafter refer to this type of narration as 'indirect interior monologue'. In general, one can say that the conclusive form + 'thinks' (*shūshikei* + *to omou*), or some equivalent thereof, corresponds to direct interior monologue, while the continuative form + 'thinks' (*ren'yōkei* + *omou*), or some equivalent, corresponds to indirect interior monologue.[5]

In Japanese, however, the distinction between direct and indirect discourse is not so clear as it is in English. The narrator's voice frequently intrudes into a character's discourse (usually interior monologue), shading the character's thoughts with the narrator's intonations. Thus the entire narration tends to become reported speech.[6] This is similar to a third type of discourse in English, which Dorrit Cohn has termed 'narrated monologue'.[7] She describes this kind of narration, which is similar to the German *erlebte Rede* and the French *style indirect libre*, as 'the rendering of a character's thoughts in his own idiom, while maintaining the third-person form of narration'.[8] Cohn illustrates these three modes of discourse as follows

> DIRECT STATEMENT: He said: 'I did not come here yesterday.'
> INDIRECT STATEMENT: He said that he had not gone there the
>   day before.
> NARRATED MONOLOGUE: He had not come here yesterday.[9]

Note the changes in spatial and temporal loci: from *come* to *gone*, from *here* to *there*, from *yesterday* to *the day before*. Cohn points out that narrated monologue is a grammatically distinct mode peculiar to written narration; this is further demonstrated by Ann Banfield in her analysis of the 'free indirect style' (*style indirect libre*).[10] Both Banfield and Cohn remark that narrated monologue, or free indirect style, contains demonstratives and adverbs associated with the present tense and the character's own spatial locus, thus clearly distinguishing it from indirect discourse.[11] The modal complexity of Japanese is reflected by the lack of such clear categories of discourse. The grammar of reported speech does not require agreement of verbal tense, and spatial and temporal referents may be ambiguous. An example of modern Japanese will demonstrate this (a corresponding construction in classical Japanese could be postulated, but an actual sentence of classical Japanese would be much less likely to include a stated subject, which would compound the ambiguity).

> *Kare wa kyō mata koko ni konai to itta.*
> He said, 'I won't come here again today.'

Removed from any context, it is not clear whether *koko* ('here') refers to the location of *kare* ('he') or that of the reporting speaker who is telling us, 'He said ...', although the latter would be the more usual interpretation. The same is true of the verb *konai* ('won't come'), which signifies motion toward the speaker—but which speaker? The adverb of time, *kyō* ('today'), may refer to the temporal locus of *kare* or of the reporting speaker. There is a further ambiguity in the Japanese which is not present in English: the subject of the verb *konai* may or may not agree with the subject of *itta* ('said'). This ambiguity may be removed by inserting *jibun* ('himself') as the subject of *konai*, but then the expression no longer renders his words directly and so no longer corresponds to direct discourse. Of course, in English reported speech these two subjects do not necessarily agree, but the ambiguity as to whether they do or not is limited. (In the last example below, the two pronouns 'he' may or may not refer to the same person.) The following possible meanings and more are all contained in the single Japanese example:

He said, 'I won't come here again today.'
He said, 'I won't go there again today.'
He said, 'I won't come here again tomorrow.'
He said, 'She won't come here again today.'
He said that he wouldn't come here again today.

Thus the possible renderings of one sentence of apparently direct quotation are manifold. This phenomenon is directly related to the concept of *ba* or *bamen*, 'linguistic situation'.

In English, direct speech, indirect speech, and narrated monologue are grammatically distinct. The lack of such clear differences in classical Japanese makes the transition from one to the other smoother and more easily accomplished, and hence a more natural feature of prose style. Saeki Umetomo demonstrates that even what appears to be direct quotation in classical Japanese prose, marked at the end of the quoted expression by *to*, *nado*, or *tote*, is often shaded to reflect the point of view of the reporting speaker.[12] Direct quotation is at least theoretically possible in modern Japanese, and parallel constructions could be made in classical Japanese as well, and might occur in Japanese translations of Western novels, for instance. But in practice, the speaker reporting someone else's words would normally adapt those words, relating them to his own spatial and temporal loci—that is, to the viewpoint of the reporting speaker.

The subtle fusion of descriptive narration (*ji no bun*) and interior monologue is indeed one of the most prominent characteristics of the prose style of the *Genji*.[13] It is this indeterminacy in the Japanese language which makes possible the intensity with which we, as readers, see the fictional world of the narrative tale (*monogatari*) through the eyes of the characters within the work.

What is called *kansetsu wahō* ('indirect discourse') in Japanese, particularly in the case of interior monologue, does not correspond to indirect speech in English; it is much closer to the free indirect style or narrated monologue. Both Japanese indirect discourse and narrated monologue may contain a number of constructions that cannot appear in indirect speech in English but are characteristic of direct discourse: expressive elements and constructions, incomplete sentences, and different dialects or languages in introductory and quoted clauses (in Japanese, the latter corresponds to the use of honorific language),[14] as well as expressions such as *ureshi* and *kanashi*, which normally occur only in first-person discourse. Furthermore, the demonstrative elements referring to the time or place of the reported speech act do not, in Japanese, necessarily belong to the locus of the reporting speaker.

Thus while there is not an exact grammatical correspondence between narrated monologue, or free indirect style, as Cohn and Banfield define them, and what I term indirect interior monologue (*kansetsu-shiki shinnaigo*) in classical Japanese, the concepts are close enough in terms of literary function for us to be able to compare the use of this technique in literatures as widely separated as those of eleventh-century Japan and twentieth-century Europe. Cohn describes this function, stating that in narrated monologue, '... we move closer to the possibility of rendering ... thoughts and feelings of a character ... not explicitly formulated in his mind [i.e., as spoken expression]. [It reveals] that part of the psyche which is hidden from the world and half-hidden from the censoring self; it can also more readily show the mind as recipient of passing images and sensory impressions than the more rhetorical first-person monologue.'[15] In addition to the function that Cohn ascribes to it, narrated monologue also allows the penetration of another voice—the voice of the narrator—into the text at the same time as that of the character whose thoughts are being recorded. This interpenetration of voices permits ironic distance to open up in a context where we least expect it, when we believe ourselves to be confronting directly the souls of the characters.

It is impossible to discuss narrative voice or point of view without encountering the problem of the narrator's identity. There should be no difficulty in accepting the premise that the narrator of a work of fiction is not the same as the historical personage who produced the work during some certain (although perhaps indeterminable) period. Until recently, Japanese scholars did not usually make this distinction. The narrator of the *Genji* is not the eleventh-century personage we know as Murasaki Shikibu. The work is a created entity, and if there is indeed a narrator within the work, that narrator is created by the author and thus is not the same as that author. The way or extent to which the narrator within a text may express the views of that historical personage whom we call the author can be determined only after we have examined that text and the workings of the narrator within the text. In regard to a work as far removed from us in time and conventions as the *Genji*, it is perhaps futile to try to determine the thoughts of the personage Murasaki Shikibu, based on the scattered facts we have about her life, and it would be a serious error in critical methodology to project these ideas back onto the text in attempting to interpret it.[16] In order to avoid confusion in the discussion that follows, I shall call this historical personage (for example, Murasaki Shikibu) the 'historical author', and deal with him (or her) no further in this essay.

What do we mean by the term 'narrator'—one who narrates, recites, tells a tale? The word has concrete and personal overtones; the narrator is not simply a disembodied voice—the subject of a given utterance—but a voice that implies a certain rhetorical attitude toward the narration itself, and beyond that, a particular grammatical relation to the object of narration and to the recipient of the narrative. Hence the narrator speaks within the conditions of a certain linguistic situation (*ba* or *bamen*). This linguistic situation—the speech act or paradigm of linguistic performance—is defined as a triangular relationship: a speaker, a topic, and a situation or listener (recipient). That the speaker is saying something to the recipient, with the intention of influencing him with respect to the topic, is central to the concept of the narrator. The necessity of inventing an impersonal, declarative style of written Japanese attests to the particular importance of the linguistic situation in Japanese.

For centuries, the use of *kambun* (Japanese-style Chinese) filled this need; in the twentieth century, the *de-aru* verb form, which never appears in natural spoken Japanese, has replaced *kambun* for expository writing. Since the Heian period, the language of personal communication has been quite distinct from that of official exchanges and records. The strength of the linguistic situation (*bamen*) in Japanese has been discussed at length by the linguist Tokieda Motoki.[17] The influence of the reporting speaker on what appears to be direct quotation (see p. 378, above) and the ease with which descriptive narration blends into interior monologue in classical Japanese prose indicate the force of the linguistic situation and the difficulty in speaking from a position outside of it in Japanese. Whereas in English the free indirect style is a special characteristic of *written* narrative, grammatically distinct from the language of the speaker-recipient paradigm, in Japanese the influence of the narrating voice on the discourse of individual characters—whether in direct or indirect discourse—is a result of that very relationship. The linguistic situation asserts itself in Japanese in a context which in English specifically denies the speaker–addressee relationship—in passages where the voice of a character blends with and is shaded by that of the narrator.

As a result of this feature of Japanese, because an impersonal mode of narration rarely occurs in Heian-period prose, the narrator acquires an importance perhaps unique to classical Japanese literature—not only in *monogatari* ('narrative tales') but in modes which are usually thought of as essentially dramatic, such as noh and *jōruri* (puppet plays). The predominant voice of the narrator is heard well into the twentieth century in the *shi-shōsetsu* (the 'I-novel').

We can identify the narrator (*katari-te*) as the subject of expression in passages where the voice of a narrating persona is evident. In the classical *monogatari*, the most obvious examples are those passages traditionally referred to as *sōshiji* ('narrator's commentary'), in which the narrator addresses the reader directly, stepping away from the characters of the tale, interpreting that world, judging the characters and their actions, for the reader. Here the narrator is the speaker within the linguistic situation that is the tale. We recognize the voice of the narrator by both semantic and linguistic means. The following passage, the conclusion of the 'Yūgao' ('Evening Faces') chapter of the *Genji*, is one of the most frequently cited examples of narrator's commentary.

> *Kayō no kuda-kudashiki koto wa, anagachi ni kakuroe-shinobi-tamaishi mo itōshikute, mina morashi-todome-taru o, nado mikado no mi-ko naramu kara ni, mimu hito sae katao-narazu, mono-homegachi naru to, tsukuri-goto-mekite tori-nasu hito mo mono-shi-tamaikereba namu. Amari mono-iisa ga naki tsumi, sari-dokoro naku....*
> [I, 'Yūgao', 269. 11–15]

His efforts to conceal this kind of troublesome thing were pathetic and so I had not let them come out, but precisely because there are even people who think the whole thing is a fiction, wondering, Just because he is the emperor's son, why do even people who know him tend to praise him and think he has no faults? [I have written like this.] There is no way to avoid the sin of gossiping....

If we look at the meaning of this passage, the subject of the expression *mina morashi-todometaru o* ('and so I had not let them come out') cannot be one of the characters who is the topic of the narrative, for the words refer to the very making of the narrative.[18] The expression *amari mono iisa ga naki tsumi, sari-dokoro naku* ('there is no way to avoid the sin of gossiping') can refer only to a persona who sees herself as the maker of the narrative and declares herself to be such, that is, the narrator.

There are also linguistic (grammatical) signs that point to the narrator persona. The use of the honorific verb *tamau* (applied to Genji's actions in the phrase *kakuroe-shinobi-tamaishi mo*—'his efforts to conceal'—and to some unidentified 'people' in the phrase *hito mo mono-shitamaikereba*—'because there are people') reflects the linguistic situation, in which the speaker's social relation to both the addressee and the topic is expressed. Furthermore, the causal construction in this phrase can be attributed only to a subject who comments about, forms conclusions about, the people who are criticizing Genji, and about the making of the narrative; the causal construction points to the reason for making the narrative the way it is. The emphatic particle *namu* following this construction (which I have translated as 'precisely') also derives from spoken discourse and is a further indication of the presence of a speaking subject explaining something or affirming his view to the addressee, that is, a narrator.[19] Finally, the verbal suffix *–keri* in *tamaikereba* implies a certain degree of objectification, of drawing away from the topic, or interpreting or explaining to the addressee on the part of the speaker or subject of the expression.[20]

These signs of the speaking subject or narrator occur not only in extended passages of commentary, or *sōshiji* ('narrator's commentary', in which the narrator expresses an opinion about a given topic or about the process of making the tale, for example, comments that explain that the narrator has omitted certain details), like that at the end of 'Yūgao', but also in passages considered by many contemporary Japanese scholars as simple description (*ji no bun*).[21] Here the narrating voice often makes conjectures about a character's thoughts or about the causes or results of a certain situation. These conjectures cannot be attributed to any character within the story itself and must be ascribed to the narrator. They are indicated, usually at the end of the sentence, by verbal suffixes such as *–kemu*, *–beshi*, and *–meri*. Rather than constituting a comment in themselves, they express a tone or mode in the narration which we recognize as belonging to the narrating voice. Honorific language (*keigo*) used in relation to the characters and their actions also reflects an attitude on the part of the narrator toward the characters. This attitude reflects the linguistic situation (*bamen*), in which a subject (the narrator) addresses a recipient (the reader or listener) about an object (the character whose action is being reported).[22] Thus the voice in such passages is necessarily personified. The attempts to define *sōshiji* as an independent and fixed entity have contributed to the obscurity of the problem of narrative voice in the *Genji*.[23] In fact, the concept of *sōshiji* may not be a useful one for such a discussion. In passages usually thought of as *sōshiji*, as well as those in which *–kemu*, *–beshi*, *–meri*, *–keri*, etc., appear, we can identify the voice as that of the narrator. If their functions are different, and it is not at all clear that they are, the voice is fundamentally that of a personified narrator. Within one passage we may find a number of different narrators, one commenting on the activities of another, but the voices remain on a level different from that of the characters within the world of the narrative, as well as from that of the reader and the author. In reading the *Genji*, however, it is evident that this persona we have called the narrator is not only inconsistent in point of view, but is neither omniscient nor omnipresent. It is not the narrator who ultimately controls the narrative. We can either accept the position that there is no such transcendental being that unifies the text as a whole, or take the view that there is such an entity, the essence of which is not expressed in the text.[24] For example, we may consider every narrative a discourse: 'a speech-act supposing a speaker and a listener, and in the speaker an intention to influence the listener in some way.'[25] This is the view voiced by Tzvetan Todorov, one that is literary rather than linguistic. He remarks, *'l'oeuvre est en même temps discours: il existe un narrateur qui relate l'histoire; et il y a en face de lui un lecteur qui la perçoit.'* He further specifies that by *'oeuvre'* he means every work of fiction.[26]

In passages or narratives where there are no linguistic signs of the narrator in the text, the narrator (the subject of the discourse that is the text itself) may be said to be effaced.[27] It is this subject of the discourse (narrative text) which Mitani Kuniaki terms the *washa* (literally, 'the one who speaks', or 'the speaker of the text') in order to distinguish the narrator (*katari-te*), who appears as a persona in the text, from the giver of the narrative, whose existence is wholly functional and underlies the entire text.[28] The *washa* refers to that by which we see the text as one, that which underlies the structure and makes it a whole. In a sense this highly abstract concept of an invisible speaker of the text has much in common with what Wayne Booth calls the 'implied author', the image the author creates of himself as he writes, not the historical author but the author as the one who controls the narrative.[29] But Booth's idea is basically that of a persona, while Mitani's remains an abstract, even metaphysical, function, and Todorov's concept is fundamentally closer to linguistics.

What is particularly valuable about Mitani's study is that he has drawn a clear distinction between the narrator whose voice is heard in the text, and the speaker of the text which is the subject of expression of the narrative as a whole. Furthermore, according to Mitani, the presence of the narrator (or narrators) in the *Genji* is a way of dealing with the opposition between the Japanese language itself, in which the linguistic situation is so strong a feature, and the nature of narrative, which has a subject of expression that is essentially transparent and neutral. The narrator expresses that aspect of the language which is controlled by the linguistic situation.[30]

The speaker of the text plays no direct role in our interpretation of the text as a work, but as the subject of the text, the point of view of the *washa* is that of the text as a whole. We can say that the point of view (and the voice) of the speaker of the text coincides with that of certain characters in certain passages. However, the *washa* as an abstract function has no voice in the sense of personal expression. Thus while we may speak of the voice or point of view of the speaker of the text, this must be understood to mean that in a particular passage the *washa* is the only subject of expression, but does not have a personified voice like that of the narrator or characters. For example, in passages of descriptive narration we might say that the voice is that of the speaker of the text.

FUNCTIONS OF NARRATIVE VOICE IN 'UKIFUNE' AND TO THE LIGHTHOUSE

THE 'Ukifune' chapter depicts the events preceding Ukifune's attempted suicide. Rather than 'events', perhaps we should say the conflicting emotions leading up to her decision and action—not only Ukifune's responses to her situation and reflections on it, but also those of her mother, of Niou, Kaoru, Ukon, Jijū, and others. Precisely because the crisis is impending, it is her inner life and that of those around her that are of importance to us. This chapter represents the characters' thoughts and emotions, their *kokoro*, in the form of interior monologue to a greater extent than almost any other chapter in the whole *Genji*.[31] It is characterized by frequent shifts in point of view, the view of the speaker of the text coinciding first with that of one character, then another. As a result, although these features are not peculiar to 'Ukifune', they play a conspicuous role here, and we can thus easily grasp the irony that these techniques create. The observations that I have made and the conclusions that I have tentatively drawn are not intended to be applied to 'Ukifune' as opposed to other chapters in the *Genji*, but I hope that they may illustrate some aspects of that chapter which are characteristic of the Uji chapters in general and, to a certain extent, of the *Genji* as a whole.

In many cases, the characters' hearts are revealed through direct discourse (direct interior monologue) and the voice heard is entirely that of the characters thus depicted. However, sometimes this voice blends in with that of the narrator, whose presence in these monologues appears, for example, in the form of honorific language applied to the subject of the monologue, in syntactic constructions that require reasoning about the situation or thoughts revealed, by exclamations that could be attributed to either the character or the narrator. There are also occasions when the voice of the character fuses with a passage of descriptive narration that precedes or follows it. In the latter case the interior monologue becomes indirect, ending not in the quotative particle *to* but with some other syntactic construction that makes the monologue a subordinate part of the passage as a whole.[32]

The importance of these distinctions lies in the recognition of different degrees of aesthetic distance between the reader and the world of the tale; they constitute the irony of the work, as Konishi Jin'ichi has pointed out.[33] Not only does the intrusion of the narrator's voice distance us from the characters, but even in passages of direct interior monologue, where we are confronted with their thoughts unmediated by the narrator's voice, the distance between the characters themselves shows us the irony of their situation. The creation of this aesthetic distance is certainly one of the functions of the shifting point of view in the Uji chapters and in the *Genji* as a whole. The narration is not controlled by a single point of view through which we see the events and characters of the narrative, nor by a single narrator who consistently tells us how to interpret those events and characters. Although the voice of a narrator is often heard, the identity of that persona and her relation to the characters within the work are ambiguous, sometimes appearing on one level of the narrative, sometimes on another. However, when the narrator does speak out, her words often take the form of a conjecture about a character or his actions.

The shifting narrative voice in 'Ukifune' and in the Uji chapters as a whole has its closest counterpart in Western literature in the novels of Virginia Woolf, particularly in *To the Lighthouse*.[34] The inner life of the characters plays a central role in both works, an inner life revealed to the reader not by means of the so-called stream of consciousness technique (which depicts less organized levels of consciousness) but by means of a flowing prose style which often exhibits a high degree of literary self-awareness.[35] While the narrative voice shifts from character to character to narrator to a non-personal subject we have called the speaker of the text, both works possess a certain degree of stylistic unity, in part created by the use of narrated monologue, in which a character's voice blends into that of the narrator or into descriptive narration. The diction of monologue, dialogue, and descriptive narration is basically the same; while the content of different characters' thoughts may vary, the language in which that content is expressed displays few individual characteristics. This evenness of texture extends also to the use of nature imagery; in *To the Lighthouse* and Woolf's other novels (especially *The Waves*) an image is often associated not only with one particular character but appears in the thoughts of several and in descriptive passages as well. In 'Ukifune', and in all of the Heian narrative tales (*monogatari*), the unity of imagery is dictated to a great extent by the conventions of *waka*. Characters may respond differently to one image, but nevertheless the image is the same.

On the whole, in *To the Lighthouse* the point of view shifts more slowly than in 'Ukifune'; passages associated with one character's vision are longer. The following passage illustrates the type of ambiguity often found in Woolf. The entire incident is part of Mrs Ramsay's recollection of a walk to town with Charles Tansley, provoked by his irritating remark, 'There'll be no landing at the lighthouse tomorrow.'

> ... she made him feel better pleased with himself than he had done yet, and he would have liked, had they taken a cab for example, to have paid for it. As for her little bag, might he not carry that? No, no, she said, she always carried *that* herself. She did too. Yes, he felt that in her. He felt many things, something in particular that excited him and disturbed him for reasons which he could not give. He would like her to see him, gowned and hooded, walking in a procession. A fellowship, a professorship, he felt capable of anything and saw himself—but what was she looking at? At a man pasting a bill. The vast flapping sheet flattened itself out, and each shove of the brush revealed fresh legs, hoops, horses, glistening reds and blues, beautifully smooth, until half the wall was covered with the advertisement of a circus; a hundred horsemen, twenty performing seals, lions, tigers.... Craning forwards, for she was short-sighted, she read it out ... 'will visit this town,' she read. It was terribly dangerous work for a one-armed man, she exclaimed, to stand on top of a ladder like that—his left arm had been cut off in a reaping machine two years ago.
>
> 'Let's all go!' she cried, moving on, as if all those riders and horses had filled her with childlike exultation and made her forget her pity.
>
> 'Let's go,' he said, repeating her words, clicking them out, however, with a self-consciousness that made her wince. 'Let us go to the circus.' No. He could not say it right. He could not feel it right. But why not? she wondered. What was wrong with him then?[36]

The section begins with a description of Tansley's feelings, but the words, 'had they taken a cab for example', seem to render his thoughts more directly, while the following two sentences clearly represent dialogue. Again, 'Yes, he felt that in her. He felt many things,' must be a rendering of his thoughts, while the amplification of those thoughts seems to come from outside the scope of Tansley's consciousness. The next sentence again represents his thoughts, as his fantasy about Mrs Ramsay admiring his future accomplishments is interrupted by her attention turning to the circus poster. The description of the poster might reflect Tansley's point of view as he follows Mrs Ramsay's gaze, or hers, or both, but the explanation, 'for she was short-sighted', seems to stem from the narrator rather than either of the characters. Mrs Ramsay's words are followed by another explanation of her mood ('as if ...') by the narrator, and then Tansley's repetition of her exclamation. But 'No. He could not say it right' could be either Tansley's own self-conscious thoughts, or Mrs Ramsay's observation of him. 'He could not feel it right' seems to render his own discomfort at his inability to respond spontaneously, but with the following line we are clearly listening to Mrs Ramsay's voice.

In this passage, almost entirely indirectly narrated, the ambiguity of the narrative voice is quite marked. By means of this kind of ambiguity Virginia Woolf suggests an absence of space between the characters, and between the characters and the narrator, implying an ultimate unity of human life within nature, or within the artist's vision of it, as it is Lily Briscoe's vision that finally rounds out the novel.

While the similarities between Virginia Woolf's technique and that of 'Ukifune' are striking, there are of course important differences that are significant for our interpretation of the works themselves. Perhaps the primary point of contrast for the purposes of our discussion is the effect on the reader of the shifting narrative voice. Woolf's novels, particularly *Mrs. Dalloway*, *To the Lighthouse*, and *The Waves*, use different perspectives to show the underlying communication between people. As old Augustus Carmichael and Mrs Ramsay both admire a dish of fruit, 'she saw that Augustus too feasted his eyes on the same plate of fruit, plunged in, broke off a bloom there, a tassel here, and returned, after feasting, to his hive. That was his way of looking, different from hers. But looking together united them' (p. 146). Again, as Mrs Ramsay contemplates the approaching marriage of two young people whom she has brought together, she feels a oneness with those around her (pp. 170–71).

In 'Ukifune', however, in spite of the fluidity of style and the flow, even within one sentence, of narrative voice from one persona to another, that very flow emphasizes the distance between characters by placing them in close juxtaposition and thus showing us the unbridgeable gaps that exist between them. While in Woolf's novel we see the continuity of thought and feeling between one character and another, in 'Ukifune' the uniformity of diction reveals disjunctions in thought, misunderstandings, and, even in dialogue, a lack of receptiveness, an active turning away from each other. This basic isolation of one human being from another in the Uji chapters of the *Genji* may reflect a Buddhist view of the universe that sees all human relationships as ultimately empty, salvation as a final rejection of such entanglements.

Thus Ukifune seeks salvation by turning her back on all former relationships. Onna San no Miya ('The Third Princess', Kaoru's mother), who loves neither Genji nor Kashiwagi and is even more isolated than Ukifune, also becomes a nun. Ukifune's father, Hachi no Miya ('The Eighth Prince'), wanders in purgatory, unable to enter paradise, because he cannot free himself from his attachment to his other two daughters, even though he abandons them before his death to enter a monastery.[37] Although Ukifune does indeed love, her conflict isolates her from those she loves. Can we believe that any of these characters is truly saved? Genji takes orders after Lady Murasaki's death, but the fact that the event is not part of the narrative de-emphasizes it and suggest a different kind of religious feeling, one that is fully realized only with the completion of a rich life of involvement in this world. Perhaps the *Genji monogatari* is saying that salvation is meaningless if it is obtained only by rejecting all human ties.

This fundamental contrast between Virginia Woolf's works and the *Genji* is apparent in two other aspects. The use of narrated monologue, directly related to shifts in voice, in Woolf helps to create that underlying unity discussed above by relating characters to each other through similarities in prose style and imagery. In 'Ukifune' it also provides a certain kind of unity of the text: the very fact that there is a narrator (even though not consistent, or even several narrators) avoids the complete fragmentation of the text by fulfilling the requirements of the linguistic situation through the persona of the narrator, thus supplying at least an apparent continuity. Through honorific language the prose of the *Genji* necessarily reflects a personal voice; the fusion of interior monologue and descriptive narration is a natural consequence of the Japanese language itself, but in English this is achieved only through the creation of a special grammar.

Whereas in *To the Lighthouse* the indirectness of the technique allows us to see aspects of the characters which they themselves would not ordinarily verbalize, in 'Ukifune' these passages often end in remarks by the narrator that point out for us the ironic distance we have been shown through direct interior monologue. In the former, the images of nature serve to reinforce that all-embracing unity between man and nature, as also among men (for example, in the 'Time Passes' section of *To the Lighthouse* and the interchapters in *The Waves*); in the latter, however, while nature reflects the moods of individual characters and is subsumed by them, sometimes providing a link between them, at the same time such images also point to the insurmountable distances between one human being and another. Such is the scene when Kaoru and Ukifune are both gazing at the river: while he thinks of Ōigimi, she is lost in thoughts of Niou (see pp. 396–97, below). A different kind of distance, one in a sense created within the dimension of the fictional world, one expressed by the characters themselves and not simply of the reader's perception, arises between Ukifune and Niou in their exchange of poems about the snow.

Niou: *Mine no yuki*
         migiwa no kōri
         fumi-wakete
         kimi ni zo madou
         michi wa madowazu

Treading the snow in the peaks, the ice on the banks, I am lost in you, though I didn't lose my way here.

Ukifune: *Furi-midare*
          migiwa ni kōru
          yuki yori mo
          naka-sora nite zo
          ware wa kenu-beki
          [VI, 146. 2–7]

More than the snow which falls in whirling flakes, freezing along the banks, I am suspended in mid-air and must vanish.

While Niou uses the image of snow to express his frustration at not being able to see her, Ukifune uses it to reflect her desire to dissolve into nothingness, her desire for death. Thus, although man may be a part of nature to the extent that it reflects his most subtle feelings, it provides no consolation, no sense of oneness. Nature is internalized, yet at the same time reflects man's isolation.

TEXTUAL ANALYSIS: A DESCRIPTION OF NARRATIVE VOICE

As a result of the following analysis of one section of 'Ukifune', I shall present a synthesis of the material associated with each point of view of the main characters (in the section that I have chosen, Ukifune and Kaoru). Every reader performs this synthesis and interpretation for himself in a work of fiction— particularly when there is no narrator consistently present, telling us throughout the work how to interpret it. But we cannot make any such interpretation without understanding the various levels and degrees of distance between the characters themselves, between the characters and the narrator, between the narrator and ourselves, and between the narrator and the speaker of the text. Although the narrative voice of the text coincides with that of Ukifune during her direct interior monologues, and for a moment we see things from her point of view, the intervention of the narrator, the shift to Kaoru's point of view, moving away from Ukifune as interior monologue blends into description, all distance us from her, and through this very subjective method of narration, enable us to make our own 'objective' view of the fictional world.

The aim of my analysis is twofold. It is first of all descriptive: to identify the shifting narrative voice within a selected passage and to see how such transitions are effected. Secondarily, it is interpretative. However, the kind of interpretation I have outlined above can be accomplished only with a much broader foundation, on the basis of an analysis of the Uji chapters as a unit or perhaps the *Genji* as a whole. Hence my conclusions in this respect will be tentative and limited. I have selected this particular passage of 'Ukifune' because it is a unit of manageable length for this kind of analysis, because it contains clear shifts in point of view depicted in the interplay of successive interior monologues, and because even within a unit of this length irony is quite evident. I do not mean to suggest that the narrative techniques revealed by my analysis are peculiar to or characteristic of only the 'Ukifune' chapter, as opposed to the rest of the *Genji*; rather, my focusing on this passage may shed some light on the work as a whole. The following is not a polished literary translation but a literal rendering which I hope reflects the syntax of the original sufficiently to make the analysis intelligible.

I have attempted to retain the aspects of the verbs as they appear in the original text to the extent that this is possible, although it is contrary to usual practice. The use of a verbal aspect that roughly corresponds to the present indicative in English is usually explained as a 'historical present' and always translated into the past tense in English; however, changes in verb aspects in Japanese reflect changes in the speaker's relation to the content of the discourse, and thus are important for our study. These shifts in verbal aspect in Japanese narrative works are analogous to the effect of changes in tense in nineteenth-century Russian works pointed out by Boris Uspensky in his detailed examination of point of view, *A Poetics of Composition*. In his discussion of the alternation of verb tenses in Leskov's story, 'Lady Macbeth of the Mtsensk District', he notes,

... the present tense is used to fix the point of view from which the narration is carried out. Each time the present is used, the author's temporal position is synchronic—that is, it coincides with the temporal position of his characters. He is at that moment located in their time. The verbs in the past tense, however, provide a transition between these synchronic sections of the narrative. They describe the conditions which are necessary to the perception of the narrative from the synchronic position.[38]

A full discussion of Japanese verbal aspects is beyond the scope of this article, but it should be noted that although Uspensky speaks of 'temporal position', this really points to aesthetic distance between narrator and character. Similarly, in the *Genji*, the use of verb aspects that may refer to past time—perfective suffixes such as *–ki*, *–tsu*, *–keri*, *–kemu*—seems to indicate an increase in distance between the narrative voice of the text (and hence the reader) and the characters, while the use of aspects that can be interpreted as referring to the present often appears to effect a decrease in that distance. However, in the *Genji* the correspondence is not nearly so exact as in Leskov's work.[39] I have followed the NKBT text.[40]

(1) *Taishōdono, sukoshi nodoka ni narinuru koro, shinobite owashitari. Tera ni hotoke nado ogami-tamau. Mi-zukyō sesase-tamau sō ni, mono-tamai nado shite....*

When things at court had settled down a bit, the major captain, as usual, slipped away inconspicuously and came to Uji. At the temple he worships the Buddhas; to the monk who chants sutras for him, he gives alms and so forth....

The passage opens with an impersonal view of Kaoru; there is no emphatic or exclamatory particle, no verbal suffix, to indicate the narrator's presence.

(2) ... *yūtsugata, koko ni wa shi-nobitaredo, kore wa wari naku mo yatsushi-tamawazu, ebōshi nōshi no sugata, ito ara-mahoshiku kiyoge nite, ayumi-iri-tamau yori, hazukashige ni, yōi koto nari.*

... and toward evening he comes here secretly. However, he, for his part, has not taken great pains to conceal his rank. His figure in informal cap and robe is flawless and refined, and from the time he steps into the room, the care he takes with everything is so special that one feels overwhelmed by his presence.

Yūtsugata ('toward evening') constitutes a neutral transition, for with *koko ni* ('to here') we move into Ukifune's spatial locus. *Hazukashige* ('one feels overwhelmed') implies a perceiving sensibility; although there is no specific reference to Ukifune, we begin to wonder here who is the subject of this emotion.[41] Moreover, *kore wa* ('he, for his part') is a comparison with Niou, a comparison made perhaps by a narrator but also of course reflecting Kaoru and Niou as seen through Ukifune's eyes. This is brought into sharp focus with the first word of the next sentence, *onna* ('the lady'). The transition from description narration (1), an impersonal view of Kaoru, to Ukifune's thoughts is effected by his spatial movement toward her, by references to her spatial and psychological locus (*koko, kore*), and by the adverb *hazukashige*, which strongly suggests a perceiving consciousness within the narrative world that is affected by Kaoru's appearance and behavior.

> (3a) *Onna, ika de mie-tatematsuramu to suramu, to, sora sae hazukashiku osoroshiki ni, anagachi narishi hito no ōn-arisama, uchi-omoi-ideraruru ni....*

The lady, wondering, How shall I ever be able to face him? is ashamed, terrified of the sky itself, but in spite of this, she recalls the presence of him who had been so impetuous....

The shift to Ukifune's point of view is confirmed by a brief direct interior monologue, *ika de mie-tatematsuramu to suramu* ('How shall I ever be able to face him?'). Here the point of view of the text coincides with her and the distance between us and Ukifune is reduced to its minimum. We draw away from her a bit with the words, *sora sae hazukashiku osoroshiki ni* ('even the sky itself is terrifying, making her ashamed'), but we can also read it, 'even the sky itself is shame-making, terrifying', taking it as Ukifune's thoughts, so the distance is not great. Ukifune's point of view is maintained in the following passage, to (4), *kokoro-bososa* ('misery'), but the distance between us and her shrinks and stretches as the voice is sometimes clearly Ukifune's, in direct interior monologues, at times farther from her as her monologues become indirect narration.

> (3b) *... mata kono hito ni mie-tatematsuramu o omoi-yaru namu imijū kokoro-uki. Ware wa toshigoro miru hito o mo, mina omoi-kawarinu-beki kokochi namu suru, to notamaishi o, ge ni, sono nochi, mi-kokochi kurushi tote, izuku ni mo izuku ni mo, rei no ōn-arisama narade, mi-zuhō nado sawagu-naru o kiku ni, mata ika ni kikite obosamu....*

... even just imagining how could she meet this one is terrible wretchedness. He did say, 'My feelings about all of the ladies I have been seeing for so long seem to be changing completely.' Hearing that, indeed, since that time, saying that he does not feel well, he does not treat any of them as usual, and that people are making a great deal of commotion, saying prayers for his recovery and so forth, I wonder what would he feel if he heard about this?

We can read the above narration as one continuous passage of direct discourse depicting Ukifune's thoughts (... *o kiku ni* can also be read as 'when she hears', moving the point of view just outside of Ukifune's range). The words *o omoi-yaru namu imijū kokoro-uki* ('even imagining that is terribly painful') could be interpreted as the voice of the narrator. However, in the entire section I am analyzing, we almost never hear the narrator's voice clearly, so it seems more appropriate to say that in this passage Ukifune's point of view, the narrator's, and our own are so close that at times they are indistinguishable. This is even more effective in reducing the aesthetic distance than removing any such ambiguity. Niou's state after he returns to the capital could not be perceived directly by Ukifune; in order to retain Ukifune's voice here, it is represented as hearsay transmitted to her by some third party—presumably one of her serving women.

There is a brief bit of description, *to omou mo ito kurushi* ('even wondering about this is extremely painful'), and then the narrative voice again coincides with that of Ukifune in an extended passage which directly modifies *kokoro-bososa* ('misery'), a characterization of Ukifune's state not made by her but by the impersonal voice of the speaker of the text:

(3c) *Kono hito hata, ito kewai koto ni, kokoro-bukaku, namamekashiki sama shite, hisashikaritsuru hodo no okotari nado notamau mo, koto ōkarazu, koishi kanashi to oritatanedo, tsune ni ai-minu koi no kurushisa o, sama yoki hodo ni uchi-notamaeru, imijiku iu ni wa masarite, ito aware, to hito no omoinu-beki sama o, shime-tamaeru hito-gara nari. En naru kata wa saru mono nite, yuku sue nagaku hito no tanominu-beki kokoro-bae nado, koyo naku masari-tamaeri. Omowazu naru sama no kokori-bae nado, mori-kikasetaramu toki nanome narazu imijiku koso abekere. Ayashū, utsushi-gokoro mo nō oboshi-iraruru hito o, aware to omou mo, sore wa ito aru-majiku karoki koto zo ka shi. Kono hito ni ushi to omowarete, wasure-tamainamu....*

But this person, too, has a way with him that is quite out of the ordinary; he is deeply considerate and his figure is graceful, and when he apologizes for his long neglect, his words are few. Although he is not outspoken, exclaiming, 'How precious! How adorable!', his genteel way of speaking of the sorrows of a love in which the two do not often meet is superior to passionate exclamations; his character is such that anyone would certainly think, How moving!, of his figure. His charm is a matter of course. His character is one a woman could depend on for a long time, and is incomparably superior. If he should happen to hear of my own wild infatuation, it would surely be terrible indeed. Even to think longingly of the person who loves me so madly is truly a frivolous thing that must not be....

The absence of emphatic and exclamatory particles in the first half of this section allows us to read it as either Ukifune's point of view or that of the text (and hence ours), as in section (3b). But these weighings of Kaoru's elegant reserve against Niou's effusiveness would seem to be taking place within Ukifune. This is supported by the use of *kono hito* ('this person') in both (3b) and (3c) (in both cases it refers to Kaoru), which points to Ukifune's spatial and psychological locus. Furthermore, we may also see the lack of emotion in the narration itself (indicated by the sparsity of emphatic expressions) as reflecting the absence of passion in Ukifune's relation to Kaoru. The emphatic constructions toward the end of the passage, *nanome narazu imijiku koso abekere* ('it would surely be terrible indeed') and *ito aru-majiku karoki koto zo ka shi* ('truly a frivolous thing that must not be') stress the presence of the speaker of these expressions, whom I take to be Ukifune, since nothing opposes interpreting the voice as hers. These phrases could be read as expressions of the narrator, but the whole of section (3) is so clearly Ukifune's point of view that I see no reason to think that the narrator suddenly intrudes here.

(4) ... *kokoro-bososa wa, ito fukō shiminikereba, omoi-midaretaru keshiki o* ...

... because the misery of being thought odious and being rejected by this person sinks into her very deeply, she is distraught; observing her state, he thinks ...

With *kokoro-bososa* ('misery'), the description of Ukifune's state, we move away from her; it is not she who reasons about it, forming the causal construction, *shiminikereba* ('because it sinks into her'), but the narrator; this direct representation of the reasoning process must be attributed to a personified voice, and not simply to the speaker of the text, which has no persona and thus cannot be the source of a judgment—the formation of a cause–effect statement. The distance between Ukifune and us widens further with the word *keshiki* ('state', 'appearance')—the visible reflection of inner emotion. It is this reflection of Ukifune's inner state that Kaoru sees. The point of view has thus shifted from an internal to an external view of her, and that point of view becomes Kaoru's.[42]

> (5) ... *tsuki-goro ni, koyo-nō mono no kokoro shiri, nebi-masarinikeri, tsure-zure naru sumika no hodo ni, omoi-nokosu koto wa araji ka shi....*

> ... over the past few months, she has come to understand the true nature of things and has matured. Because of the tedious place in which she lives, her thoughts must certainly leave nothing unexplored....

Here the voice is clearly his, as this section is immediately followed by *to mi-tamau* (the quotative particle *to* plus 'he thinks'). His monologue is straightforward and simple syntactically. The verbal suffix *–keri* and exclamatory particles *ka shi* emphasize the presence of a speaking subject.

> (6) ... *to mi-tamau mo kokoro kurushikireba tsune yori mo kokoro-todomete katarai-tamau.*

> .... he thinks; since even to see this is extremely painful, more attentatively than usual he speaks intimately to her.

In (6), the point of view shifts slightly from an internal to an external view of Kaoru. Again it can only be the narrator who forms the causal construction.

In the preceding silent exchange between Ukifune and Kaoru we see the pattern of their other, verbal, exchanges. Some external manifestation of Kaoru is the occasion for Ukifune's reflections about him and Niou. On the other hand, her mood, as it appears to Kaoru, is completely misunderstood. He interprets her distress as the result of his failure to visit her frequently enough, and immediately begins to talk about the new life he is planning for her. He blames her mood on the place, the desolation of Uji (*tsure-zure naru sumika no hodo ni*, 'because of the tedious place in which she lives'), and his solution to her problems is a new place. He tries to comfort her as one would a child. When Kaoru speaks to Ukifune directly, he speaks of external things only:

> (7) *Tsukurasuru tokoro, yōyō yoroshū shi-nashitekeri. Hito-hi namu mi-shikaba, koko yori wa kē jikaki mizu ni, hana mo mi-tamaitsu-*

beshi. Sanjō no miya mo chikaki hodo nari. Akekure obotsukanaki hedate mo, onozukara ara-majiki o, kono haru no hodo ni, sarinu-bekuba watashitemu to omoite-notamau mo ...

'The place I am having built for you is gradually taking shape. I saw it the other day, and the river is more agreeable than here and you will also be able to see the cherry blossoms. The Palace of the Third Ward is also near by. The separation between us which is so unsettling, day and night, will, of itself, cease to be. And so, some time this spring, if things go well, I will move you.' When he speaks his thoughts ...

Although he says he is moved by her pain, he does not address himself directly to her feelings, nor indeed say anything about his own. His speech simply indicates his intentions, and attempts to make her feel more secure about the future. Kaoru's words, like Ukifune's air of distress, do not convey what is behind them; he does not succeed in communicating what he wishes, the stability in his plans for her future, gradually being realized in this building project. Instead, his words serve as an occasion for her recollection of Niou's words and his plans for her:

(8) ... *kano hito no, nodoka naru-beki tokoro omoi-mōketari, to kinō mo notamaerishi o, kakaru koto mo shirade, sa obosuramu yo to, aware nagara mo, sonata ni nabiku-beki ni wa arazu ka shi, to omou kara ni, arishi ōn-sama no omokage ni oboyureba, ware nagara mo, utate kokoro-u no mi ya, to omoi-tsuzukete nakinu.*

... she thinks, That person was saying just yesterday, 'I've thought of a place where you should be able to feel at ease,' but he must be thinking that way without knowing about this situation, and although it is heart-rending, I certainly must not yield to him. While she thinks this, an image of the way he had looked rises up before her and she has to admit to herself, What a wretched lot!, and continuing to feel this way, she bursts into tears.

The contrast between Kaoru's words and Ukifune's thoughts about Niou is stressed by the syntactic connection between them: *notamau mo kano hito no ... to kinō mo notamaerishi* ('when he says this, she thinks, That person was saying just yesterday...'). The transition from one voice to the other is provided by Kaoru's words. Direct speech does not function here in the expected way, as a means of conveying the thoughts of one person to another.

That function is denied here by the juxtaposition of Kaoru's words and Ukifune's thoughts of Niou. She does not, however, totally ignore Kaoru's words; she takes something from them (the idea that he is planning to move her into the city) and her own feelings develop around that kernel. In a similar way she uses the imagery and diction of the poems addressed to her to reject what they say. With the word *nakinu* ('she bursts into tears') the distance widens once more between us and Ukifune, and we see what Kaoru sees and responds to: the visible manifestation of her inner state. But even though he sees the external signs, the real source of her outburst is not communicated to him—her despair at what she believes to be the necessity to reject Niou and at the same time her inability to do so. Again Kaoru misunderstands the expression of this despair and interprets it as unhappiness at his neglect.

We have seen in sections (5) and (6) that Kaoru is saddened by what he considers her newfound maturity, her new understanding of human relations. He feels responsible for having left her alone so long in so inhospitable a place, but at the same time he seems to long for the old calm and compliant Ukifune:

(9) *Mi-kokoro-bae no, kakarade oiraka narishi koso, nodoka ni ureshi-kari-shika. Hito no ika ni kikoe-shirasetaru koto ka aru. Sukoshi mo oroka naramu kokorozashi nite wa, kō made mairi-ku-beki, mi no hodo michi no arisama ni mo aranu o nado …*

'When your disposition was not like this and was calm, I was relaxed and happy. What have people been telling you? If my intentions were in the least bit frivolous, neither my own position nor the condition of the road is such that I could come here like this.' Saying things like this …

Her earlier submissiveness is giving way to something that he can neither control nor understand. Perhaps he senses something contrary in her outburst (indeed it is her longing for Niou and deception of Kaoru that are the source of her agony). He frequently, if not always, thinks of her as a substitute for Ōigimi, but when she asserts her own identity by not conforming to an expected pattern, he can no longer manipulate her for his own ends—that is, treat her as an image of Ōigimi. Not only do his words fail to communicate reassurance to her, but as if to emphasize the distance between them, he seems not to expect a reply from her. He moves away from her and lies down by the veranda, directing his attention away from her:

(10) ... *tsuitachi-goro no yūzukuyo ni, sukoshi hashi-chikaku fushite nagame-idashi-tamaeri. Otoko wa, suginishi kata no aware o mo oboshi-idete, onna wa, ima yori soitaru mi no usa o nageki-kuwaete, katami ni mono-omowashi.*

... as it was a moonlight evening around the first of the month, he lay down near the edge of the veranda and was gazing out. The man recalls his longing for the past, while the lady laments the new grief that has been added to her lot, and each is sunk in painful thoughts.

Kaoru's monologue (9) serves as a transition away from Ukifune's view, but in (10), rather than shifting the narrative voice to Kaoru, both he and Ukifune are described neutrally. The words *katami ni mono-omowashi* ('each is sunk in painful thoughts') crystallize the ironic distance between the two, and between them and us: we know that Ukifune is thinking of Niou and Kaoru of Ōigimi, but neither of them has any idea of the other's thoughts (nor do they seem to care here). The neutral perspective provides a bridge to what appears to be a purely descriptive passage:

(11) *Yama no kata wa kasumi-hedatete, samuki susaki ni tateru kasa-sagi no sugata mo, tokoro-gara wa ito okashū miyuru ni, Uji-bashi no haru-baru to mi-watasaruru ni, shiba-tsumi-bune no tokoro-dokoro ni yuki-chigaitaru nado, hoka nite me-narenu koto-domo nomi tori-atsumetaru tokoro nareba, mi-tamau tabigoto ni, nao, sono kami no koto no tadaima no kokochi shite, ito kakaranu hito o mi-kawashitaramu dani, mezurashiki naka no aware ōkaru-beki hodo nari. Maite koishiki hito ni yosoeraretaru mo, koyo nakarazu, yōyō mono no kokoro shiri, miyako-nareyuku arisama no okashiki mo, koyo naku mi-masarishitaru kokochi shi-tamau ni....*

... the mountains are shrouded in mist, and the figure of a crested heron standing on a cold sandspit—because of the character of the place—seems especially lovely; Uji Bridge can be seen in the distance, and boats piled high with brushwood ply back and forth; because it is a place where only things like this are brought together, things he is used to seeing nowhere else, every time he looks at it those days past seem present to him; even if he were exchanging glances with someone who was not like this, the rare sympathy between them would surely be deep. But as she is the very image of someone dear to him, it is all the more special.

Gradually she has come to understand the nature of things. He feels that the charm of her appearance, which has become more sophisticated, is now beyond compare....

This depiction of the river scenery at Uji seems at the beginning to be pure description narration, but gradually the reader senses the presence of a perceiving subject which at last becomes focused on Kaoru. The clause *ito okashū miyuru* ('seems especially lovely') implies a subject to which it so seems; with the clause, *shiba-tsumi-bune no tokoro-dokoro ni yuki-chigaitaru nado, hoka nite me-narenu koto-domo nomi tori-atsumetaru tokoro nareba* ('because it is a place where only things he is used to seeing nowhere else, like boats piled high with brushwood plying back and forth, are brought together'), we know that it is Kaoru who is perceiving this scene. His feeling that the past is present is not only explained to us in this passage but shown to us directly (if we are good readers): Kaoru gazes at a similar scene the first time he exchanges poems with Ōigimi, when he watches small boats laden with firewood passing back and forth and reflects on the transience of human life.[43]

The past and present exist simultaneously both for Kaoru and for us, but while this juxtaposition enhances his enjoyment of the present, for us the effect is quite different. We cannot help but sense his distance from Ukifune, a gulf created by his longing for the past. Although we, too, see the Uji River through his eyes, our point of view does not quite coincide with his. This ambiguity is present also in the text: while the point of view is clearly Kaoru's, the voice never becomes so. Verbs of seeing (*mi-watasaruru*, 'can be seen in the distance', and *me-narenu*, 'not used to seeing'), which have no honorific suffixes attached to them, can be interpreted as general statements, while verbs that can refer only to Kaoru as the subject end in the honorific *tamau* (*mi-tamau tabigoto ni*, 'every time he looks', and *kokochi shi-tamau ni*, 'he feels'). These honorifics reflect the narrator's point of view and consciousness of Kaoru's rank—a narrator who speaks about Kaoru from a standpoint very close to him. But in another clause in which we would expect a similar honorific, there is none: *sono kami no koto no tadaima no kokochi shite* ('those days past seem present to him'), suggesting that the voice here is Kaoru's own (in which case we might read it, 'those days past seem present to me'), as do the following clauses. However, the usual signs of direct interior monologue are missing (exclamatory and emphatic particles, and verbal suffixes that point to the presence of a speaking subject), nor does the passage end with a quotative particle, but becomes an extended modifier for *kokochi shi-tamau* ('he feels'). Here, the honorific suffix indicates the narrator's voice. The transition from (10) to (11) is reflected from a neutral point of view, thus minimizing the syntactic break at *omowashi* ('lost in thought'). Although there is one conclusive form (*shūshikei*) within the passage describing Kaoru's feelings (*'hodo nari'*), there is no shift in point of view here; so again the syntactic break is de-emphasized. Syntactic units do not correspond closely here with shifts in perspective. Hence these shifts take place within the almost unbroken flow of words.

(12) ... *onna wa, kaki-atsumetaru kokoro no uchi ni moyōsaruru namida to mo sureba ide-tatsu o....*

... but on the lady's part, the tears which have welled up because of her accumulated feelings are about to fall....

Although Ukifune's feelings are described to us, we see barely more of her than Kaoru himself can see. The source of her pain is not stated here because it is not visible to him. Again he misinterprets her distress, thinking she is upset by his negligence.

Kaoru's poem characteristically includes no expression of emotion, no direct statement of his own feelings:

(13a)   ... *nagusame-kane-tamaitsutsu,*
             Uji-bashi no
             nagaki chigiri wa
             kuchiseji o
             ayabumu kata ni
             kokoro sawagu na.
             Ima mi-tamaitemu to notamau.

... but being unable to comfort her, he says, 'The enduring vow of Uji Bridge will not decay. Don't let your heart be torn by what you fear. Now you will surely see—'

In verse, as in prose, Kaoru's speech is unadorned. This is evident if we compare Kaoru's poem with that of Niou about the snow (see p. 389, above). The former is a straightforward request that she not hesitate to rely on him. In her answering poem, although she has not misunderstood, she rejects his attempt to comfort her.

(13b)   *Taema nomi*
             yo ni wa ayōki
             Uji-bashi o

kuchisenu mono to
nao tanome to ya

'There is nothing but gaps in this world. Are you really telling me
to rely on that dangerous Uji Bridge as something that will not
decay?'

Ukifune deliberately misleads him by implying that she cannot depend
on him, thus reinforcing his previous misinterpretation of her state. In this
way, her poem also fails to communicate. We see the poem without an
accompanying view of her thoughts; it is thus seen from Kaoru's point of
view. We have no access to her real reaction to his poem because he himself
does not. Although there are subtle shifts in voice, the point of view remains
with Kaoru.

He does not reply to Ukifune's expression of insecurity. Although he
finds it harder than ever to leave her, his concern over what people would say
if he stayed longer overrides any sense of her feelings:

(13c) *Sakizaki yori mo ito mi-sutegataku, shibashi mo tachi-tomara-*
mahoshiku obosaruredo, hito no mono-ii no yasukaranu ni, ima sara
nari, kokoro-yasuki sama nite koso, nado oboshi-sashite, akatsuki ni
kaeri-tamainu. Ito yō mo otonabitaritsuru ka na, to, kokoro-gurushiku
oboshi-izuru koto, arishi ni masarikeri.

It is more difficult to leave her than ever, and although he feels he
would like to stay even for a little while longer, since he is uneasy
about what people might say, making an effort to think, It would
be foolish now. When I can relax .... at dawn he returned to the
capital. Recollecting, She certainly has grown up, was more
painful than ever.

Here again, the point of view is Kaoru's throughout, but the voice
varies, sometimes coinciding with his, sometimes reflecting the narrator's
presence. The first two clauses (through *tachi-tomara-mahoshiku*, 'wanting to
stay'), which in the Japanese are parallel adverbial constructions, constitute
an indirect monologue. Following *obosaruredo* ('although he feels'), we see his
thoughts directly. The last direct quotation of his thoughts, *ito yō mo*
otonabitaritsuru ka na ('she certainly has grown up'), also re-emphasizes his
lack of understanding of her. Thus even in passages in which we are
linguistically closest to a character, when the narrative voice is wholly his, we
are conscious of ironic distance. The distance between us and Kaoru is

stressed by the closing of the whole section, marked by the verbal suffix *–keri*. Here, the narrator describes Kaoru's feelings, *to, kokoro-gurushiku oboshi-izuru koto arishi ni masarikeri* ('recollecting ... was more painful than ever'), which we know to be based on a misunderstanding, and rounds off the sentence in a way that points both to the presence of the narrating voice and to the fact of narration. The section thus concludes in a way that is typical of many of the chapters of the *Genji*, where by various means the narrative points to itself.[44]

FROM ANALYSIS OF THE TEXT TO INTERPRETATION OF THE WORK: FIRST STEPS

FROM the above analysis of narrative voice in a short section of 'Ukifune', it is possible to form a synthesis of the insight gained from it about each of the two characters, a synthesis which is at the same time an interpretation of the text. Obviously there are aspects of Kaoru and Ukifune that do not appear at all in this passage; thus my remarks are necessarily tentative. In order to interpret fully even this small part of the text, we must read it in light of the rest of the Uji chapters, if not the *Genji* as a whole. Although I have attempted to limit my analysis to the selected passage, the interdependent structure of the text has required that I refer to an earlier chapter in order to make a particular scene intelligible.[45] But we can gain a considerable degree of understanding of the mutual relationship of the two characters from an examination of this brief section.

The first glimpse we see of Ukifune shows us that she responds negatively to Kaoru. This is quite clear from her first interior monologue, and is also suggested by the preceding transitional passage that describes the impression he makes on some, as yet unnamed, observer. Her embarrassment and fear of Kaoru are contrasted with her passionate love for Niou, whose warmth is repeatedly reflected in Ukifune's thoughts about him. While she notes, one by one, the praiseworthy aspects of Kaoru's character, her frequent attempts to suppress her memories of Niou and her feelings for him leave no doubt that it is Niou that she loves.[46]

But it is not only Ukifune who responds without passion to Kaoru's calmer virtues. We also see him as she does. The opening section (1) shows us his dispassionate nature; his situation is described as *nodoka nari* ('calm')— Kaoru himself is referred to by the same adjective at the beginning of the chapter (vi, 99.10). He presents a striking contrast to Niou, who, in the immediately preceding passage, thinks he will die of love (vi, 133. 5–6). Kaoru, on the other hand, is in no great hurry to see Ukifune. When business matters are not too pressing, he finds time to go to Uji; when he arrives, he does not rush immediately to her quarters but goes first to the temple, prays, spends some time with the priests, and, finally, when he has taken care of these other responsibilities, he stops in to see her. The very absence of interior monologue here suggests that he is not thinking of anything relevant to the story of Ukifune.

When his thoughts are exposed to us, two points emerge clearly: his repeated misunderstanding of Ukifune, and his preoccupation with Ōigimi. We cannot censure Kaoru for not knowing the real source of Ukifune's unhappiness, but because we do know we cannot simply accept Kaoru's judgment that she has matured; that judgment is based on ignorance. Rather than being pleased by this change in her, he reproaches her for it, for she no longer responds in the way he expects, and he cannot control her. Kaoru is deceiving Ukifune in not telling her about his attachment to Ōigimi, and deceiving himself in continuing to see Ukifune as an image of Ōigimi. The ironic distance thus established between us and Kaoru prevents our identifying with him too closely, and in effect prevents our taking Kaoru as the hero of the Uji chapters. His longest interior monologue in the chapter, when he discovers the deception of Ukifune and Niou (VI, 165–167), reveals some of the most unattractive aspects of his character, reinforcing the irony.

It is not only Kaoru who practices deception. Ukifune's agitation provokes his poem, an attempt to console her. But her answering poem, far from revealing her real emotions as we have seen them through her interior monologues, conceals the conflicts within her. According to her poem, she doubts the endurance of Kaoru's vow; however, we know that it is not his unreliability that distresses her, but her own and Niou's. It is the very fact of Kaoru's dependability which makes him so clearly a better potential husband than Niou, that requires her to reject Niou and creates her conflict. Ukifune's words are opposed to her feelings. This contrast becomes vivid for us through the juxtaposition of two forms of direct utterance—direct speech (here in the form of a poem) and direct interior monologue, the latter supported by narrated dialogue. If descriptive narration had been our only source of information about her thoughts, we would not feel the contrast with the words so strongly as we do when we see her thoughts directly, from her own point of view. Because we see directly, we understand the irony of her poem. It is more difficult to understand Ukifune's role in the work than it is to evaluate our relation to Kaoru. At times we may identify with her, but, in the end, we stand apart from her. While we may view her with sympathy, it is mixed with censure toward her indecisiveness. However, the distance we thus experience is not of the same quality as the sharp irony with which we must regard Kaoru's protestations of fidelity and piety. Ultimately, our point of view and that of the work as a whole do not coincide with that of any of the characters in the Uji chapters. Through the use of multiple points of view, by placing in apposition the consciousnesses of Ukifune and Kaoru, we are distanced from both of them. The irony of their words thus becomes vivid.

The narrative voice shifts, then, from character to character, to descriptive narration, to the voice of a narrator. While interior monologue brings us face to face with the characters, descriptive narration provides a background against which we see them as objects, on the one hand, and on the other confronts us with what the characters themselves see. The latter kind of description begins as narration in which the voice is not personified, but as the passage proceeds the point of view becomes that of one of the characters. Thus, to a certain extent, descriptive narration serves to move us away from the characters, insofar as their movements and thoughts are described in summary. But as this kind of description (particularly of nature) takes on the intonation and orientation of a certain character, we move closer to him, and when the narrative voice then blends with his in direct interior monologue, we face him directly.

However, when the voice is personified as a narrator, the distancing effect is stronger than in passages of description. The auxiliary verb –keri calls attention to the presence of a personified subject, that is, a narrating voice, particularly in conjunction with the emphatic particles namu, zo, and koso. In addition, there are auxiliary verbs such as –beshi, –meri, and –kemu, which indicate conjecture on the part of the narrating voice about the subject of the main verb (see p. 382, above). For example, in the expression omoi-yoru nari-kemu ka shi (VI, 177.3, 'it must be that she thought of it'), it is not the subject of the verb 'thinks' (here, Ukifune) that speculates, but the narrator who is explaining Ukifune's thinking. Causal constructions perform the same role. This kind of speculation about a character's motives or actions places the narrator within the same dimension as the character (that is, the narrator is not omniscient) and at the same time objectifies him, thus creating distance between us and him. The technique has close parallels in *To the Lighthouse*.[47] In Auerbach's words, Woolf is deliberately 'obscuring and even obliterating the impression of an objective reality completely known to the author' precisely in order to create a more real reality.[48] In the *Genji*, also, the very humanness of the narrator who wonders about Ukifune's motivations functions to establish the reality of the fictional world.

As the voice of the narrator becomes more insistent, unquestionably distinct from that of the character being described and obviously personified, the character is objectified and our distance from him is at its maximum.[49] We can see this in the sentence, kano mimi todome-tamaishi hito-koto wa, motomai-idenu zo nikuki ya (VI, 145. 7–8, 'it is really hateful that he does not mention that word that caught his ear'), in which the narrator condemns

Niou for not mentioning to Ukifune that he overheard Kaoru repeating a poem about his longing for the lady of Uji Bridge.[50] Both of these techniques of distancing—descriptive narration and narrator's commentary—are relatively infrequent in 'Ukifune' in comparison to other chapters of the *Genji*; however, they do occur often enough to form a significant aspect of the narrative method in 'Ukifune'.

Thus the shifting of narrative voice in 'Ukifune', in contrast to similar techniques in Virginia Woolf's *To the Lighthouse*, while drawing us closer to the characters within their world also creates irony and controls the aesthetic distance among the characters themselves, and between the fictional world and us, the readers. A study of narrative voice in the *Genji* as a whole should indicate an increasing refinement in the uses of aesthetic distance and irony; even on the basis of a cursory reading, there seems to be a fundamental difference between the degree and consistency of the irony directed toward Hikaru Genji and the distance between us and the major characters in the Uji chapters, particularly Kaoru. However, such conclusions must be the result of a much broader critical examination of the *Genji*. I have confined myself in the present study to a selected passage from the 'Ukifune' chapter. Although my analysis is extremely limited, it has revealed important elements in the relationships of major characters within the fictional world as well as significant aspects of narrative method.

NOTES

1. Roland Barthes, 'An Introduction to the Structural Analysis of Narrative', in *New Literary History*, vi: 2 (Winter 1975), p. 261.

2. Robert Scholes and Robert Kellogg make this assumption the starting point for their discussion of point of view in *The Nature of Narrative*, Galaxy Books, Oxford U.P., 1968, p. 240.

3. Tamagami Takuya, '*Genji monogatari no dokusha: monogatari ondoku-ron*', in *Genji monogatari hyōshaku*, Kadokawa Shoten, 1964–6, *Bekkan* i, *Genji monogatari kenkyū*, 1966, pp. 247–65.

4. All quotations from the text are from Abe Akio *et al.*, ed., *Genji monogatari* (*Nihon koten bungaku zenshū* Shōgakukan, 1970–76. Unless noted otherwise, all references are to the 'Ukifune' chapter. For the general reader, corresponding chapter titles in English have been included, from Edward G. Seidensticker, tr., *The Tale of Genji*, Alfred Knopf, New York, 1976, 2 vols.

Nakano Kōichi—cites ii, 'Usugumo' ('A Rack of Cloud'), 438. 8–14, as evidence against the viability of Tamagami's theory ('*Genji monogatari no sōshiji to monogatari ondoku-ron*', in *Genji monogatari*, i (*Nihon bungaku kenkyū shiryō sōsho*), Yūseidō, 1969, pp. 206–7).

In this case the narrator cannot in any way be interpreted as a lady-in-waiting who either witnessed the event or heard it from another lady who was a direct witness, but, according to Nakano, must be more transcendental and omniscient than any of the three narrators Tamagami proposes.

5. Although Saeki Umetomo only draws this conclusion in relation to adjectives, we

can expand it to refer to reported discourse in general and particularly to interior monologue. See Saeki Umetomo , '*Chokusetsu wahō to kansetsu wahō*' , in *Jōdai kokugo-hō kenkyū*, Daitōbunka Daigaku tōyō kenkyū-jo sōsho, #3, 1966, pp. 42–3.

6. This is the reverse of Russian narrative, in which the tone of the reported speech casts a shadow on the embedding narrative and influences even the narrator's tone. See V. N. Volosinov, 'Reported Speech', in Ladislav Matejka & Krystyna Pomorska, ed., *Readings in Russian Poetics: Formalist and Structuralist Views*, MIT Press, 1971, pp. 167 ff.

7. Dorrit Cohn, 'Narrated Monologue: Definition of a Fictional Style', in *Comparative Literature*, xviii: 2 (Spring 1966), pp. 97–112.

8. Cohn, pp. 97–8.

9. Cohn, p. 104.

10. Ann Banfield, 'Narrative Style and the Grammar of Direct and Indirect Speech', in *Foundations of Language*, x (1973), pp. 1–39, esp. pp. 10 ff.

11. Cohn, p. 105; Banfield, p. 10.

12. Saeki, p. 33.

13. See Suzuki Kazuo , '*Genji monogatari no hōhō, buntai: shinnaigo no mondai*' in *Genji monogatari*, ii (*Kōza nihon bungaku*), Kaishaku to kanshō, bessatsu (May 1978), pp. 163–84.

Throughout his essay, a re-examination of a survey of modes of discourses in the *Genji*, Suzuki reiterates that this fusion is typical of the *Genji* (see pp. 167 ff). He also notes the use of direct interior monologue and indirect interior monologue and their frequency in other major Heian-period *monogatari* (pp. 174 ff).

14. Banfield, pp. 7–8.

15. Cohn, p. 110.

16. Wayne C. Booth, *The Rhetoric of Fiction*, University of Chicago Press, 1961, pp. 151 ff.

17. Tokieda Motoki , *Kokugogaku Genron: Gengokateisetsu no Seiritsu*, Iwanami Shoten, 1941, pp. 38–56.

18. It is possible to consider the subject of this expression different from that of the causal construction and the comment at the close of the passage, but for the purposes of our discussion it does not make any difference whether there is one or more narrators in this sense.

For remarks on the possibility of multiple narrators in this passage and that at the beginning of the 'Hahakigi' ('The Broom Tree') chapter, see Mitani Kuniaki, '*Genji monogatari ni okeru "katari" no kōzō: "washa" to "katari-te" aruiwa "sōshiji" ron hihan no tame no Joshō*', in *Nihon Bungaku* , xxvii:11 (November 1978), p. 46.

19. For a discussion of the significance of the particle *namu*, particularly in combination with the verbal suffix *–keri*, see Sakakura Atsuyoshi, *Bunshō to hyōgen*, Kadokawa Shoten, 1975, pp. 24–41.

20. Sakakura, p. 18.

21. Mitani, p. 43.

22. See above, p. 378.

23. Some of these attempts to define *sōshiji* from the earliest sources to the present are discussed in Takahashi Tōru, "'*Katari*" no hyōgen kōzō: iwayuru sōshiji ni tsuite', Genji monogatari, ii (*Kōza nihon bungaku*) Kaishaku to kanshō, bessatsu (May 1978), pp. 119–38.

24. The former is the position of Banfield, pp. 25 ff., who argues on grounds of transformational grammar that in the free indirect style there can be no other subject of expression than the subject named in the given expression.

S.-Y. Kuroda, in his essay, 'Where Epistemology, Style, and Grammar Meet: A Case Study from the Japanese', in S. Anderson & P. Kiparsky, ed., *A Festschrift for Morris Halle*, Holt, Rinehart & Winston, New York, 1973, also argues that there can be no omniscient narrator who speaks directly to the reader because the free indirect style has a unique grammar which is 'essentially different from the paradigmatic linguistic performance' (p. 387).

25. Emile Benveniste, *Problèmes de linguistique générale*, Gallimard, Paris, 1966, p. 241. Benveniste does not hold that every narrative is a discourse, however.

26. Tzvetan Todorov, '*Les categories du récit littéraire*', in *Communications*, 8 (1966), pp. 126 & 147.

27. Tzvetan Todorov, *The Poetics of Prose*, Cornell U.P., 1977, pp. 27–8.

28. Mitani, pp. 39 ff.

29. Booth, pp. 70–71 & 151.

30. Mitani, pp. 43 & 44.

31. According to Suzuki's analysis, pp. 170–72, the average percentage of interior monologue per chapter is 11.2%; that in 'Ukifune', 17.6%. In the *Genji*, this is exceeded only by 'Kagero' ('The Drake Fly'), 22.1%.

32. For a detailed discussion of the fusion of interior monologue with the embedding descriptive narration, see Akita Teiji, '*Genji monogatari no naiwa*', *shinwa kokubun*, 2 (December 1969), pp. 1–21.

33. Konishi Jin'ichi '*Genji monogatari no shinri byōsha*' in Yamagishi Tokuhei & Oka Kazuo, ed., *Genji monogatari kōza*, Yūseidō, vii, pp. 44 ff.

34. Erich Auerbach's discussion of *To the Lighthouse* first suggested to me a possible analogy between Woolf's work and the Uji chapters of the *Genji* (and perhaps the entire work). He calls the technique found in Woolf and some other 20th-century novelists 'multi-personal representation of consciousness', noting that the most important difference between Woolf and earlier novelists who rendered inner views of their characters is that while the earlier writer, 'with his knowledge of an objective truth, never abdicated his position as the final and governing authority.... The essential characteristic of the technique represented by Virginia Woolf is that we are given not merely one person whose consciousness (that is, the impressions it receives) is rendered, but many persons, with frequent shifts from one to the other.... The design of a close approach to objective reality by means of numerous subjective impressions received by various individuals ... is important in the modern technique....'

Erich Auerbach, *Mimesis: The Representation of Reality in Western Literature*, Doubleday, Anchor Books, Garden City, New York, 1957, p. 474.

I am greatly indebted in my discussion of Virginia Woolf's works to James Naremore's fine study, *The World Without a Self: Virginia Woolf and the Novel*, Yale U.P., 1973, esp. pp. 112–50. For further detailed analysis of changes in point of view in *To the Lighthouse*, see Mitchell Leaska, *Virginia Woolf's Lighthouse: A Study in Critical Method*, Columbia U.P., 1970, pp. 47–58.

35. For a basic study of stream of consciousness, see Robert Humphrey, *Stream of Consciousness in the Modern Novel*, University of California Press, 1954, esp. pp. 2 ff. For a discussion of conflicting views on the subject, see Naremore, pp. 63–76.

36. Virginia Woolf, *To the Lighthouse*, Harcourt, Bruce & World, Harvest Books, New York, 1955, pp. 15 & 20–21. Due acknowledgment is made to the Author's Literary Estate and The Hogarth Press for permission to quote this passage. This quotation and all further citations refer to the edition cited above.

37. After his death, Hachi no Miya appears in dreams to both Naka no Kimi and Azari (v, 'Agemaki' ['Trefoil Knots'], 301.3 & 312.4).

38. Boris Uspensky, *A Poetics of Composition: The Structure of the Artistic Text and Typology of a Compositional Form*, University of California Press, 1973, p. 71.

39. To my knowledge, no one has discussed the *literary* significance in shifts from past or perfect aspects to what may be called present aspects of the verb in classical Japanese narrative. There are many *linguistic* studies of individual verb suffixes, and comparisons of

ki and *keri*, for instance (see n. 19, above), but they do not deal with the changes in narrative aspect that I have touched upon above.

40. See n. 4, above. The section in question corresponds to vi, 133.7–137.15.

This passage corresponds to Tamagami Takuya, *Genji monogatari hyōshaku*, xii, pp. 89–94; Akiyama Ken, *Genji monogatari* (*Nihon koten zenshū*), Shōgakukan, 1976, vi, 133.7–136.9; Yamagishi Tokuhei, ed., *Genji monogatari* (*Nihon koten bungaku taikei* 18), Iwanami Shoten, 1963, v, 230.12–233.15.

41. Tamagami, xii, p. 92, takes this whole clause, from *ayumi-iri-tamau yori* ('when he steps into the room'), to be Ukifune's point of view.

42. For definitions of external and internal points of view and a discussion of their functions, see Uspensky, pp. 83–5.

43. v, 'Hashihime' ('The Lady at the Bridge'), 141.8–11.

44. Earl Miner, 'Narrative Units in the *Genji monogatari*: "Ukifune" in its Context', unpublished manuscript.

45. This very necessity to refer back to other parts of the text makes it clear that the *Genji* is essentially a *written* work. See the reference to Tamagami's theory of the work as performance, pp. 375–76, above.

46. For a discussion of Ukifune as she appears throughout the Uji chapters, and in particular her relations to Kaoru and Niou, see Takahashi Tōru, '*Sonzai-kankaku no shisō: "Ukifune" ni tsuite*', in *Nihon bungaku*, xxiv: 11 (November 1975), pp. 79–80. Takahashi supports my reading of Ukifune's feelings.

47. See especially the famous passage beginning, 'Never did anybody look so sad' Woolf, p. 46.

48. Auerbach, p. 472.

49. Konishi, pp. 53 ff., discusses the creation of aesthetic distance in the *Genji* by means of the manipulation of point of view and the use of personified narrators. He states, however, that in general the point of view in the *Genji* is omniscient, with which I cannot agree. There is a fundamental difference between omniscient narration, which implies a consistent point of view throughout a text and at the same time a *personified* subject of expression that freely makes judgments about the characters, and the kind of multiple-point-of-view narration that characterizes the *Genji* and the novels of Woolf, Faulkner, and Joyce.

50. Similar expressions by the narrator about the characters occur throughout the chapter. See vi, 139.7–9; 149.12–13; 162.14–15; 169.12; 177.1–3.

IVAN MORRIS

Aspects of 'The Tale of Genji'

T he first psychological novel in the literature of the world is also one of its longest. In its original form *The Tale of Genji* consisted of fifty-four books or chapters, which were separately bound and which, as the complaint in the *Sarashina Diary* reminds us, often circulated independently. Arthur Waley's translation, which does not expand the original (and from which one of the books is missing), has some 630,000 words; this makes Murasaki's novel about twice as long as *Don Quixote, War and Peace*, or *The Brothers Karamazov*, though only two-thirds the length of *A la recherche du temps perdu*.

The action is spread over three-quarters of a century and involves four generations. There are about four hundred and thirty characters, not counting messengers, servants, and anonymous members of the working class. Most of these characters are related to each other,[1] and early commentators devoted years to the sisyphean task of producing genealogical tables in which almost every character in the novel was included. The tradition has been maintained by modern scholars: Ikeda's recent *Encyclopaedia of the Tale of Genji* has over seventy closely-printed pages of genealogy. Murasaki belonged to a rigidly stratified society in which family connexions were all-important, and while working on the novel she must have kept her own charts to show how her huge cast of characters were related. For never once is she inconsistent about the relationship of even the most obscure people in her book.

From *The World of the Shining Prince: Court Life in Ancient Japan.* © 1964 by Ivan Morris.

This methodical approach is even more striking in Murasaki's time scheme. There is hardly a passage in the entire novel that we cannot identify in terms of year and month and in which we cannot determine the exact age of each of the important characters.[2] Occasionally Murasaki will depart from straight chronological order in telling her story. The events in one chapter, for example, may occur before those in the previous chapter ('flashback'), or two chapters may overlap. But such deviations are deliberate and there is never any confusion. Commentators have subjected the time scheme of the novel to the minutest scrutiny. They are, one feels, almost hoping to find some inconsistency; until now they have been unsuccessful.

This precision is one aspect of Murasaki's talent for organizing her voluminous material in the most effective way. It immediately puts her work in a different category from *The Tale of the Hollow Tree*, the only extant precursor in the field of lengthy prose fiction. For one of the things that makes *The Tale of the Hollow Tree* so hard to read, and ultimately so unreal, is its disorganized construction and its chaotic time scheme.

The Tale of Genji does not ramble on amorphously as a haphazard sequence of loosely connected episodes. It is true that the books tend to be more independent than the chapters of most modern novels, especially since there is often a gap of several years between them; yet to view the work as a series of vaguely related short stories (as some critics have done) seems to me completely off the mark. Like the individual books of which it is composed, *The Tale of Genji* is an artistic unit whose shape has been carefully and deliberately designed. It is so constructed that the entire work can be resolved into certain general divisions, which represent its beginning (Books 1–12), its middle (Books 13–41), and its end (Books 42–54) and into a number of significant sub-divisions whose various chapters are closely bound together by the coherent development of character and event.[3]

Above all, *The Tale of Genji* is constructed about a set of central ideas or themes, the historical theme of Fujiwara power, for example, and the human theme of impermanence, which combine to give it an artistic unity. This is one of the aspects (the use of realistic psychological detail is another) that allow us to describe Murasaki's work as a 'novel', a term that cannot be applied to any of its exact precursors.

One device that Murasaki uses with particular effect is anticipation or build-up. Frequently she will hint at the existence of some character long before that person enters the action of the novel, or she will adumbrate some sequence of events that is to take place many years in the future. There is a scene in one of the early books, for example, in which Prince Genji and a young friend stand on a hill and discuss the beauties of the countryside in the distance. 'If one were to live in such a place,' exclaims Genji, 'one could really ask for nothing more in this world!'[4] Here Murasaki anticipates, not without irony, the events that are to happen eight years (and seven books) later. For the landscape at which Genji gazes so fondly is to be the place of his forlorn exile from the capital. His friend then tells him the story of the strange old lay priest of Akashi and of his attractive little daughter. This arouses the young prince's curiosity, as well as the reader's, and paves the way for Genji's love affair with Lady Akashi and for all the complications that this entails in later years.

Sometimes Murasaki will speak about a character never mentioned before as though the reader already knew all about him. In the hands of a skilful writer this device can produce a curiously realistic effect and, as Arthur Waley has pointed out, it was used by Proust. Murasaki's more usual method of build-up, however, is to make different characters speak about someone from their respective points of view long before the person in question actually appears on the scene. For example, Kaoru hears various reports about Ukifune, the tragic heroine of the last five books, many years before he actually meets her. It is not until we have formed a fairly clear picture of the girl that she enters the action.

By far the best-known case of anticipation in *The Tale of Genji* occurs in Book 2 when Genji and his young friends meet on a rainy night to discuss the different types of women they have known and to compare their merits. This passage, with its detailed comments on various sorts of women that are to figure in the novel, has often been regarded as a key to the organization of the entire work, not unlike the first movement of a symphony in which the composer may suggest the themes that he intends to develop later.[5] In fact the 'discussion on a rainy night' does not have nearly such a mechanical function as this might suggest. Of the many types of girl that the young gallants describe, only one can be identified with a specific character in the novel. This is Yūgao, the simple young woman whose love affair with Genji and whose weird death are described in the following two books. One of Genji's friends mentions that he has had an illegitimate child with Yūgao; mother and child have both disappeared and he has been unable to track them down. Here is another case of anticipation; for the child in question turns out to be Tamakazura, who enters the action of the novel seventeen years later.

Another aspect of Murasaki's style that serves to tighten the structure of her narrative is the deliberate repetition of situations, settings, and relationships between characters. *The Tale of Genji* contains certain patterns of action that occur with variations at widely separated points of the narrative, not unlike the motifs in a musical composition. Here again we are reminded of *A la recherche du temps perdu*[6] with its subtle use of internal 'rhythms'.

One of the best ways to understand the carefully balanced architecture of Murasaki's novel is to note how she places different characters, or sometimes the same character, in successive situations that 'correspond' with each other. Thus, when Genji finds out that his young wife, Princess Nyosan, has been seduced by Kashiwagi and that the little boy (Kaoru) whom everyone takes to be his own son and heir is in fact the result of this affair, he realizes that history has repeated itself to an uncanny degree. For some thirty years earlier Genji himself had seduced his father's new consort, Lady Fujitsubo, and she had given birth to a boy (Reizei), who was accepted as the Emperor's son and who as a result came to the throne illegitimately. As Genji holds the little child in his arm, it occurs to him that the old Emperor may secretly have known and suffered about Fujitsubo's unfaithfulness, in much the same way that he himself is now tormented by what Nyosan has done.[7] The same pattern continues to unfold in later years. Just as Reizei was racked with doubts about his paternity, to the extent that he eventually resigned the throne, so when Kaoru grows up he is obsessed with the feeling that there was something strange about his birth, and this serves to intensify the neurotic aspect of his character.

There are many cases like this in which a pattern that has been developed in the early part of the novel, when Genji is the hero, is repeated with variations in the Kaoru books. For example, the relationship between Genji and Yūgao finds its echo, as it were, in the love affair between Kaoru and Ukifune some fifty years later. In each case the hero's interest is aroused by hearing about an attractive girl who belongs to a far lower social class than himself. It is only after careful anticipation that Murasaki puts her on the scene. The hero meets her by chance and is almost immediately captivated (Books 4 and 49). The love affair begins in the lady's humble town dwelling; and in the morning the hero lies listening to the unfamiliar street noises. He abruptly decides to move his mistress to some more isolated place and despite the protests of her attendants he takes her in his carriage to a gloomy country house. In both cases the relationships are marked by a sense of strangeness and end in tragedy. It is not surprising that such closely parallel situations should contain what Waley describes as 'balancing scenes', like those in Books 4 and 50 when Murasaki describes the sounds of the peasants and the pedlars. The emphasis in the two scenes is on the unfamiliarity of the common surroundings in which the hero suddenly finds himself. Both men are fascinated by the street sounds, which in Genji's case are able years later to evoke the memory of his love. These are the scenes:

> (Book 4) '... the dwelling, so different from those to which Genji
> was accustomed, seemed strange to him. It must have been nearly

dawn. From the neighbouring houses he could hear the uncouth voices of workers who were just waking up: "Oh, how cold it is!" "We can't count on much business this year. It's a poor look-out for our hauling trade." "Hey, neighbour, wake up!" With such remarks they set out noisily, each to his own pitiful job.'

(Book 50) 'Soon it appeared to be dawn, but instead of the song of birds, Kaoru heard the raucous and unintelligible cries of pedlars calling out their wares from near the main street while they passed by in large groups. As he looked out at them staggering past in the dawn light with their loads, they appeared like phantoms. The experience of having passed the night in this simple dwelling seemed most strange to Kaoru.'[8]

Murasaki's deliberate repetitions are never as obvious as this may suggest. Nor are they exact. Psychological realism demanded that different types of people react differently in the same situation; however parallel the patterns may be, it is unthinkable that we should, for example, find a resolute character like Genji handling a love affair with the diffidence and deviousness of a Kaoru.

The use of 'sustained imagery' (the repetition, that is, of a single central image in both the narrative passages and the poems) can also serve to connect different parts of the novel that are widely separated in time, or to tighten the structure of a particular series of books. Throughout the novel, for instance, Murasaki rings the changes on the image of dreams and thereby evokes one of her central themes—the nebulous, unreal quality of the world about us, and the idea that our life here is a mere 'bridge of dreams' (the title of her final book), over which we cross from one state of existence to the next.[9]

Another example of sustained imagery is the river at Uji, which figures prominently in the last ten books. This section (commonly known as the 'Ten Books of Uji') occupies a special place in the writing of The Tale of Genji. It is marked by tightly-knit narrative and by a most effective use of psychological detail and of imagery. In almost every sense, indeed, it represents the climax of Murasaki's style. (This having been said, the reader should perhaps be warned that the following discussion is focused on one particular aspect of the Uji books and that their tone is not nearly so monotonous or insistent as an abstract of this kind might lead one to believe.)

The main setting is a house in the little hamlet of Uji, where the religious recluse, Prince Hachi, lives with his two attractive daughters. The

Prince's residence, though less than ten miles from the bustle and brilliance of the capital, presents so isolated and depressing an aspect as to become the very crystallization of that mood of melancholy which increasingly dominates the novel and its characters. The theme of death is constantly in the foreground. Indeed, the action of the Uji books centres on the deaths, or supposed deaths, at Uji of the Prince's wife, the Prince himself, his elder daughter, and his step-daughter, Ukifune. Meanwhile the survivors are depicted as becoming more and more imbued with the gloom of the place. They toy with the idea of leaving the house and moving to the capital, but this is hardly easier for the Prince's daughters than it was eight centuries later for the sisters in Chekhov's tragedy.

The very name Uji ('Forlorn') is symbolical of the sorrow that pervades the house. This is not lost on any of its inhabitants; sometimes, in fact, they almost seem to revel in the thought that their village is true to its name.[10]

The mood of Uji is reflected in the imagery. The dreary weather of the village—the winds and rains, the snow flurries and blizzards, the clouds and the gathering mist—mirrors the emotions of the characters, and is contrasted with the relatively benign and cheerful conditions in the capital beyond the hills. Murasaki also evokes the atmosphere of the place by numerous sound-symbols that in *The Tale of Genji* are invariably associated with sorrow. Such are the cry of the deer (that strangely poignant sound that has so greatly moved Japanese poets over the centuries), the slow tolling of the distant temple bell, the call of the wild geese, the rush of the waterfall, the wailing of the wind in the oak trees.

Of all the images that symbolize the atmosphere at Uji none is used more consistently and with greater effect than that of the river outside Prince Hachi's house. As the central image of these final books, it serves to evoke the grief and tragedy that dominate the house at Uji and its inhabitants. On his first visit to the place Kaoru is struck by the noise of the river directly outside the Prince's house: 'The fierce sound of the water and the lapping of the waves against the river bank boomed terrifyingly in his ears.'[11]

In the following book the roar of the water is combined with those other doleful aspects of nature into which the girls merge themselves during their grief at Prince Hachi's death:

'Now they had reached the ninth month of the year, and the sisters felt that their lives had turned into an unending night. The sight of the rainswept hills and fields brought tears to their eyes and made the sleeves of their robes still wetter than before. The rustle of the falling leaves as they swirled against each other in the air, the roar of the water in Uji River, the sound of the waterfall like a gushing torrent of tears—it all seemed to blend into a dirge, filling the girls with dismay. How could things go on like this? Was there to be no end to this existence of theirs?'[12]

The elder sister is overcome by a particularly intense bout of melancholy: 'Everything seemed unutterably sad, and she felt herself drifting along with the sound of the water.'[13]

Murasaki was always interested in the effects that the same scene could have on different characters. When Kaoru's rival, the comparatively ebullient and extroverted Prince Niou, pays his first visit to Uji, he is delighted by the place; for, as Murasaki points out, 'he was always susceptible to new forms of beauty'. His main objective is to seduce the younger daughter, but as a true Heian gentleman he is bound to be impressed by the natural setting: 'He watched the wreath of mist drifting over the water and the boats laden with brushwood as they sailed along the river leaving white swirls in their wake. A strange place to live, he thought, but not without a charm of its own.'[14] But later in the day the mood of Uji begins to tell on him and he sees the river in a new light: 'The sound of the water seemed to have lost its pleasant tone, and now as the mist cleared and the ancient Bridge of Uji emerged into full view he began to feel that there was something harsh and friendless about these shores.'[15]

Ukifune's tempestuous destiny lends itself perfectly to expression in terms of the river imagery. The girl's life is repeatedly associated with the river that flows ominously outside the house at Uji, where her new lover, Kaoru, has brought her to live. He is rarely able to visit her, and Ukifune spends most of her time in a state of gloomy solitude that is only occasionally interrupted by the arrival of a messenger from the capital. During the rainy season Kaoru sends a poem in which the central image is Uji River. It is hardly a cheering tonic.

'How fare you by those far-off shores
(Lost no doubt in doleful thoughts)
While the never-ending rains
Swell the fierce waves that surge outside your house?'[16]

In her reply Ukifune maintains the image and she also refers to a well-known poem about a gliding boat (which incidentally is the origin of her name)

'So smoothly glide my boat
That if it were to merge into the waves
Who would there be to say he saw a ripple on the water's face?'

For the first time the idea of drowning, of merging with the water in death, is suggested.[17]

When Ukifune finally decides that her predicament has become impossible (her two lovers, Kaoru and Niou, are both expecting to move her to the capital and the dates of departure are only a few days off), it follows both realistically and symbolically that she should decide to drown herself in Uji River, which has become the symbol of her tormented life. Now the image and reality have become a single texture, and the events move fast, with a degree of inevitability that we would never find in a haphazard narrative of actual happenings. Ukifune has overheard her mother, who is visiting her at Uji, tell one of the old ladies in the house that, if her daughter should become involved in any more difficulties, she will never be able to see her again. Ukifune's cup is full. She knows that a most appalling situation is approaching. Although Kaoru and Niou are supposed to be bosom friends, neither has told the other about his relations with Ukifune. Soon they will find out, and then both men will desert her in disgust. And she can no longer count on her mother for support. Clearly there is only one solution 'Oh that I might lose this body of mine!'[18]

During all this time the roar of the swollen river can be heard outside, and now the girl listens as her mother and the old lady discuss it:

'Ukifune's mother had begun to respond to the fearful roar of the river. "Really," she said, "this was an odd place to build a house. Some stretches of the river are far less rough than here. How terrible to have to live year after year with that sound always in one's ears." Never before had the river seemed so formidable.'[19]

It is at once symbol and reality that Ukifune should now resolve to join the large number of people who have ended their lives in Uji River. A recurrent image has become a reality: the fierce waters, which have always represented the mood of sorrow and tragedy at Uji, become the real agent of the culminating disaster.

In her final poem Ukifune once more uses the river imagery:

'Though this poor body sink into the waves,
My sinful name, alas, will not stay down,
But float up to the water's top for all to know.'[20]

The river continues to appear as a symbol of tragedy long after Ukifune's supposed suicide. In Book 52 two inhabitants of Uji stand watching the river swirl by outside the Prince's house and hear in its noise a

constant rebuke to Ukifune for having committed suicide.[21] Later in the
same book Kaoru, unbearably agitated by the noise of the waters, sets out for
the capital in the middle of the night, rather than remain alone in Uji with
the picture in his mind of Ukifune lying on the river bed: 'So long as he
heard that sound he was unable to put his mind to rest for a single
moment.'[22]

Yet he cannot keep away from Uji. In the following book a Captain of
the Guards tells about having seen Kaoru at Prince Hachi's house:

> 'As His Excellency stood near the river, he gazed into the water
> and wept. Then he went into the house and wrote a poem which
> he attached to one of the pillars. It said
> > "Not even her faintest shadow shows upon the river's face,
> > Only my swelling tears that no dam will keep back."'[23]

The scene is spiced with irony; for Ukifune, far from lying at the bottom of
Uji River, is safely ensconced in the next room, where she is eavesdropping
on the Captain's conversation.

                              *   *   *

Long as *The Tale of Genji* may be, it is the merest ant-hill in comparison
with the mountains of commentaries and scholarly studies that have grown
up about it. According to Professor Ikeda, more than ten thousand books
have been written about *The Tale of Genji*, not to mention innumerable
essays, monographs, dissertations, and the like; in addition there are several
Genji dictionaries and concordances, and hundreds of weighty works in
which Murasaki's novel has been used as material for the study of subjects
like Heian court ceremony and music. The basic textual commentary
belongs to the early thirteenth century and consisted of fifty-four ponderous
tomes, one for each of Murasaki's books; of these only a single volume is
extant. Subsequent commentaries were rarely less than a thousand pages
long; Ikeda's recent *Tale of Genji Encyclopaedia* has some 1,200 large, closely-
printed pages, of which about one hundred are devoted to listing earlier
commentaries. No other novel in the world can have been subjected to such
close scrutiny; no writer of any kind, except perhaps Shakespeare, can have
had his work more voluminously discussed than Murasaki Shikibu.

This flood of exegesis started about one generation after Murasaki's
death, when people were beginning to recognize certain difficulties in
understanding her novel. A good deal of the early work was aimed at pointing
out the overall unity of the fifty-four books. Genealogies were drawn up to

explain how closely the huge cast of characters were related to each other; the systematic sequence of events was demonstrated by means of elaborate chronologies. The next main task was to list the thousands of quotations and references to literature and history that occur throughout the novel. The role of quoted poems was recognized as particularly important in Murasaki's imagery. While civil war raged throughout Japan, many a medieval scholar spent his years patiently ferreting out poems in obscure anthologies or private collections from which Murasaki may have derived her quotations.

As the world of *The Tale of Genji* receded into the distant past, the language of the novel began to present ever greater difficulties. The first Genji dictionary dates from the fourteenth century, and much of the work during the Muromachi period was devoted to linguistic interpretation. The study of manuscripts and the comparison of different versions also became important, as scholars tried to establish a definitive text of the work. By now Genji scholarship had largely become the preserve of certain aristocratic families, and we are confronted with the strange tradition of secret commentaries and secret texts, which would be handed down in particular schools like precious heirlooms. Various 'Genji problems' were listed, and each school would have its own arcane interpretations, jealously guarded from other schools and imparted only to trusted disciples. A good deal of the effort of the medieval scholars was devoted to the exhilarating task of demolishing the work of rival groups.

One of the great centres of Genji studies was the 'southern court' in the richly blossomed hills of Yoshino, where during a good part of the fourteenth century a rival line of emperors maintained itself in opposition to the 'northern court' at Kyoto. Many of the 'southern' emperors were noted for their erudition in the field of Genji scholarship, which of course greatly added to its prestige. It became customary at Yoshino for groups of noble *cognoscenti* to meet in full court dress, often in the presence of the emperor, and for one of them to read aloud from the text, stopping occasionally to interpret an obscure passage or to expatiate on some literary subtlety.

The Yoshino scholars were mainly interested in *The Tale of Genji* as a work of art, whereas the groups in Kyoto tended to use it as a basis for linguistic and historical studies.[24] These two opposing trends have continued throughout the course of Genji scholarship, but the most valuable work, like that of the great nationalist scholars in the Tokugawa period, has always involved a blending of the 'literary' and the 'academic' approaches. The flow of both types of studies has continued unabated until the present day, and Professor Ikeda's voluminous work (both textual and interpretative) will undoubtedly rank among the most valuable in this field during the past eight centuries.

Confronted with this formidable mass of scholarly material, the reader sometimes feels that, far from helping him to enter into the delicate spirit of *The Tale of Genji*, it imposes a block between him and the original novel. Indeed, as one wades through some of the more turgid commentaries, one wonders whether they are not trying to open a fragile persimmon with a hydraulic drill. Of course it would be the height of churlishness to question the value of the work by these generations of patient scholars; without it the novel would be as impenetrable as an Easter Island inscription. But it is important to remember that Murasaki was an artist, not a chronicler (still less a scholar), and that *The Tale of Genji* must be enjoyed above all as a work of literature, not as a source of information.

To what extent can we really understand what she was writing about? It has sometimes been suggested that the modern Western reader is so divorced from Murasaki in time and space, in patterns of thought and expression, in custom and in sensibility, that she might as well have belonged to a different planet, and that what we derive from the work of this court lady of tenth-century Japan can be only the palest approximation of what she intended to convey. According to this argument, even the modern Japanese reader, the child of Westernized industrial society, is hardly less cut off from the world of the shining prince than we in the Occident.

I do not subscribe to this view. Indeed, it seems to me, one of the remarkable things about this novel of a millennium ago is how readily we can enter into the thoughts and feelings of its characters and respond to the total vision of life that its author communicated. The more we know about the times—social organization, religious ideas, marriage customs, literary conventions, and so forth—the greater our understanding will be. Yet, even with the most elementary knowledge of the Heian background, the sensitive reader can grasp the psychology of a character like Kaoru, for example, and appreciate the close connexion between beauty and sorrow that is an underlying theme of the novel.

Many things that seemed important to Murasaki (calligraphic skill, for instance, or the court hierarchy) have little relevance in the present day; yet, when it comes to vivifying a character by psychological detail, or using imagery to evoke the feelings that death can inspire, she seems close to us and 'modern' in a way that no previous writer of prose fiction can approach.

But is our present text of *The Tale of Genji* what Murasaki actually wrote? It is a complex matter and this is not the place to discuss it in any detail. The earliest extant manuscript dates from the middle of the twelfth century, over one hundred years after Murasaki was writing; it could hardly be more inaccurate and incomplete. Our first full text of the fifty-four books belongs to the fourteenth century, and varies in many ways from the manuscripts on which most modern texts are based.[25] The rival schools of medieval Genji scholars had their own texts, which they guarded like military secrets. It was not until relatively recent times that the various manuscripts could be correlated and compared for accuracy.

Considering this rather confused history and the difficulties of producing reliable copies of Japanese 'grass writing' script, we might expect the most bewildering discrepancies between the different versions. In fact a study of Ikeda's textual correlations suggests that they are remarkably close and that most of the differences are matters of detail which have little bearing on the overall content or significance of the novel. Of course such correlations do not tell us how faithful the texts are to the sentences that Murasaki committed to paper one thousand years ago. Failing a monumental literary discovery, this is something we shall never know. The consensus among modern Japanese scholars, however, is that the printed texts of *The Tale of Genji* may for all literary purposes be regarded as quite close to the original.[26]

The real barrier between the modern reader and *The Tale of Genji* is not any corruption of the text, nor any confusion of theme. It is a far more direct one: the difficulty of the language in which the novel is written. Since this language is virtually pure Japanese, one might expect that at least for Murasaki's countrymen it should present no insuperable hardships. The trouble is that during the past seven centuries both the literary and spoken languages of Japan have become so thoroughly impregnated with Chinese vocabulary and constructions (not to mention the recent flood of linguistic imports from the West) that Heian Japanese has become quite as remote as the Anglo-Saxon of *Beowulf* is for the average Englishman. Most people in Japan who read *The Tale of Genji* nowadays use the modern-language version by the eminent novelist, Tanizaki Junichirō; and some, including as prominent a literary man as Masamune Hakuchō, find Arthur Waley's translation more comprehensible than the original text.

The main trouble does not arise from the length and complexity of the sentences, nor from the massive agglutinative verb forms, the involved honorific usage, and the host of obscure particles. With a certain amount of patience we can work all this out systematically and remember it. What we can never hope to surmount is the fantastic lack of specificity in Heian writing. The Japanese language in general lacks the precision of which Chinese is capable and which is the glory of some Indo-European languages. But in the *kanabun* literature of the Heian period—including, alas, the work of Murasaki Shikibu—this obscurity can reach nightmare proportions. Proper names are rigorously avoided. Direct speech is common, but the speaker hardly ever indicated. As often as not we have to guess at the subject of the sentence, and sometimes the subject will change half-way through without any warning. The mutually exclusive categories that we take for granted in European languages—past and present tense, affirmation and question, singular and plural, male and female (as identified by personal names and pronouns), doubt and certainty—have little relevance in Heian Japanese; sometimes it is not even clear whether the sentence is positive or negative.

This reluctance to be specific, which has given so much trouble to commentators and readers of Heian literature, results partly from the intimate connexion between this literature and classical Japanese poetry—a poetry that is marked by extremely laconic wording and an overwhelming reliance on imagistic suggestion. It also results from the 'closed' nature of upper-class Heian society. The members of Murasaki's society always preferred the allusion to the statement, the hint to the explanation. This applies most conspicuously to poetry and poetic quotations, but it also affected their everyday speech, their occasional writings (diaries and notes), and the vernacular literature in which their lives were described. For people who live in a small, closed society, like that of the Heian court, the entire range of experience will be so familiar that the briefest hint will suffice to convey one's meaning, and any systematic exposition of one's thoughts is regarded as otiose, even boorish. Language becomes a sort of shorthand, immediately understood by those who are 'in', vague and slightly mysterious to the outsider. The same phenomenon can be found in almost any small, closed group, but in the court society of Heian Japan this economy of expression was carried to extraordinary lengths and profoundly influenced the literature, which was an intimate part of that society.

Another reason that Heian writing impresses the modern reader as being so vague is the poverty of the vocabulary that Murasaki and her colleagues had at their disposal. Like many languages in an early stage of development, tenth-century Japanese was endowed with an extremely rich grammatical apparatus but a relatively limited choice of words. This applies especially to abstract adjectives. The result is that certain words tend to be greatly overworked and to lose all precision of meaning. Modern English, of course, has its share of such words ('interesting', 'nice', 'good'), but the conscientious author uses them with the greatest caution. Heian writers, on the other hand, almost seem to revel in the repetition of the same emotive words, whose range of meaning is so widely and thinly spread as to make accurate communication impossible.[27] In the sentence on p. 282, for example, the word *ayashi* is used no less than three times, with the successive meanings of 'remarkable', 'outlandish', and 'disagreeable'. This by no means exhausts the possible translations of the word. Among its many other senses is 'absurd', and it is quite possible that this, rather than 'distasteful', is what

Murasaki intended here—a typical example of how lack of verbal specificity can obscure meaning for readers of a later age. I have chosen this particular sentence because it illustrates not only the repetition of words but many other characteristics of Heian literary style, and may suggest to what an extent Murasaki's language can act as a barrier to our understanding. It is not regarded as one of the difficult passages.

The scene is that in which Prince Niou secretly sets out for Uji to pay his first visit to Ukifune, whose charms have been vaguely reported to him by Kaoru. Since it was Kaoru who originally introduced him to the Uji household, he feels a certain compunction about seducing his friend's mistress—but not enough to deter him. A fairly literal translation will be followed by a more literary one; the words in square brackets are not in the original, but have to be added if we are to understand anything at all:

> 'recalling all sorts of things [and thinking] what an underhand thing this is to the person/people who joining [his/their] heart/hearts (*kokoro*) [with me] to a remarkable (*ayashiki*) extent led me and since even in the capital [he] was not under any circumstances able to go about indiscreetly without people/a person knowing wearing an outlandish (*ayashiki*) disguise and though the feelings [of him] who was on the horse were fearful and guilty since [his] heart (*kokoro*) was advanced in the inquisitive direction thinking as [he/they] came deep into the hills when how will it become to go back without even meeting would indeed be unsatisfying (? lonely) and disgraceful (? absurd = *ayashi*) [his] heart (*kokoro*) was stirred up'[28]

Out of this loose sequence of vague phrases, in which the subject is never once mentioned, and which of course has no punctuation whatsoever, the following emerges:

> 'Various thoughts occurred to Niou. He recalled how remarkably helpful Kaoru had been in introducing him to Uji in the first place. Even in the capital Niou was never in a position to come and go as he pleased without people knowing about it, and for this expedition he had put on an outlandish disguise. Now as he rode up to Uji his feelings of guilt towards Kaoru were mixed with a sense of fear. Yet his was an unusually inquisitive temperament, and as they came deeper into the hills he grew more and more excited. When would they arrive, he wondered, and how were things likely to turn out. Perhaps he would have to

go back to the capital without even having met Ukifune. How frustrating that would be-and what a disgrace!'

Heian style poses special problems for the translator. Should he try to stay close to the original Japanese and convey at least some of its imprecision to the Western reader? Or should he make everything as clear and specific as possible, interpreting (and if necessary reorganizing) the author's thoughts, as well as translating the words? In *The Tale of Genji*, as in all translation, it is a matter of striking the proper balance between the extremes. The two versions of the passage on p. 282, however, may suggest that any pedantic attempt at an 'accurate' translation is doomed to failure. One of the splendours of Murasaki's work is the beauty of its language, and, unless the translator is able to suggest this fact, he will not have done his job properly. Paradoxically this means that he must get away as far as possible from the original language and recast it in a style of his own that he considers appropriate to the work in question. In so doing he is bound to obscure the nature and the character of the original. But, when the main interest of the book is literary, an 'accurate' translation will obscure it in a far more damaging way-by making it unreadable.

Arthur Waley's version of *The Tale of Genji* represents the freest possible type of translation. Indeed the word 're-creation' would be more appropriate; for he has brought Murasaki's novel to life as a great work of English literature in its own right. As Waley himself has said, so much is inevitably lost in translating from classical Oriental literature that the translator must give a great deal in return. This is precisely what he has done in *The Tale of Genji*. Purists may object that in the process he has entirely changed the spirit of the original, in particular by making it all seem more modern and 'sophisticated' than it really is. I do not believe that a careful comparison with the Japanese text substantiates this view. Certainly Waley has played fast and loose with the structure of Murasaki's prose and, wherever necessary, has eked out the laconic wording of the original with explanatory phrases and sentences of his own. Yet often when one imagines that he has gone off entirely on his own tack, for instance by ascribing some improbably modern psychological motive to one of the characters, a comparison with the original will reveal that he has been scrupulously faithful to Murasaki's meaning.

Many aspects of Waley's technique will become clear if we compare his version of the passage on p. 282 with the other translations:

'It all seemed strangely familiar. Who was he with that second time? Why, of course, with Kaoru; and he became slightly

uncomfortable when he remembered all the trouble his friend
had taken to bring him and Kozeri together. "I am afraid he
would think this rather an odd way of repaying his kindness,"
Niou said to himself. Even in the Capital his position made it
extremely difficult for him to amuse himself as he chose, and he
was used to going about at night with the utmost secrecy. But the
present occasion demanded even greater precautions. He was
heavily disguised in clothes of a most awkward and unsightly
kind, and was compelled to sit for hours in the saddle—a thing he
particularly disliked. But he had a vast fund of curiosity, and as
they drew nearer and nearer to Uji his excitement became so
intense that he hardly noticed the tedious windings of the
mountain road. How was it going to turn out? Was it so certain
after all that it was his girl? However, that did not really matter.
He only wanted to know. But was that all? Certainly if she proved
to be someone different he would feel extremely flat on the way
home.'[29]

Waley's interpretation of the last part of the sentence is different from
that of the commentators on whom I have relied; but such is the nature of
the original that variants of this kind are all too possible. Leaving aside these
moot points of interpretation, we find that, while Waley could hardly be
more flexible in his handling of the original, he does not change its essential
meaning.

Does he improve on Murasaki's style? This of course is entirely a
matter of taste. Waley has produced a new style, totally unrelated to the
original, and it would be possible to prefer this style, just as some people
profess to find Wilhelm von Schlegel's German better than the English of
William Shakespeare. What is certain is that he has exploited Murasaki's
writing to the fullest possible advantage, making explicit the many subtle
psychological touches that are merely implied in the original. He has
changed the loose, meandering language of the Japanese into a precise and
limpid idiom, in which we need never stop to wonder about the identity of
the speaker or any of the other crucial points that Murasaki fails to specify.
The verbal monotony of the original has been overcome by using the
bounteous resources of modern literary English.

In doing all this Waley may have lost some of the poetry and the
particular charm of Murasaki's writing. In its place he has given us a text that
can be readily understood and appreciated for its own admirable style. And
it is thanks to this that Murasaki's novel, so long obscure even to its own
countrymen, has become one of the few great works of Oriental literature to

be widely known, and even read, in the West. Any attempt to reproduce the style of the original would almost certainly have made *The Tale of Genji* the preserve of the specialist—and he in any case could presumably read it in Japanese.

*   *   *

One question that has engaged the many generations of Genji scholars is the extent to which Murasaki derived her material from actual life. Should her novel be read as a *roman à clef* in which the characters represent people with whom she was personally acquainted or about whom she had heard? Successive commentators have had their pet theories about the models on whom Genji and the other principal figures are supposedly based. At least twenty people have been named as the source for Prince Genji alone. They include Ariwara no Narihira (the famous ninth-century poet, Adonis, and lover), Emperor Murakami, Sugawara no Michizane, and even such improbable candidates as Po Chü-i and the Duke of Chou.[30]

The main contender for the honour, however, is Michinaga's nephew, Korechika, the attractive young nobleman whose rapid rise in the world was followed by sudden disgrace and exile owing to the machinations of his Fujiwara enemies.[31]

When we come to the heroine of the novel, Murasaki, the obvious identification is with the writer herself. According to early commentators, they both had sensitive, retiring dispositions, both were plagued by disagreeable stepmothers—and above all they had the same name. The trouble with this theory is that the name 'Murasaki' was almost certainly applied to the writer because of the character in her novel, not vice versa. Besides, the Murasaki Shikibu we see in the diary is a very different person indeed from the sweet, gentle girl who figures as the main heroine of *The Tale of Genji*. What seems far more likely is that, in describing her fictional heroine, Murasaki Shikibu projects an ideal—the ideal of the type of woman she would have liked to be and, above all, of the sort of life she would have liked to lead. Prince Genji's lifelong devotion to the heroine also seems to belong to the realm of romantic idealization rather than to the harsh realities of polygamous society.

In discussing the art of fiction with Tamakazura, Genji makes a remark that throws some light on this question of models: 'I am quite sure,' he says, 'that the author does not write about specific people, giving all the circumstances of their actual lives.'[32] The trend among modern scholars has been to move away the simple type of correlation, according to which each character in the novel represents a single historical figure, and to substitute a more complicated system of sources. The character and life of Prince Genji, for example, are shown to be based on those of numerous eminent exiles of the Heian period: his good looks and attractive personality relate him to Korechika; his artistic skill, to the great Michizane; his family name, to Minamoto no Takaaki. In the later books the principal model for the hero may well have been the resplendent figure of Fujiwara no Michinaga himself.

A similar use of multiple models can be found in the case of Genji's pompous son, Yūgiri. So far as personality is concerned he appears to have been based on Michinaga's eldest son (whom Murasaki incidentally mentions in her diary as good potential material for a character in a novel),[33] but his career is closer to that of the younger son.[34]

Although a few of the minor figures in *The Tale of Genji*, especially certain ladies-in-waiting and priests, may have had single, specific models, it is likely that the principal characters are based on a variety of people whom Murasaki had known or heard about, and that often she may not have been aware of these sources. Conversely, several aspects of a single historical person, Michinaga, for example, may have been applied to different characters in the book. The creation of people in fiction is far from being the mechanical process that some commentators and critics seem to suggest. In Murasaki's novel, as in Proust's, it is surely a mistake to identify single individuals as the sources for any of the important characters. In so far as there were models they were almost always composite.[35]

Scholars have also found a number of events in *The Tale of Genji* that appear to be taken directly from actual happenings at court. Genji's exile is given as an example, but, since this was a fairly common form of punishment in Murasaki's time, it is hard to relate it to any particular historical case. The more specific correlations usually refer to somewhat trivial particulars—the Emperor's eye trouble in Book 14, for example, and the details of the ceremony of presenting swords on the Princess' birthday.[36] There are also some entries in Murasaki's diary describing actual events that later find their way into the novel. These too are rather insignificant. A description of an incense competition in Book 32 is closely parallel to one in the diary (summer of 10008), and Tō no Chūjō's amazement at finding his daughter asleep in the middle of the day (snoozing was frowned on in aristocratic circles) appears to echo Murasaki's own shock when she comes on a friend of hers indulging in a noonday nap.

There is a more important question than that of specific models for characters and events: does *The Tale of Genji* as a whole present a reasonably faithful picture of Heian society? If we are using Murasaki's novel as a source of social history, the question becomes crucial.

The first point is that the people in *The Tale of Genji* represent only a minute percentage of the inhabitants of tenth-century Japan. With few exceptions they belong to the aristocracy, who numbered a few thousand out of a population of several million. Their lives were as remote from those of the common people as is a Maharaja's from that of an untouchable. A modern scholar (a Russian as it chances) has emphasized the contrast between the elegant luxury in the urban court circles and the poverty and barbarism that prevailed elsewhere in Heian Japan. He compares the flourishing, beautifully planned city of Heian Kyō with the primitive settlements in the provinces, the glittering mansions with the squalid huts, the lofty learning and the exquisite works of art with the bestial ignorance and the primitive household utensils, the magnificent tree-lined avenues with the rough tracks that served for transport in the countryside.[37] He has no doubt exaggerated the splendour of life in the capital by accepting the contemporary idealizations at face value. Yet on the whole his contrast is valid, and we must never forget that what Murasaki describes in her novel was almost totally inapplicable to the vast majority of the population.

Besides, even the aristocratic world is not fully described. Hardly anything is said about affairs of state and politics, let alone about the economic activities that permitted this class to maintain its power. (In exactly what form did they extract income from their land, for instance, and how much did they pay their retainers?)

In short, Murasaki's interest is almost exclusively focused on the private, emotional, and aesthetic lives of a select group of aristocrats. She would no more have thought of entering into the feelings of a peasant than would a novelist nowadays try to describe what a horse or a cow was thinking; and to discuss the economic life of her people would have seemed as preposterous as for a modern writer to give details about his characters' thymol turbidity.

Far from regretting this, however, we should be grateful that in her novel she did not venture into realms about which she and her female contemporaries could have little reliable information. Murasaki wrote about the sides of life that she knew from her own direct experience; and, if the result is a one-sided representation of a period, so is that of a great modern author like Proust.

Making allowance for a certain measure of idealization, especially in the depiction of a character like Prince Genji, we can be fairly confident that what *The Tale of Genji* does describe it describes realistically. There is no discrepancy between the image that the novel gives us and what we know of contemporary conditions from chronicles, diaries, and other sources. With immense care and detail Murasaki depicts the world as she saw it. She tells us, for instance, exactly what it was like to be a jealous woman in a polygamous society where jealousy was the most scorned of all emotions, and what a sensitive man might experience when confronted with the demands of his various wives. Her novel does not attempt to give a full picture of a period (few successful novels do); but it does provide an authentic picture of a beautiful and most intriguing world.

NOTES

1. See Appendix 4.

2. These identifications are often extremely complicated. Murasaki does not mar her novel by periodically referring to dates, ages, etc. On the other hand, as Motoori points out in *Genji Monogatari Tama no Ogushi* (pp. 531–63), it appears that in each book she deliberately introduced certain events that can be situated in point of time, usually by reference to the age of the hero. This aspect of her work has been exhaustively examined by Japanese scholars, and most of the standard commentaries contain detailed chronological charts (e.g. Part III of Motoori, op. cit.).

3. Once Hachirō finds that the novel falls into six sub-divisions:

(i)	Books	1–7	Genji's life until he is 19;
(ii)	"	8–13	his disgrace and downfall;
(iii)	"	14–33	his recall to the capital; the splendour of Genji's life reaches its apex;
(iv)	"	34–41	the decline of Genji's fortunes, owing to a series of emotional shocks (Nyosan's seduction, Murasaki's death, etc.);
(v)	"	42–49	introduction to Kaoru and Niou;
(vi)	"	50–54	Ukifune's appearance on the scene and the tragic rivalry for her affections.

Within each of these sub-divisions there is a definite sequence of events running from book to book, even though there may be time-gaps between the books; and in each case there is a break in the action between one sub-division and the next. Onoe Hachirō, N.B.T. ed. of *Genji Monogatari*, vi. 20–23.

4. N.B.T. ed., vi. 116–17.

5. Thus, according to Baron Suematsu, the real purpose of *The Tale of Genji* is 'to portray the different shades of female characters, as set forth in [the judgement on a Rainy Night] and thereby to show the fickleness and selfishness of man'. Suematsu Kencho, *The Romance of Genji*, Introduction. And so we have yet another 'motive' for Murasaki's novel.

6. Cf. E. M. Forster: '... whereas the story appeals to our curiosity and the plot to our intelligence, the pattern appeals to our aesthetic sense, it causes us to see the book as a whole.' Because of its patterns even a vast, rambling novel like Proust's has an unmistakable unity: 'The book is chaotic, ill constructed, it has ... no external shape; and yet it hangs together because it is stitched internally, because it contains rhythms.' *Aspects of the Novel*, pp. 138, 151.

7. N.B.T. ed., vii. 153–4. The repetition of this particular pattern was emphasized by traditional Genji scholars as an example of the moral intention of the work (the theme of karma and retribution). Motoori indignantly countered their view and insisted that Murasaki's aim was to describe the sense of *mono no aware*, which emerges most poignantly in unhappy love-affairs of this kind. Motoori Norinaga, op. cit., p. 516.

8. N.B.T. ed., v. 88 and vii. 669.

9. See pp. 113–14.

10. E.g. N.B.T. ed., vii. 675, 710, 759.

11. Ibid., pp. 399–400.

12. Ibid., p. 436.

13. Ibid., p. 463. This is a curious use of imagery; I have given a literal translation of *mizu no oto ni nagaresou kokochi shitamau.*

14. Ibid., p. 491.

15. Ibid., p. 492.

16. Ibid., p. 710. The poem contains a conventional play on words: *nagami* = (i) long rains, (ii) lost in thought; *harenu* = (i) does not clear up (of rain), (ii) gloomy, doleful.

17. Listed among the love poems later included in the *Shinchokusen* anthology. Later when Ukifune disappears her attendants find a letter that she has written to Niou, and from the single word *majiranaba* ('if it were to merge') recognize the Floating Boat poem and realize that she must have drowned herself. Such were the advantages of knowing one's poetry.

18. N.B.T. ed., vii. 715–16.

19. Loc. cit.

20. Ibid., p. 732.

21. Ibid., p. 740.

22. Ibid., p. 758.

23. Ibid., p. 831.

24. Ikeda Kikan, *Genji Monogatari Kōza.*

25. The two main textual traditions are the *Kawachi Bon*, on which the earliest complete extant manuscript (the *Hirase Bon*) is based, and the *Aobyōshi Bon* (Blue Cover Copy), which is the source of most modern printed texts. Both date from the early 13th century. Ikeda has provided an exhaustive 8-volume correlation of the various texts: *Genji Monogatari Taisei.*

26. Oka, op. cit., p. 560.

27. Typical words of this kind are *aware, kokorobososhi, okashi* (Sei Shōnagon's favourite), *warinashi, namamekashi, kuchioshi.* This tendency has not entirely disappeared from modern literature, and is one of the less fortunate legacies of classical Japanese.

28. N.B.T. ed., vii. 23–24. Throughout the novel Murasaki deliberately varies the length of her sentences. This rather long one is followed by a simple sentence of about a dozen words. (See also p. 119, n. 1.)

29. Arthur Waley, *The Bridge of Dreams*, pp. 128–9.

30. Ikeda Kikan, 'Genji Monogatari' in *Nihon Bungaku Daijiten.*

31. See Appendix 4 and pp. 56–59.

32. N.B.T. ed., vi. 261.

33. Ibid., ed., iii. 269.

34. Tezuka Noboru, 'Genji Monogatari no Moderu' in *Kokugo to Kokubungaku,* i (no. 1), 12–31 and (no. 2) 19–44.

35. Mr. Painter's conclusions about the models for characters in *A la recherche du temps perdu* apply remarkably well to *The Tale of Genji.* George Painter, *Marcel Proust,* Vol. I. He finds numerous models for most of Proust's main characters. Baron de Charlus, for example, is related to Baron Doasan, Aimery de la Rochefoucauld, Robert de Montesquiou, and Prince Boson de Sagan. Conversely a single real person may become the basis for more than one character in the novel, e.g. Madame Émile Strauss (née Halévy) for Duchesse de Guermantes *and* Odette Swann, Madeleine Lemaire for Madame Verdurin *and* Madame de Villeparisis.

36. Ikeda, loc. cit.

37. N. I. Konrad, *Yaponskaya Literatura v Obraztsakh i Ocherkakh,* 1. 38.

H. RICHARD OKADA

Speaking For:
Surrogates *and* The Tale of Genji

I begin this discussion of surrogates in *The Tale of Genji* and what I shall call the problematic of "speaking for" with two questions. The first is one posed, seemingly ages ago, by Roland Barthes, who asked, "Where does the writing begin? Where does the painting begin?" The second is one Edward Said asked more recently: "Who speaks? For what and for whom?"[1] The two questions trace a movement from a perspective in which the subject was removed, to a postcolonial one, in which it takes center stage, figuring a mode of questioning that retains its cogency today. The heritage of the missing subject and the question of agency were problematic in so-called poststructuralist analyses, which were assailed for an inability (if not an alleged outright refusal) to address urgent historical or political concerns as they sought to displace traditional notions, for example, of a transcendental "I." The critique of "Orientalist" discourse inaugurated by Said, in its interrogation of how subjects remain disempowered to enunciate and narrate, remains not only salutary but also absolutely crucial in a postfeminist, postcolonial, post–Cold War world.

It might be argued that Barthes's intuition of Japan as a "country of writing," or "empire of signs," retains a certain relevancy for a nation with putatively noncentered gardens, meals, and cities, where the wrapper, the mask, the clothing constitute the "message." "Japan" has also been read as a

From *Crossing the Bridge: Comparative Essays on Medieval and Heian Japanese Women Writers.* © 2000 by Barbara Stevenson and Cynthia Ho.

nation where one's various "positions"—social, marital, scholastic, occupational, etc.—seem constitutive of selfhood, where the Western advocacy of essentialized selves gives way to selves determinable by sites of occupancy. Barthes's gaze, however, does not extend to a study of subject position or the gender of the observer, the manipulator of the signs and the masks, nor does it engage in a meaningful way with the questions of how, by whom, when, and for what purpose Japan has been constructed as possessing those characteristics. In an essay on the puppet theater, for example, Barthes registers only the (Bunraku) master's exposed, "civic" face, which to him signifies an "exemption from meaning."[2] Such easy removal of manipulators from the spheres of meaning exposes the mechanisms to various manipulations: by Western scholarship that, accountable to nothing outside of a deep-seated, institutionalized need for rational and ethical consistency, can assume the master's place and speak for, that is, appropriate for its own purposes, the eminently detachable Japanese signs.[3] It is at those moments of Western appropriation that Said's questions return to haunt the writer of Empire of Signs.

In contrast to Barthes, Said has been concerned with "representation," not only as a mimetic question but as one anchored firmly in the critique of historico-political imperatives of European national construction and imperialist expansion. The issues Said raises in a more recent work like *Culture and Empire* revolve around the notions of "interdependence" and what he calls the "contrapuntal," taken from his extensive knowledge of and experience with music.[4] In other words, the study of what we normally refer to as "literature," and in particular the "novel," ought not to be embarked upon under the common aegis of hermetic, literary categories, but those categories must be seen in their interrelation to such questions as power, empire, and geography. The exclusions that have been systematically carried out within institutionalized, scholarly investigations must be reexamined. Those factors that have been excluded, then, when given proper voice, would form contrapuntal moments to the work of mainstream scholarship.

Revisionist readings of exclusionary maneuvers are, of course, also at the heart of certain feminist critiques of patriarchy, for the study of how the non-West is positioned in Eurocentric discourse is analogous in many ways to how "women" are positioned in patriarchal discourses. As subservient nodes mappable on a Self–Other paradigm, both have been exploited and marginalized, sacrificed for interests other than their own. We must also remember that despite the compelling analogies, feminist criticism has not always (although things have changed drastically in the past few years) attended sufficiently to questions of race and ethnicity; conversely, analyses of race, ethnicity, and the nation-state have not always attended to questions of gender. The predominant feminist subject position has often been that of the white, middle-class woman, whereas minority or ethnic writers have often ignored questions of "women," or "woman," and of gender. The problems involved in thinking feminist and postcolonial (and postmodern) critiques in tandem are many and difficult. The growing list of writers who have addressed the question include Judith Butler, Rey Chow, Diana Fuss, Chandra Mohanty, Biddy Martin, Trinh T. Minh-ha, Craig Owen, Linda Nicholson, Denise Riley and, of course, Gayatri Spivak (the list goes on).

One important question taken up by feminist writers is the problem of negotiating the terms "woman" and "women." The simple acknowledgment of gender is insufficient because that move is complicit with a tendency to group all women, no matter of what country or time period, together and then to characterize them, often condescendingly, as "oppressed," "victimized," etc. Chandra Mohanty is one who has alerted us to the difficulties and dangers in her now classic essay, "Under Western Eyes."[5] In Japan, where *The Tale of Genji* has received, albeit primarily through male appropriations, attention similar to what readers in the West accord a sacred text, authorial gender almost never plays an operative role in the countless commentaries and analyses on the text. One Japanese scholar has suggestively argued that perhaps the multiauthor (and different gender) thesis—for example, that the last third of the narrative was written by a man, perhaps Marusann Shikibu's father—results from the fact that scholars could not bring themselves to believe that a woman had written the *Genji* text all by herself.[6] He is the exception, however. The more prevalent view is represented by comments that feminism in the West was a necessary result of women having been downtrodden for centuries, whereas feminism is precluded in Japan because the grand works by Heian women have always been treasured by Japanese scholars!

In any case, as Mohanty and others like Judith Butler and Denise Riley argue, the category "women" is not a prediscursive, universalizable entity but must be negotiated as something more like a discursive effect, which means that in each case "women" must be situated, not necessarily or solely in its/their own historical context, since the accessibility and reproduction of such a "context" is extremely problematic, but rather within a theoretically informed reading that takes as its inaugural moment the constructedness of all so-called historical representations. As Riley states, "... 'women' is historically, discursively constructed, and always relatively to other categories which themselves change; 'women' is a volatile collectivity in which female persons can be very differently positioned, so that the apparent continuity of the subject of 'women' isn't to be relied on; ... for the individual, 'being a woman' is also inconstant, and can't provide an ontological foundation."[7] Following those initial insights, we must also account, in a serious way, for the necessary and fundamental intervention of the analytical present and for the subject position of the observer, who must then divest herself/himself of the illusion of standing at a neutral or Archimedian point, ontologically based (or biased), outside either the discourse in question or the putative object of knowledge that the discourse itself has constructed.[8]

SURROGATES, "SPEAKING FOR," AND SCHOLARSHIP

If we refuse to subscribe to the notion of "objective" or neutral, Archimedian stances of research, the question of "speaking for" and of the "surrogate," a particular point of emphasis in what follows, should be a constantly troubling one for anyone engaged in scholarly studies. Let us return to the most recognizable aspect of the problem famously characterized by Edward Said as a condition of representative modes known as "Orientalism."[9] The West deemed it necessary to speak for (represent) the East since the latter was thought to be incapable of speaking for (representing) itself.[10] Beyond the "Orientalist" framework per se, in virtually every case where one person or group speaks for another person or group, the question ought to be a crucial one. It goes to the heart, for example, of studies involving gender (men speaking for women), ethnicity (dominant groups speaking for minority groups), theory (Marxist thinkers speaking for the "masses"), and scholarship in general (scholars speaking for their objects of study).

In post–World War II Japan studies, scholars have rarely attended to the problems involved in Western interpretations of Japan, where Orientalist paradigms have at times been strong.[11] Japanologists confidently spoke for Japan to such an extent that it is believed that the first Nobel prize in literature for that country would not have gone to Kawabata Yasunari in 1968 had it not been for the work of his able translator and spokesperson, Edward Seidensticker. More recently, in the economic world the phrase, "the Japan that can say no," seems to indicate that things have fundamentally changed, that Japan now has a true voice, can speak for itself, so that concern about Japan's ability to speak in any other realm (cultural, political, historical) is even less necessary that it was before. Such an optimistic diagnosis, however, overlooks the fact that the phrase fixes Japan's position as primarily one of negative reaction (a kind of power often accorded to women), a dynamic in which power still remains situated in the "outside," the West.

In this essay, I shall focus on the act and position of "speaking for," as it concerns the crucial role of narrators and "surrogates" in/of *The Tale of Genji*, keeping in mind its significance for scholarly stances in general, and as it relates to my own analytical position. I would argue, first of all, in what might seem a contradictory gesture given what I've stated above, that the concern for giving the other/native a true or proper voice is misguided at best. As critiques of so-called cross-cultural analysis suggest, the very framework of the cross-cultural installs two positivities between which the researcher apparently is freely able to "cross." The installation of two positivities, however, effects the simultaneous construction of two identities that are ahistorical and monolithic, self-identical each to itself, with each possessing its own distinctive characteristics. To be attentive to "speaking for" and to surrogates should not, then, result in the search for ways to give the other a true voice but to recognize that, in an important sense, there is only ever "speaking for." When a native Japanese scholar produces an interpretation of a *Kokinshū* poem or a *Genji* passage, for example, rather than speaking authentically for "Japan," it might very well be the case that the person is speaking just as much for his/her training in Western poetics and criticism. Similarly, the status of the researcher who is supposedly able bidirectionally to traverse two reified entities must be tirelessly questioned.

What we need, then, might be called "positional" readings that would add to Said's questions—"Who speaks? For what and for whom?" which are, after all, an asking after surrogates—a chronotopic and geopolitical query: that is, "Where and at what point in time is the speaker/researcher situated?" when the act of "speaking for" is performed. The aim would be, for example, to complement the need to historicize modernist readings of premodern texts with the impulse to demystify the possibility of any neutral or detached position that can truly speak for itself.

SURROGATES AND *THE TALE OF GENJI*

Relevant to the matter at hand, the issues raised by the one who "speaks for" in the *Genji* text often involves the question of the surrogate, which is always marked by the sign of "fiction": critical, genealogical, historical, or otherwise. The term "surrogate" embraces the *Genji* narrators who speak for the author as well as for the vast number of attendants and other intermediaries who facilitated the smooth functioning of Heian aristocratic society, the broader kinship networks and their relation to power and desire, and such familial, privatized (or otherwise construable as feminist) matters like motherhood and reproduction. Such attention to the surrogate would move us beyond an initial, important awareness of the author's gender and attempt to read it against the following: the imperial salons in which learned women like Murasaki Shikibu served and tutored their mistresses and recited and wrote their narratives—that is, their privileged spaces and special statuses deriving from their function as special attendants to their mistresses (empresses or other high-ranking royal women); their daily responsibilities as verbal/scriptive intermediaries—they often composed poems and messages on behalf of their patrons and acquaintances; their emergence out of the middle ranks (that is, fifth and sixth out of eight bureaucratic ranks) of officialdom; their unofficially acquired learning; their inferable views of the disaffected level of royalty called the "Genji," the dominant Fujiwara clan (Northern Branch), the imperial household, and their own social class. As a counterpoint to their unquestioned privilege, it would also begin to investigate the ways in which they were forced to sacrifice themselves for the welfare of their family lineages, the extent of their knowledge and awareness of the political world around them, and their feelings of sympathy for other disaffected members of society, including those former members of royalty, the "Genji," and those political figures sent into exile.

"Speaking for" in Heian Japan

Talented and learned women like Murasaki Shikibu, Sei Shōnagon, and Izumi Shikibu went to the palace as tutors and attendants to high-ranking women.[12] Born into illustrious scholarly families, they had access to great funds of learning and knowledge. While in court service and at other times, they were called upon, perhaps on a daily basis, to compose poems and letters for their mistresses, and they wrote texts that later were viewed as epitomizing the flowering of Heian (read "native" as opposed to Chinese) culture.[13] In an important sense, these women have been made by later writers (mostly male) to speak for (or, in a positivist mode that still dominates much academic thinking, "reflect") a culture that is assumed to have been always in place even though what they are actually speaking for are their newly forged cultural creations, certain political figures (political and otherwise) with whom they sympathized, as well as their ability to speak in the first place. Moreover, the practice of adopting males to carry on a paternal lineage is common throughout Japanese history. The Fujiwara, other hegemons, and leaders of artistic schools (tea, flower arrangement, etc.) regularly resorted to male adoption to maintain their family lineages, as many people still do so today. My point here is that adoption involves the insertion of a "fictional" sign, a surrogate, that displaces a "natural" order. Those same hegemons, moreover, rather than seize power directly, elected to rule through surrogates in the form of a son, for the most part, of the imperial family. Finally, in terms of the role of mothers, it was common practice for Heian families to hire wet nurses who became surrogate mothers to the newborn children.

The logic of the surrogate, therefore, thoroughly subtends Heian society and also the *Genji* text with its narrating in a "woman's hand."[14] Exploration of the surrogate should enable us to interconnect the complexities that arise at the intersections of the narrating, the represented narration, and the social class of the narrators, who serve as authorial surrogates. Such a reading should also begin to displace major male figures like Genji and Kaoru from positions of centrality accorded them by a received, masculinist scholarly tradition (both Japanese and Western), as well as the position of the neutral researcher installed in patriarchally oriented scholarship.[15] It would also inhabit the oxymoron that the empowerment of Heian salon women must only be a strategic and contingent one and, as one byproduct, the Genji figure would come to seem less the grand or romanticized male, the heartthrob of Heian women, than as a contingent representation who can only move "forward" in the text with the aid of female surrogates who "serve" (in all senses of the word) to put him in his place(s). Finally, the manner in which we address the issue can enable us to displace the self–other binarism in cross-cultural study mentioned above and figure our objects of study in a nonimperializing, nontotalizing manner.

It would not at all be difficult to demonstrate that the depiction of the Shining Genji is a far cry from the heroic, saviorlike way that many writers have preferred to describe him. Indeed, Genji's actions are more bumbling, blind, mistake-ridden than genuinely solicitous, heroic, or "ideal."[16] In keeping with the theoretical positions discussed above, such a demonstration of the displacement of Genji and other male figures should not involve a counter-installation of the women (whether main character or intermediary) as central or powerful but rather the move ought to mark, among other things, the congruence or convergence of subject positions of author with her chosen narrators and also with my own observational stance(s) in relation to the representations effected by the text. On the one hand, for example, the privilege of the Heian middle-rank women and my privilege as a university professor are not incidental; on the other hand, the author's, the narrator(s)'s, and my own positions of analysis (in my case, furthermore, as an Asian-American male) are inscribed by marginality. There are, of course, important differences, such as the sacrifices Heian women were forced to make for the sake of their family lineages and their mode of writing. The following will trace the act of speaking for and the role of surrogate at different registers in the text.

A SURROGATE WRITING MODE

The phonetic mode of writing known as *kana* (syllabic symbols derived from Chinese characters to write the Japanese language) was explicitly distinguished from the *kanbun* (which included Chinese as used in China and Japanese versions of Chinese) mode; the latter, both masculine and foreign, was considered to be, ironically, the marked mode. The *kana* mode was gendered feminine and referred to as *onna-de*, "woman's hand," although men also used it extensively.[17] The unprecedented situation enabled women, especially those from middle-rank families, to represent themselves in a "hand" ceded to them, what at first glance appears as a kind of *écriture féminine*, often misleadingly associated with Luce Irigaray, Julia Kristeva, and Hélène Cixous.[18] The fact that Heian sociopolitical power was wielded by male members of a certain branch of the Fujiwara clan and other important realms of male domination should immediately temper any overreading of the ultimate political and other effects of the woman's hand for Heian times, yet it undoubtedly allowed Heian women a degree of freedom and confidence of representation in contrast to the *kanbun* mode, and in a manner vastly different from the French feminist theorists', or my own, relation to Western patriarchal discourse. Furthermore, it is significant for what follows that the Japanese term *ka-na* derives from *kari-na*, which means "temporary, provisional, or nonregular name," and comes to designate explicitly a system of phonetic symbols taken to "temporarily stand-in," that is, be surrogates for, something else; Chinese characters, on the other hand, were designated as *ma-na*, or "real or regular name." While the surrogate condition would hold true for either case, *ka-na* or *ma-na*, the former makes explicit the fundamentally surrogate function of writing itself.

SURROGATE NARRATING

At a broader level of narration, a surrogate movement with far-reaching consequences can be found in *The Tale of Genji* in the second chapter, "The Broom-tree." In the famous section known as "The rainy night critique of ranks," four young men (Genji and three cohorts) are fortuitously brought together owing to a directional taboo, and they use the occasion to discuss the merits and demerits of women. Most scholars focus on what the men's speech takes as its object—women, their qualities, and their classifiability into three ranks—but a narratologically and gender-informed reading might trace the more complex network that comprises author, narrator, the narrating men, and their primary objects, all of which are, of course, the effects of discursive representations. The narrator places men in her own subject position as surrogate narrators, as we can infer from the text that the narrating act is the proper domain of women. As I've argued elsewhere, the at times inflated disquisitions of the men do not end in closure, and the men fail at their avowed goal of drawing clear distinctions, especially concerning women of the middle rank, which is the rank of the author, the narrators, and their listening colleagues, the last being most likely a primary audience for the tale.[19] Due to the resulting gaps and disjunctions, humor and irony are prevalent throughout the "critique." Genji himself remains silent, even falling asleep or pretending to at one point, and is in fact objectified and even feminized as he becomes the focus of the other men's gazes, which in turn become the focus of the gazes of the narrator and her assumed colleagues. The objectification of Genji stands in contrast to the staged inability of the male narrators to achieve their goal of defining unequivocally the ideal middle-rank woman, whom we can take to represent (speak for) the women controlling the narrative in the first place. The male narrations, then, as they demonstrate the difficulty men have of "speaking for" the women, also serve to valorize the *Genji* mode itself that is, narrating [*monogatari*] as a surrogate mode that pursues (indeed, is destined only to pursue) but cannot achieve closure.

The extended instance of surrogate narrating in the "Broom-tree" chapter, then, provides a counterpoint to and a displacement of the narrating in the first chapter, "The Paulownia Court." Whereas the latter presents a "beginning" based on the representation of a "natural" birth—that is, Genji's—the former creates figures out of a surrogate narrating that enact the displacement of the "natural" (regarding births and other matters) with ones fashioned out of language and narration, a narrating that plants figural seeds whose effects will be disseminated throughout the narrative and continually displace the Shining Genji whose fictional status, as we now see, is an already displaced one early in the tale. The men's speech, realized in *kana* narration, is further displaced by that scriptive mode that, as noted above, itself already enacts displacement. The displacement enacted by the second chapter, moreover, does not simply overturn what had occurred in the first chapter. Genji's mother, for example, is soon replaced by Fujitsubo, a stepmother who becomes a lasting obsession for Genji. The narrative, then, while inaugurating the first "step" relationship in the text, also puts into play a concomitant desire for the person who occupies the surrogate position. It demonstrates that at the "origin" there is already a powerful displacement at work through the figure of the surrogate and that the surrogate can be a prime focus of desire.

SURROGATE RELATIONS

Let us now keep in mind the question of the author's social position and her mode of writing, and further problematize the issue by considering the dizzyingly complex "step–," "foster–," or otherwise surrogate and substitutive positions (stepfather/mother, foster daughter, etc.) found in the narrative. A sampling of examples of step– or surrogate relations involving most of the major characters produces the following: Fujitsubo is stepmother to Genji, Koremitsu's mother is surrogate mother (as his wet nurse) to Genji, Utsusemi [Lady of the Locust-shell] is stepmother to the Governor of Kii, Genji is stepfather (and stepmother) to Murasaki, Ukon is surrogate mother to Yūgao [Evening Faces], Yūgao's wet nurse is stepmother to Tamakazura, Genji is stepfather to Akikonomu (the Rokujō Lady's daughter), Genji is surrogate "father" to Tamakazura, Princess Ōmiya (Tō no Chūjō's mother) is surrogate mother to Yūgiri (Genji's son by his official wife, the Aoi Lady), the Orange Blossoms Lady is surrogate mother to Yūrigi, Murasaki is surrogate mother to the Akashi Princess, the Reizei emperor is surrogate father to Kaoru, a wet nurse is surrogate mother to Kashiwagi, Jijū is surrogate mother to the Third Princess, Bennokimi is surrogate mother to Ōkimi[20] and Nakanokimi, the Hitachi Governor is stepfather to Ukifune, the Uji nun is surrogate mother to Ukifune. One category of surrogate characters crucial to the *Genji* text and embedded in the above list is that of wet nurses and their own offspring, who are raised together with their charges. Important ones include Koremitsu's mother (Koremitsu is Genji's closest attendant), Yūgao's nurse, Kashiwagi's nurse, Jijū [Third Princess's nurse], and Bennokimi. Admittedly, the practice of enlisting wet nurses was so common among Heian aristocrats that their pervasive presence should come as no surprise. The extent to which they are made to function narratologically in *Genji* is remarkable, however.

The above ought to show that something more than coincidence is at work insofar as virtually all the important characters in the narrative are associated in some fashion with surrogate positions. The resulting deflection away from blood ties to surrogate or foster ones embeds, it can be argued, a posture of critique: of officially arranged marriages (which, with one exception—the Uji Eighth Prince—does not produce harmonious relations), of motherhood as defined by Heian aristocratic society, and of the very maintenance of house lineages themselves.

MURASAKI

Symptomatic is the case of Murasaki. Easily misrecognized by readers who tend to romanticize her as part of an ideal Genji–Murasaki pair, she is actually represented as the victim of a series of deprivations, among the most important being the early loss of her mother, separation from her father, and the inability to bear children. As if mimicking her already surrogate marital status, she is allowed only the position, albeit an important one, of foster mother, for the Akashi Princess and her son, Genji's grandson, Niou. As she raises her charges, she must continually experience pain for the sake of the male Genji's own fortunes.

The inverse of Murasaki's position is represented by the "real" mothers who are prevented from "mothering": Genji's mother, Yūrigi's mother (Genji's official wife), the Akashi Lady, Yūgao, the Third Princess, the Eighth Prince's wife, and so on. Their situations, in which the "real" or "natural" is effectively displaced, undermine attempts to establish a biologically determinate ground for women. For the narrators of the tale, as for many modern feminists, a critique and demystification of motherhood as a woman's "natural" domain or function can be taken as a focal point of the narrative. The narrators negotiate a space where the problematic of the surrogate can be deployed to name the displaced blood ties that intertwine continually with fictional and political concerns and intertexts.

HIKARU GENJI

Now we can reexamine the character of Hikaru Genji. As mentioned above, Genji is not only deprived of his royal status but is also left motherless. Fujitsubo fills the maternal gap when she becomes his stepmother, although a rhetorical movement also constructs them *like* sister and brother (another rhetorical move had constructed Fujitsubo *like* Genji's mother, the Kiritsubo Consort, for whom she, Fujitsubo, becomes a surrogate).[21] In accord with the Heian practice of assigning wet nurses to children, Genji is placed in the care of Koremitsu's mother. The two surrogate mothers then serve two narrative purposes.

First, Koremitsu's mother provides a narrative link to another character when Genji pays a visit to her when she is ill, because it is then that he meets Yūgao, "Evening Faces," who was introduced earlier in the narrative by Tō no Chūjō's rainy night narrating mentioned above, and who happens to be residing temporarily next door to Genji's ailing nurse. A woman who has lost both parents, Yūgao soon dies of a mysterious spirit possession while with Genji and leaves behind a daughter also mentioned by Tō no Chūjō. Since she is living in the western half of the capital (*nishi no kyō*) with Yūgao's wet nurse, the child's whereabouts are unknown to Genji. He recruits Ukon, Yūgao's attendant, for his own entourage at the Nijo Mansion as a kind of keepsake (surrogate) for her mistress. Ukon is the daughter of another of Yūgao's wet nurses and a surrogate sister to her; she is the one who will recognize the daughter many years later. We will learn at that time that the girl, Tamakazura, had remained in the care of her mother's nurse when the woman accompanied her husband to his new post as junior Assistant Governor-General of Dazaifu in Tsukushi (present-day Kyushu).[22]

Second, Genji's other stepmother, Fujitsubo, provides a link to Murasaki when Genji's desire for this other surrogate mother takes the form of a transference of that desire to her niece. Like Genji, Murasaki, who is often considered the major female character in the narrative, is motherless and has been abandoned by her father, Fujitsubo's brother, a prince who will be continually on opposite political sides to Genji. When Genji first espies the niece, she is still a child in the care of a surrogate, her maternal grandmother. After learning of her relation to Fujitsubo and encouraged by her close physical resemblance to his surrogate mother, Genji abducts her just as her father is about to reclaim her. Intent on molding her, Galatea-like, according to his wishes as he learned from his friends during that rainy-night conversation, he first makes her his foster daughter; then, after she grows up a bit, he forces himself on her and makes her one of his wives. Murasaki thus becomes a surrogate for her aunt, just as the aunt was a surrogate for Genji's mother. Fashioned according to a masculinist ideal, she is forced to "speak for" women who are victims of male desire. She is not Genji's official wife (she can't displace Yūrigi's mother, the Aoi Lady) but rather a sign of the fictive, educated (that is, created) by Genji to be his ideal partner, despite her "secondary" status.[23] She is also destined continually to be displaced by other women in Genji's amorous affairs: Oborozukiyo, the Akashi Lady, the Third Princess, etc. As if abiding by a logic that prevents two motherless characters from having children, Genji and Murasaki are fated to be a childless couple. While it is possible to read their childless condition in a romanticized manner as a sign of the intensification of their mutual "love," the text makes it clear that Murasaki's childless state frees her to perform her all-important surrogate role. The devastating consequences of her surrogate status are brought home to her (and to the reader) when she must return her charge, the Akashi Princess, to her mother when the girl goes to court.[24]

TAMAKAZURA

The above linkages now allow us to establish the following analogy: Murasaki is to Fujitsubo as Tamakazura is to Yūgao. Based on her inextricable ties to the situation of the surrogate and of "fiction," one can argue that Tamakazura is one of the two most important characters in the narrative—the other is the character even more thoroughly inscribed by the sign of the surrogate, Ukifune (see below). Born of Tō no Chūjō's narrating, Tamakazura will occupy, among others, the position of surrogate for Yūgao when Genji, whose memory of the mother is enduring, discovers her. When we meet her in "The Jeweled Chaplet," we learn that she had been taken to Tsukushi by Yūgao's nurse, who also regarded her as a surrogate, a keepsake for the mother, and that she was whisked back to the capital by a stepbrother just as a provincial strong man was about to force her to become his bride. Ukon accidentally meets Tamakazura while on a pilgrimage to Hase Temple[25] and reports her discovery to Genji, who installs her in a "supplementary" status in his elaborately designed Rokujō Mansion.[26] There she is figured by Genji as his foster daughter: that is, he keeps her identity a secret from her "real" father, Tō no Chūjō, and pretends, to the woman's great discomfort, that she's his own daughter. He then puts her on display in his mansion so that he can enjoy the reactions of the men who come around in pursuit of her. As he taught Murasaki how to be the ideal wife, so he tries to teach Tamakazura how to be the ideal lover, or at least a woman who can effectively lure men. In marked contrast to Tamakazura, the Rokujō Lady's daughter, Akikonomu, is also installed in the mansion but is given her own quarters (southwest). Hers is also a surrogate position vis-à-vis Genji, but she stands as an unequivocally "real" foster daughter, so to speak, since she plays a crucial political role in the narrative as Reizei's empress. As I argue elsewhere, Tamakazura is also connected to exile both as a result of her being taken to Dazaifu as a child and her intertextual association with the *Bamboo-cutter* tale.[27] As such, the seemingly supplementary or "ornamental" aspect of her figuration signals a different narrative register as she deflects attention away from the overtly political and serves to effect a narrative and genealogical transformation: she displaces Genji's narrative lineage with that of Tō no Chūjō's. Furthermore, a firm connection between the surrogate and fiction/storytelling is made in the famous discussion of narratives in the "Fireflies" chapter. The contrast during the discussion between Genji's remarks to his surrogate daughter, Tamakazura, filled with references to the suasive and displacing effects of literature, and those to Murasaki regarding Murasaki's surrogate (and Genji's "real") daughter, the Akashi Princess, that is primarily of a didactic and/or pragmatic (that is, politically motivated) nature, are striking.[28] Let us now turn our attention to the last ten chapters of the narrative.

A SURROGATE TOPOS AND KAORU

A second important displacement at the narrative (and topological) level, matching the one in chapter 2 discussed above, occurs from the "Lady at the Bridge," the first of the so-called "Ten Uji Chapters." The narrative topos shifts from the capital to a place southeast of it at Uji, a name suggestive of "gloom" [*ushi*], as well as "inside" or "interior" [*uchi*].[29] This time the narrative doesn't stage a discussion of surrogates, but rather explores relentlessly the surrogate position and its implications for women.

First of all, the "fatherless" Kaoru, the main male figure of the Uji chapters and a sign and effect of Genji's displacement, hears about the Eighth Prince because he keeps company with the retired Reizei emperor, who has served as a surrogate father to him after the death of his real father, Kashiwagi (Kaoru, whose mother is the Third Princess, the last of Genji's wives, is believed to be Genji's son). Thus the narrator brings together Reizei and Kaoru—one the "fictional" son of the Kiritsubo emperor (actually Genji's son), the other the "fictional" son of Genji (actually Kashiwagi's son). The Eighth Prince, Genji's half-brother, has been devoting himself to the study of Buddhism with an abbot who happens to be a close acquaintance of Reizei. The prince lives in a kind of self-imposed exile at Uji looking after his two daughters, Ōkimi and Nakanokimi. Since his wife, with whom he had an unusually (for the Genji narrative) close and practically monogamous relationship, died giving birth to the second daughter, he has been a surrogate mother to them, as has Bennokimi, the daughter of Kashiwagi's wet nurse.

The network of surrogates here is as complex as it is important: Bennokimi, who had been a surrogate sister to Kashiwagi, is a cousin on her father's side of the deceased wife of the Eighth Prince. As a relative of the prince's wife, Bennokimi came into his employ as guardian and surrogate mother to the prince's two daughters after being away from the capital for ten years (her mother had died soon after Kashiwagi did). We learn that she was also a close acquaintance of the daughter of the Third Princess's wet nurse, Jijū.[30] In other words, a motherless daughter (Bennokimi) of a surrogate (Kashiwagi's nurse) is now a surrogate to two motherless daughters and an intimate associate with another surrogate's daughter. The interrelations among the surrogates are important because, as a result, Bennokimi was able to gain access to the entourages of both Kashiwagi and the Third Princess, thereby becoming privy to the secret of Kaoru's birth, a secret that she begins to divulge to Kaoru in the "The Lady at the Bridge." We learn that she was entrusted by Kashiwagi on his deathbed with a written testament of sorts that she hands over to Kaoru. The narrative installments, spanning several meetings, in which Bennokimi relates Kaoru's past and her own identity to him, are continually referred to by various words that mean "old tales," references that further associate the surrogate with the fictive and with storytelling—an evocation of Tamakazura is unmistakably evident here.[31]

Kaoru belongs, let us remember, to the lineage of his grandfather, Tō no Chūjō. His "real" father, Kashiwagi, was the oldest son of Tō no Chūjō and his official wife, the latter a daughter of the Minister of the Right (we learn this in the "Evening Faces" chapter). His mother, the Third Princess, carries on the line of the Suzaku emperor who was the son of Genji's mother's nemesis, the Kokiden consort, herself a daughter of a Minister of the Right. At the start of the "Uji chapters" we have, in other words, a character, Kaoru, who represents ("speaks for") lineages that sought to oust Genji's political faction. Genji himself only "fathers" Kaoru in a displaced manner, and since Murasaki never had any children of her own, Genji's lineage gets displaced by other, politically opposing, lines. The Eighth Prince, moreover, had been the victim of a failed attempt by Kokiden to displace Reizei as emperor. With such genealogies and political events at play, it is not surprising that the characters that emerge in the "Uji" chapters are fated to experience miscommunication (even noncommunication), misery, and tragedy.[32]

ŌKIMI AND NAKANOKIMI

I shall now examine the question of the surrogate as it relates to the main Uji women. The Eighth Prince's daughters Ōkimi and Nakanokimi have lived in isolation in Uji until Kaoru enters their lives. The fatherless Kaoru is interested in the motherless Ōkimi, the older daughter, but she steadfastly refuses to yield to him. More important, she urges Kaoru to accept her sister Nakanokimi in her place, but Kaoru refuses to accept this surrogate. Their relationship becomes more complicated when the Eighth Prince dies, leaving behind ambivalent statements about his wishes for his daughters and the role he wants Kaoru to play in their lives. Reminiscent of the Suzaku emperor's comments to Genji about the Third Princess, the Prince's remarks only serve to deepen the misunderstanding between the two characters involved. Ōkimi interprets her father's words as a warning never to leave the confines of Uji, whereas Kaoru believes the Prince was asking him to become their guardian—that is, a surrogate for himself. Kaoru remains strongly attracted to Ōkimi but, perhaps due in part to the circumstances of his birth and also to the fact that he was initially interested in the Prince as a surrogate father with whom he could study Buddhist texts, he cannot act forthrightly and claim her as his own. After the Prince dies, Ōkimi abandons hope for herself and begins to play the role of surrogate father/parent for her sister. Kaoru, meanwhile, has become enlightened through Bennokimi's narrations, not about Buddhist texts but about the secret of his birth, and has come into possession of the writings left behind by his "real" father, Kashiwagi. When Ōkimi dies, in a manner in which she practically wills her own death, her sister is left surrogate-mother-less, vulnerable to the whims of the world and of men.[33]

The play of surrogates continues its complex movement as we near the introduction of Ukifune in "The Ivy." Kaoru had countered Ōkimi's plans by getting the ever eager Niou to be his surrogate and occupy the younger sister. Niou eventually marries Nakanokimi, but Kaoru's strategy only manages to drive a wedge between the two sisters and does not produce the desired effect as Ōkimi maintains her attitude of resistance and dies, as noted above. Meanwhile, Niou is pressured into marrying Yūrigi's daughter, Rokunokimi, who displaces Nakanokimi and leaves the latter miserable (more so since she's now pregnant) with no strong backing. Rokunokimi's stepmother is Kashiwagi's widow, the latter looked after by Yūrigi, who plays the role of surrogate for his ill-fated friend. Kaoru likewise is pressured into marriage, in his case to one of the emperor's daughters, the Second Princess.[34] The mother is dead when we meet her, and the emperor (Suzaku's son and Genji's son-in-law)—in an echo of his father's marrying off his daughter, the Third Princess, to Genji—sees in Kaoru a source of support for the motherless child. Kaoru passively agrees to the marriage.

Socially and emotionally displaced, Nakanokimi finds the equally troubled Kaoru a more than eager confidant and writes to him when she can no longer endure her situation with Niou. Kaoru had earlier spoken of turning the Uji house into a temple, and Nakanokimi had expressed a desire to make offerings of sutras or images of the Buddha. Kaoru had been regretting his decision to enlist Niou to be his surrogate for the sister Ōkimi had tried to make into a surrogate for herself and the attention incites him to action. He quickly visits her chambers and, finding himself unable to restrain his desire, especially when she hints that she would like him to take her to Uji, and convincing himself that her voice sounds just like Ōkimi's, he takes hold of Nakanokimi's sleeve. Shocked at his behavior and at his belated attempt to make her a surrogate for Ōkimi, but unable to reject him openly, Nakanokimi begins to be more wary of Kaoru's intentions. When he visits her again in a fit of nostalgia for Ōkimi, he speaks of his desire to have a "likeness" [hitokata] or portrait of Ōkimi offered at Uji.[35] The two discuss the implications of likenesses and Kaoru refers to a craftsman who made flowers fall from the sky. At that point, Nakanokimi refers to Ukifune by way of repeating different words for surrogates: hitokata and also "memento" [katami].[36] Nakanokimi's strategem works and Kaoru's curiosity is piqued by the story of this woman reported to resemble Ōkimi.[37]

UKIFUNE

In Ukifune the narrative rewrites Tamakazura, as this half-sister of Ōkimi and Nakanokimi radically extends the figure of the surrogate. Like Tamakazura, Ukifune emerges out of a character's narration, but this time as a clearly constructed "image" conjured up by language and as the narrator's (that is, Nakanokimi's) surrogate. Like Tamakazura, she has been living in a far-off province as a stepdaughter, in her case of the Governor of Hitachi. She is "fictional" in a genealogical sense: her "real" father, the Eighth Prince, refused to acknowledge her existence and that of her mother, who ended up marrying the governor. By contrast, Tamakazura's father, Tō no Chūjō, didn't exactly abandon her, although he doesn't seem to have been too solicitous of her welfare, but lost track of her whereabouts. Having been raised away from the capital and suddenly appearing in the narrative, her figuration participates as does Tamakazura's in the *Bamboo-cutter* intertext.[38] She is the focus of several suitors who make life miserable for her but, in contrast to Tamakazura, she rejects all of them. She herself is rejected by one suitor trying to curry favor with the governor when he discovers that she is only the stepdaughter of the wealthy man; the suitor, who speaks for those who subscribe to the preeminence of blood ties, turns his attention to Ukifune's half-sister because the latter is the governor's real daughter. The steadfast Kaoru, who sees Ukifune primarily as a surrogate (for Ōkimi and Nakanokimi), and the impetuous Niou, who can't keep his hands off of any interesting woman, pursue her relentlessly and their attentions end up driving her to what she sees as only a dead end. Completely at a loss, she attempts to kill herself.

To a greater degree than the other female characters, the narrator marks Ukifune by aspects of the surrogate and the copy. First, more than any other character, she is shown engaged in the practice of calligraphic brush-writing, known as "writing practice" [*tenarai*]. The common practice of copying (even meticulous tracing) the style of a well-known calligraphic model involves a repetitive process that, over time, begins to blur the lines between "original" and "copy." Moreover, as a circular loop that begins and ends with the aim of improving one's "style," it also problematizes the function of writing as "communication." In Ukifune's case, she writes poems that in different circumstances would be sent to someone else, but the narrator often remarks that she wrote the poem "by way of writing practice." What she writes, in other words, does not participate in a communicative act. Her words "speak," but only as a copy that never reaches anyone.[39]

Also, as mentioned, Ukifune tries to end her life but the narrative will eventually reveal that she has been saved by strangers. Immediately after the incident, the narrator states at the beginning of "The Drake Fly" that her surrogate Uji family, to translate literally, "were in an uproar searching for her absence [or, nonpresence]."[40] Moreover, unaware of her whereabouts or that she is even alive, they perform the rite of "cremation," but the fiery pyre engulfs only an absent, "fictional" body. In her sudden disappearance she is again linked with Tamakazura and Kaguya-hime. At the beginning of the next chapter, "At Writing Practice," we learn that she is found dazed at the base of a tree by a party headed by a bishop of Yokawa; Kaguya-hime was found at the base of a bamboo stalk. Her rescuers refer to her as a "changeling," a term used for Kaguya-hime (it was also used by Nakanokimi when she first mentioned Ukifune to Kaoru).[41] She then becomes the surrogate daughter of a woman who had recently lost her own daughter and is taken by the woman's party to Ono, at the foot of Mt. Hiei.[42]

Unable to die, then, Ukifune becomes death's surrogate. Her life after her "death" is accordingly marked by "silence" (although, echoing Yūgao, "silence" was a part of her character from the beginning[43]), which performs the ultimate displacement of language, of narrative, of the very narrative that, like Kaoru and Niou, would force her to speak for others, would enclose her. As the narrative moves towards its end, Ukifune only grows more determined to remain silent, refusing to respond to direct questions about her background or to answer letters.[44] In her silent, dreamlike state after her "death," a state in which the past and memory would all be erased (she continually pleads amnesia), she eludes her pursuers and refuses to be co-opted back into a life in the capital. All she is left with is her speechless, homeless, and still thoroughly surrogate condition.

While the desire for surrogates instituted at the beginning of the narrative remains intact with Ukifune, the position of the surrogate itself has become greatly transformed. As the narrator spoke for the surrogates, or "surrogate-ness," in the text, those figures effectively served to displace a host of variations, at different narratological levels, on what might be construed as the "natural"; or, to put it another way, the position of the "stand-in," through a maneuver that has global implications for the narrative, and for scholarly study in general, comes to be the naturalized one. With Ukifune, however, we meet a character so completely inscribed by the mark of the surrogate that she can only exist as a figure that defies reclamation as either "body" or "form"—a body without form and a form without a body. After suffering constant dislocation, she finally finds herself in a realm in which desire for her body has ended in frustration (neither Kaoru nor Niou can "possess" her), but also one in which the anticipated reinstitution of her form (into society, into language) will also end in failure. She has taken Buddhist vows to sever her ties with the world but we never get the sense that even that break is a final one; she is not in the world but she cannot be completely out of it either.

SURROGATE CONCLUSIONS

What conclusions can we begin to draw, then, from the pervasiveness of the surrogate, "foster/step" situations in the *Genji* text, and as they relate to the act of "speaking for"? First, they provide a different, more inclusive perspective on a notion familiar to *Genji* readers: substitution.[45] As analyzed by scholars, substitutive links, such those between the Kiritsubo Consort, Fujitsubo, and Murasaki, remain at a structural level that neither displaces Genji as the main focus of those links, nor is able to address the question of the "original." The problematic of the surrogate enables us to realize the illusory nature of the "original" itself, fully inscribed as it is by the fictional, as we realign the statuses of the women represented with those doing the representing. In other words, it allows us to trace the complex interrelations between surrogate status and kinship, on the one hand, and the act of "speaking for" (narrating position and representation), on the other.

Second, we begin to see that the pervasiveness of the represented surrogates echoes the very status of the woman's hand: a writing that was never exclusively a feminine domain but relegated to women, as if they were male surrogates writing at a transitional discursive moment before that writing is ultimately (re)appropriated by men. Ki no Tsurayuki's strategy of assuming the woman's hand to write the *Tosa Diary* in 935 can be seen as a move to relegate the hand to women, but as male surrogates, an ironic early attempt to appropriate and keep control (ultimately, to speak for women) of the hand for men.[46] The learned, middle-rank women recruited as intermediaries (surrogates) of one kind or other to serve at the palace, were the temporary caretakers of texts that come to be regarded as a great (if not the greatest) flowering of Japanese literary culture.

Third, and expanding on the second point, the problematic of the surrogate and the act of speaking for is also, as I suggested earlier, intimately tied to the notion of "fiction," which often occupies a surrogate position relative to a putative "reality"; or, in the case of *The Tale of Genji* text, to official histories and other texts written in Chinese. The ability to construe *monogatari* as "fictive," or even allegorical, as specifically asserted in the *Genji* text itself, suggests that the reading I am proposing is not based simply on tenuous, arbitrary, or irrelevant connections.

Finally, the problematic of the surrogate should allow us to think of the broader networks of narrative and their relation to the world without falling back on monological, essentialized positions, such as essentialized narrators/authors or Self–Other binarisms, since the position of the surrogate itself always already undermines those positions. In other words, the fictiveness of the surrogate becomes a figure for negotiating a realm of positionality where identities are continually destabilized. If we can maintain the problematic of the surrogate as we go about our daily lives, it should enable us to interact with others in a new light. On the one hand, the unquestionably valid desire of women and ethnic minorities to maintain a kind of identitarian assertiveness and equality must not keep concealed incommensurabilities of position, privilege, and power embedded in dominant Eurocentric discourses. On the other hand, those already placed in positions of dominance need to relearn and relocate their privilege in ways that foreground their own virtual dependence on contingency and surrogate status. My own surrogate status, as I speak for Heian women's writing, ought also to help undermine my privilege as a university professor.

NOTES

1. Roland Barthes, *Empire of Signs*, trans. Richard Howard (New York: Hill and Wang, 1982), p. 21; and Edward Said, "Representing the Colonized: Anthropology's Interlocutors," *Critical Inquiry*, 15, no. 2 (Winter 1989): 212. Said's questions serve to put Japan into a global context.

2. I am referring to Barthes's suggestive essay, "Lesson in Writing," in *Image, Music, Text*, trans. Stephen Heath (New York: Hill and Wang, 1977), p. 173. Exile has always been a subtext of Said's writings; see Edward W. Said, *Culture and Imperialism* (New York: Alfred A. Knopf, Inc., 1993), p. xxvi.

3. Cf., "Why this rejection [of 'parts or all of the conceptual apparatus we inherited from nineteenth-century Europe; including ... certain elements and logics of the conceptual apparatuses based in traditional movements of human liberation; including, of course, feminism']? ... our ways of under-standing in the West have been and continue to be complicitous with our ways of oppressing." Alice Jardine, "Opaque Texts and Transparent Contexts: The Political Difference of Julia Kristeva," in *The Poetics of Gender*, ed. Nancy K. Miller (New York: Columbia University Press, 1986), p. 99.

4. See Said, *Culture and Imperialism*, p. 51. I am citing the "contrapuntal" heuristically here since I wish to displace the traces of the self–other binary that often subtends Orientalist criticism.

5. Chandra Mohanty, "Under Western Eyes: Feminist Scholarship and Colonial Discourses," in *Third World Women and the Politics of Feminism* (Bloomington: Indiana University Press, 1991).

6. See Mitani Kuniaki, "Seiritsu kōsō ron to josei besshi" [On the Original Shape of the Narrative and the Denigration of Women], in *Genji monogatari o dō yomu ka* [How Do We Read *The Tale of Genji*?], a special issue of *Kokubungaku kaishaku to kanshō* (Tokyo: Shibundō, 1986): 208.

7. Denise Riley, *Am I That Name? Feminism and the Category of Women in History* (Minnesota: University of Minnesota Press, 1988), p. 2.

8. See Myra Jehlen's essay, "Archimedes and the Paradox of Feminist Criticism," in *Feminist Theory: A Critique of Ideology*, eds. Nannerl O. Keohane, et al. (Chicago: The University of Chicago Press, 1982), pp. 189–215.

9. Edward W. Said, *Orientalism* (New York: Pantheon Books, 1978).

10. "The exteriority of the representation is always governed by some version of the truism that if the Orient could represent itself, it would; since it cannot, the representation does the job, for the West, and *faute de mieux*, for the poor Orient," Said, *Orientalism*, p. 21.

11. An enduring attitude among many Japanologists has been to honor the findings of Japanese scholarship but to treat them as raw material for the more important work of interpretation or translation (the classic form of "speaking for" in Japanology) carried out

by Western scholars. Notable exceptions to the paradigm are Naoki Sakai, *Voices from the Past* (Ithaca, NY: Cornell University Press, 1992); Mitsuhiro Yoshimoto's forthcoming study of Akira Kurosawa; and the important essay by H. D. Harootunian, "America's Japan/Japan's Japan," in *Japan in the World*, ed. Masao Miyoshi and H. D. Harootunian (Durham, NC: Duke University Press, 1993), pp. 196–221.

12. All three lived during the final decades of the tenth century and the first decades of the eleventh. Murasaki Shikibu left behind, in addition to the *Genji* text, a "diary" and a poem collection. Sei Shōnagon is the author of *The Pillow Book of Sei Shōnagon*. Like Murasaki Shikibu, Izumi Shikibu also left behind a "diary" and a poem collection. See, *Murasaki Shikibu: Her Diary and Poetic Memoirs*, trans. Richard Bowring (Princeton, NJ: Princeton University Press, 1982); *The Pillow Book of Sei Shōnagon*, trans. Ivan Morris, 2 vols. (New York: Columbia University Press, 1967); and *The Izumi Shikibu Diary: A Romance of the Heian Court*, trans. Edwin Cranston (Cambridge, MA: Harvard University Press, 1969).

13. Composing for someone else was actually a practice common to males as well.

14. *Onna-de*. See the discussion below on *kana* writing.

15. For a different view of the women and Genji, see Norma Field, *The Splendor of Longing in The Tale of Genji* (Princeton, NJ: Princeton University Press, 1987).

16. Genji "fails," for example, in his relations with women like Utsusemi [Locust Shell Lady], Asagao [Morning Glory Lady], Fujitsubo, Yūgao, Suetsumuhana [Safflower Princess], Tamakazura, and the Rokujō Lady. Even his successes, the narrator seems to imply, are never unconditional.

17. With the imperially sanctioned compilation of the Japanese poetry collection, *Kokin wakashū* in 905, *kana* became the official mode of writing for poetry. See, *Kokinshū A Collection of Poems Ancient and Modern* (Princeton, NJ: Princeton University Press, 1984).

18. See the discussions of the three writers in Toril Moi, *Sexual/Textual Politics: Feminist Literary Theory* (London: Methuen, 1985).

19. *Figures of Resistance: Language, Poetry, and Narrating in The Tale of Genji and Other Mid-Heian Texts* (Durham, NC: Duke University Press, 1991), chapter 8.

20. Also referred to as Ōigimi, which is the way Seidensticker translates it in *The Tale Genji*.

21. See *Figures of Resistance*, pp. 192–196.

22. Seidensticker translates the man's position as "deputy viceroy of Kyushu." *The Tale of Genji*, trans. Edward G. Seidensticker (Alfred Knopf,1976; hereafter cited as *TTG*): p. 387.

23. Genji's marriage to Aoi takes place in "The Paulownia Court," *TTG*, pp. 17–19. High-ranking men often had numerous wives but only one "official wife." Marriage with the official wife was usually arranged by both sets of parents for strategic (political) purposes. As a consequence, other wives had to compete with each other for the attentions of their husband. For a celebrated portrait of the feelings of a nonoffcial wife toward both her husband and her competitors, see *The Kagerō Diary*, trans. Sonja Arntzen (Ann Arbor: Center for Japanese Studies, The University of Michigan, 1997).

24. "Murasaki trust now give up the child who had been her whole life. How she wished that she had had such a daughter, someone to be with in just such circumstances," *TTG*, p. 531.

25. A temple far south of the Heian capital that was popular among women as a place for Buddhist worship and retreat.

26. He positions her as a marginal element in the Orange Blossom Lady's quarters in his Rokujō Mansion. See my discussion of Tamakazura in *Figures of Resistance*, chapter 9. The description of Genji's mansion is found in "The Maiden," *TTG*, pp. 384–386.

27. In the tale, Kaguya-hime [Shining Princess] comes to earth for a time, is cared for

by an old bamboo-cutter and his wife, is pursued by suitors all of whom she rejects, and in the end returns to the moon. For an English translation of the tale by Donald Keene, see Thomas Rimer, *Modern Japanese Fiction and Its Traditions* (Princeton, NJ: Princeton University Press, 1978): pp. 275–305.

28. "What would Tamakazura have made of the difference between his remarks to her and these remarks to Murasaki?" *TTG*, p. 438. The Japanese emphasizes Tamakazura's displeasure were she to hear of Genji's remarks. Vol. 3 of *Genji monogatari*, Abe Akio, et al. eds., vols. 12–17 of *Nihon koten bungaku zenshū* (Tokyo: Shōgakkan, 1972–76; hereafter, *GM*): p. 207.

29. The aspect of "gloom" derives from a *Kokinshū* poem, no. 984, by the Monk Kisen: "My hut lies southeast of the capital / thus I live apart / at a place with mountains people associate with gloom." The suggestion of "inside" derives from the fact that premodern manuscripts do not contain diacritical marks, as modern punctuation provides, to distinguish a voiced sound from an unvoiced sound: thus, a word written *u-chi* could be read either *u-chi* or *u-ji*.

30. *TTG*, p. 789.

31. Here are a few examples. In "The Lady at the Bridge," we are given the following terms: *mukashi no monogatari* [old narratives], *GM*, vol. 5, p. 136 (*TTG*: "story of long ago," p. 812); *furu monogatari* [ancient narratives], *GM*, ibid., p. 138 (*TTG*: "ancient story," p. 789); and, *mukashi gatari* [old tales], *GM*, ibid., p. 151 (*TTG*: "tale of long ago," p. 795). In "Beneath the Oak," we get these: *towazugatari* [unasked for tale], *GM*, ibid., p. 174 (*TTG*: omitted); *monogatari* [narratives], *GM*, ibid. (*TTG*: "story," p. 806); *on-monogatari* [narratives], *GM*, ibid., 190 (*TTG*: "things to say," p. 812); and, *on-furu monogatari* [ancient narrative], *GM*, ibid., p. 191 (*TTG*: "your story," p. 812).

32. Genji's lineage, as a result of his union with the Akashi family, does succeed when the Akashi Princess gives birth to a boy who is appointed crown prince. That line, which produces Niou, is clearly subordinate to the narrative focus on Kaoru, the Eighth Prince, and the prince's daughters.

33. Ōkimi's death occurs in "Trefoil Knots," *TTG*, p. 867.

34. The Second Princess' mother is the third "Fujitsubo" consort in the narrative. The second was the mother of the Third Princess.

35. The word can mean "likeness," or refer more specifically to images used in lustration ceremonies. Nakanokimi mentions Ukifune in "The Ivy," *TTG*, pp. 915–917.

36. Kaoru speaks of wanting a "changeling" [*henge no hito*] a word that connects Ukifune, of whom he will learn immediately, with Kaguya-hime. Seidensticker translates *hitokata* as "image," and *katami* as "legacy," *TTG*, p. 916.

37. Tamakazura's existence was also first revealed by way of a narration.

38. "She was like an angel that had wandered down from the heavens and might choose at any moment to return," *TTG*, p. 1051. Here, the narrator actually speaks from the nun's position: "She felt as if she had witnessed the descent of a heavenly being from the skies," *GM*, vol. 1, p. 287. And, "The whole sequence of events was as singular as the story of the old bamboo cutter and the moon princess," *TTG*, p. 1051. Here, too, the narrator speaks from the old man's and the nun's positions: "She [the woman] felt even more amazed than the old bamboo cutter had when he discovered Kaguya-hime," *GM*, vol. 6, p. 288. Finally, she refers in a poem, not meant for anyone, to people in her past as inhabiting a "moon capital" [*tsuki no miyako*], *GM*, p. 291. The reference is obscured in the translation: "Who in the city, now bathed in the light of the moon," *TTG*, p. 1053.

39. Examples of Ukifune at writing practice include the following: *TTG*, pp. 1053, 1062, 1069, 1070, and 1070.

40. Cf. "The Uji house was in an uproar. Ukifune had disappeared and frantic

searching had revealed no traces of her," *TTG*, p. 1012. The Japanese is more suggestive of Ukifune's fundamental condition since, even when she was present, her surrogate status was equivalent to an "absence."

41. *GM*, vol. 6, p. 269–270; *TTG*, p. 1044; see also note 31.

42. "She yearned for a companion to remind her of the one now gone [her daughter]. And she had come upon a hidden treasure, a girl if anything superior to her daughter," *TTG*, p. 1052. The Japanese contains the word "keepsake" [*katami*], which Ukifune becomes, *GM*, p. 288. The woman is the bishop's sister, *TTG*, p. 1047.

43. Just before Kaoru learns of Ukifune's existence, he had remarked that he "wished to find a soundless village," *GM*, vol. 5, p. 436. Seidensticker translates it "Let me have a Silencetown somewhere," *TTG*, p. 915.

44. The nun asks her questions soon after they discover her, but "The girl did not answer," *TTG*, p. 1048. "'Throw me back into the river,' she had said, and there had been not a word from her since," ibid., p. 1049. "She has not said a word," ibid. Other examples of her silence can be found on pp. 1057, 1059, and 1078.

45. Norma Field makes much of the notion of "substitution" in *The Splendor of Longing*.

46. An English translation of *The Tosa Diary* is available as *A Tosa Journal* in *Classical Japanese Prose*, compiled and edited by Helen Craig McCullough (Stanford, CA: Stanford University Press, 1990), pp. 73–102.

ESPERANZA RAMIREZ-CHRISTENSEN

The Operation of the Lyrical Mode
in the Genji Monogatari

The dominant lyrical strain in the *Genji monogatari* prompted the pre-modern *Genji* scholar Motoori Norinaga to call it a work of *mono no aware*, "the pathos of things," or their immanent power to move us. Although the *Genji* is a prose narrative whose principal concern is to tell a story or sequence of stories, it does not therefore progress as an ordered series of actions that follow each other with the logic of causality from beginning to end, not even within the boundary of a single episode. Instead the narrative progression is curiously diffuse. It is constantly interrupted by the evocation of momentary impressions or frozen into static scenes which specify a particular mood, emotion, or thought. Its climaxes are not those in which the hero commits the fatal irretrievable act that unleashes the forces of destiny. They are rather those moments of heightened emotion in which outer and inner worlds are fused together in a transfiguring metaphor or pattern of images.

All these would seem to suggest that the *Genji* is a hybrid genre in which narrative is being employed for lyrical or poetic ends. This in itself ought not to surprise anyone in view of the fact that the *monogatari* ("tale") proper is generically related to the *uta monogatari* ("poem-tale") and *uta nikki* ("poetic diary") in which prose functions as a narrative context for poetry, and that these hybrid genres ultimately point to the poetic anthology whose *kotobagaki* (brief prose introductions) provide a contextual frame for the

From *Ukifune: Love in the Tale of Genji.* © 1982 by Columbia University Press.

poems themselves. What is surprising, however, is the sheer monumentality of the structure which the author causes to rise out of this ambivalent device; the way the narrative is at once diffused and sustained by imagistic moments which transcend their particular contexts to echo and foreshadow other moments in the narrative the way a lyric poem deploys word-images in patterned arrangement.

In what follows, I should like to examine how these poetic moments operate in relation to the narrative's constituent elements of plot, character, and point of view. My study is limited to the first three chapters of the so-called *Uji jūjō*, the Uji stories comprising the final ten chapters of the *Genji*.[1] The *Uji jūjō* is about the hero Kaoru's successive involvements, all thwarted, with the sisters Ōigimi, Nakanokimi, and Ukifune. Its first three chapters, "*Hashihime*" ("The Lady of the Bridge"), "*Shii ga moto*" ("Beneath the Oak"), and "*Agemaki*" ("Trefoil Knots"), relate Kaoru's love for Ōigimi from its inception to its tragic conclusion in Ōigimi's death.

"*HASHIHIME*"

"At that time there was an old Prince who lived isolated and forgotten by society" (4-297-5).[2] Thus begins "Hashihime," with a long narrative exposition introducing the reader to Prince Hachi: his lineage, political downfall, and consequent abandonment by supporters; the birth of his eldest daughter Ōigimi, the death of his wife after the birth of their second daughter Nakanokimi, and his gradual turning away from society and toward the religious life. Interspersed are descriptions of the two daughters, the potential heroines: "In appearance Nakanokimi was of such surpassing loveliness that one almost feared for her. Ōigimi was of a quiet and intelligent disposition; there was in her manner and appearance an air of refinement and indeed, of concealed depths. Of the two she was more clearly the aristocrat" (4–299–4). There is a brief reference to the Prince's overgrown garden, a physical correlative to his fallen fortunes and a presaging of the wild, untamed nature of Uji. Soon the exposition narrows down to the Prince's sessions with his daughters, when he teaches them the genteel accomplishments. There is another contrastive description of the princesses' character traits, later to acquire a momentous significance in their distinct destinies: Ōigimi was "quick and adept and showed a deeply serious attitude," while Nakanokimi was more "relaxed, with an appealingly helpless and shy manner" (4–301–1). And finally the narrative closes in and expands on one such scene in the life of the widowed Prince and his two motherless children.

On a day in spring, he sat gazing at the pond where in the soft and clear sunlight the ducks swam happily about, their voices cooing to each other as wing alighted on wing. It would have been an ordinary enough scene in former days, but now it was with envy that he gazed at those inseparable pairs. He was giving his daughters a music lesson. They seemed so small and pretty as they bent over their instruments, plucking a melody whose sound, somehow sad and appealing, brought tears to his eyes.

Uchisutete	"Parting our joined
Tsugai sarinishi	Wings, she flew away,
Mizudori no	The waterbird;
Kari no kono yo ni	Why were her young left to
Tachiokurekemu.	Linger in this transient world?

The heart grows weary," he added softly, brushing away the tears. He was a very handsome-looking Prince. The years of religious austerities had thinned and emaciated him but they had also enhanced the graceful nobility of his appearance. Dressed in a soft, faded court robe out of concern for the princesses' upbringing, there was in his manner a courtliness so natural it quite put one to shame.

Ōigimi had quietly drawn the Prince's inkstone toward her and was writing characters on it as if practicing her hand. "Set them down here," said the Prince, giving her some paper, "one does not write on an inkstone." Embarrassed, she wrote:

Ikade kaku	"Why did it have
Sudachikeru zo to	To leave its nest like this,
Omou ni mo	I wondered;
Uki mizudori no	And now how well I know
Chigiri o zo shiru.	The bitter fate of the waterbird!"

It was not a good poem, but the circumstances were very moving. Her handwriting showed promise, even though the characters were not as yet smoothly flowing. "My young Princess too should write one," said the Prince, and as she was still a bit childlike it took a long time before she was finished.

Naku naku mo	"Though he wept and wept,
Hane uchikisuru	Had not Father enfolded me
Kimi naku wa	In his wings,
Ware zo sumori ni	I would have remained
Narubekarikeru.	In the nest unhatched."

Their robes were soft and faded from wear. With no one to attend them, the time must seem lonely and tedious indeed, yet how appealing they were in various ways. Seeing them thus, how could he help but feel pity and pain for their sad state?

(4–301–4)

This is the first tableau that slows down the narrative exposition. It is an extended lyrical passage with no direct bearing on the action of the story; it could have been omitted without upsetting the causal–temporal sequence of the plot. Nevertheless the narrator chooses to focus on this emotive scene in order to direct the reader's sympathy to the three characters who are going to play such a crucial role in the hero Kaoru's life. She does this by investing them with a soft aura of pathos and gentility. This aura is raised by the content of their poems of course, but it is also influenced by the soft spring sunlight and the image of the ducks swimming in the pond under its beneficent warmth. The pathetic appeal is raised by the estrangement of the three characters from all this warmth and light. Figuratively speaking, they lead their lives in shadow; the domestic felicity of the family of ducks, swimming wing to wing, has been broken in their case by the death of the wife and mother. On the other hand, the very presence of the images of spring sunlight and waterbirds invests the characters and their situation with the appealing qualities associated with these images. Like the waterbirds, the princesses are small, innocent, and appealing. The picture of the Prince going over a music lesson with them, his concern and solicitude for them, suggest a warm, tranquil, and idyllic family scene. And the genteel grace of the characters is enhanced, even idealized, by their association with the soft spring sunlight. In short the metaphorical juxtaposition here between external setting and the characters' situation works in two ways; the two terms of the metaphor are related by association and similarity as well as by an intuition of the disparity between them.

The mechanics of this passage demonstrate a pattern that will reveal itself to be the most typical one in the operation of the lyrical mode. First an external setting is described, expressly or implicitly through the eyes of the character looking at it. Simultaneously—or before or after, it does not matter which—the character's situation is similarly described. And then a metaphorical fusion occurs in which the elements of the setting become the vehicle for the character's emotion, usually as expressed by the poem he composes at that point. The natural scene thus becomes charged with his emotion, and his emotion in turn is objictified through the scene. Over and over again, we will find in the *Genji* that physical descriptions of scenery are potential or realized metaphors; the setting that frames the characters or the action serves at the same time as their image.

The poems of the two sisters in this passage function also to maintain the contrastive characterization noted earlier. Ōigimi, innately more serious, already shows in adolescence a pessimism which is to become obsessive in the course of the story. Nakanokimi, more dependent as younger sister and less given to brooding, shows a positive attitude in being grateful for her father's protection and realizing that she could have fared worse. We see here the germ of the tragic and comic plots which will develop in a parallel manner in the next two chapters.

After this lyrical interruption, the narrative exposition resumes with an account of the Prince's genteel upbringing and unfortunate fall from society. It then comes to a momentary pause to contemplate the final deprivation that leads to his removal to Uji.

> And then his mansion burned down. The shock of it, coming on top of all his sorrows, was more than he could bear, and having no other place in the capital suitable to live in, he moved out to the fine little mountain villa he had in the village called Uji. In his mind he had already turned his back on the world but now that the time had come to leave the capital sorrow overcame him. The villa lay by the Uji River, within the deafening roar of the waters rushing past the fishing weirs nearby. It was not wholly conducive to quiet meditation but where else could he go? And so letting himself be borne along the turning current of the springtime flowers, the autumn leaves and the flowing river, more than ever now he gave himself up to reveries. "Cut off from the world here in my final retreat in the hills, how I wish that the person of old dwelt by me still," he thought, for memories of her were never far.

Mishi hito mo	"She who dwelt
Yado mo keburi ni	Beside me, my home, all have
Narinishi o	Turned to smoke;
Nani tote waga mi	Yet why is this body
Kienokorikemu.	Still languishing behind?"

Such longing consumed him, for he had nothing left to live for.

(4–301–11)

This passage is a pivotal one. It transports us from the capital into Uji, not only physically but also temporally through the reference to the passing seasons and flowing water. And the poem that comes at its end is also a summing-up: by making an allusion to the Prince's dead wife, it recalls the main burden of the first narrative unit ending in the spring day scene and unites it with the second narrative unit which comes to a head in the destruction of the house. From the framework of the narrative progression then, the poem functions like an epilogue to the story of the Prince's life in the capital, an echo of events that transpired, from the vantage point of Uji, in another time and place. A poem coming at the end of a narrative sequence thus has the power to draw together the most significant aspects of the experience related therein. It combines with its emotive function the aesthetic one of ordering events into a pattern of images.

The passage above continues:

> To his abode surrounded by range upon range of mountains, no one came to visit. Only mean peasants and rustic woodcutters would occasionally venture in to offer their services. As he passed the days and nights gazing "on peaks where the morning mists never lift."

(4–304–6)

The last phrase in an allusion to *Kokinshū* 935:

Kari no kuru	On peaks where the
Mine no asagiri	Wild geese pass, the morning
Harezu nomi	Mists never lift;
Omoitsukusenu	And of dark thoughts there is
Yo no naka no usa.	No ending in a world of gloom.[3]

This second description of Uji focuses on its physical isolation, especially as symbolized by the thick mist that constantly hovers over it, enshrouding it. As the allusion to *Kokinshū* 935 indicates, the mist image is being used as the objective correlative of a mind (Prince Hachi's here) immobilized by persistent gloomy thoughts from which it is unable to break out. Again and again in the Uji stories this image is going to recur in various contexts and nuances, but its central connotation of confinement and immobilization will remain the same. The other salient feature of Uji is the river introduced in the previous passage. Sinister, disturbing, and perilous, the river too is a leitmotif that flows through the Uji chapters and reaches its climax in "Ukifune".

    The Prince's enforced isolation is somewhat mitigated by his friendship with the Abbot of a monastery in the neighboring hills. It is this Abbot who in one of his visits to the capital informs the Retired Emperor Reizei of Prince Hachi's saintly life at Uji. That conversation, during which Kaoru was present, is the first real element of plot in the story, since it directly leads Kaoru to seek Prince Hachi's religious guidance and signals the beginning of those fateful ties between the capital and Uji, symbolized also by the poetic exchange between Reizei and Prince Hachi.

    Kaoru's psychological motivation for seeking Prince Hachi's guidance is, as we know from the "Niou miya" chapter, his long-standing desire to renounce the world and devote his life to religion. This desire stems from a vague awareness of something shameful in the circumstances of his birth; a fearful suspicion, so much more malevolent because concealed, that he is in fact not Genji's son at all: "When he was a child there had been whispers whose import he could but dimly comprehend; they had always disturbed him, he yearned to know what it all meant, but there had never been anyone he could ask. He could not even hint to his mother of his vague suspicions, so dreadful they were, and so they remained in his mind, a constant torment" (4–223–9). As the recognized child of Genji and the Third Princess, Kaoru is surrounded by powerful relatives. The incumbent Emperor is his uncle, the Empress his half-sister. The Retired Emperor Reizei looks after him like a father, sponsoring his coming-of-age ceremonies and assuring that his promotions are rapid. He is the favorite companion of the princes of the blood, Niou and his brothers. And so "it was but natural that society should make much of him; his worldly success was so brilliant as to be almost dazzling, but he had no heart for any of it and remained sunk in melancholy thought" (4–224–12). Between Kaoru and the world that showers him with such favors hangs the unresolved shadow of his birth. Inwardly tormented by a dark secret that may not be revealed, he seeks to escape into the monastic life where the nature of his birth is immaterial, and where he may atone for whatever sin was committed in bringing him to life.

    Kaoru's otherworldliness is viewed romantically by the society around him: "Indeed his life was so favored from the very start that he seemed not to have been born for this world; there was something about him that made one think of a Buddha temporarily incarnated in human form. One could not have said where in his face or figure the beauty and distinction lay; there was just this terribly fascinating air, this inscrutable reserve that seemed to hint

of wordless depths, and made him seem like no ordinary mortal"
(4–225–11). A romantic figure indeed, and a potential tragic hero. And there
is his inexplicable fragrance to complete the mystery. Kaoru is much sought
after by the ladies at court, "but in his heart there was the dreadful
knowledge about himself and the vanity of existence that kept him from
indulging his feelings in romantic affairs; he was so restrained in everything
that he became known for his mature, deliberate character" (4–228–6).
What amorous affairs he has had have been merely casual ones that have not
endangered his ultimate resolve. Or as the narrator remarks, "Was it
because there was no one to captivate his heart that he was so wise?"
(4–228–2).

This is then the high-minded, scrupulous young man who comes to Uji
to study the Buddhist Law with Prince Hachi. Through his eyes we get
another impression of Uji.

> There were mountain villages where the mind could find rest
> and tranquility, but here the tumultuous sounds of the water and
> the echoes of the waves could not have soothed the troubled
> thoughts, nor could the nights of wildly blowing wind have lulled
> one enough to dream. It was indeed a setting to tear the mind
> from worldly attachment, suitable for a monkish hermit like the
> Prince, but what must his daughters feel in such a place? Might
> they not be lacking in ordinary feminine gentleness?
>
> (4–308–16)

This is the second passage having to do with the Uji River. In the first, as we
have seen, a brief reference was made to the flowing river in conjunction with
the passing seasons, emphasizing the ineluctable passage of time. This
passage is an elaboration of the river's auditory aspect: its tumultuous sound
frustrates dreaming, and we are to understand "dream" here in the Buddhist
sense—ignorance of the inherent nullity of human craving and desire. The
river's noise constantly shocks one into wide-awake contemplation of bare
reality. The author has clearly conceived the wild, unaccommodated nature
of Uji in contrast to the cultured, man-made gardens of the capital, such as
Genji's four-seasons garden which is made to accommodate itself to man's
reassuring view of nature and of himself. The author's description of the Uji
scenery establishes the symbolic landscape for Ōigimi's character, its strain of
harshness and lucidity that refuses to be drawn into that most beguiling
illusion, love. Kaoru's fleeting curiosity about the princesses is very apropos,
it turns out, but at this point his mind is fixed on his resolve. Hereafter he

comes faithfully to see Prince Hachi, motivated solely by an earnest desire to train himself in Buddhist detachment.

But three years later his life suddenly takes an unexpected turn. It is late in autumn. Prince Hachi leaves his house for a retreat at the monastery. Not knowing this, Kaoru is suddenly moved by a desire to see him. What happens next is what "Hashihime" is all about.

> In the deep of night while the waning moon still hung in the sky, he set out secretly from the capital, dressed simply and with no official attendants. He went on horseback and since the Uji house was on this side of the river, he did not need to bother about crossing by boat. When he came into the mountains, thick mists rolled in to obscure his path, and as he groped his way through the dense trees a stormy wind would send huge drops of dew splattering from the wildly scattering leaves until he was thoroughly soaked and chilled, and he had no one to blame but himself. Unused to such secret excursions, he felt somewhat afraid, but also excited.

Yamaoroshi ni	"From leaves that cannot
Taenu konoha no	Hold before the mountain storm
Tsuyu yori mo	The dewdrops fall—
Ayanaku moroki	Yet more weakly fall my tears,
Waga namida kana.	For no reason."

> When they came to a village he enjoined his men to keep silent; it would be bothersome if the peasants were roused from their sleep, he said, and as he rode between brushwood hedges he tried to restrain the hoofs of his horse as they splashed into some tiny rivulets in the dark, but his own fragrance carried in the wind and caused some to wake up in wonder at "the sweet smell of the unknown master." As he approached the house, the notes of an instrument he could not identify came floating chill and clear in the night air. He remembered hearing that the Prince often played music with his daughters, but had never had the opportunity to hear the Prince's renowned *koto*. Now was a good chance, he told himself, and then realized, as he passed through the gate, that the sound was from a *biwa*. It was tuned to the *ōjiki* mode, which was ordinary enough, but was it perhaps due to the air of the place that he felt as if it were something rare and new? The sound the plectrum made as it played down across the

strings and up again had a certain purity and distinction. Now
and then a *koto* would join in, its note fresh and appealing.

(4–311–1)

This passage is full of poetic suggestion (*yojō*); it resounds, so to speak, with
potential implication. When Kaoru enters the mountains to Uji, he starts
floundering. His sight is obscured by the mist, he cannot see the way, he loses
his direction. He is confronted by an unsettling experience, one couched in
terms of a natural event: the wind that blows down upon the trees and
scatters the dew which is powerless before it. The same is true of Kaoru; he
is reduced to a state of vulnerability and also, we should note, excitement.
The identification Kaoru/tears–trees/dew is explicit in the poem, which goes
further by saying that Kaoru weeps for an unknown reason (*ayanaku*). In the
vocabulary of Japanese poetry, dew/tears signify longing, in the sense of love-
longing, or grief. This poem then, or the whole passage for that matter, is a
foreshadowing motif. It anticipates Kaoru's falling in love with Ōigimi in the
following scene. One can also see it as a synoptic motif in the sense that the
Ōigimi cycle is primarily the story of a man who loses his direction. Kaoru
comes to Uji in search of the ways of Buddhist liberation from worldly
attachment. Instead he falls into love, the greatest bind of all.

This passage is interesting in other ways. It is, strictly speaking,
unmotivated. There is nothing in the handling of Kaoru's character up to this
point to prepare us for his emotions here. We have been given to understand
that he is sober and mature, that he kept himself under strict control. Yet
here he is, weak, susceptible, and in tears—and all because of the scenery.
There is also the added complication of the poem. It is presumably a kind of
soliloquy that he intones or thinks to himself, but its suggestive implications
raise the problem of point of view. Obviously Kaoru himself cannot know the
reason for his tears, but the narrator must have meant her "well-versed"
readers to see what they allude to. What we have here, in other words, is a
paradoxical situation in which a character intones a poem whose implications
are opaque to himself but transparent to the reader. A way out of this
dilemma would be to consider the whole passage as an extended metaphor or
allegory manipulated by a concealed omniscient poet-narrator, and existing
on a quite different level from the ordinary one in which consistency of
characterization is the prime consideration. From the point of view of the
plot, the action is almost a gratuitous one—Kaoru on his way to Uji. That
the author expands it at such length should alert us therefore to its supra-
narrative, that is to say its poetic function. Viewed from this angle, the
passage reveals itself to be about a man's symbolic encounter with forces
beyond his control. The real Kaoru is momentarily transformed into a

symbolic type-figure belonging to the mythopoeic structure of courtly love as adumbrated in the poetic anthologies: the man floundering in the darkness of uncontrollable longing (*madoi*) and suffering a loss of his usual identity in the process. Kaoru is seen through a romantic aura; he is imaged as a lover in disguise on his way to an amorous tryst. His fragrance floats in the night air, rousing the peasants to wonder, and significantly enough, it mingles with the notes of music from the Uji house. The union of scent and sound: what could be more ephemeral or, as it turns out, more symbolic of the spiritual idealism of the Kaoru–Ōigimi affair.

The passage thus has its own inner logic when viewed as metaphor. Nevertheless it is instructive to raise the question of narrative consistency, since it enables us to discriminate precisely what the author is doing, and how the lyrical mode operates within the narrative. Briefly: an event that is part of the temporal sequence of the plot (Kaoru on his way to Uji) is transformed into a poetic motif that crystallizes the significance of the particular moment, yet breaks out of it to implicate future events, and finally the whole story itself.

The passage above is a prelude to the first crucial event in the story of the Ōigimi cycle: the *kaimami* scene, in which Kaoru catches a glimpse of the Uji princesses and falls in love. This scene introduces the basic conflict motivating the rest of the plot development. Kaoru is unexpectedly deflected from his determined path to spiritual liberation, and it remains to be seen whether religion or love will win out in the end. What is pertinent here, with regard to *Genji*'s lyrical orientation, is that this crucial event in the plot is again conceived as a metaphor.[4] *Kaimami* literally means "peering through a gap in the hedge," and refers specifically to a man catching a glimpse of a woman behind a barrier. The barrier does not have to be a hedge or fence; it may be a screen, curtains, blinds, or, figuratively, mist, clouds, or darkness, but in all cases the psychology is the same: that of the momentary, elusive glimpse that leaves the subject yearning for more. Such moments recur in Japanese romantic tales and in poetry, hence I think we are justified in seeing them as a kind of archetypal motif signifying the inception of love. It is clearly being employed so in this scene, where we have in fact not only the motif in its classic guise—Kaoru pushing the gate of the fence slightly ajar and peering at the princesses—but other images that mirror it. There is the fragment of music that tantalizes him and is to recur on two more occasions hereafter, the second time in a significant context in "Shii ga moto." Then there is the moonlight suddenly appearing from behind the clouds, and momentarily illuminating the princesses' faces through the mist. "Come moonlight forth again" [*mata tsuki sashiidenamu*] (4–315–4), whispers Kaoru, thus illustrating the dynamic principle behind the *kaimami*: that a momentary pleasure generates its own desire for repetition, a fugitive glimpse ever strives toward a completed vision, and absence strains toward presence. In a sense the impression of a well-sustained plot in the Ōigimi cycle from the first to the third chapter is due to the sheer energy generated by this motif whose fulfillment is repeatedly postponed until at last it reaches its idealized sublimation in Ōigimi's death. Kaoru's tragedy then is the very paradoxical one that in losing Ōigimi he remains forever suspended in the illusionary potentiality of the *kaimami* stage. Prevented from seeing the affair to its hollow conclusion, he remains forever enchanted, a victim of permanent nostalgia for a dream whose end eluded him (the *mihatenu yume* motif of poetry). And it is this nostalgia of course that in turn generates the subsequent Uji chapters.

The *kaimami* falls together in this scene with a related motif, that of the "hidden flower," the beautiful woman discovered in some remote and uncultivated place.[5] ("'So it is true. The world does have in store such affecting things, hidden away in the shadows,' thought Kaoru, his heart almost leaving him" (4–315-2). Interestingly, this conjunction occurs as early as the *Ise monogatari*, whose first episode is about a courtier who goes hunting in Kasuga village, where he catches a glimpse of two beautiful sisters through the hedge and becomes so ecstatic he tears off a strip of his wildly patterned robe to accompany his poem about the disorder of his heart. The significance of the "hidden flower" motif lies, I think, in the psychology of surprise, the excitation caused by the juxtaposition of the familiar with the unfamiliar, the known with the unknown. Remote and strange, Uji represents a world wholly different from that of the courtly society of the capital. And so what a marvelous discovery it is to find there ladies who embody precisely the courtly ideal. Where Kaoru had expected some rustic maidens (we remember that on his first visit to Uji, he wonders fleetingly whether the princesses were not perhaps lacking in grace), it is with a shock of recognition that he finds the ultimate in aristocratic poise. This is how he sees them when, told that a gentleman was outside, they withdrew from his gaze into the inner room: "They showed no signs of being upset; calmly, unobtrusively, they went in, their motions, which allowed not even a rustling of silk to be heard, so exquisitely delicate that his heart almost ached with the loveliness of it all. Such high-born dignity and grace [*ate ni miyabikanaru*] filled him with admiration" (4–315-6). The appeal of the "hidden flower," its very uniqueness, lies in its existence within an unfamiliar context. The music he hears is tuned to the common *ōjiki* mode, but it is made uncommon by the *place* in which he hears it.

The enchantment Uji weaves around Kaoru is by no means over. Hardly has he regained his bearings when Bennokimi appears. Bennokimi is apparently a sorcerer figure and medium of fate; it is she who reveals to Kaoru his real parents' tragic destiny, and in a sense presides over its reenactment in the unfolding Kaoru–Ōigimi story. She is still at Uji years later during its equally unfortunate sequel, the tragedy of Ukifune.[6] As a sorcerer figure, she mesmerizes Kaoru with stories of the past. Their significant theme, moreover, is love or *aware*, the forces that generate worldly attachment and bind the soul to the vicious circle of *karma* whereby the past forever repeats itself. Bennokimi begins to unfold the story that by its very concealment had preoccupied Kaoru's imagination since childhood, whose dire import had made him turn to religion and ironically to Prince Hachi and Uji. Kaoru is both repelled and attracted: "It was strange, a story in a dream; it was as if a medium had poured out an unbidden tale while in a trance; it was weird, he thought, but as it had to do with things that had disturbed him all these years, he was also very fascinated" (4–320–15). But it is growing light, he has to leave without hearing the real core of the story, knowing only that it concerns his birth.

> "I am still unable to grasp precisely what it all means ...," he said, and as he stood up, there came the distant booming of the bell from the mountain temple where the Prince was. The mists hovered thickly about. Clouds covered the slopes and he felt sadly that they formed a barrier to his longing. It pained him too to imagine what the princesses must be feeling. Were there any sorrows left that they had not had to endure? No wonder they were so reclusive.

Asaborake	"In the faint dawn
Ieji mo miezu	I cannot see the way home,
Tazunekoshi	And Makinoo Hill
Makinooyama wa	Which I came to visit
Kiri kometekeri.	Lies shrouded in mist.

How lonely it is," he murmured, half-turning back, and his hesitant figure as he stood there....

(4–321–4)

[Ōigimi replied:]

Kumo no iru	"It is a time
Mine no kakeji o	When the trail up the peak

Akigiri ni	Where clouds dwell,
Itodo hedatsuru	Recedes ever farther from us
Koro ni mo aru kana.	Behind the autumn mist."

There was just the faintest suggestion of a sigh in her voice that
spoke of no ordinary sorrow and touched him deeply. By itself the
place had little to offer by way of amusement but of sorrows it
had many.

(4–322–1)

Kaoru's poem, like the one before, is highly suggestive; its implications,
however, are not potential but regressive, pointing to the significance of
events that have just occurred. The things hinted at in the previous passage
have come to pass; the reason for his ineffable feelings of fear and excitement
has now been revealed. Kaoru is but dimly aware that something has
happened to him: presumably for him the words of his poem mean exactly,
and only, what they say; but the reader is of course disposed by the
omniscient narrator to interpret this passage symbolically. Its overriding
impression is one of hesitation and uncertainty. He should go home, but
Bennokimi's unfinished story holds him in thrall, as does his brief glimpse of
the Uji sisters. The mist that obscures his way home and separates him from
the Prince is an image of his state of mind, his confusion and loss of control
as he stands hesitating on the brink of the yawning, ever-turning circle of
inga. Although he longs for the enlightened guidance of Prince Hachi, he is
unable to break out of these internal mists. The sound of the temple bell that
reminds him of his true direction is very far away: religion is remote. Ōigimi's
poem is very similar in context and imagery to Kaoru's; both are motivated
by a feeling of being isolated from the reassuring presence of Prince Hachi
and religion, and they form a kind of duet.

He went to the western wing where the guard had prepared a
place for him, and sat there gazing out at the river.
    "See how excited they are, down at the fish weirs."
    "But doesn't it seem to you that the fish have avoided the trap?
The fishermen look disappointed." His men were conversing
knowledgeably about the local scenery.
    Poor-looking boats laden with brushwood came and went past
each other in the river, each boatman eking out a pathetically
meagre livelihood adrift upon the perilous waters. "Life is
uncertain for everyone, when you think about it. How can I
presume that I alone am not adrift, but 'seated calmly in my

jeweled pavillion'?" he thought to himself, and was lost in reflection for a while. Then he called for an inkstone and wrote her a poem.

Hashihime no	"Drawn to the sorrows
Kokoro o kumite	Of the Lady of the Bridge,
Takase sasu	My sleeves grow moist
Sao no shizuku ni	In the drops of spray from
Sode zo nurenuru.	The oar plying the shoals.

How sadly she must gaze on such a scene." ... She was embarrassed by the poverty of her letter paper with its undistinguished scent, but at such a moment, she reflected, what mattered was to deliver a quick reply.

Sashikaeru	"The Ferryman of Uji
Uji no kawaosa	Plying his oars day in
Asayu no	And day out,
Shizuku ya sode o	In the drops of spray will his
Kutashihatsuramu.	Sleeves rot away at last?

My very being is cast adrift...." It was a beautiful hand. Her ways leave nothing to be desired, he thought, entranced.

(4–322–8)

The conversation among Kaoru's men about the poor catch at the weirs functions on the first level to illustrate his thoughts about the fishermen's uncertain livelihood, but the detail about fish not drawn to the trap is, on the allegorical level, also an allusion to Kaoru's own precarious situation in being drawn to the snares of emotional attachment here in Uji.[7]

The river motif which has occurred twice before takes center stage in this passage. The natural scenery is transformed into an allegorical image: everyone is a boatman cast adrift upon the uncertain river of life, or destiny. Presumably, Kaoru feels that he and Ōigimi are united under the burden of this universal human destiny; he because of the tragic circumstances of his birth, and she because of her father's political downfall that forced them into exile in Uji. And he imagines that life is even more unbearable for her since she spends her days before the very emblem of this dire message. His poem is sympathetic. Ōigimi's reply closely parallels his in content and imagery; again as in the previous pair we have the impression of a duet, two tonalities of the same melodic figure, with Ōigimi's poem being much darker. It focuses on the interminable quality of her sorrow, and its inevitable result: not only her sleeves, but her "very being is cast adrift"—that is, she is saturated through and through, waterlogged. The image is portentous, not only of her own death, but later of Ukifune's attempted suicide by drowning. It is a typical poem for Ōigimi; we remember that her first poem, in the sprint day scene, was equally pessimistic, equally aware of the bitter fate of the waterbird." Shrouded in the gloomy mist of Uji and "drowning" in the torrents of its river, she is a true creature of the place, the very goddess of the Uji Bridge whom Kaoru's arduous efforts are finally unable to dislodge from her shrine of sorrow.

This is a good place to consider the theoretical question of the operation of poetry within a narrative context. Typically, a narrative progresses in a linear manner through the chronological unfolding of the plot. Narrative, as the French critic Jacques Riviere has observed, is "the surge toward that which does not yet exist."[8] Every moment in it is a new moment adding information to the old in order to reveal the story and the characters' development in a sequential progression. This progression may also be seen as a metonymical one; the author moves from the action to its setting, from the character to its environment in the course of the narration. Plot-character-setting are in contiguous relationship to each other just as the constituent elements of a sentence, noun-phrase and verb-phrase, are seen to be in an external, contiguous relationship governed by the rules of combination called syntax. As we have seen in the passage just quoted, or in earlier ones for that matter, the setting does not remain a mere metonymical adjunct to plot and character, but is in fact transmuted into their metaphorical equivalent, their mirroring image. This is eminently a demonstration of the poetic process or function.[9]

Poetry is distinct from narrative because it progresses through paradigms which elaborate a single emotion or thought. The parts of a poem are in an internal relationship of equivalence, both phonologically through meter, and semantically through metaphor. What happens in the passages under consideration is that the poetic function is being superimposed upon the narrative progression, slowing it down and transforming its constitutive elements (plot-character-setting) into paradigmatic transparencies of meaning. The paradigm, by reiterating the same message in various reifications, endows the narrative with a certain permanence, and at the same time a certain ambiguity and richness.

Let us examine more closely the operation of this poetic function in the passage quoted above. As soon as Kaoru makes the connection between himself and the boatmen, between the river and his own life, the scenery that is a constitutive element in the narrative's temporal sequence is transformed into a metaphorical equivalent of his situation. His poem imitates the scenery in its use of synecdochic details and associative words that evoke it. "Moist," "drops of spray," "oar," and "shoals" are all images belonging to the semantic field of river and boat in the description. "Heart" (or sorrows) and "sleeves," however, make us realize that the water images are merely being used in a manner of speaking. The double entendre hinges on the verb *kumu*, which means both "to draw water" and "to guess and sympathize with another's feelings." We look at the poem again and realize that it is a reification of an earlier statement about Uji's hold on Kaoru: "the place had little to offer by way of amusement but of sorrows it had many"; it also recalls Kaoru's situation as a fish drawn to the snares of emotional attachment, alluded to in the beginning of the quoted passage. In Ōigimi's poem, the Ferryman of Uji (= boatman = herself) "plying his oars day in and day out" echoes "boats ... came and went past each other" in the initial description. "Drops of spray" and "sleeves" repeat Kaoru's words, and the fragment of an envoi, "My very being is cast adrift," echoes "boatman ... adrift upon the perilous waters." The whole passage then, the prose as well as the poetry, is a series of resonant paradigms, and we can see it as a single poem. The narrative progression is frozen before the external scenery while a single melodic line is repeated in various modulations to give the poetic message resonance and depth. We have seen how these two poems, while belonging ineluctably to their present context, also implicate what went before and comes after, even finally suggesting the pattern of the whole story. This is true of all the poems considered so far, and I think it is responsible for attenuating the force or dynamism of the plot. The poems do this by suggesting the direction of the plot even before the events themselves are narrated. They are imagistic signposts which by enabling us to see a meaningful design in the story at any one point in its progression weaken the surge of expectation regarding what yet remains unrevealed.

The shifting and ever-widening implications of the poems create an ambiguity with regard to the exact nature of the poetic message and the point of view behind the poems, most of which are after all composed by a particular character and addressed to another in a specific instance in the story. It has been noted earlier that the tender sensibilities displayed in Kaoru's poems are somehow inconsistent with his characterization in the "Niou miya" chapter as a sober and scrupulous young man, indeed somewhat of a prig. The same traits are revealed here in "Hashihime" when he protests his honorable intentions to the guard and in his amazing speech to Ōigimi, with its mixed tone of offended dignity and self-righteous reprimand, ending in a highly unusual request for her friendship.

There is in fact an ironic juxtaposition between Kaoru's inner feelings and reactions in the lyrical passages, and his imperfect comprehension of them as manifest in his outward behavior. The impression of irony suggests that it is misleading to identify the poetry solely with the character who composes it. That it integrates so well with the prose and reflects so succinctly the design of the narrative indicates the presence of the author-narrator's point of view as well. Furthermore it seems necessary to distinguish between the "I" of the character as we know him within the story and the "lyrical I," the persona which is a formal, impersonal identity to the degree that the poem's author (i.e., the character) is never completely identical with the poet. It is precisely this distinction that renders it plausible for a character to express a sensibility that goes against his social personality, while paradoxically revealing his inner self.

Poetic distance is related to the nature of poetry as conventionalized ritual in the society the author depicts. Kaoru can feel free to unmask his emotions, something he would not ordinarily do, under the guise of impersonal identity lent by the convention of the poetic exchange. The same goes for Ōigimi, who is so embarrassed that she has only barely managed to utter one single sentence up to this point, but who nevertheless composes two poems that lay bare the very soul of her sorrowful existence in Uji. That the characters themselves apprehend the poems partly as conventional artifacts is I think also evidenced by the unexpected manner in which they receive them. In the two instances quoted here, Kaoru appears to be concerned less with the content of Ōigimi's poem than with the tone of voice in which she intones it, or with her calligraphy. It is as though he would discover her true feelings not in the poem itself, ultimately a figure of speech, but in the supra-linguistic factors that endow it with the speaker's private emotion.

To summarize then, the ambiguity of the poems arises from their bearing three points of view: those of the character, the character as impersonal poet, and the author-narrator. The character as such, in projecting himself into the poetic persona, is not necessarily aware of the full implications of his poem. Or to put it in another way, the character assumes a persona that disguises him from himself as well as from the character to whom he addresses the poem, while simultaneously revealing himself to us through the author-narrator's orchestration of the poem with the complex of the narrative. Not all the poems in these three chapters are so richly ambiguous; I have omitted from discussion those that operate only on one level, as ordinary dialogue couched in figurative terms and bound only to a specific instance, without implicating progressively wider contexts.[10]

"*SHII GA MOTO*"

The "Hashihime" chapter centers around the inception of Kaoru's love for Ōigimi. It also introduces the motifs against which the events of the two subsequent chapters are to be interpreted. Our discussion of the significance of these patterns of imagery may have obscured the fact that the hero himself is only dimly aware of these same significances, although he is much moved by what he has just experienced in Uji. "He realized weakly that the world was after all hard to renounce" (4–323–15), says the narrator of Kaoru as he comes away from Uji, but after recounting what he saw to his friend Niou, he immediately falls back on his old resolve, apparently unaware of any break in his own self-confident control.[11]

The crucial event in "Shii ga moto" is the death of Prince Hachi and Kaoru's promise to look after his daughters. Kaoru makes this promise when he goes to see Prince Hachi in the seventh month following the spring of Niou's visit. The scene of the conversation between the two men is particularly interesting because of the overwhelming impression of irony which culminates in the poetic exchange that ends the scene. In the first place, when Prince Hachi makes the request that Kaoru should come and visit the princesses after he is gone, Kaoru graciously accedes—"A single word from you [*hitokoto nite mo*], and I would never neglect them" (4–346–14); but he has some reservations about his own lack of desire to remain in the world. Now this scruple can only strike the reader as ironic when juxtaposed against the whole bearing of the "Hashihime" chapter. Furthermore, having just asked a young man to look after his daughters, the Prince then proceeds to deliver a speech on none other than the topic of the evil influence of women, "a suitable companion for a moment's pleasure, but planting the seed of passion in men's hearts" (4–347–11). And Kaoru, with a singular lack of self-awareness, hardly realizes the significance of the Prince's speech, but instead expresses his desire to hear more of that fragment of music (*hitokoe kikishi onkoto no ne*) (4–348–6) he had first heard that early dawn of the *kaimami* scene. Prince Hachi then conceives the idea of bringing Kaoru and his daughters together, significantly enough, by asking them to play a melody for him. Thus when the poems celebrating the contract made between the two men emerge at the end of all this, they acquire a peculiar and powerfully ironic ring because of the superimposition of the quite different promise suggested by the *kaimami* motif of love-longing.

Ware nakute	When I am gone,
Kusa no iori wa	This hut of grass may
Arenu to mo	Fall to ruin;

Kono hitokoto wa   But this one promise, I feel,
Kareji to zo omou.   Will not wither.

[The Prince]

Ikanaramu   When will it
Yo ni ka karesemu   Ever wither, this but
        Nagaki yo no   Of grasses
Chigiri musuberu   Twined with a promise
Kusa no iori wa.   Made for all time.

[Kaoru]
(4–348–15)

These poems, unlike those previously quoted, do not utilize imagery from the external setting. Their effect depends upon the context of the conversation of which they are a part, pulling together its two strands to create a symbolic, synoptic reiteration that is also the climax of the scene. The felt superimposition of the *kaimami* motif on the explicit theme of the poems is a good illustration of the "contagious" influence of the prose context on the poem, and vice versa. Especially because there is no overt image in the poems themselves to evoke the *kaimami*,[12] this becomes a striking instance of the poetic, resonant effects made possible solely through the associative power of elements in contiguity. In general the imagistic continuity from prose to poetry that we found in "Hashihime" is not always so explicit in subsequent lyrical passages. The poems are still mirroring images reflecting the feeling or thought in the preceding prose section, but not necessarily the external setting. As before, however, they draw together the threads of the narrative plot into a total synoptic image or metaphor, contracting them and endowing them with a heightened symbolical meaning. The difference, which is between images picked from the actual setting and those summoned from the mind, is worth noting, but it does not alter the paradigmatic character of the poems in relation to their prose context.

With the death of Prince Hachi in the following eighth month, the paradoxical promise signified by the poems above comes into operation. It now becomes Kaoru's solemn obligation to look after the princesses, who are wholly defenseless but for his protection. In a word, Kaoru contracts the very bond (*hodashi*) that to the end prevented Prince Hachi from realizing his most cherished desire of complete liberation from worldly attachments. And ironically, he is also put in a position of being able to rationalize his budding desire for Ōigimi.

Kaoru's first visit to Uji after Prince Hachi's death throws the princesses into acute discomfort, a shyness the cause of which is hinted in the narrator's use of suggestive imagery: "To the shadowy regions where they wandered distraught with grief, he came in shining with a radiance so dazzling that they were embarrassed and unable to respond to his solicitous queries" (4–360–9). The same imagery figures in Ōigimi's explanation for their reticence: "Still wandering in a grievous dream from which it is hard to awaken, we shrink from gazing at the light of the sky" (4–360–16), and in Kaoru's reply: "To tell the truth, I think you are being far too scrupulous. It would be wrong of course if you were to feel like prancing cheerfully out into the light of the sun and moon, but as it is your behavior leaves me bewildered and uncertain as to what I should do" (4–361–4).

From the very beginning of this passage, the narrator suggests that it is not only her grief that causes Ōigimi to retreat into her shell but also a maidenly reserve before Kaotu himself, who is imaged here with a radiance suggestive of romance. There is a finely nuanced shift in attitude between seeing Kaoru as protector, which he has been all along, and as the handsome young man that he actually is. Ōigimi in her fastidious mind cannot reconcile these two figures, and therefore she cannot allow herself to depend on Kaoru; this is the meaning of her poem below. The love-longing that colors Kaoru's sympathy, investing him with the romantic aura from which Ōigimi shies away, is palpable in the evocation of the kaimami motif just before he intones his poem.

It was a pitiful shadow that was dimly outlined through the black curtains, and as he imagined how grief-stricken she must actually be, the figure he had glimpsed that autumn dawn rose fleetingly in his memory. He murmured as though to himself,

Iro kawaru	"Seeing the altered
Asaji o mite mo	Hue of the withered weeds,
Sumizome no	I am moved to imagine
Yatsururu sode o	Those sleeves now wasting
Omoi koso yare.	In a black pall of grief."
Iro kawaru	[She replied] "Altered in hue,
Sode o ba tsuyu no	My sleeves provide a lodging
Yadori nite	For the dew,
Waga mi zo sare ni	But I myself find
Okidokoro naki.	No place to rest.

'The threads that come loose...,'" she whispered, but her voice
faltered, and trailed off. She seemed to be having great difficulty
in controlling herself, and was withdrawing into the inner room.
He longed to call her back, but it was not the time, he thought,
pity welling in his heart.

(4–362–2)

By the time of his next visit in the late winter, however, Kaoru is already
firmly set on a path that is the exact opposite of the one that had first brought
him to Uji four years earlier. This time his reception is warmer; Ōigimi is
more talkative, so enchanting in fact that Kaoru, unable to endure the
thought that their relationship should remain at a standstill, realizes that it
must be deepened: "'I can't let things remain like this between us (a shocking
change of heart indeed),[13] they *must* change!' he told himself as he sat before
her screen" (4–368–6). But amazingly enough, contrary to what the reader
expects, he proceeds to disclose not his own feelings but Niou's, although it
does seem possible that the latter part of his long-winded speech is actually
a description of himself in the guise of his friend. But its real subject and
intent are ambiguous, and Ōigimi's reaction is entirely understandable:
"'Well. What can I say? You have run on and on in a rather tantalizing way,
and I must confess that I can't think of what to answer,' she said, and there
was a light laugh in her voice that he found attractive" (4–370–1). Kaoru
hastens to make himself clear, but blunders only deeper into indirection.

> "I do not think that you yourself need feel called upon to
> receive his suit. It is enough that you as an elder sister appreciate
> my goodwill in thus braving the snow to visit. No, I believe he is
> drawn to someone else. He has been sending occasional notes
> too, I hear, and yes, by the way, it is not clear to me. Which of
> you has been answering them?"
>
> It was not the sort of thing she could have done even in jest,
> but the thought that she might just as easily have answered Niou's
> letters—for they meant nothing to her, filled her with such shame
> and embarrassment that she was unable to reply.

Yuki fukaki	"Along the mountain
Yama no kakehashi	Trail covered deep with
Kimi narade	Snow, I see
Mata fumikayou	No other footprints
Ato o minu kana.	Aside from your own."

She wrote instead, and pushed the note toward him. "Such indirections serve only to increase my uncertainty," he complained.

Tsurara toji	"Riding my horse
Koma fumishidaku	Whose hoofbeats break the ice
Yamakawa o	Of the mountain river,
Shirubeshigatera	I shall cross first,
Mazu ya wataramu.	Leading the way for another.

That I have come is a sign, not so shallow as to 'reflect even the image...,'" he added.[14]

Taken by surprise, she became uncomfortable and was not up to any reply. She did not seem impossibly cold and remote, yet neither was there in her manner any suggestion of that affectedness so com mon to young women of the day. He judged her to be a lady of quiet and graceful attitudes, someone in fact who was no different from what he imagined he would like a woman to be. But each time he hinted of his feelings she pretended not to understand. Embarrassed, he began instead to talk earnestly of things that happened long ago.

(4–370–4)

This passage constitutes an admirable model of the workings of Kaoru's mind. The beginning of it is especially powerful in the way it dramatizes the stark contrast between the force of his inner intention and desire as revealed in his thoughts as he sits before Ōigimi's screen, and the amazingly irrelevant words that he subsequently utters ("Niou is very angry with me" 4–368–9). What this whole passage reveals is that Kaoru is unable to approach his own feelings directly. He needs a protective covering, and this he finds in Niou. Under the pretext of discussing Niou's attitude to women and love, he manages, willy-nilly, to allude to his own feelings, but the cover-up continues until at one point he allows his own self to peek through, almost incidentally it seems, by appending a brief remark to his own poem. He alludes to his feelings by alluding to another poem, and what could be more indirect than that? And from Ōigimi's point of view, this fragment of a revelation is unexpected. Kaoru's long, ambiguous discourse has not exactly prepared her for it, and she is alarmed instead of being beguiled. The workings of Ōigimi's mind are apparently no different from Kaoru's. She too is self-possessed as long as her feelings are not involved. It is because she does not think that Kaoru's speech has anything to do with herself that she even finds it slightly amusing. But as soon as the question directly touches her, she too employs a protective mechanism, that of a poem.

We find here an interesting case of a character deliberately exploiting the poetic distance discussed earlier. Ōigimi is so embarrassed by Kaoru's tactless question that she is unable to reply in the same vein, that is, in the ordinary language of dialogue prose. Instead, by couching her reply in the formal language of poetry, she is able to distance herself from it. She not only answers Kaoru's question unambiguously but through poetry manages to do it with a poise and wit which adequately cover up the embarrassment she really feels. It is perhaps not too far-fetched to see Kaoru's reaction to her poem as evidence of his awareness that the language of poetry is not a completely forthright one. He proceeds to employ it himself, with an ambiguity that simultaneously masks and reveals his own feelings. As in his earlier speech, he makes Niou the dominant subject, and himself the minor one. The ambiguity lies in the word *mazu*, which clearly means his coming ahead, before Niou, as Niou's guide to Nakanokimi, but which can also mean that first, or to begin with, he has his own mission with Ōigimi herself. He clarifies this ambiguity, as we have seen, by the pointed allusion to another poem. It is interesting to note that Kaoru's scolding remark about Ōigimi's poem shows a deplorable lack of sensitivity to feminine shyness and reserve. Indeed his wooing is marked throughout by a bewildered mixture of earnestness and obtuseness.

Kaoru may express himself by indirection, but there is no doubt at all that at this point his original resolve to attain religious detachment has given way before the dark, entangling forces of love. The scene following the one above embodies his realization of what he has lost. This is the climactic scene to which the whole chapter has been moving, and it includes the "title-poem." Like the *Hashihime no* poem, it is preceded by a brief anticipatory dialogue, about the old night guard's feeling of vulnerability now that Prince Hachi is dead, his grief at losing the "shelter" (*kage*) of the Prince's protection. Kaoru's situation is the same (his poem uses the same image of shade, shelter), only his loss is not material but spiritual.

He made the guard open Prince Hachi's room and saw that the dust had settled thickly everywhere. The Buddhist image with its flower ornaments stood as splendid as before, but the prayer dais where he had seen Prince Hachi at his devotions had been taken away, and the spot swept clean, and bare. "When I accomplish my resolve...," he remembered having vowed to the Prince.

Tachiyoramu	"Beneath the oak
Kage to tanomishi	I had hoped to draw near
Shii ga moto	For shelter,
Munashiki toko ni	Now there is only
Narinikeru kana.	An empty room."

(4–372–10)

This scene is to all intents and purposes the end of this chapter, which centers on Prince Hachi's death and the changes it causes in the lives of the people around him. Kaoru's guide and mentor is gone, he himself has taken another path, the lessons and training have come to nothing. The image of *munashiki toko*, symbol of a mental space once full of aspiration, now barren with the emptiness and futility of human life and effort, is an extremely effective one. The poem is full of regret for a thwarted renunciation.

"*AGEMAKI*"

From the vantage point of "Agemaki," the first two chapters constitute a long preparatory section, an overture as it were to the main movement which is the love story of Kaoru and Ōigimi. The progression of the three chapters suggests an analogy to the *jo-ha-kyū* structure of Japanese musical and dramatic compositions. "Hashihime" with its imagistic prefigurings would be the anticipatory *jo* section, "Shii ga moto" which introduces changes in the protagonists' actual situation would be the *ha* section (in music the gradual weaving in of new motifs and rhythms), and "Agemaki" the climactic *kyū* section which impels the story to its most intense development and brings the foreshadowing images of "Hashihime" to their fullest realization. It is revealing of the distinctly poetic Japanese sense of structure that the climax comes, not at the point of the change that governs the subsequent development of the plot, but where the protagonists are finally fused with their metaphors: Kaoru as the eternal wanderer in the darkness of madoi, and Ōigimi as the transfigured goddess of the Uji Bridge.

With the "Agemaki" chapter, we come to the love story itself: Kaoru's wooing of Ōigimi, the obstacles that appear on the path of his desire, his tremendous efforts to overcome them which lead to but a brief, illusory moment of victory before the dark forces return to lead the story to its predestined, tragic end. We should observe at the outset that poetry and lyrical prose do not play as dominant a role in "Agemaki" as in the previous chapters, except near the end, and there they are decisive in revealing the poetic significance of the whole cycle. It is as if the author-narrator, having already established the patterns of imagery and the motifs which will provide the meaning framework for the story, were now settling down to the business of actualizing it. In the greater part of the chapter, instead of the heightened expression of emotional moments achieved by lyrical prose, we have an incisive power of analysis demonstrated in the interior monologues of the protagonists, and the intellectual energy generated by their long, contentious dialogues. The Kaoru–Ōigimi love story is conceived as a battle of wills, and wits, which makes it a peculiar love story indeed, as compared with the others in the *Genji*. In fact it owes its absorbing power to its very deviation from the normal course of a love affair, and to the protagonists' atypical characterization as romantic hero and heroine. Kaoru, with his sobriety and compulsive reticence, is incapable of winning his love by seduction and passionate demonstrations. He tries instead to convince her by reasoned words and exemplary deeds. As the narrator writes near the end of "Shii ga moto": "Our earnest fellow's character was quite singular. He hoped to make her his own, but with infinite patience he was resolved not to act imprudently nor give her cause for alarm as long as she had not softened in her heart toward him. And he hoped too that she would eventually realize his fidelity to her father's wishes" (4–375–8). He apparently confuses gratitude with love, just as he confuses his love with his duty to look after the princesses.

Ōigimi's character is just as singular. She appears to be cast in the role of the "harsh mistress" whose iciness spurs her lover to feats of daring and invention. (Kaoru not only engineers the Niou–Nakanokimi affair, he even dares to challenge the powerful political opposition for her sake.) Although reared in the remote mountains, she possesses a social poise and wit which she employs to hold Kaoru at bay, while simultaneously exciting his admiration. But this is only half the story. Ōigimi is to the very end the "hidden flower" figure of the "Hashihime" chapter; she combines the courtly, aristocratic ideal of poise and social grace with the reclusive shyness, the simplicity and inexperience of a maiden brought up apart from society. That she belongs to Uji accounts for her painful awkwardness and feelings of inadequacy before the rich, courtly figure of Kaoru. That she is at the same time a princess and true aristocrat accounts for her excessively fine scruples and her concern for decorum, which in turn motivate her energetic resistance.

The "title-poem" of this chapter appears at its beginning and assumes the nature of an emblem for it, since the chapter is all about Kaoru's efforts to exchange marriage vows with Ōigimi (the significance of tying a "trefoil knot") and her persistent refusal. The trefoil knot, though never really tied, assumes an ironic significance at the end, as it comes to represent Kaoru's permanent attachment to Ōigimi's memory. This emblematic image is anticipated by several allusions to poems with the related images of threads, spinning, and twining. It is also firmly wedded to its context, since the princesses are in this opening scene sewing ornaments for the memorial services on the first anniversary of their father's death. Kaoru's poem too is very appropriate; it is conceived as a kind of *gammon*, a petition or prayer to the Buddhist gods, while he is actually engaged in writing such petitions for the ceremonies.

> Kaoru sat writing the petitions that were to be offered during the memorial services along with sutras and Buddhist images, and while he still had the inkstone before him, he also wrote:

Agemaki ni	"Into a trefoil knot
Nagaki chigiri o	That is tied to seal an
Musubikome	Enduring vow,
Onaji tokoro ni	May these threads meet
Yori mo awanamu.	And together entwine."

> He pushed the poem beneath the blinds. Not again, thought Ōigimi, annoyed.

Nuki mo aezu	"A frail thread
Moroki namida no	That cannot hold the
Tama no o ni	Jewels of tears
Nagaki chigiri o	That weakly fall, how can
Ikaga musubamu.	It bind an enduring vow?"

> "'But if they do not meet...,'" Kaoru whispered. He looked hurt as he gazed off into space.

> (4–382–4)

Ōigimi's reply to Kaoru's "marriage proposal" sounds like a rejection, but on somewhat ambiguous grounds. On the level of objective images, the sense of her poem is clear enough, but its rational meaning is more difficult to grasp. She seems to be saying that her broken, sorrowful life cannot stand up to anything as concrete as a marriage arrangement, but in any case its main attitude is, as usual, pessimistic. She is not exactly saying "yes" or "no"; she is simply unable to consider the proposal. She gives her reasons in the ensuing dialogue: her father had left no instructions about What she was to do under such circumstances, which leads her to conclude that he intended her to pass her life in Uji, resigned to a fate different from ordinary people. And therefore she did not know one way or another how she should receive his proposal. The reasoning here is significant. In the whole course of this wooing, the matter of whether or not she likes Kaoru never comes into question. On one or two occasions, we are indeed informed that she does not dislike him, that if he had been just some ordinary man and not the superior being that he is, she might have yielded to him. But the whole matter of her emotions seems to be beside the point. It seems to be of more relevance that Kaoru vanquish her scruples than win her love.

The peculiarities of the two protagonists emerge once more in the scene where they spend the night together. It would be difficult to find another "first-night" scene in the *Genji* that is as absorbing in its combination of ironic wit and *tendresse*, of delicate reticence and candor, passion and sympathy. In a novel, where such encounters impress the modern reader as little more than legitimate rape—with the hero exercising force or guile to overcome the heroine, who promptly wilts away or offers but passive resistance to the inevitable (all this of course delineated with the proper romantic ambience)—the encounter between characters who must be viewed as unconventional by standard Heian practices strikes one as somewhat more human and realistic. It starts when Kaoru, for once unable to restrain himself, goes behind Ōigimi's screen. She is incensed.

> "So this is what you mean by an 'unencumbered talk'? I would never have expected such audacious behavior from you!" she taunted him, but her manner only served to increase his admiration.
> "It is precisely because you persist in not understanding what I mean that I thought I would show you. But pray tell me, what exactly were you thinking of, to call my behavior 'audacious'? I swear by the Buddha here—come now, stop trembling so. I am determined not to force your heart, and although people will not believe such an unlikely situation as this, I shall probably spend the rest of my life playing the eccentric fool." Stroking the black hair that fell loosely in the bewitching light, he saw that she was as entrancing as he had imagined....
> Weeping in chagrin and despair, she was extremely pathetic. It must not be like this, he thought to himself, I must wait until she softens in her own heart toward me. Pained at her distress, he calmed the turmoil in his breast and tried to comfort her.
> "Not knowing what you really felt, I have allowed an uncommon

familiarity between us. You show a lack of consideration in forcing me to show myself in these mourning robes, but I realize too that my own carelessness was to blame and find no comfort in the thought," she said reproachfully. She was vexed by the thought of how she must look, caught unguarded in her shabby robes under the lamp-light; it was too dismal and embarrassing.

"I understand that you must think me inconsiderate. I am ashamed and can think of nothing to say to excuse myself. It is natural of course that you should bring in the matter of your mourning robes, but do you think it right, when you have had evidence of my feelings all these years, to make of your mourning an excuse to act as if we have just met? Such prudence dazzles me with its fine excess," he declared.

(4–389–16)

Kaoru's hesitation at the crucial point, where a hero like Genji would have plunged on, proves fatal. This hesitation is subject to ambiguous interpretation; on the one hand it seems rather admirable, and on the other quite deplorable, but whatever else it is, it is surely in character and from a modern viewpoint quite human. What is truly deplorable is Kaoru's persistent misunderstanding of Ōigimi's reactions. He forecloses by his obtuseness every little possibility of Ōigimi's acting the woman with him; he argues where he should woo. Thus rebuffed, woman-like she has no other recourse but to her pride. And this is her tragedy. There is a moment later in the chapter when this subtle point comes across very well. On Nakanokimi's third nuptial night, the house is in a flurry of delighted preparation. Nakanokimi is at her most beautiful, Niou is the very image of the romantic hero. And during this night Ōigimi lies all alone, a forlorn figure excluded from brightness and romance, and reflecting sadly on her passing youth and beauty.

Toward dawn of the abortive night with Kaoru, a lyrical strain appears, woven into the dialogue. The sound of the flapping of birds' wings nearby, the dawn bell ringing far away, and later the cock's crowing are all pulled together in Kaoru's poem, a masterpiece of restraint and delicate suggestion.

Yamazato no	"Many things
Aware shiraruru	That touch the heart are
Koegoe ni	Brought together
Toriatsumetaru	In the sounds of the mountain
Asaborake kana.	Village at daybreak."

She replied:

> Tori no ne mo   "Mountains beyond
> Kikoenu yama to   The reach of even the bird's
>   Omoishi o   Song, I thought;
> Yo no uki koto wa   Now the world's sorrows
> Tazunekinikeri.   Have come to visit."
>
>   (4–394–5)

These are hardly what one would expect of *kinuginu* ("morning after") poems, ideally, in the formal tradition of Japanese love poetry, expressions of the lovers' regret that the night has been so brief, that the cold dawn should break upon the warmth of shared robes. Kaoru's poem may not be so irrelevant; it projects a persona still nostalgically suspended in the emotions of the night; "the sounds of the mountain village" at dawn are just that much more affecting because of what transpired during the night. But Kaoru is alone in his enchantment. Ōigimi herself is wide awake, with that lucidity the narrator has related to the power of the Uji River's roar to shock one into reality. For her, not a whit beguiled, the previous night is merely an unwelcome intrusion into her quiet and monkish (*hijiri-dachitaru* as she puts it in "Shii ga moto") existence in Uji. These two poems, like those that opened the chapter, are oddly at cross purposes. This is a characteristic of all the poems exchanged by Kaoru and Ōigimi in "Agemaki," and is in striking contrast to their lyrical, harmonizing duets in "Hashihime." Such a contrariness reflects of course the battle of wills that is the subject of this chapter. Similarly, the unconventional character of their love story can be measured by the degree to which their "love poems," of which there are not many—only three more pairs after the one above—deviate from the readers expectations based on the courtly poetic tradition. The deviation is especially apparent in comparison with the poetic exchanges of Niou and Nakanokimi, whose love affair follows the normal course, and whose poems therefore are equally conventional protestations of fidelity and longing. In a sense then we can say that the tragedy of "Agemaki" is essentially that of atypical characters caught in an all too typical situation in which they are unable to cope.

The final showdown in the battle of wills between the protagonists comes when Kaoru, in a scheme to counter and also accommodate Ōigimi's plan that he marry Nakanokimi, marries her off to Niou instead. Having disposed of that problem, he expects Ōigimi to bow to the inevitable by accepting him for herself. Though initially shocked and angered by Kaoru's audacity, Ōigimi later begins to relent toward him. Influenced by the romantic aura of Nakanokimi's nuptials and Niou's apparent sincerity, her attitude softens, evoking rare moments of hope in this otherwise dark chapter. To Kaoru at least it must seem that his efforts are soon to be rewarded, for he becomes confident enough to think of bringing Ōigimi to the capital as soon as the rebuilding of his mothers Sanjo mansion is completed. To the reader too it is a welcome thought to contemplate Kaoru's ultimate salvation from a lonely, tormented existence by marriage to the woman he loves and admires, and on the other Ōigimi's liberation from the gloomy and mentally constricting influence of Uji. "Agemaki" would then have confirmed itself as a kind of comedy of manners after all, which ends in the reassimilation of the erring protagonists into society. Kaoru would then have realized that his earlier rejection of the world was but an affectation based on ignorance of truly meaningful human relationships, and Ōigimi's narrow scrupulousness would have been tempered by a worldly wisdom arising from experience in society.

But this was not to be. The autumn-foliage excursion, Kaoru's best and grandest scheme, which was to be the final coup in his series of exploits to bring the "hidden flower" to the capital, quickly reverses itself to be the final blow for himself and Ōigimi.[15] It confirms her against marriage and in the suspicion of the inferior position she and her sister occupy vis-à-vis court society. High-minded and proud, she cannot tolerate the insult, nor endure the guilt she feels in allowing her parent's memory to be so dishonored. She decides to die.

From this point onward, the story moves into the autumnal and elegiac mood as the portentous motifs and patterns of meaning laid down in "Hashihime" fulfill their dark promise. The energy of the realistic dialogue which takes up the greater part of the chapter is replaced near the end by a subdued lyricism. Here all those implacably frustrating encounters between the protagonists, otherwise ultimately incomprehensible, emerge as a necessary condition for the author's completed poetic vision. In the story's tragically glorious finale, where the hero still stands enchanted on the threshold of a promise never to be betrayed, because it has gone forever beyond fulfillment, the true idealistic nature of the Kaoru–Ōigimi romance is finally revealed. Dream triumphs over reality. The disenchantment, the bitterness and reproach that characterize the final stage of the conventional love affair, will never come to pass for the protagonists.

The final irony in Kaoru's characterization also becomes apparent in the story's end. The religious aspirant who blundered into the path of love undergoes there a similar *askesis* (a severe training in the renunciation of a physical consummation persistently withheld) until at the point of final deprivation, the spirit gleams with a beauty born of suffering and tears. (It is just this beauty that Niou remarks in Kaoru near the end of the chapter.) The lyrical progression of Kaoru's emotions from the point when Ōigimi falls seriously ill ranges from the forlorn *sabi* of a pale morning of frost to the twilight darkness of utter desperation at her impending death, and thereafter borrows the imagery of moonlight and snow to symbolize the purity of a transfigured passion.

> Shimo sayuru
> Migiwa no chidori
>   Uchiwabite
> Naku ne kanashiki
> Asaborake kana.

> In the chill frost
> Along the riverbank the
>   Plovers complain,
> Their cries echoing sadly
> In the dim white dawn.
>
> (4–458–3)

> Kakikumori
> Hikage mo mienu
>   Okuyama ni
> Kokoro o kurasu
> Koro ni mo aru kana.

> In deep mountains
> Where no light breaks through
>   The whirling clouds,
> My heart, as each day ends,
> In heavier darkness sinks.
>
> (4–460–6)

> Kurenai ni
> Otsuru namida mo
>   Kainaki wa
>   Katami no iro o
> Somenu narikeri.

> The crimson of
> Blood, my tears flow but
>   Impotently,
> For they may not dye my robe
> The black hue of remembrance.
>
> (4–465–2)

> Okureji to
> Sora yuku tsuki o
>   Shitau kana
> Tsui ni sumubeki,
> Kono yo naraneba.

> Loath to be left
> Behind, I long to follow the
>   Moon down the sky;
> In a world dimmed of its light
> Forever I cannot dwell.
>
> (4–466–4)

> Koiwabite
> Shinuru kusuri no
>   Yukashiki ni
> Yuki no yama ni ya
> Ato o kenamashi.

> Wracked with a hopeless
> Passion and yearning for the
>   Medicine of death,
> I would enter the Snowy Mountains
> And leave no traces behind!
>
> (4–466–9)

The end of "Agemaki" is Kaoru's only moment of tragic glory in *Uji jūjō*. In subsequent chapters, deprived of the sense of purpose that Ōigimi had given him and simultaneously estranged forever from his youthful religious resolve, his personality verges on dissolution. He becomes merely another man who has missed his true vocation and is reduced to the half-hearted pursuit of substitutes.

Ōigimi's character, like Kaoru's, undergoes a kind of poetic resolution as she fuses in the reader's imagination with Hashihime, the guardian goddess of the Uji Bridge, the lady of sorrows prefigured in the first chapter, and the woman deprived of love suggested in the *Kokinshū* poem.[16] Near death, Ōigimi seems to merge with the spirit of Uji, with its gloomy mountains and river, its wild winds, its declining seasons of autumn and winter. She becomes, as it were, spiritually transfigured at the moment of her final renunciation; her beauty takes on greater mystery and depth.

> At dusk the sky darkened in clouds and rain, and harsh gusts of wind ploughed beneath the trees. In the harrowing sound, the painful thoughts of what was past and what was to come ran on and on in Ōigimi's mind as she sat, half-reclining, in an attitude of singular refinement. Upon her white robe her black hair flowed down in a smooth cascade with not a strand out of place, although it had not been combed since her illness. The increasing pallor of her face with the days had merely deepened its air of mystery. The eyes that gazed rapt into the distant unknown, the pale cast of the brow—one would have liked to show such beauty to someone of informed sensibility.
>
> (4–449–8)

In the plot's poetic-aesthetic resolution, Ōigimi is also portrayed as the embodiment of ascetic passion, a woman wracked by a willfully thwarted desire and realizing her being in deprivation, in order that body be transformed into spirit. This is the significance of her dying scene (4–461–4), in which her corporeal frame literally dissolves into a pure, unearthly beauty.

It is interesting to note that here in the first three Uji chapters, the author seems to be moving toward the medieval aesthetic of *sabi*, a concept of beauty founded on a deliberate denial of material richness in favor of plainness, a plainness that conceals spiritual richness. The concept of *sabi* is almost certainly associated with the spiritual training and ascetic disciplines (*shugyō*) of the Buddhist aspirant, and it is not impossible to see in the whole development of the Ōigimi cycle, in particular the "Agemaki" chapter, a romantic analogy to *shugyō* in the trials undergone by the two protagonists.

We note that even their characterization is related to the sabi concept: Ōigimi's understated beauty is contrasted to Nakanokimi's more immediately attractive one; Kaoru's appearance does not have the outward beauty of Niou but somehow fascinates because of its suggestion of hidden depths. In fact the whole atmosphere of the Ōigimi cycle is informed by *sabi*—the dreary scenery of Uji, the austere villa of Prince Hachi, the sombre seasons of autumn and winter, Ōigimi in dull mourning robes, and so on.

Doubtless the early medieval poet Teika, whose *Genji* text forms the basis of most modern editions (those belonging to the *aobyōshi* line), was inspired by Murasaki's conception of the Hashihime figure when he composed the poem which in its numinous evocation of a woman remote from any consummation of physical desire, indeed in its merging of her spirit with the landscape of Uji, provides a most fitting epilogue to the Ōigimi cycle.

Samushiro ya   For her straw mat bedding
Matsu yo no aki no   The Lady of the Bridge of Uji now
Kaze fukete   Spreads the moonlight out,
Tsuki o katashiku   And in the waiting autumn night
Uji no Hashihime.   Still lies there in the darkening wind.[17]

NOTES

1. So-called because Uji, the mountain village south of the capital, is their principal setting.

2. The text used for the translations is Yamagishi Tokuhei, ed., *Genji monogatari*, 5 vols. (Tokyo: Iwanami Shoten, 1958–63; *Nihon koten bungaku taikei*, vols. 14–18). For commentary and problems of interpretation however I have preferred to use Tamagami Takuya, ed., *Genji monogatari hyōshaku*, 14 vols. (Tokyo: Kadokawa Shoten, 1967). Hereafter Tamagami; citations indicate volume and page number.

3. Saeki Umetomo, ed., *Kokinwakashō*, vol. 8 of *Nihon koten bungaku taikei* (Tokyo: Iwanami Shoten, 1958). Hereafter *Kokinshō*. I have otherwise desisted from taking up the problem of poetic allusions and have merely indicated their presence with quotation marks.

4. Throughout this essay, I use the word "metaphor" or "motif" to mean an instance in a literary text in which an objective image, whether thing, act, or situation, is implicitly or explicitly being employed to represent a state of mind.

5. The term "hidden flower" is from Edwin A. Cranston, "Aspects of the *Tale of Genji*," *Journal of the Association of Teachers of Japanese* (May/September, 1976), 11(2/3): 183–89.

6. In the "Ukifune" chapter, during a conversation with Ukifune's mother Bennokimi describes her own presence as "inauspicious," a reference to the tragic fates that befell those she had served: Kashiwagi, Prince Hachi, and Ōigimi. (5–249–3)

7. A similar reference to fish and traps is made on his next visit to Uji in the Tenth Month, and there the correlation is more direct (4–328–2).

8. Riviere as cited in Ralph Freedman, *The Lyrical Novel: Studies in Herman Hesse, Andre Gide, and Virginia Woolf* (Princeton: Princeton University Press, 1963), pp. 7–8. I

found this book valuable in suggesting how the problem of lyricism in a narrative genre may best be approached.

9. "The poetic function projects the principle of equivalence from the axis of selection into the axis of combination." Roman Jacobson, "Linguistics and Poetics," in Richard and Fernande De George, eds., *The Structuralists from Marx to Levi-Strauss* (New York: Doubleday, 1972), p. 95. The axis of selection refers to the series of paradigms or semantic cognates from which linguists posit that a speaker selects the words he then combines to form a sentence.

10. I shall also omit from the discussion of the next two chapters the poems and lyric passages belonging primarily to the subordinate Niou–Nakanokimi "comic" plot which develops contrapuntally to the tragic story of Kaoru and Ōigimi. Some of these omitted poems are significant in illuminating the spring–autumn and capital–Uji polarization implicit in the poetic design of the three chapters.

11. In the curious conversation with Niou (4–325ff.), what Kaoru is really doing is projecting his own excitement about the Uji sisters on Niou in order to laugh at him, and thereby also at his own susceptibility. Psychologically speaking Kaoru's action is a form of defense mechanism; Niou is in a sense his alter-ego.

12. Tamagami (10.206) sees a double-meaning in *hitokoto* (literally, "a word," i.e., a promise) in the fourth line of Prince Hachi's poem, since that word may also mean "a fragment of music."

13. The parenthetical comment is apparently the narrator's interpolation.

14. An allusion to the following poem in the *Kokin rokujō*, II, "A Mountain Well": "Asakayama / Kage sae miyuru / Yama no i no / Asaku wa hito o / Omou mono ka wa." ("Shallow the mountain well / That reflects even the image of / Asaka Mountain; / Can you think my feelings / For you could be so shallow?") (Cited in Tamagami, 10.276). The same poem appears in *Manyōshō* 16:3807, with a slight variation in the last two lines.

15. The autumn-foliage excursion, in which Niou and a party of courtiers were to have paid a formal visit to the sisters across the river, was part of Kaoru's plan to legitimize Niou's secret marriage to Nakanokimi by making it public and presenting the court with a *fait accompli*. His scheme was foiled, however, when Yūgiri's elder son suddenly arrived with a large retinue to escort the party back to the capital on instructions from Niou's mother, the Empress. It should be noted that Yūgiri, the powerful Minister of the Left, intended Niou as potential Crown Prince to marry his own daughter, Rokunokimi.

16. *Kokinshō* 689: "Samushiro ni / Koromo katashiki / Koyoi mo ya / Ware o matsuran / Uji no Hashihime." ("As she spreads her / Lonely robe upon the straw / Matting, tonight too / Does she wait for me, the / Lady of the Bridge of Uji.")

17. Shinkokinshō 420. The translation is from Robert Brower and Earl Miner, *Japanese Court Poetry* (Stanford, Stanford University Press, 1961), pp. 276 and 454.

ROYALL TYLER

"I Am I": Genji and Murasaki

There I was, she thought, completely miserable, and he, simple pastime or not, was sharing his heart with another! Well, I am I!"[1] So Murasaki no Ue silently assures herself in the "Miotsukushi" (Channel Buoys) chapter of *The Tale of Genji*, when injured by Genji's talk of the Akashi Lady. She is Genji's wife, and the Akashi Lady has just given Genji a daughter conceived during his exile. Murasaki's words (*ware wa ware*, "I'm *me!*") are the seed of this essay. They sharply affirm the distinctness of her own existence.

Murasaki's protest is a surprise, even unvoiced. She is Genji's private discovery and his personal treasure. Her fate in life depends so entirely on him that she might be a sort of shadow to him, without a will of her own, and yet at this critical moment, and two later ones like it, she resists him. This essay is about the pattern of give and take between her and Genji at these moments, and its consequences.

The essay will dwell at greater length on Murasaki than on Genji because readers in recent decades have not agreed on her nature or her significance. I will therefore establish her position in the work as I read it, encouraged by Akiyama Ken's remark that studying her, more than any other character, gives access to the essence of the tale.[2] However, my purpose will always be to follow how she and Genji affect one another and to suggest the significance of their relationship in the two-thirds of the work that cover

From *Monumenta Nipponica*, 54, no. 4 (Winter 1999). © 1999 by Sophia University.

their lives. This is therefore a reading of the lives of Genji and Murasaki as a couple.[3]

Three critical junctures in the relationship between Genji and Murasaki are central to this reading. Shimizu Yoshiko called them Murasaki's "perils."[4] They are Murasaki's hurt when she learns about the Akashi Lady ("Akashi" and "Miotsukushi"); her fear when Genji courts Princess Asagao ("Asagao," The Morning Glory); and her shock when Genji marries Onna Sannomiya, the "Third Princess," the daughter of Retired Emperor Suzaku ("Wakana 1," "Wakana 2", New Herbs: Part One and Part Two). These scenes are well recognized in writing on Murasaki, and I am not alone in treating them as a set; but while others who mention them see them as roughly equal and isolated from one another, I find the interaction between Murasaki and Genji following the same pattern in each, with analogous but graver consequences each time. Genji talks to Murasaki about another woman who is or has been important to him; Murasaki resents it; her anger upsets Genji; and Genji's effort to calm her miscarries because it is at least in part blind and self-serving.[5]

Like many others I raise the question of why Genji seeks with Akashi, Asagao, and Onna Sannomiya the tie that so disturbs Murasaki, when he already has in Murasaki herself a wife who meets his personal ideal and for whom he sincerely cares. I propose that Genji's desire for all three is connected less with erotic acquisitiveness than with aspiration to glory.

First, Genji's tie with the Akashi Lady, and the consequent birth of their daughter, opens for him the way towards that highest pinnacle of advantage accessible to a commoner: to be the maternal grandfather of an emperor. Although reaching this peak—an aspect of his destiny fostered by her father's devotion to the deity of Sumiyoshi and announced by prophetic dreams—does not depend entirely on his will, it requires from him a cooperation that he gives gladly. What Murasaki sees, however, is attachment to a rival who, to make things worse, gives him a child when she herself cannot.

Second, Asagao and then Onna Sannomiya promise Genji a rounding out of his success, one that might be called less political than representational. By the time he begins courting Asagao seriously, let alone by the time he accepts to marry Onna Sannomiya, his supremacy is secure. Politically he does not need them, but I believe that he still wants one and then the other above all to seal his increasingly exalted station. Nothing the narrator (as distinguished from the author) says about Genji, or presents him as saying or thinking, directly confirms this, but while others have taken her words or those she attributes to Genji as literally authoritative, I suggest looking past them to other hints that she gives, or to her silences.

The Genji of my reading is a flawed man like others, although far more gifted, whose public ambition comes into conflict with his private affection. Murasaki's personal quality makes her his equal, and her value to him, as well as her valuation of herself despite his slights, makes this conflict a vital theme running through the tale.

After reviewing the way Murasaki has been received, I will discuss the penchant for so-called jealousy (*shitto*) that distinguishes her. I will then turn to her childhood and her marriage to Genji. The main part of the essay concerns the three "perils" mentioned and discusses them in chronological order.

PERCEPTIONS OF MURASAKI

Murasaki means so much to Genji for so long that one easily assumes her to be the heroine (*onna shujinkō*) of part one of the tale ("Kiritsubo", The Paulownia Court, through "Fujinouraba", Wisteria Leaves; chapters 1–33) and part two ("Wakana 1" through "Maboroshi", The Wizard; chapters 34–41). However, Matsuo Satoshi argued in 1949 that she is no more prominent in part one than any of the other women in the tale and does not play a central role until "Wakana 1."[6] In fact, Matsuo saw no connection between the Murasaki of parts one and two. Although his thesis became widely accepted, many writers later on proposed a qualified continuity after all. In 1993, after exhaustively discussing whether or not Murasaki is the *onna shujinkō* of both parts, Nagai Kazuko concluded that she is.[7] Still the doubt remains.

In any case, many do not respond to Murasaki. Tanabe Seiko wrote that when young she found her tiresomely perfect; Enchi Fumiko called her too "sheltered" to be a romantic heroine; Ōba Minako omitted her from her list of "female characters who have a brilliance, a strange beauty, and a romantic quality befitting the heroine of a *monogatari* (tale)"; and Norma Field wrote of her studied "banality."[8] Modest and untouched by scandal, she can seem colorless and perhaps even tediously privileged. However, it is also true that the text describes her repeatedly as a woman of extraordinary beauty, kindness, intelligence, and warmth, and that some Japanese writers describe her as an "ideal woman." Among those who take her this way, Shigematsu Nobuhiro evoked her with particular success in the text's own terms.[9]

Only one writer seems to have found Murasaki worse than dull. Matsuo Satoshi described her in part one as coarse, ignorant, vain, petty, cold, and incapable of self-reflection; while in part two, he wrote, she "coldly" asks Genji several times to let her become a nun, knowing perfectly well that such requests wound him, then "betrays all his hopes" by "coldly" dying.[10]

Matsuo's hostility is not mentioned by those who praise his contribution to *Genji* studies, but it obviously influenced his evaluation of Murasaki's importance. His mirror image is the feminist critic Komashaku Kimi, with her passionate attack on Genji and her correspondingly militant defense of Murasaki.[11]

JEALOUSY AND SELF-AFFIRMATION

Murasaki's silent "I am I!" conveys a pang of jealousy, and her recurring jealousy (*shitto*) is a theme in the Japanese literature about her.[12] The word is not quite fair to her, however, since it takes Genji's part: it is what he sees, while hurt, fear, and anger are what she feels. What she protests is an injury done her by the person for whom she cares more than anyone else in the world and on whom her well-being depends.[13] A symptom of her predicament in life is that in principle it is beneath her dignity to express such feelings at all.

Ware ("I"), even alone, occurs in many expressions that might not flatter a woman like Murasaki, for it easily suggests self-affirmation in a manner that the tale does not normally associate with feelings proper to a lady. The opening paragraph of "Kiritsubo" says of the women who were jealous of Genji's mother, "Those others who had always assumed that pride of place was properly theirs ["who thought pridefully, Me!"] despised her as a dreadful woman."[14] *Ware wa* ("Me!") conveys not only the emotions of "those others" but their vulgarity in comparison with Genji's mother.

Waka poetry associates the expression *ware wa ware* with a sharp awareness of self in the vicissitudes of a private love affair. In three of four occurrences that are earlier than the tale a male speaker laments that because of love's longing he has lost his "self,"[15] while in the fourth a woman stolen from one lover by another feels estranged from any "self" she may properly possess.[16] However, two of three poems roughly contemporary with the tale use the words as Murasaki does in "Miotsukushi." The full expression in both is *kimi wa kimi ware wa ware* ("you are you, I am I"). Izumi Shikibu evokes the distinction between "you" and "me" only to deny it ("Since nothing comes between us [to make us] 'you are you, I am I,' how could our hearts be separate from one another?"),[17] but Ben no Menoto affirms the distinction sharply: "You are you, I am I: that is the way for us, although we pledged ourselves to each other for life."[18] Murasaki's "I am I," which evokes especially "my" dignity in a private relationship, conveys the same mood.[19]

For many Japanese readers Murasaki's jealousy is her salient trait. Genji himself seems to enjoy it, despite his complaints, at least until the "Wakana" chapters; it gives her a piquancy that he savors. Tanabe Seiko remarked that it is what animates her and makes her human.[20] Shigematsu Nobuhiro contended that no woman as intelligent as Murasaki could fail in her situation to be jealous,[21] and Komashaku Kimi noted with pleasure that Genji's treachery and oppression had not after all "killed" Murasaki's sense of self.[22]

Murasaki certainly remains herself throughout her life, but however discreetly she conveys her strongest feelings, they little become a lady of her standing. No avowed expression of jealousy is ever associated with Aoi, Genji's original wife; and the jealousy of Rokujō, a high-ranking lover who comes into dramatic conflict with Aoi, is so far beneath her dignity that in life she is not even conscious of it. Mitoma Kōsuke, who wrote of jealousy in Heian literature that ladylike behavior forbade it, observed that Toshikage's daughter, the ideal heroine in *Utsubo monogatari*, never shows any such feelings, and that jealousy never appears in *Ise monogatari*. He suggested that Murasaki gets away with it only because she is so beautiful.[23]

Since Murasaki's jealousy compromises her, some writers sympathetic to her feel obliged to explain it. They observe that her expressions of jealousy are fair and loyally meant, which undoubtedly they are. After all, the famous "rainy night conversation" (*amayo no shinasadame*) in "Hahakigi" (The Broom Tree) enjoins a woman to let her straying husband know tactfully that she knows and cares, and so to win back his affection.[24] However, the rainy night conversation explicitly does not discuss women of the "highest class" (*kami no shina*), to which Aoi and Rokujo belong. Is Murasaki then not of this class? Feeling the difficulty, Akiyama Ken assigned her at least as a girl to the "middle class" (*naka no shina*) instead.[25]

On the other hand, the temper that helps to make Murasaki's standing ambiguous also makes her accessible. As Tō no Chūjō remarks in the "rainy night conversation," "It is among those of middle birth that you can see what a girl really has to offer and find ways to tell one from another."[26] Murasaki's tendency to resist Genji over certain of his affairs gives her a similarly distinct individuality, which is why some recent Japanese readers have admired her as a woman of independent spirit. Baba Taeko, for example, wrote that her sense of self gives her a remarkably contemporary appeal.[27] At the same time, Murasaki is of such high birth and station that "middle class" will not really do. I will suggest that Murasaki's jealousy is a manifestation less of intrinsic personality than of contingent social predicament.

THE CHILD MURASAKI

Many writers fail to see the mature Murasaki in the child. Tanabe Seiko wrote that what Genji glimpses through the fence, when he first discovers

Murasaki, "has graven a little girl's appeal in the hearts of the Japanese," but she noted nothing individual in the scene; in fact, she held that until Genji's exile Murasaki remains a "doll bride." Akiyama Ken similarly called the young Murasaki a "living doll" without individual traits.[28] However, others disagree. For Ōasa Yūji and Shigematsu Nobuhiro, Murasaki is recognizably herself from the very beginning.[29]

Genji discovers Murasaki when he visits a healer in the hills north of Kyoto ("Wakamurasaki", Lavender). As soon as he sees her he wants her. That she is a little girl does not matter, for he sees the grownup already and is willing to wait. Her resemblance to his great and inaccessible love, his father's empress Fujitsubo , captivates him above all.

In a way, Murasaki satisfies the adolescent longing that Genji felt at the end of "Kiritsubo," when he "kept wishing with many sighs that he had a true love to come and live with him"[30] at his mother's home, now rebuilt after her death. Five years later, the "rainy night conversation" that broadens his knowledge of women includes this piece of advice from Sama no Kami (the "guards officer"):

> "It's probably not a bad idea to take a wholly childlike, tractable wife and form her yourself as best you can. You may not have full confidence in her, but you'll know your training has made a difference."[31]

The idea of living apart from the world with a true love, and of forming her to his own ideal, is therefore present in his mind by the time he first spies Murasaki:

> In came running a girl in perhaps her tenth year, wearing a softly rumpled mountain rose layering over a white gown and, unlike the other children, an obvious future beauty. Her hair cascaded like a spread fan behind her as she stood there, her face all red from crying.
>
> "What is the matter?" the nun [her grandmother and guardian] asked, glancing up at her. "Have you quarreled with one of the girls?"...
>
> "Inuki let my little sparrow go! And I had him in his cage and everything!" declared the indignant little girl.
>
> "Oh come, you are such a baby!" the nun protested. "You understand nothing, do you! Here I am, wondering whether I will last out this day or the next, but that means nothing to you, does it! All you do is chase sparrows. Come here!"

The girl sat down.

"You hate even to have it combed," said the nun, stroking her hair, "but what beautiful hair it is! Your childishness really worries me, you know. Not everyone is like this at your age, I assure you."

Child though she was, the girl observed the nun gravely, then looked down and hung her head. Her hair as she did so spilled forward, glinting with the loveliest sheen.[32]

Genji soon discovers that her father is Fujitsubo's elder brother and her mother a wellborn lady (now dead) with whom this gentleman had an affair. All her qualities therefore suggest that she will fulfill the promise of her looks. By birth she is worthy, she has a pleasing vividness of presence, and she does not talk back. He has seen her accept a scolding with downcast gaze and gathered that she would accept his guidance meekly, too. He therefore dreams straight away of making her his own. "How he would love to have her with him," the narrator says, "and bring her up as he pleased!"[33]

Cheekiness is certainly not in Murasaki's nature, but she is not passive. She has a temper, she is possessive about her pet sparrow, and the way her grandmother's plight fails to quell her high spirits suggests character and a mind of her own. That so lively a girl should accept her grandmother's rebuke suggests more depth than simple docility: the capacity to honor her elders and to recognize that she is wrong. If she can do that, she can also see that someone else is wrong and respect herself for being right. Although not vain, she has the intelligence to be justly proud. Genji senses that quality in her, too.

It is unusual that Genji should be able to observe Murasaki so directly and then imagine taking her home. She is of good birth, she is pretty, she is delightful, and she knows right from wrong, but what really allows him to dream on is that she is so poorly protected. She has no *ushiromi* , no one to uphold her interests in a ruthless world, because her mother is dead and because her father does not dare to provoke his ill-tempered wife (her stepmother) by recognizing her. Her grandmother resists Genji's interest in Murasaki because she fears how he might treat her; but when she, too, dies, Murasaki is left with next to no prospects. Her father then makes up his mind at last to bring her home, but Genji makes off with her first. Her father has no idea where she has gone. While people gather that Genji now has someone living with him, no one knows who she is or suspects her to be a child.

Genji could not have abducted Murasaki if she had been her father's recognized daughter, nor might he then have been so keen to have her, since success would have made him responsible to a second father-in-law. (His wife, Aoi, is still alive.) As it is, she passes from having a doubtful future to being Genji's own—what? Some might say property, others true love, but either way her life is what he will make it. A woman in the tale who fears being seen from the outside (perhaps the blinds of the room are up) may exclaim, *arawa nari!* ("Anyone could see us!"). Murasaki is figuratively *arawa* to Genji. She is his in a way the well-screened and guarded Aoi could never be, and this suggests that she is more or less disreputable.

That a prince's daughter just ten years old should not be seen to act with Murasaki's charming spontaneity is a shame, and no one could really criticize her for what she does or the narrator for what she tells. Still, once Genji has taken her home, and she has accepted him, her innocent affection leads her to behave in ways unlike those expected of a young lady. As Shimizu Yoshiko noted, Murasaki behaves like a wanton when Genji's plan to go out one night makes her sulk and fall asleep on his lap. Aoi's women pass on rumors of such goings-on disapprovingly to their mistress. Shimizu also suggested that Aoi, whose gentlewomen do not know that Murasaki is a child, may look down on Genji for his playfulness, his susceptibility, and his insistence on demanding from herself the same kind of intimacy.[34] In this way Murasaki's situation in her early years tarnishes her a little, just as her jealousy may raise an eyebrow later on.

MURASAKI'S MARRIAGE

An inadequately protected girl in the tale, and still more those to whom her future matters, may fear that a suitor means only to toy with her. Genji's approaches appall Murasaki's grandmother because she cannot believe he is serious and clearly suspects him of strange desires. No one would believe him today, either, but he has no intention of treating Murasaki lightly or of misbehaving, nor does he do so. Wakashiro Kiiko, among others, acknowledged the honorable character of his conduct when she wrote, "If Genji were an insensitive man he could never have waited so patiently for the little girl to grow up."[35] His abduction of Murasaki is certainly startling (Enchi Fumiko found it "uniquely manly and quite wild"),[36] but in the long run it is no offense against *her*. While some might condemn him for depriving her of her autonomy, and so on, she really has none to lose, and no hope otherwise of anywhere near so good a marriage. Her stepmother would certainly see to that, lest Murasaki overshadow her own daughters.

Having treated Murasaki from the start with affection and respect, Genji at last consummates his marriage with her in the same spirit. By contemporary standards, it is true, he rapes her. Setouchi Jakucho called it rape,[37] and many teachers or students in *Genji* classrooms may agree. Norma Field wrote of "a betrayal both horrifying and humiliating."[38] Komashaku Kimi allowed that Murasaki is remarkably innocent to take Genji for no more than a father, but she charged him nonetheless with callously failing to explain to Murasaki what he wants and of treating her like a mere "pet." She wrote that while from his standpoint, the dominant male's, he does nothing wrong, from Murasaki's he commits rape.[39]

Such condemnation of Genji is uncommon, however, at least in print. Most writers never mention the issue. Tanabe Seiko wrote of finding the marriage consummation scene wonderfully sexy, and Wakashiro Kiiko, who acknowledged Murasaki's dismay, observed only that the author had perfectly captured "a girl's feelings" (*onnagokoro*).[40] That is all.

In truth, Murasaki's relationship with Genji has been no more frivolous than his with her. She does not even notice his attempts to stir her interest once he believes her ready. "Pleased to see that his young lady had turned out perfectly in all ways," the narrator says, "he began to drop suggestive hints, for he judged that the time had now more or less come; but she gave no sign of understanding."[41] The risqué character of her situation is beyond her, and for years Genji has refrained from pressing her. She is his chosen companion for life, and he is patient. His decision to act ends her innocence, but not a word in the tale suggests that she holds it against him later on, nor does it upset anyone else at the time. Her women, who had assumed that the event happened long ago, are merely surprised, and once the marriage cakes are eaten her nurse weeps with happiness, since under the circumstances nothing obliged Genji to go through a marriage ceremony at all.

As Murasaki enters womanhood she is therefore all she should be. Her purity, untainted by any breath of desire, proves her quality, just as Genji's patience towards her proves his. To respond to his advances and consent to first intercourse she would have to divine what intercourse is and feel drawn to it, but if she did, she would not be a perfect young lady.[42] That she is still perfect after years of sleeping beside him, and he therefore a perfect gentleman towards her, has something of the fairy tale about it, but what matters is that each should be fully worthy of the other. Since they are, it is up to Genji to act. That is why he who loves her is only charmed by her outrage, and why the issue never comes up again.

Unhappily, marriage does not make Murasaki secure, despite Genji's good will. She will always lack influential backing, having no children of her own will always leave her a little vulnerable, and the flaw in her background will become a more and more pressing issue as Genji rises in rank.

THE CRISIS OVER AKASHI

In his twenty-sixth year Genji goes into exile at Suma, leaving Murasaki at
home, in charge of his affairs. Their three-year separation is painful to her
(she is only nineteen when he returns), but it never occurs to her that he
might not be faithful. Meanwhile, at Suma and then Akashi, he misses her
and hesitates to take the opportunity that the Akashi Lady's father is so eager
to press upon him. Still, he yields in the end to the exotic enchantment of the
place and to the lady's personal distinction, so unexpected in a provincial
governor's daughter. He returns from Akashi understandably full of his
experience, and especially of thoughts of the lady and the child she is soon to
bear.

Genji and Murasaki are no sooner reunited than, "deeply content, he
saw that she would always be his this way"; and yet at that very thought "his
heart went out with a pang to [Akashi] whom he had so unwillingly left."

> He began talking about her. The memories so heightened his
> looks that [Murasaki] must have been troubled, for, with "I care
> not for myself," she dropped a light hint that delighted and
> charmed him. When merely to see her was to love her, he
> wondered in amazement how he had managed to spend all these
> months and years without her, and bitterness against the world
> rose in him anew.[43]

Despite the wonder of rediscovering Murasaki, anticipation of the birth, and
then the thought of his new daughter, prolongs the enchantment. Genji
cannot wait to see the little girl, for a prophetic dream has already let him
know that she is a future empress and that in her his own fortunes are at
stake.

However, Murasaki does not yet know about the birth, and Genji does
not wish her to hear of it from someone else. To mask all it means to him he
behaves like a guilty husband, first claiming indifference and a commendable
resolve to do his tedious duty, then passing to diversionary reproaches.

> "So that seems to be that," he remarked. "What a strange and
> awkward business it is! All my care is for another, whom I would
> gladly see similarly favored, and the whole thing is a sad surprise,
> and a bore, too, since I hear the child is a girl. I ought really to
> ignore her, I suppose, but I cannot very well do that. I shall send
> for her and let you see her. You must not resent her."
>
> She reddened. "Don't, please!" she said, offended. "You are

always making up feelings like that for me, when I detest them myself. And when do you suppose I learned to have them?"

"Ah yes," said Genji with a bright smile, "who can have taught you? I have never seen you like this! Here you are, angry with me over fantasies of yours that have never entered my head. It is too hard!" By now he was nearly in tears.[44]

Fearing Murasaki's rebuke, Genji takes the offensive so that she is obliged to defend herself instead. Still, it is true that she does not quite understand. The child means more to him than the mother, and in time he will have Murasaki adopt her for that reason. Meanwhile, Murasaki remembers "their endless love for one another down the years.... and the matter passed from her mind."

In the ensuing silence Genji goes on, half to indulge his feelings and half to pursue loyal confidences, and in so doing he manages to hurt Murasaki after all.

"If I am this concerned about her," Genji said, "it is because I have my reasons.[45] Were I to tell you about them too soon, you would only go imagining things again." He was silent a moment. "It must have been the place itself that made her appeal to me so. She was something new, I suppose." He went on to describe the smoke that sad evening, the words they had spoken, a hint of what he had seen in her face that night, the magic of her koto; and all this poured forth with such obvious feeling that his lady took it ill.

There I was, she thought, thoroughly miserable, and he, simple pastime or not, was sharing his heart with another! Well, I am I! She turned away and sighed, as though to herself, "And we were once so happy together!"[46]

The pattern of this conversation with Murasaki recurs in the two other crisis passages that I have identified. There, too, it is once the danger seems to have passed that Genji indulges in reminiscing about his women, especially Fujitsubo in the second and Rokujō in the third. In each case someone then becomes angry: Murasaki above, then the spirit of Fujitsubo, and finally the spirit of Rokujō. The role played by these three women in these scenes suggests their critical importance to Genji himself.

The injury Murasaki feels is of course painful, and her response springs from a fine quickness of spirit, but the scene is still touched by the lyrically beautiful anguish of those exile years. She is hurt but not yet in danger. No provincial governor's daughter, not even one as unusual as the Akashi Lady, can actually threaten her.

ASAGAO: THE MATTER OF GENJI'S MOTIVE

Three years after the birth of Genji's daughter, Murasaki discovers that her distress then was nothing to what she feels now as Genji courts Princess Asagao. She has been quite happy in the meantime: the Akashi Lady has come no closer, Genji has pursued no new affairs, and she has had the joy of adopting the little girl. Genji, now palace minister (*naidaijin*), has not yet built his Rokujo estate (Rokujoin), but he is already the key figure at court.

Genji has known the highly respected Asagao for years. She is first mentioned in "Hahakigi," where he overhears women "discussing a poem that he had sent with some bluebells to the daughter of His Highness of Ceremonial, although they had it slightly wrong."[47] He seems to have attempted a liaison with her already in his youth, but although he kept in touch with her after that, she refused all new approaches. Once she had become Kamo priestess (in "Sakaki", The Sacred Tree) he pressed her nearly to the point of scandal, considering that a priestess properly remained untainted by any suspicion of such concerns. When her father's death obliges her to resign ("Asagao"), she retires to his house, where she begins the life of Buddhist devotion that her priestly role at the Kamo shrine forbade. She clearly does not mean to marry. Social constraints discouraged the daughter or granddaughter of an emperor from marrying anyway, and besides, she long ago noted that Genji only toyed with Rokujo and decided that she would not risk that happening to her.

She has hardly retired from Kamo when, without a word to Murasaki, Genji lays siege to her. He has always liked her, it is true. In "Aoi," for example, the narrator observes that Genji "was struck by how truly in her case 'distance is the secret of lasting charm.' Distant she might be, but she never failed to respond just as she should."[48] However, this does not sound like passion. What does he want with her? There seem to be two lines of thought on the question. One, the simpler, is associated with Saitō Akiko. The second, dominant and more complex, was proposed by Shimizu Yoshiko and developed by other scholars, including Akiyama Ken and Suzuki Hideo.

Saitō suggested that Genji had always been drawn to Asagao by the difficulty of success and had courted her even at Kamo for the same reason he made love to Oborozukiyo (with whom he began a perilous affair in "Hana no en", The Festival of the Cherry Blossoms): because of the risk.[49] The "Asagao" chapter begins: "The Kamo priestess had resigned because of her mourning. Genji, whose peculiarity (*kuse*) it was, as always, never to break off a courtship he had once started, sent her frequent notes."[50] Saitō gathered from this that Genji's initial approaches to her are only "lukewarm"[51] and that her rejection is what challenges him to conquer her resistance at all costs; and Norma Field agreed that Genji pursues Asagao because "her very resistance poses a challenge he cannot overlook."[52] While Saitō's reading recognizes the urgency of Genji's interest in Asagao and the need to explain it, the explanation it offers lacks substance. Genji resembles a mechanical toy blocked, wheels spinning, by a wall. He has no intelligible motive except a refusal to give up, which is implausible for so shrewd and powerful a courtier.

Several years earlier, Shimizu Yoshiko had suggested that Genji courts Asagao out of nostalgia for Fujitsubo.[53] Fujitsubo has died only recently ("Usugumo", A Rack of Cloud), in the third month of Genji's thirty-second year, and "Asagao" begins in the ninth month of the same year. Genji must feel her loss deeply, even though the text does not say so. The first time he visits Asagao, he finds at her house the Gen no Naishi over whom he and Tō no Chūjō quarreled comically fourteen years before (in "Momiji no ga", An Autumn Excursion). According to Shimizu, this reminder of a past now lost—the world of his father's court—wakens vivid memories of Fujitsubo, and he thereafter courts Asagao as his sole surviving link to those days. He desires Asagao because she is now to him a token of Fujitsubo.

In the chapter's closing scene, which Shimizu discussed at length, Genji and Murasaki sit with blinds raised before their frozen, moonlit garden, deep in snow. Murasaki has expressed her fears about Asagao, and Genji has sought to allay them. Then, having sent the girls of the household down into the garden to roll a snowball, he begins to talk about Fujitsubo, who once did the same, and even to contrast her favorably with Murasaki (her niece). Next he muses about some of his other women. When he has finished, Murasaki speaks a poem, and Genji sees her with new eyes:

> Leaning forward a little that way to look out, she was lovelier than any woman in the world. The sweep of her hair, her face, suddenly brought back to him most wonderfully the figure of the lady he had loved [Fujitsubo], and his heart, which had been somewhat divided, turned again to her alone.[54]

That night, Fujitsubo comes to him in a dream and reproaches him bitterly.

Shimizu Yoshiko held that Genji's memories of Fujitsubo spill forth willy-nilly before the snowball scene, and that he only goes on talking about the others (Asagao, Oborozukiyo, and Akashi) to cover his indiscretion. As he talks, he realizes that Murasaki looks exactly like Fujitsubo, and his longing (*koi*) for Asagao vanishes. However, Fujitsubo, who truly loved him, has heard him from the afterworld. She feels not only insulted that he should speak of her to another woman but jealous that, to him, the other woman should have now become, as it were, she; hence she reproaches him in his dream. Shimizu did not wonder why Genji pursues Asagao with such tenacity, nor did she seem to believe that Murasaki's fears, which she hardly discussed, ever had substance.

A few years after Shimizu published her essay, Imai Gen'e analyzed Murasaki's poem in order to illuminate her mood in the chapter:[55]

kōri toji	Frozen into ice
ishima no mizu wa	water among the rocks
yukinayami	flows no longer,
sora sumu tsuki no	while the bright moon, aloft,
kage zo nagaruru	courses through the sky.[56]

Having shown that the poem had always been read simply as an evocation of a beautiful winter scene, Imai argued that in reality it conveys deep distress: it is Murasaki who is "frozen into ice among the rocks" and Genji who "courses through the sky" (spends night after night away, courting Asagao), far from her. Imai demonstrated that Genji misrepresents his interest in Asagao to Murasaki and that she recognizes his duplicity. He also stressed that Murasaki is upset about Asagao and that while Genji has not actually done anything yet, so that he has nothing definite to tell her, her anxiety is understandable. Imai held that his silence, which is meant only to spare her feelings, alarms her more than would the truth.

Thus, while Shimizu gave Genji a motive and Imai understood the depth of Murasaki's distress, both considered her fears in the end unwarranted. Their Genji may do as he pleases and is not accountable to Murasaki, and as long as he has not actually succeeded in committing Asagao to himself she has nothing to worry about.

Akiyama Ken's interpretation of "Asagao,"[57] published soon after Shimizu's essay appeared, shared Shimizu's belief that the snow scene resolves some key tensions and Saito's that Genji's pursuit of Asagao is helplessly compulsive. His main emphasis, however, was on the operations of the author, for he found Asagao's sudden appearance in the foreground of the narrative hard to explain except as an authorial device to remind Murasaki of her insecurity vis-à-vis Genji and so to prepare for "repositioning" her (*suenaoshi*) in the tale. He argued that Genji is upset over the way he failed to resist trying (in "Usugumo") to seduce Akikonomu, the daughter entrusted to him by Rokujō, and over the way he is now unable not to pursue Asagao;

and he suggested that thanks to Genji's absorption in thoughts of Fujitsubo, these tensions are resolved for him in the snow scene. When he sees Murasaki as Fujitsubo the "repositioning" is complete. Murasaki is no longer a substitute for Fujitsubo, but herself, in full, and once the chapter is over Fujitsubo will all but disappear from the tale.

Recently, Suzuki Hideo continued this line of thinking in a further attempt to define the significance of the chapter. Taking Genji's reassurances to Murasaki ("There is nothing serious to any of this")[58] at face value, he proposed that the author contrived the "device" of the closing passage about the snow and the moon in order to settle Murasaki's fears. Rejecting Imai's understanding of Murasaki's poem, he wrote that in this scene Genji successfully draws her into harmony with his own attunement to the "nature surrounding their solitude." He held that when Genji sees Murasaki as Fujitsubo, "and his heart ... turned again to her alone," she becomes for him, and will remain thereafter, what Fujitsubo had been.[59]

Shimizu, Akiyama, and Suzuki held that in the snow scene Genji renounces his attachment to Fujitsubo in favor of Murasaki and that thereafter Fujitsubo ceases to figure in the tale.[60] Even in the closing lines of "Asagao," however, Genji longs to share Fujitsubo's lotus throne in paradise. She and Murasaki still do not seem to be identical, and Genji's attachment to her memory does not seem to have been ended by that single rush of feeling. Moreover, the Shimizu reading in particular has Genji's interest in Asagao extinguished by that moment under the winter moon, when it is not. At the beginning of the next chapter ("Otome", The Maiden), the following spring, Genji is still writing to Asagao and sending her gifts, the narrator is still claiming that he never meant to force her, the Fifth Princess, Asagao's aunt, is urging her to marry him, and she herself is still afraid that her gentlewomen will take things into their own hands.[61] In fact, eight years later (early in "Wakana 1"), bystanders are still saying, "One gathers that [Genji] deeply desires a lofty alliance, and that he has so little forgotten the former Kamo priestess that he still corresponds with her."[62] They assume that Genji's preoccupation with Asagao remains unresolved because he still does not have a proper wife.

None of the readings just outlined acknowledges the practical consequence if Genji were to succeed with Asagao: both his life and Murasaki's would be profoundly altered. In getting behind her curtains—those of a princess of unassailable standing—he would marry her, and he would then have to treat her properly as his wife. At his age and with his experience he could not doubt this or hope to get away with less. (The disasters associated with Rokujō stem from his having tried to do just that with her.) No wonder that Murasaki is beside herself with apprehension. She understands the gravity of what he is up to, and his silence, far from sparing her feelings over an affair of no lasting importance, confirms that he understands it too. The truth is too awful to confess. He must want to marry Asagao.

Rumor supports Murasaki's fears. "He is courting the former Kamo priestess," people said, "and the Fifth Princess has no objection. Those two would not go at all badly together."[63] This is how Murasaki first hears, from her gentlewomen, about Genji and Asagao. Those spreading the rumor approve the match, as does the Fifth Princess, because Asagao, unlike Murasaki, is fully worthy of Genji in rank.

The Fifth Princess explains her position near the beginning of "Otome":

> "I gather that [Genji] has been keen on you for ages," she observed to her niece [Asagao] when they met; "it is not as though this were anything new for him. [Your late father] regretted your life taking another course, so that he could not welcome him; he often said how sorry he was that you ignored his own preference, and there were many times when he rued what you had done [in becoming the Kamo priestess]. Still, out of respect for the feelings of the Third Princess [Aoi's mother] I said nothing as long as [Aoi] was alive. Now, though, even she, who did command great consideration, is gone, and it is true, I simply do not see what could be wrong with your becoming what [your father] wished, especially when [Genji] is again so very eager that this seems to me almost to be your destiny."[64]

In other words, Asagao's father wanted to marry his daughter to Genji and did not consider Genji's existing marriage to Aoi an obstacle; and the Fifth Princess agreed, even though she refrained from seconding him aloud. Both assumed that Asagao outranked Aoi, even if the prestige of Aoi's mother and the power of Aoi's father (the minister of the left) might have made the marriage politically tricky to bring off.[65] Meanwhile, the Fifth Princess says nothing at all about Murasaki, who for her does not count. Social "common sense" simply does not give Murasaki the weight to be taken seriously as Genji's wife.

This, I believe, is the problem that Genji knows he can no longer ignore,[66] and the reason why he courts Asagao in the "Asagao" chapter. Perhaps Asagao's prestige was even part of the reason why he began courting her in the first place, all those years ago. One might imagine one or two available princesses promising him by this time even higher prestige, but the tale mentions none, and under these circumstances Genji's long relationship with Asagao does indeed explain his present interest in her, as the opening of the chapter suggests. She has the rank, and he likes her. She is an old friend. He therefore moves quickly to court her when she returns from Kamo not because she reminds him of Fujitsubo, but because she is now there to be courted as she had not been before.

Long ago Genji chose Murasaki himself, without reference to social convention, although he then found her birth adequate. She is the emblem of the private autonomy on which he insists. However, as he rises he realizes that autonomy outside the accepted social structure is not sufficient, and he comes to wish to conform to this structure in order to turn it to the ends of his own sovereignty. Therefore, if "Asagao" does mark a change, that change is not in Genji's view of Murasaki but in his view of himself and of what his position requires. The death of Fujitsubo and the reappearance of Asagao in private life wean him from the idea that to make one's own way one must break the rules, as he did before with Murasaki and Fujitsubo, and persuade him to act. That moment before the snowy, moonlit garden may remind him that in Murasaki he has Fujitsubo after all and so console him for his failure with Asagao. However, his love for Fujitsubo, too, was irregular, and having Murasaki is still not enough. That is why in time he will marry Onna Sannomiya.

ASAGAO: THE SCENE BETWEEN GENJI AND MURASAKI

Genji says nothing to Murasaki about his pursuit of Asagao partly because, for him, his ambition to marry Asagao has no connection with his love for Murasaki, and partly because he knows that this time he is in earnest. Murasaki, who learns what he is up to only through rumor, says nothing either. Her silence, too, measures the seriousness of the matter. She is not just hurt but frightened. Noticing her changed mood, Genji reproaches her as before, though with sharper deceit.

> One evening, overcome by the empty hours, Genji decided on one of his so-called visits to [Asagao's aunt].... "I gather that the Fifth Princess is unwell, and I thought I might pay her a call," he said, on one knee before [Murasaki]; but she did not even look at him. Her profile as she played instead with her little girl suggested that something was wrong. "You are looking strangely unlike yourself these days," he said. "I have done nothing. I have been staying away a bit because I thought you might find the same old salt-burner's robe dull by now. Now what can you possibly have been making of that?"

"Familiarity often breeds contempt," she replied and lay down with her back to him.... She lay there thinking how naive she had always been, when such things as this could happen.... As she watched him go, ... she ached unbearably to think that he might really be leaving her.[67]

The way she turns her back recalls the *ware wa ware* of three years ago. His conduct is beyond words. She can hardly speak to him.

Further, decisive rebuffs from Asagao leave Genji undaunted, but when Murasaki's continuing torment troubles him and draws him back towards her after all, at first reluctantly, this crisis, too, begins to pass.

"You are looking curiously unlike yourself—I cannot imagine why," Genji said to her, stroking her hair.... "You are quite grown up now, but you still think seldom of others, and it is just that way you have of getting their feelings wrong that makes you so dear." He tidied a wet lock of hair at her forehead, but she turned further from him and said not a word.

"Who can have brought you up such a baby?" he asked. What a shame it was, when life is short anyway, to have her so upset with him! But then daydreams would sweep him off again.... "Please understand that you need not worry." He spent the day trying to make her feel better.[68]

That night a brilliant moon illumines the snow, and Genji waxes eloquent as he strives for reconciliation.

"More than the glory of flowers and fall leaves that season by season capture everyone's heart," he said, "it is the night sky in winter, with snow glittering under a brilliant moon, that in the absence of all color speaks to me strangely and carries my thoughts beyond this world ..."[69]

Although justly famous, his praise of winter is not a good sign. He is becoming overwrought.

Keen to act and to be amused, Genji sends the girls down to the garden to roll their snowball, while exaltation sweeps him on to dream aloud about Fujitsubo. It is not that the thought of Fujitsubo, having filled his mind all the time he courted her stand-in, Asagao, has at last spilled over into words. His thoughts of Fujitsubo and his interest in Asagao are unrelated, belonging as they do to the realms of private feeling on the one hand and public ambition on the other. Having failed with Asagao, he seeks solace and reassurance in memories of Fujitsubo, and he also seeks to bring Murasaki closer to him by confiding in her. Thus he flirts not only with betraying what Fujitsubo was to him but with taking her name in vain, so to speak, by putting her memory to the ends of his own self-satisfaction. "The smallest thing she did always seemed miraculous," he says. "How one misses her on every occasion! ... She made no show of brilliance, but a talk with her was always worthwhile.... No, we shall never see her like again." He then goes straight on to compound his fault towards her and Murasaki by comparing Murasaki explicitly, and unflatteringly, to her and then to Asagao.

> "For all her serenity, [Fujitsubo] had a profound distinction that no other could attain, whereas you, who despite everything have so much of the noble *murasaki*,[70] have a difficult side to you as well and are perhaps, alas, a little headstrong. The former Kamo priestess's [Asagao's] temperament seems to me very different. When I am lonely, I need no particular reason to converse with her, and by now she is really the only one left who requires my best of me."[71]

A discussion of Oborozukiyo and others follows, without comparisons. In the guise of confiding in Murasaki, Genji has complacently reviewed his secure emotional assets while simultaneously placating her and reminding her that she depends on his indulgence. Nonetheless, her protest has worked as a loyal wife's was supposed to in the "rainy night conversation": it has convinced him of his folly and returned him to her. After a day spent talking her round, he has come round himself. Having indulged in calling up the image of Fujitsubo he sees that Murasaki, there before him, has exactly her quality. This is not a new discovery for him. He has made it before, when failure to grasp some petty prize has opened his eyes again to the treasure he already has. Disappointment with Onna Sannomiya will affect him the same way. By then, however, it will be too late.

Later that night Genji falls asleep thinking of Fujitsubo, and his performance earns its reward when "he saw her dimly—it was not a dream— and perceived her to be extremely angry. 'You promised never to tell, yet what I did is now known to all. I am ashamed, and my present suffering makes you hateful to me!'"[72] He awakes with a pounding heart to hear Murasaki crying out, "What is the matter?"

Murasaki's challenge to his willful ways has provoked a play of ambition, treachery, love, conceit, cajolery, and contrition with an eerie outcome, and this pattern will recur in connection with Onna Sannomiya.

Murasaki's open unhappiness over Asagao recalls her behavior as a girl, when her sulking persuaded him to stay home instead of going out for the night. While her conduct then appeared wanton, she was really only an innocent child, and her feelings in "Miotsukushi" or "Asagao" are of course natural to any wife. Still, to Genji's mind, especially when he compares her to Fujitsubo or Asagao, the sharpness of her temper is a flaw, even if an attractive one. It is the inner counterpart, and perhaps the consequence, of her flawed origins. "Who can have brought you up such a baby?" he asks. The girl he reared himself, hoping to form her entirely to his will, has a will, an "I" of her own. She has "a difficult side to her" (*sukoshi wazurawashiki ki soite*) and is "perhaps, alas, a little head-strong" (*kadokadoshisa no susumitamaeru ya kurushikaran*). That could not be said of Fujitsubo, who despite her great depth "never put herself forward" (*moteidete rōrōjiki koto mo mietamawazarishikado*). Supremely distinguished, she betrayed no sharp glint of wit or temper. No more does Asagao who, for all her stubborn refusal to engage with Genji, seems otherwise to be utterly bland. These two great ladies do not have Murasaki's "prickles." Murasaki is too proud, cares too deeply for Genji, and depends on him too much to hold her peace; while Genji, more headstrong even than she, loves her too much either to ignore her or to scold her outright. It is the exceptional strength of the bond between them that allows their story to grow through crises like these towards real tragedy.

ONNA SANNOMIYA: PRELIMINARY REMARKS

At the beginning of "Wakana 1" Retired Emperor Suzaku, who feels he has little longer to live, longs to find his favorite daughter the "protector" (husband) she needs. By accepting that role, Genji will profoundly affect the rest of Murasaki's life as well as his own. Onna Sannomiya in her thirteenth or fourteenth year is still a child. "How I wish for someone to take this princess in hand and bring her up the way [Genji] did [Murasaki]," he says to her nurses.[73] Actually, she is a niece of Fujitsubo, like Murasaki; and like Murasaki once she is young for her age. Unlike Murasaki, however, she is in her own person a hopeless nonentity. Nonetheless, before leaving the world to prepare for death, Suzaku gives her almost everything he owns. She is a prize coveted by the most ambitious young men of the court.

To most readers Genji, whether hero or villain, is the lover, the man of endless charm and wandering fancy, whose unerring style and taste define a courtly age. He is seen less often as a man of power. One must make an effort to remember that after returning from exile he remains a merciless and effective enemy of all those who turned their backs on him at the time. The author seldom, and only in passing, evokes him as statesman or political patron, a maker and breaker of men. He is that too, however. Early in "Wakana 1," Retired Emperor Suzaku, who knows whereof he speaks, puts it lightly but well.

> "Yes," he said, "it is true, [Genji] was exceptional [in his youth], and now, in his full maturity, he has still more of a charm that reminds one just what it means to say someone shines. When grave and dignified he has so superbly commanding a presence that one hardly dares to approach him, and when relaxed and in a playful mood he is sweeter and more engagingly amusing than anyone in the world."[74]

The enchanting lover and host commands at will terror and awe.

The reader glimpses this Genji directly in "Wakana 2." Aware of Kashiwagi's transgression with Onna Sannomiya, Genji has nonetheless been expressing publicly the most generous affection for him; but the reader also knows that he, who now holds the title of honorary retired emperor, is outraged beyond forgiveness. Genji then hosts a party that the frightened Kashiwagi must attend and singles him out for attention with a venomous show of friendly banter.

> "The older you are, the harder it gets to stop drunken tears," Genji remarked. "Look at [Kashiwagi], smiling away to himself— it is so embarrassing! Never mind, though, his time will come. The sun and moon never turn back. No one escapes old age." He shot a glance at [Kashiwagi], who seemed far less cheerful than the others and really did look so unwell that the wonders of the day were lost on him....

Kashiwagi goes home ill, thinking, "I am not that drunk, though. What is the matter with me?"[75] He soon takes to his bed, and few months later he is dead. As *Mumyōzōshi* puts it, Genji has "killed him with a glance."[76] One does not trifle with such a man.

The "light" (*hikari*) of Hikaru Genji, which for most readers evokes beauty, grace, and so on, may also therefore mean danger. Kashiwagi is already dying when he confides to Kojijū, the gentlewoman who knows his secret, "Now that [Genji] knows what I have done I shrink from the prospect of living—which, I suppose just shows how singular his light is.... As soon as I met his gaze that evening my soul began to wander in anguish, and it has never come back."[77] Genji has extraordinary potency and charisma.

However, that does not shield him from error. He may simply err more gravely than lesser men.

In marrying Onna Sannomiya he does so. His error is to believe that he can achieve perfect prestige by adding to his panoply the last ornament it lacked (a suitably exalted wife) while at the same time keeping true love (Murasaki). In acquiring the first, a worldly prize that the world will insist he keep, he begins to lose the second, which has to do only with the heart; and as he does so he begins to lose himself. He soon compromises himself in the eyes both of Suzaku and of society at large, for despite his decision to marry Onna Sannomiya, his love for Murasaki will prevent him from honoring Suzaku's daughter as he should. Furthermore, his inability to tear himself away from Murasaki when at last she becomes ill leaves the door open to Kashiwagi's violation of Onna Sannomiya. That incident of course remains secret, but its consequence is that Onna Sannomiya becomes a nun, which underscores for all to see how inadequate her life with Genji has been. Genji's marriage is therefore a private tragedy with respect to Murasaki and a public failure with respect to Onna Sannomiya.

ONNA SANNOMIYA AND MURASAKI

Many writers on Murasaki and Onna Sannomiya have noted that the two make a contrasting pair, and almost all agree that Genji accepts Onna Sannomiya because of her link to Fujitsubo;[78] although some point out also an element of pity for Suzaku, and Oasa Yuji suggested that Genji hopes for a new Murasaki. Oasa called the marriage an attempt on Genji's part to relive the past, hence a mistake, since reliving the past is impossible. Fukasawa Michio found in the stark contrast between the glory of Genji's Rokujō estate and the miseries caused by the advent of Onna Sannomiya the key theme of the tale, and he held that the "occasion" of these miseries is none other than Murasaki's jealousy.[79]

Murasaki's jealousy—that is to say, her growing wish to disengage herself from Genji—is certainly central to the tragedy that begins to unfold in "Wakana 1," even if it is not the cause. This is the third and most serious of Murasaki's three "perils." Akashi was no threat, even if the inexperienced Murasaki thought she was. Asagao resembled distant storm clouds that melted into the sky. However, Onna Sannomiya really does move into Rokujoin, and she is far more exalted in rank than Asagao. "By birth [Asagao] is worth what I am," Murasaki assures herself in the "Asagao" chapter (in other words, "My father is a prince, too!"); but she knows that is not the whole truth and must conclude, "I shall be lost if his feelings shift to her."[80] Onna Sannomiya allows not even that spark of hope. Insignificant in her person, she is of crushing rank. Murasaki can only yield in silence. This time the slightest protest, being senseless, would only demean her further.

As already noted, many who have written on Murasaki recognize a more or less sharp difference between the Murasaki of the pre-"Wakana" chapters and the one awakened, as it were, by the marriage to Onna Sannomiya. The sheer volume of text on Murasaki in "Wakana 1" and after seems to have convinced many that there is something different about her. Haruo Shirane's statement that "Murasaki does not become a major character in the novelistic sense until part two, when she confronts the uncertainty of love and marriage,"[81] represents a widely held view. More recently, Nagai Kazuko wrote that the "child" Murasaki does not become a "woman" until "Wakana 1," when she is shocked to discover a peril she had not noticed before: the fragility of her position as Genji's wife.[82] I find this view puzzling. The Murasaki I have discussed so far has obviously been a woman before "Wakana 1," and she has long known that her position is fragile. She is prominent in the "Wakana" chapters not because she has suddenly grown up, but because the crisis she faces is graver and because, this time, it profoundly affects Genji as well. Still, the writing in the "Wakana" chapters is qualitatively different, as Ōasa Yūji, Akiyama Ken, and many others have observed.[83] The reader has seen nothing before like the long passage (Suzaku's deliberations over a husband for Onna Sannomiya and his conversation with Genji) that opens "Wakana 1." Perhaps that is why, to some, Murasaki appears to have changed.

Apart from being acutely aware that she has always lacked her father's recognition, hence his support, Murasaki learned long ago that Genji is not to be trusted, whatever he may say. She makes that clear in "Kochō" (Butterflies), four years before the events of "Wakana 1," in connection with Tamakazura, Tō no Chūjō's lost daughter whom Genji recently brought to live at his Rokujō estate:

> Genji was more and more thoroughly smitten. He even spoke of [Tamakazura] to [Murasaki]. "What an extraordinarily attractive person she is!" he said....
>
> To [Murasaki], who knew him well, this sort of praise betrayed a heightened interest, and she understood. "She does seem to be quick," she said, "but I pity her if in her innocence she ever trusts you too far."
>
> "And what about me should encourage her not to?"
>
> "Oh come now! Do I not remember the misery your ways have so often caused me?" She smiled.
>
> She misses nothing, does she, thought Genji; and he said, "But

you have it all wrong! She herself could hardly fail to notice!" He said no more, for he knew he was in trouble; and now that she had seen through him he struggled in vain to make up his mind what to do, while reflecting ruefully at the same time on his own warped and deplorable disposition.[84]

DECORUM AND DISCRETION

The narrator in *The Tale of Genji* often cites Genji's "peculiarity" (*kuse*), as she does in the opening passage of "Asagao," to excuse or explain his behavior. The word resembles a wry apology, as though to say, "No, one cannot approve, but on the subject of so great a lord I can hardly say more, and besides, the things he does make such a good story." When the narrator represents Genji himself, she may go so far as to let him acknowledge a "warped and deplorable disposition," but the effect is similar. The author of *Mumyozoshi* likewise remarks that it is not for her to criticize Genji, even though there are many things about what he does that one might wish otherwise.[85]

What are these things? Every reader can imagine some, and of course the *Genji* narrator actually spells some out, to a degree. Early on, one assents to the proposition that Genji's *kuse* is in the realm of *irogonomi* (gallantry, a penchant for lovemaking): it is romantic. More precisely, it is a compelling urge to seek to make love to certain women. However, the subjective content of that urge in particular cases remains undisclosed. Why, really, does Genji (or would a living man in Genji's place) find Akikonomu or Tamakazura all but irresistible? How does he weigh her attraction and the consequences of success? Both are of course daughters of former lovers, which suggests the erotic nostalgia stressed by Ōasa Yūji.[86] Still, one can imagine other motives as well, for example, a wish in the case of Akikonomu secretly to appropriate yet another woman destined (like Oborozukiyo, but higher in rank) for the emperor; or, in that of Tamakazura, to leave his mark less on Yūgao's daughter than on Tō no Chūjō's. The narrator could not possibly attribute such thoughts to him. Then there is Utsusemi. Very well, Genji was experimenting after the "rainy night conversation," and he took Utsusemi's flight from him as a challenge. Naturally he felt driven to win, especially since he had nothing at stake in the matter except his self-esteem. As already noted, however, talk of his *kuse*, or the claim that "[Asagao's] coolness maddened him, and he hated to admit defeat,"[87] does not suffice fifteen years later, when Asagao is a respected princess and he has recently been offered the office of chancellor. Discretion seems to have restrained the author from attributing to Genji the ambition, and the maneuvering to achieve that ambition, without which his actions make little sense.

Norbert Elias confirmed in his classic study of court society that discretion, reticence, and caution are essential to the courtier's failure or success.[88] Court society is a network of hierarchical relationships sustained by a sophisticated etiquette that is not vain show, but the substance of each courtier's (male or female) legitimate concern; for skill yields heightened prestige, and a lapse can mean social ruin. The courtier strives to avoid betraying his own feelings, while divining the motives and feelings of others.

As to Genji himself, the veil, or filter, that intervenes between him and the reader is therefore double. First, he veils himself from others—nothing in the tale contradicts Elias on this point—and is also likely, for the sake of self-respect, to veil his motives at times from himself. Second, the author of the tale (through her narrator), and even the author of an appreciation of the tale (*Mumyōzōshi*), protect him because, fictional or not, he is a great lord in the very court society to which they themselves belong. The representation of Genji, as of everyone else in the tale who "is anyone," is therefore bound to be compressed in dynamic range and painted in permissible colors. Elias's arguments on this matter apply well to the work. The author recounts about her hero, in the earlier chapters, all sorts of more-or-less scandalous stories of which her narrator often claims to disapprove, but these do not actually breach decorum because Genji at the time is relatively junior and because in any case it is made quite clear from the beginning that they do not impugn his essential dignity. Later, when he rises to palace minister (in "Miotsukushi") and beyond, his risk-taking will cease as far as the audience knows.[89] The commentators would then have it prolonged not by continuing maneuvers to enhance his prestige, as Elias leads one to expect of the most successful courtier, but by nostalgic pursuit (Asagao) or acceptance (Onna Sannomiya) of only coincidentally prestigious women—women who arouse no passion in him but merely represent someone else for whom he felt passion in the past. This seems improbable, as long as one is looking through the text towards a man who might actually have lived.[90]

Two simple and parallel examples of narratorial reticence prompted by considerations of rank are the passages in which Genji at last gains access to the agonizingly shy Suetsumuhana and then to the Akashi Lady.

In "Suetsumuhana" (The Safflower), Genji goes straight in to Suetsumuhana through a door that his confederate, her gentlewoman Myobu, has locked "with her own hands." While so glaring an inconsistency suggests a textual flaw, the narrator's insistence on the way Myōbu locks the panel probably means simply that, for the benefit of Suetsumuhana, she makes a great show of locking the panel but does not. To say this outright would be indecent and would also offend the dignity of a princess. In any case, the narrator never flags a deception; instead, she places one thing next to another in the listener's mind.[91] Yes, Myobu is shocked by Genji's behavior. "How awful of him! And he promised he wouldn't!" she thinks and slips off to her room. However, that does not mean that she did not leave the panel unlocked; it only means that she did not think Genji would simply force himself on her mistress.

The second example occurs in "Akashi." The Akashi Lady's father, playing the role of Myobu in "Suetsumuhana," though more eagerly, has contrived to bring Genji to his daughter. Shocked, the Akashi Lady "entered the neighboring room and somehow fastened the sliding panel so securely that he made no move to force it open." That sounds conclusive, but the text continues, "And yet that could not very well be all. Elegantly tall, she had such dignity that he was abashed ..."[92] How does he get in? Surely her father, who foresaw the difficulty and is there to remove it, opens the panel for him.[93] However, this explanation is not only indecent but an affront to the future mother of an empress, and the narrator therefore leaves it up to the reader.

ONNA SANNOMIYA: SUZAKU SEEKS A SON-IN-LAW

In "Wakana 1" the author had to give Genji Onna Sannomiya as she gave him Suetsumuhana and the Akashi Lady: without visible impropriety. She had to make Onna Sannomiya his without convicting him of greed. She did so above all by putting the discussions and negotiations of the issue in the first person—that is, in words spoken or thought by the interested parties themselves. Neither Genji nor Suzaku could possibly express himself plainly to the other on so momentous an issue; surely few great nobles have ever done so in any aristocratic society. In fact, one can probably assume that two such men discussing such a topic will never tell each other the whole truth. That is why they, and especially Suzaku, need advisers on the matter: informed bystanders who can speak not diplomacy but sense.

In "Asagao," "people" were saying of Genji and Asagao, even before Murasaki had heard what Genji was up to, that "Those two would not go at all badly together." No writer on the chapter mentions these rumors, but they count. Early in "Wakana 1" the rumors about Genji's feelings are louder and more explicit, and Suzaku's main adviser in the matter, one of Onna Sannomiya's nurses, is unambiguous on the subject. In one passage she first discusses Genji's son, Yūgiri, then Genji himself:

> "The middle counselor [Yūgiri] is extremely serious," she replied
> [to Suzaku]. "For all those years his heart was set on that young
> lady [Kumoi no Kari], he never gave any real sign of looking

elsewhere, and now that he has her he will be still less likely to waver. Judging from what they say about him, His Grace is the one who remains as susceptible as ever to what any woman may seem to offer. Moreover, one gathers that he deeply desires a lofty alliance, and that he has so little forgotten the former Kamo priestess [Asagao] that he still corresponds with her."[94]

Those who favor as Genji's motive either the link with Fujitsubo or simply his *kuse* of not giving up may well ignore such a passage. Ōasa Yūji, who mentioned it, granted that the nurse has Yūgiri just right, but he wrote that "Her words [on the subject of Genji] are clearly no more than a nurse's petty, irresponsible assumption." The reader understands that Genji's courtship of Asagao sprang from a "retrospective passion," he continued, but the bystanders in the tale are less well informed and so cling to mistaken ideas. He concluded, "Ordinary people are hardly capable of understanding Hikaru Genji's inner feelings (*naimen*).[95]

A little later, the nurse receives from her brother, a left middle controller (*sachuben*), an account of this gentleman's private conversation with Genji. The brother confirms what she has already said and remarks, "I gather His Grace [Genji] often jokes privately about feeling that while his glory in this life honors this latter age beyond what it deserves, when it comes to women, he has escaped neither censure nor personal disappointment."[96] The nurse therefore reports to Suzaku that, according to her brother, "His Grace would undoubtedly welcome the idea [of the marriage], since it would mean the fulfillment of his own enduring hopes." Nonetheless, Akiyama Ken doubted that the nurse believes what she says, refused to take her brother's conclusion seriously, and dismissed Genji's remarks about being disappointed as just what Genji apparently claims they are: jokes.[97] If they are jokes, they are in very poor taste.

If Genji is really confined to *irogonomi*, his motivation is too limited to account for his success. Male mammals have two related and consuming interests: mating and hierarchical advantage. The second generally takes precedence in the long run. Mitoma Kosuke explained the significance of *irogonomi* by saying that the *chōja* (the dominant human male) is required to be fertile and should not be devoted to just one woman; and in this connection he cited *Tsurezuregusa* to the effect that the gentleman should have a taste for love.[98] Very well, but that taste, not ambition and the will to glory, was the one Yoshida Kenkō felt the need to enjoin. He took ambition for granted. Advantageous mating is a privilege or a duty of power, not a prerequisite for it. Before favoring many women, the *chōja* must do what he must to become and remain a *chōja*. A male so caught up in *irogonomi* as to have no thought of rising in rank and privilege would be not only unintelligible but nonviable. Since Genji is manifestly viable, the nurse must be right about him, too: he does indeed desire a "lofty alliance."

In the pages of "Wakana 1" that culminate in Genji's acceptance of Onna Sannomiya, what Genji thinks and says, if taken at face value, suggests that he agrees to the marriage out of compassion for her father, although a private attraction to this relative of Murasaki and Fujitsubo encourages him as well. No other motive is seen to enter his mind.

Little by little, in a later talk with the nurse's brother, Genji convinces him that he does not "entertain the idea [of marrying Onna Sannomiya] himself." Instead he recommends that Suzaku present her to the emperor. "No doubt," he concedes, "she will find there earlier arrivals to be reckoned with, but no matter; they do not constitute an objection."[99] This idea is both implausible (of course the others are a threat—quite enough in the tale makes that clear) and sycophantic ("*Your* daughter is beyond the reach of petty jealousy"). Genji must know that Suzaku will reject it and mean that he should. He wants to provoke Suzaku into approaching *him*, which Suzaku does.

The decisive conversation between Suzaku and Genji is a model of diplomatic understatement. Genji, for whom it would be presumptuous and undignified to betray an active interest in Onna Sannomiya, studiously avoids doing so. This time he rejects the idea of giving her to the heir apparent on the grounds that the heir apparent, once emperor, would be unable to favor her specially, and he urges Suzaku instead to choose her a suitably reliable, nonimperial husband. Suzaku concedes that the idea makes sense, but he rejects it and cautiously asks Genji himself "to take this young princess under your special care and work out on your own who would make a good match for her"; to which he adds, to soften his request further, "[Yūgiri] would have been well worth approaching when he was single, and I am disappointed that [Tō no Chūjō] got to him first." Suzaku, who approached Yūgiri before Genji, knows that Yūgiri is not available because of his recent marriage.

Under cover of paternal modesty, Genji now at last allows himself to go to the point, though still with studied discretion:

> "My young lord the middle counselor [Yūgiri] can be relied upon for loyal service, but he lacks experience, and I believe there are many things that he does not yet understand. Please forgive my presumption, but were I to devote myself to her welfare, she would find her life unchanged from what you have made it. My only anxiety, alas, is that since I myself have little time left, I may conceivably fail her."

Appearances suggest that Suzaku has maneuvered Genji, who seems to lack nothing, into conceding him a magnanimous favor, but it is really Genji who has let himself be caught. He has said enough. The passage ends, "With these words, Genji accepted."[100]

Murasaki has the news first from rumor, but she who bridled at Genji's Akashi adventure and who feared Asagao does not believe it. "He had seemed in earnest when he was courting the former Kamo priestess, too, she told herself, but he avoided taking courtship to its extreme conclusion. She did not even bother to ask him about it."[101] After all these years, Genji has at least her provisional trust.

Genji knows this but still does not understand the gravity of what he has done. He thinks he will redeem himself yet again, sooner or later. Nonetheless, he lets a night go by without a word to Murasaki and brings the matter up only the next day, in the voice of the man who once claimed to be bored by the birth of his daughter at Akashi.

> "His Retired Majesty is not at all well," he remarked, "and I called on him yesterday. It was all very touching, you know. The thought of leaving Her Highness, his third daughter, has been worrying him terribly, and he told me all about it. I felt so sorry for him that I simply could not refuse. I suppose people will make quite a thing of it. It is all rather embarrassing by now, and unbecoming as well ..."[102]

He watches her as he speaks, but he who sees so much now sees nothing, for he is wondering "how she would feel—she who, with her quick temper, objected to the least of his little amusements"; and that Murasaki is the one of long ago, before graver anxieties taught her silence. She does not react. She only says, mildly, "What an extraordinary thing for him to ask of you! For myself, why should I wish to dislike her? I shall be perfectly happy as long as she does not find my presence here offensive ..." Disconcerted, he lectures her anyway on the wisdom of "taking things as they really are."[103]

All on her own, Murasaki struggles to take herself in hand and to salvage her dignity. "This came on him out of the blue, she said to herself, and he could hardly avoid it; I refuse to say an unkind word in protest ... and I will not have people gather that I am sulking." Yet the shock after all reminds her of her own misfortune, and she remembers her father's wife, whose jealousy deprived her of her father. "His Highness of Ceremonial's wife is forever calling down disaster on me ...," she reflects. "How she will gloat when she hears about this!" On this turn in her thoughts the narrator comments:

Hers was no doubt a heart without guile, but of course it still had
a dark recess or two. In secret she never ceased grieving that her
very innocence—the way she had proudly assumed for so long
that his vagaries need not concern her—would now cause
amusement, but in her behavior she remained the picture of
unquestioning trust.[104]

Demeaned by Genji's betrayal, Murasaki masks her resentment. He has at
last driven her, too, to dissemble. Once the undoubted mistress of Rokujōin,
she must now defer to one who is hardly more than a child, and she does so
with such perfect attentiveness and grace that he rues the step he has taken,
particularly when he discovers that Onna Sannomiya is, to say the least, "too
dismally dull."

"Why, he asked himself, had he let anything persuade him to try setting
another beside [Murasaki]? He had imprudently allowed a wanton weakness
to get the better of him: that was why it had happened ..."[105] The narrator's
Genji hides his underlying motive even from himself, for it is beneath his
dignity, and blames what he did on mere erotic temptation. Why believe
him, when he made no effort beforehand to find out what Onna Sannomiya
was like? He wanted the ornament, not the woman. Perhaps her being a
relative of Murasaki and Fujitsubo made him more eager and dulled his good
sense, but that is no excuse for a man of his age and experience. Bitter
thoughts fill him (he feels cheated by Suzaku), and tears come to his eyes, but
the Genji we see is deceiving himself.

"I was wrong after all to be so sure of him, and I shall never be able to
trust him again," Murasaki says to herself; and when he clings to her instead
of returning to Onna Sannomiya, as duty requires, she cries, "No, no, I will
not let you do this to me!" (since people may blame her for detaining him)
and sends him on his way. To her gentlewomen she dismisses any worry that
something might spark an incident between her and the princess. "It is just
as well Her Highness has come," she insists, since he wanted her. "People
seem to be talking as though there were a gulf between us; I wish they would
not ..., and I do not see how anyone could disapprove of her." In response
they whisper to each other that their mistress is "being much too nice."[106]
And so she is. That night, while she lies sleepless but painfully still, lest her
women note her restlessness and understand, Genji (with Onna Sannomiya)
dreams of her and wakens in alarm, his heart pounding. The bond between
them, though unbroken, is stretched very taut.

Onna Sannomiya is so small and immature that one wonders about
Genji's dutiful nights with her. There cannot be much to them. At the same
time his relations with Murasaki seem to be cool as well. His frustration soon

shows when Suzaku's departure for his mountain temple leaves Oborozukiyo (a minor consort) her own mistress again. All at once, he is desperate to see her after long years apart, and nothing, least of all her own objections, can stand in his way. He has always been fond of her, and their clandestine relationship of old seems to have been particularly passionate. Now he longs for that passion again, as well as to renew a valued tie and reassert an old claim, and this probably helps to explain his extraordinary tactlessness towards Murasaki in the matter. For all his fibs and evasions she knows what he is up to. "Why, you are quite the young gallant again!" she says when he returns from being with Oborozukiyo. "There you are, reliving your past, only to leave me wondering what will become of me."107

MURASAKI WISHES TO BECOME A NUN

The contrast between Murasaki, Genji's private treasure, and Onna Sannomiya, his public prize, demonstrates the folly of vain ambition. However, when in "Wakana 2" the narrative returns to Murasaki after a gap of several years, it is at first to affirm that all is well.

> While enjoying widespread esteem, [Onna Sannomiya] had never outdone the lady in the east wing [Murasaki], for the passage of the months and years only brought that one and Genji more perfectly together, until nothing appeared to come between them.

One need not take this assurance of harmony at face value; on the contrary, as elsewhere in the tale, words as pious as these probably announce trouble. "Nothing appeared" means what it says, for despite lasting affection on both sides the old tension, though hidden, remains. Having said this much, the narrator straight away raises a grave issue.

> Even so, though, [Murasaki] quite seriously told Genji now and again, "By now I should prefer a life of quiet practice to the commonplace one I lead. At my age I feel as though I have learned of life all that I wish to know. Please allow me that."
> "That is too cruel of you, and it is out of the question!" he would reply. "It is exactly what I myself long to do, and if I am still with you, it is only because I cannot bear to imagine how you would feel once I had left you behind, and what your life would be then. Once I have taken that step myself, you may do as you please." He would not have it.108

The religious life has attracted Genji ever since his youth, at least from a safe distance, but by now Asagao and Oborozukiyo have both taken the step Murasaki has in mind, and the reader has already heard him fret that he is falling ignominiously behind. This is more competitive of him than wise. In this case his reaction is completely illogical, as Fukasawa Michio observed.[109] When Murasaki opens the door for him to do what he claims to have long wanted to do, he only accuses her of cruelty; and he will again whenever she broaches the matter. He clings to this world far more stubbornly than he would have even himself believe.

The matter continues to weigh on Murasaki's mind, and evidence of Genji's continuing favor does little after all to calm her fears for the future.

> Seeing her own prestige rise in time so high above that of all others at Rokujō, the lady in the east wing continually reflected that although the personal favor she enjoyed equaled anyone's, age bye and bye would dull her in his eyes, and that she preferred to leave the world on her own before that should happen; but she found it impossible to say so clearly, for she feared that he might condemn her forwardness.[110]

He has chided her before, after all, and the topic is no doubt an especially sore one for him now, not only because of his complex feelings about leaving the world himself, or about allowing Murasaki to do so, but because by this time Onna Sannomiya has been given a still higher court rank. When rumor has it in any case that he has not honored Onna Sannomiya enough, this has placed him under a yet heavier obligation to put her visibly above Murasaki. Despite his inclinations otherwise, he has had to make a show of spending more time with Onna Sannomiya; and Murasaki, who knows he cannot countenance her desire to become a nun, must sense also that tension over Onna Sannomiya may sharpen his reaction to any expression of her desire to do so. Meanwhile, Genji begins to divide his nights equally between the two. "This [Murasaki] accepted and understood, but it confirmed her fears, although she never allowed them to show."[111]

Soon Genji must begin teaching Onna Sannomiya the *kin* to please Suzaku, and the "women's concert" (*onnagaku*) follows. The Akashi Lady, her daughter (the heir apparent's consort), Murasaki, and Onna Sannomiya perform at Rokujo for Genji and Yugiri, his guest. Onna Sannomiya does well, thanks to Genji's patient instruction, but Murasaki plays the *wagon* more beautifully than Genji ever imagined, since he has never even heard her before on this instrument.

After Genji and Murasaki have slept the next morning "until the sun was high in the sky," Genji begins the day with a tactless remark.

"Her Highness's music on the *kin* is remarkable, isn't it!" Genji observed. "How did it strike you?"

"When I first heard a little of her playing over there I wondered about her, but she is very good now," she answered. "How could she fail to be, when you have been giving all your time to her lessons?"[112]

Murasaki is hurt that he hardly taught *her* music at all. In reply he explains that he had to teach Onna Sannomiya because Suzaku and the emperor both expected it of him, and he goes on to assure Murasaki that her own performance, and the degree to which it impressed Yugiri, made him extremely proud. This is poor consolation, however. After all, the Akashi Lady (Murasaki's old rival) also played superbly, and Murasaki knows as well as Genji that in her case as in others mastery of music has nothing to do with a lady's real weight in the world.

MURASAKI ASKS AGAIN TO LEAVE THE WORLD

As Murasaki's weariness and anxiety mount, the narrator pauses to reflect with Genji that her very quality puts her in the way of misfortune.

> What with such accomplishments as this, and the authority with which she looked after His Majesty's children, [Murasaki] was in all ways a success, so much so that Genji even feared for her, remembering the example of others, equally perfect, whose lives had not been long; for she was that rarity, someone who in every single thing she did remained beyond cavil or reproach.... She was in her thirty-seventh year.[113]

Many passages in the tale express a similar fear that someone too beautiful will not live, for perfection is ill-omened. Moreover, the almanac warns that a woman in her thirty-seventh year is particularly prone to calamity, as Genji soon reminds her.[114] His thoughts announce imminent sorrows. The way he seems to attribute these to the agencies of fate hint that he is either blind (if he does not suspect he is to blame) or patronizing (if he does but dismisses the idea); but these opening lines concern less him than her. They evoke the flower's full beauty just before the wind and rain. They are the narrator's way of introducing gently a very dark passage.

Genji seems really to have lost touch with Murasaki, for he goes on to muse aloud to her about the course his life and hers have taken, and he contrasts his sorrows and hardships with her sheltered tranquillity. His uncomprehending tactlessness is a shock, for Murasaki's distress and anxiety over Onna Sannomiya, and her efforts to betray neither, are by now all too familiar. He has never before spoken to her from so false a height.

> "It seems to me that for you, though, except for that time when we were apart, there has been little either before or after it really to cause you serious unhappiness. Whether she be empress or, of course, someone lower, the greatest lady will have her sorrows. Keeping exalted company exacts its own torment, and the will to outdo others seems to leave one no rest; whereas you, who have always lived as it were with your father, have had fewer troubles than anyone, ever. Do you realize how, in that sense, you have been more fortunate than others? No doubt it was difficult for you to have Her Highness turn up here suddenly, but you cannot have failed to notice, since it directly affects you, how much more devoted to you her coming has made me. You who understand so many things must have grasped that."[115]

Genji's dramatic, relatively unfettered life, one that could only be a man's, can hardly be compared this way to Murasaki's, restricted as it has been by all that a lady must uphold and endure. He seems to imagine that, even now, she will believe she has no troubles just because he tells her so. His speech, which in kindness to him may owe something of its tone to the pressure he himself feels, is a provocation that Murasaki cannot let pass without renouncing her own integrity and even her identity. The reader, who learned long ago that she will not do that, may feel that Genji should have learned the same.

> "As you say," she replied, "I expect that in others' eyes I enjoy favor beyond what I deserve, but a sorrow greater than I can bear has inspired all my prayers ever since it entered my life." She seemed to have much more to say but to be too embarrassed to do so.
>
> "Seriously, though," she continued, "I feel I have little time left, and the thought of spending this year, too, pretending that I do worries me very much. If you would kindly permit what I once asked of you ..."[116]

She knows quite well that she cannot raise safely, yet again, the subject of her becoming a nun, and the fact that she does so anyway shows how urgently she feels the need. Genji's response is predictably sharp.

"But that cannot be. What would my life mean without you? Not much has happened all these years, but all I ask is the joy of our being together morning and night. Do see my extraordinary affection for you through to the end."

He said no more, which hurt her, since she had heard that much before; meanwhile he, pained to see her eyes fill with tears, talked on so as to turn her mind to other things.

His words have stung her, and she is upset. Still, he concedes nothing. Instead, to distract her, he begins again to muse out loud. What he had to say before, when both were calm and he told her how lucky she was, did him no good. This time, his judgment impaired by emotion, he tries something worse. The situation resembles the one near the end of "Asagao." As though to distract her, to reassure her by censuring others, and perhaps even covertly to get back at her for contradicting his belief that she should be content, he launches into reminiscences about Aoi and Rokujō; and to these he adds the Akashi Lady as a model for Murasaki. His tactic is an affront to Murasaki and dangerous as well. When he reminisced about Fujitsubo for the same purpose, under similar but more benign circumstances, Fujitsubo came to him in a dream and reproached him bitterly. This time the result is disaster. After discussing Aoi, remarking that she was "so terribly proper that one might say she overdid it a little," Genji continues,

"[Rokujō] ... comes to mind as someone of unusual grace and depth, but she made painfully trying company. I agree she had reason to be angry with me, but the way she brooded so interminably over the matter, and with such bitter rancor, made things very unpleasant. There was something so intimidating about her that I could never enjoy with her the daily intimacies of life; I could never drop my guard, lest informality invite her contempt, and so she and I soon drifted apart. I regretted her distress when scandal touched her and her good name suffered, and in fact, considering who she was, I felt in the end that I was to blame; but to make it up to her I insured that her daughter (who of course was so destined anyway) rose to be empress, ignoring by the way a good deal of slander and bitterness, and I expect that by now, in the afterworld, she has come to think better of me."[117]

This passage did not trouble Tanabe Seiko, who wrote that, as earlier in "Asagao," Genji's reminiscing about his women successfully restores harmony with Murasaki. She felt no need to add that in due course Rokujō will possess a girl of the household to pour out her complaint against Genji. Norma Field noted the parallel with "Asagao" (reminiscences followed by supernatural visitation) but made nothing of it.[118] Otherwise the parallel is hardly mentioned, perhaps because the accepted reading of "Asagao" obscures the pattern and its consequences. When I came to translate Genji's speech I felt as though he had taken leave of his senses.

The least of his sins is that in response to Murasaki's anguish he can do little more than talk about himself, which he does under the guise of confiding to her reflections on several of his other women. This is self-indulgence. Not a word in the tale suggests that Murasaki fancies gossip, and although what he says may interest her superficially, it could hardly bring her closer to him. Imai Gen'e, discussing the parallel passage in "Asagao," cited Sei Shonagon's observation in her list of "hateful things" (*nikuki mono*) that it is hateful to hear a lover praising a former mistress, even when it all happened a good while ago.[119] There is no reason why Murasaki should feel otherwise.

A greater sin is turning the name and memory of the dead to one's own selfish purposes and disclosing their secrets to others. But that is not all. Genji actually speaks ill of them: first of Aoi, and then, above all, of Rokujō. He who twenty-five years ago witnessed what Rokujō's spirit could do, when it possessed Aoi, still has the face to "treat her," as his father put it to him reproachfully then, "as casually as [he] might any other woman."[120] While Fujii Sadakazu wrote that Genji built Rokujōin to pacify (*chinkon*) Rokujō's spirit, and others, such as Haruo Shirane and Doris Bargen, have accepted this reading,[121] I cannot, and not just because of the present scene. Genji built Rokujōin on the site of Rokujō's residence, it is true, and no doubt in part with resources that passed from her to him when he undertook to see to her daughter's future; but the place is Genji's dream and Genji's glory, not a gesture towards a late lover who "made painfully trying company." Genji's building of Rokujōin is consistent with his attitude towards Rokujō both twenty-five years ago and now. He still takes her for granted. The young man who said of the haunted mansion in "Yūgao" (Evening Faces), "The place *is* eerie, but never mind: the demons will not trouble *me*"[122] has not changed. In fact, he not only takes her for granted, he self-righteously claims to have bought her off by doing the right thing (in the end, after perilous wavering) by her daughter. Could the Rokujō the reader knows, if her wandering spirit hears him, let this pass?

Genji's talk turns next to Akashi, whom he praises as he has done several times in the past for a personal quality out of keeping with her station.

"While on the surface she yields and appears mild," he says, "she has within such unbending dignity that before her one may feel somehow abashed." To this Murasaki responds so self-effacingly that Genji is

> greatly moved to reflect that she who once had sharply resented the lady in question, now, out of pure devotion to the consort, admitted her so indulgently to her presence. "You are not without your dark recesses," he said, "but it is a wonder how well you adapt your feelings to person and circumstance."123

He is being condescending to her. A short while ago he reminded her that she had always lived, as it were, with her father, as though both were still caught in that passage of their youth, and now he talks to her as though she were still the Murasaki who protested his affair with Akashi. Moreover, he makes her only a backhanded compliment when he praises her ability to feel, as appropriate, otherwise than she really feels in the "dark recesses" where she upholds her own worth and dignity against his slights.

By highlighting certain sentiments, this discussion has inevitably made Genji sound more sharply arrogant and patronizing than he does in the original. It is important to remember at the same time that he really does love Murasaki, although other imperatives, as well as the passage of time and gradually failing judgment, have drawn him away from her. While this essay may seem at times to set the two against one another in a sort of modern confrontation, one should never forget the grace of the original, and its measured pace; and the grace, too, of the picture that Genji and Murasaki always make.

MURASAKI'S ILLNESS

That night Genji goes to Onna Sannomiya, and to pass the lonely time Murasaki has her gentlewomen read her tales. After her talk with Genji, the atmosphere is heavy with a crisis that comes quickly.

> These old stories are all about what happens in life, she thought, and they are full of women involved with fickle, wanton, or treacherous men, and so on, but each seems to find her own in the end. How strange it is, the unsettled life I have led! Yes, it is true, as he said, that I have enjoyed better fortune than most, but am I to end my days burdened with these miseries that other women find hateful and beyond endurance? Oh, it is too hard!124

She went to bed very late and as dawn came on began to suffer
chest pains. Her women did what they could for her. "Shall we
inform His Grace?" they asked, but she would not have it and
bore her agony until it was light. She became feverish and felt
extremely ill, but no one told Genji as long as he failed to come
on his own.[125]

Once, long ago, Murasaki thought, "I am I!", turned away from Genji, and
sighed. A few years later she said, "Familiarity often breeds contempt" and
lay down with her back to him. This time, when he has really done what she
feared, and she is sick with hurt and anger, she will not even tell him. Let him
return when he pleases!

Her illness will last off and on until her death four years later. Soon,
Genji moves her to Nijō, where they had first lived together, and all but
abandons Onna Sannomiya (at Rokujō) to remain by her side while the
priests pursue their rites.

In lucid moments Murasaki only spoke to reproach him, saying,
"You are so cruel not to grant me what I ask!"; but for Genji the
sorrow and pain of seeing her one instant, with his very eyes,
wearing by her own wish the habit of renunciation, rather than
parting from her at the end of life itself, would be more than he
could ever bear. "It is exactly what I have always longed to do,"
he said, "but worry about how you would feel, once you were left
alone, has constantly detained me. Do you mean to say that you
would now abandon me?" That was his only response ...[126]

Nothing has changed. What she asks is more than he can give. He cannot
allow her an independent existence and feel that he remains himself. He
cannot bear to see her "one instant, with his very eyes, wearing *by her own
wish* (*ware to*) the habit of renunciation." For love of her he cannot bear her
to have a will, a life of her own. For this many a man has deserved both pity
and damnation. At least her illness has led Genji for now to forget the duties
of his political marriage, which would be all very well, were it not that during
his absence from Rokujoin Kashiwagi violates Onna Sannomiya and
precipitates another tragedy.

THE POSSESSION

Genji has at last left Murasaki to spend some time after all with Onna
Sannomiya when word reaches him that Murasaki has died. Rushing back to

Nijō, he summons the most powerful healers, and in response to their prayers the afflicting spirit suddenly "moved into a little girl, in whom it screamed and raged while the lady began at last to breathe again."[127] It is Rokujō.

The dramatic scene that follows has generally been neglected by those who write about Murasaki and issues affecting her, and the few who mention it do so only to dismiss it. Tanabe Seiko found it "tacked on" and recalled Shimizu Yoshiko saying that the author must have written it only because her readers liked the counterpart scene in "Aoi" and wanted more. For Kojima Yukiko, the text makes it perfectly clear why Murasaki falls ill: she is unhappy about Onna Sannomiya. The possession scene, Kojima wrote, is simply a "device" to explain how the dying Murasaki can unaccountably revive and regain Genji's attention.[128]

One writer who treated the scene at length is Doris Bargen,[129] whose conclusions also amount to denying that this scene represents what the text clearly implies: a renewed intervention in Genji's life by a personage known as Rokujō. Bargen contended that the Rokujō who possesses the medium is not an autonomous entity but Murasaki's own image of a woman whose "charisma" Murasaki appropriates to "empower herself";[130] and she charged "critics" with mistakenly adopting Genji's own, biased "preoccupation with identifying the possessing spirit,"[131] when here and in the earlier possession scene in "Aoi" they and Genji should both know that the real speaker is Genji's possessed wife. However, it takes no preoccupation with anything to accept that the spirit is Rokujō. In the "Aoi" scene, the reader already knows that the spirit is Rokujō, and Genji recognizes her instantly. In this one, Genji behaves normally for someone addressed by a medium in a trance: he seeks to verify who the speaker is. His fear that he knows the answer already is all the more reason to make sure. To agree that the speaker is Rokujō is not to take Genji's side. It is simply to read what is there.[132]

There are three ways to explain the possession: Murasaki somehow provokes her relapse and Rokujō's speech to get Genji's attention back and to rebuke him, as Bargen would have it; the author arbitrarily does it for her, as Kojima suggested; or Genji's absence removes his protection from Murasaki, and Rokujō seizes the opportunity to capture his attention herself. Of these, the first is implausible, the second is uninteresting, and the third, however incredible, is the one presented as true. The spirit says:

> From on high I kept my eye on you, and what you did for Her Majesty made me pleased and grateful; but perhaps I do not care that much about my daughter, now that she and I inhabit different realms, for that bitterness of mine, which made you hateful to me, remains.

The spirit's remark that in the afterworld she cares less about her daughter than Genji assumes has a ghastly plausibility, and moreover the spirit confirms that Genji's indiscretion is the immediate reason for her renewed reproach:

> What I find particularly offensive, more so even than your spurning me for others when I was among the living, is that in conversation with one for whom you do care you callously made me out to be a disagreeable woman.

For that is just what Genji did. The spirit continues:

> I had hoped, as I did then, that you might at least be forgiving towards the dead and come to my defense when others maligned me; and that is why, since I have this terrible form, things have at last come to this. I have little against this woman, but you are strongly guarded; I feel far away and cannot approach you, and even your voice reaches me only faintly.

None of this has anything obvious to do with Murasaki. Nonetheless, it is true that in this scene Murasaki and Rokujō are briefly and eerily superimposed on one another—superimposed, not merged. That this superimposition resists explanation neither diminishes its power nor authorizes the suppression of one of the pair. To accept it is to feel doubly the heart-rending force of this, the height of Rokujō's speech:

> The weeping figure, her hair over her face, resembled the spirit he had seen then [in "Aoi"]. Shuddering with the same fear and astonishment, he took the girl's hands and held her down lest she embarrass him. "Is it really you?" he asked.... "Say plainly who you are! Or else, tell me something to make it obvious, something no one else could know. Then I will believe you, at least a little."
>   The spirit sobbed loudly.

waga mi koso	"I am no longer
aranu sama nare	what I was,
sore nagara	and yet, through it all,
sora obore suru	you are the same you
kimi wa kimi nari	who refuse to know!

> Oh, I hate you, I hate you!"[133]

The voice speaks the awful truth: indeed, Genji refuses to know. Murasaki, who does not hate him, could still say the same; on this Bargen and I agree.[134] However, she does not.

Murasaki's *ware wa ware* long ago over Akashi was akin in spirit and rhetoric to love poems that set "I" against "you." Rokujō's utterance, which does so as well, belongs to the same family: "I am no longer what I was," she says, "but you are the same you." It is the classic lover's reproach become a nightmare voice, but Genji, who has no ears with which to heed it, will let this reproach, too, pass.

MURASAKI'S DEATH

Murasaki survives another four years of crisis, weakness, and reprieve. Filled though they are in the narration with sad or tender scenes and reflections, the distance between her and Genji remains. When the worst of the possession crisis seems over, Genji, "since his lady so longed to take the tonsure, cut a token lock of her hair that she might thereby gain the strength to observe the Five Precepts, and he allowed her to receive them";[135] but this tiny concession, made under extreme duress, changes nothing.

Murasaki therefore does what the unhappy Rokujō could never do: she gathers herself to rise above things as they are. Komashaku Kimi wrote, "It is certain that, contrary to worldly appearances, Murasaki no Ue died still burdened by her misfortune, a 'woman's' misfortune."[136] There is some truth to this. In "Minori" (The Rites) Murasaki "hoped still to assume, somehow, the guise to which she aspired" and was "angry with him because it would so obviously be unkind and contrary of her to act on her own, without his permission; but she feared too that her own sins might be weighing her down." Her *ware* is not yet gone, and she still suffers. However, she who "asked nothing more of this life and, having no fond ties to detain her, did not particularly wish to stay" is also thinking of him, to whom the very thought of outliving her is appalling; for "in her heart of hearts she regretted only his pain when the bond between them failed."[137] Meanwhile, she seeks to make peace with her life as well she can under the circumstances. She has herself in hand.

Most of those who have written on the end of her life have preferred to see her this way, and some have obviously found her example inspiring. She has taken the difficult path of generosity, as her nature from the beginning disposed her to do. Feeling death approaching,

> She hastened to dedicate the thousand copies of the Lotus Sutra
> that she had had made as prayers for herself over the years. The

event took place at Nijō, which she considered her own home....
Since she had never told him it was to be so solemn, he in turn
had offered her no particular advice, and the excellence of her
judgment, and even her knowledge of Buddhist things, impressed
him profoundly; his only role was to look after quite ordinary
matters of altar adornment and so on.[138]

She has never done anything like this before, in the house she considers her
own, entirely on her own; and of course she does it magnificently. Kurata
Minoru justly observed that with this event she achieves independence, and
that the court's full attendance makes her true standing plain: yes, in the eyes
of all she really is the wife of the honorary retired emperor.[139] It is
impossible not to recall the magnificent rite of the Eight Discourses on the
Lotus Sutra held by Fujitsubo, at the end of which Fujitsubo left the world
and became a nun ("Sakaki").

With this Murasaki therefore rises at last to join Fujitsubo on the same
high plane of perfect simplicity that Genji recalled with admiration when he
described Fujitsubo to Murasaki in "Asagao": "Although she displayed no
extraordinary brilliance, a talk with her was always worthwhile, and she did
the smallest thing exactly right. We shall never see her like again." After
speaking then, he looked at Murasaki and rightly saw Fujitsubo; but in those
days he could not yet honor her as she deserved, and, alas, he never learned
really to do so. She lacked the world's unreserved approbation, and in any
case he clasped her, like everything else, too jealously to himself. It is only in
setting out on her own, within the confines of compassion towards a deeply
loved but failing man, that she becomes at last in simple reality what he saw
then, and the woman who by natural gift she has always been: like Fujitsubo,
a born empress. Some have praised her "self-transcendence" at the end,[140]
but it is better to say that she transcends nothing. Thoughts of herself drop
away—even the wonderful gifts (music, calligraphy, skill at dyeing, freshness
of taste, beauty, quick wit) that in truth she enjoyed more abundantly even
than Fujitsubo. An empress has no "I," no "prickles"; she does not deign to
commit herself to personal traits. Only sorrow remains, and concern for
others.

Lady Murasaki, who had so much on her mind, never spoke
sagely of what might be after she was be gone. She confined
herself to a few, quiet remarks about the fleeting character of life,
but the very lightness of her tone, as though the matter hardly
touched her, made it more movingly plain than any words what
sorrow she felt.... When the conversation took such a turn that

she could speak without seeming morbid, she mentioned those who had served her so well through the years and who deserved pity for having nowhere else to go. "Do give them a thought once I am gone," she said. That was all.[141]

She is beyond rank. Soon, to say good-bye, the present empress, her adopted daughter, will come to her while she lies dying, as naturally as any daughter would come to sit with her mother.[142]

There is nothing for Genji to do, nor will he ever do anything again.

CONCLUSION

I have sought in this essay to acknowledge both the grace of the *Genji* text and the way the work conveys after all the realities of life. Haruo Shirane wrote, in agreement with many others:

> In the *Genji* it is not the fulfillment or frustration of desire that becomes the focus of the narrative so much as the elegant and elaborate process of courtship.... Almost every aspect of social intercourse is transformed into an aesthetic mode.[143]

However, I do not see this in the tale. Fulfillment of desire is seldom the focus of any narrative, and certainly not for long; but frustration of it, defined to include the desire for glory, seems to me perhaps the tale's great theme, to which "the elegant and elaborate process of courtship" and so on adds an essential, unhurried refinement. Shirane continued:

> Genji becomes a great lover-hero not simply because he conquers women but because he has also mastered the "arts"—poetry, calligraphy, music—of courtship. The same applies to Genji's political triumphs, which are measured by a cultural and aesthetic code that transcends the usual notion of power and influence.[144]

Yet I do not believe that Genji owes his political success to aesthetic mastery. Nothing in the text except its supernatural elements suggests to me that Genji's rise "transcends the usual notion of power and influence," and I have argued that his maneuvering for prestige extends even to projects of alliance with prestigious women. Far from being unusual, except in the degree to which he is gifted, he adopts the methods of any courtier.

Writers on the tale take it for granted that Genji represents (or is supposed by everyone else to represent) an "ideal." Ōasa Yūji, for example, called him an "ideal figure" (*risōsha*).[145] Murasaki is taken likewise to be an "ideal woman." However, this notion of "ideal" seems to put beyond question certain things that, when examined, enrich the work and give Genji and Murasaki fuller life.

The notion of "ideal" associated with Genji is probably summed up by his peerless looks and grace, which the narrator evokes repeatedly; but his enchanting quality also diverts the audience's attention from what he is up to. Many more-or-less troubling passages end when the narrator turns the scene into a beautiful tableau, or the gentlewomen, watching him leave, whisper to each other what a wonder he is to behold. He also has superb intellectual and artistic gifts, as well as the personal charisma that gives him, in Kashiwagi's words, such a "singular light." He is never ordinary. It is this quality that gives him in all circumstances a dignity commensurate with his exquisitely ambiguous proximity to the throne. However, while his beauty in this broad sense makes him fascinating, it does not make him a model of laudable thought or behavior. He is kinder than many heroes of world literature, and perhaps than many lords whom the author knew, but his "light" is not a sign of goodness. On the contrary, it lends grace and style to that in him which may not be laudable at all. At each moment the audience sees of him what the narrator wishes seen,[146] but in the imagination the reader puts these moments together, looks beyond the words, and sees more or less distinctly a man. No one could think, talk, or write about "him" otherwise. This man as I see him is like other men, even if his gifts lift him above all others.

Naturally Genji has always stirred readers' dreams, but Murasaki lives with Genji the man. It is he who claims her, tests her, hurts her, cajoles her, lies to her, loves her, and even against her wishes never lets her go. Some have described their love, too, as "ideal" and have even called its story "the fulfillment of ideal love."[147] I wonder what they mean. Who would wish on a couple the fate of Genji and Murasaki? It is not a happy one.

Genji alone provokes this fate, moved by ambition that requires more of Murasaki than she can give him. After the abdication of Emperor Reizei ("Wakana 2"), his secret son, he entertains before the reader thoughts if not of empire, then at least of dynasty. Already the grandfather of a future emperor in the female line, he nonetheless regrets not being the same in the male:

> At Rokujō, Genji nursed his disappointment that Retired Emperor Reizei had no successor of his own. The heir apparent was his direct descendant too, it was true, but no trouble having ever arisen to disturb His Retired Majesty's reign, Genji's

transgression had never come to light, and now, as fate would have it, that line was in any case not to continue. This Genji greatly regretted, and since he could hardly discuss the matter with anyone else it continued to weigh on his mind.[148]

Thus Genji, who would really have reigned if his father had not refrained from naming him heir apparent, has long wished to correct this error and, so to speak, to rewrite history. Dare one imagine that he made love to Fujitsubo with that in mind? At any rate, it is to this sort of desire—one his gifts allowed him the hope of fulfilling—that he sacrifices with deep but blind sorrow the woman he really loves.

Murasaki may understand little of this, but there is much that he does not understand about her, either. She has her own destiny. If he, in a truer world than the flawed one they inhabit, is a born emperor whom only fortune has cheated of his realm, she in that truer world is his equal, and in this one suffers a counterpart misfortune. Her resistance to his three infidelities proceeds from no intrinsic trait, but only from the predicament of a flawed birth that does not match her nature. For him, reclaiming what should have been his requires such manipulation of persons and circumstances that despite both genius and supernatural favor he falls short after all. He wanted too much. Reizei has no heir, Onna Sannomiya slips from him, and these two great transgressions (against his father and against Murasaki) cost him the substance of what he is and has.

Murasaki, as beautiful as he, has never for a moment been ordinary either. Still, she is a woman, and her different destiny depends on his. It is not just an inner matter. Despite her repeated affirmations of distinctness, she does not free herself from his appetites until his powers begin to fail and her own death approaches, and if she were not thanks to him an empress's adoptive mother, that empress's last visit to her could not seal her life. Yet in rising at the end above happiness or unhappiness she achieves something that he does not; for until lost to view he remains, like many another great man, entangled in the complexities of an extravagant pride.

NOTES

THE AUTHOR, a reader in the Japan Centre of the Australian National University in Canberra, is currently translating *The Tale of Genji*. He wishes to acknowledge the vital contributions made to this essay by Susan C. Tyler, without whose knowledge, insight, and assistance it might never have been written. He also would like to thank two anonymous referees for their encouragement and their criticism, and Alison Tokita for having kindly obtained many materials not available in Australia.

1. NKBZ 2:282 (*Genji monogatari*); S 277 (Seidensticker 1976). All translations below are mine.

2. Akiyama 1964, p. 75.

3. My conclusions had formed themselves before I studied the secondary literature, and what I read then encouraged me to pursue them. I will cite the work not only of major specialists but of junior scholars, a student or two, and fiction writers of whom some have translated the tale and some have not; for *The Tale of Genji* belongs to all.

4. Shimizu 1967, p. 44.

5. Doris Bargen, who included all three episodes in her discussion of Murasaki, pointed likewise to Genji's incomprehension and self-centeredness (Bargen 1997, pp. 109–49; see, for example, p. 137). My treatment of Murasaki parallels hers in some ways, although I share neither the foundations of her argument nor her conclusions. I will discuss this matter below under "The Possession," pp. 471–73.

6. Matsuo 1968, pp. 151–66 (first published in *Kokubungaku kaishaku to kanshō*, August 1949).

7. Nagai 1993, pp. 157–74.

8. Tanabe 1981, pp. 106–107; Enchi 1974, p. 79; Oba 1996, pp. 19–40; Field 1987, p. 175.

9. Shigematsu 1978, pp. 5–22.

10. Matsuo 1968 pp. 157–58, 165.

11. Komashaku 1991.

12. Articles devoted to Murasaki's *shitto* include Iijima 1981; Morita 1989; Saito 1973a, Saito 1973b; and Saito 1975. On her sense of self: Baba 1990.

13. Most writers accept without question Genji's view as the narrator presents it. For example, Fukasawa Michio saw in Murasaki's *shitto* the sole, precipitating cause of Genji's passage from glory to anguish (Fukasawa 1965, p. 20).

14. NKBZ 1:93; S 3.

15. *Gosenshu* (951) 518; *Shitago shu* (Minamoto no Shitago , 911–983) 187; *Asamitsu shu* (Fujiwara no Asamitsu , 951–995) 72.

16. *Gosenshu* 711, the last poem addressed to Heichu (d. 923) by his mistress, in the story about how Heichu's mistress was stolen from him by Fujiwara no Tokihira (871–909).

17. *Izumi shikibu shu* .

18. *Ben no menoto shu* 85.

19. In "Matsukaze" (The Wind in the Pines) Genji makes the same words mean something quite different. Far from accepting Murasaki's reproach, he insists that she agree to *his* definition of her standing. On returning from a visit to the Akashi Lady he admonishes Murasaki, "In rank, there is simply no comparison between the two of you. You are you, after all: remember that." NKBZ 2:412; S 330. More literally, he says, "Think, 'I am I!'" The fourteenth-century commentary *Kakaisho* observes, "He means that Murasaki should take pride in being who she is and reflect that no one comes higher than she." Tamagami 1968, p. 356.

20. Tanabe 1981, p. 127.

21. Shigematsu 1978, p. 13.

22. Komashaku 1991, p. 152.

23. Mitoma 1995, p. 76. The principle that a lady does not betray jealousy of course does not apply to a wandering spirit such as that of Rokujo.

24. Shigematsu 1978, p. 13. NKBZ 1:144; S 26.

25. Akiyama 1964, p. 77. See also Ko 1988.

26. NKBZ 1:134; S 22.

27. Baba 1990, p. 249.

28. Tanabe 1981, pp. 109, 126; Akiyama 1964, p. 82.

29. Oasa 1975, pp. 350–51; Shigematsu 1978, p. 10.

30. NKBZ 1:126; S 19. Genji is in only his twelfth year. While *omou yo naran hito* ("a

true love") has been taken to refer to Fujitsubo (S, "the lady he yearned for"), the expression is probably more speculative than that. He is dreaming of someone *just like* Fujitsubo.

31. NKBZ 1:140; S 25.

32. NKBZ 1:280–81; S 87–88. I have abbreviated the scene.

33. NKBZ 1:287; S 90.

34. Shimizu 1967, pp. 66–69.

35. Wakashiro 1979, p. 226.

36. Enchi 1974, p. 77.

37. Setouchi 1997, p. 42.

38. Field 1987, p. 174.

39. Komashaku 1991, pp. 136–38.

40. Tanabe 1981, p. 122; Wakashiro 1979, p. 228.

41. NKBZ 2:62–63; S 180.

42. The example of Tamakazura confirms that a lady could not decently agree in advance, on her own initiative, to first intercourse. In "Wakana 2" Genji reflects as follows on her marriage night with Higekuro :

> When His Excellency [To no Chujo] prevailed on an unthinking gentlewoman to help him [Higekuro] make his way in to her, she [Tamakazura] made sure everyone understood clearly that she had had nothing to do with it, that what was happening had full authorization, and that for her own part she was completely blameless. Looking back on it now, I can appreciate how very shrewd she was. It was their destiny to be together, and never mind how it began, as long as it lasts; but people would think a little less well of her if they retained the impression that she had willingly acquiesced. She really did it very, very well. (NKBZ 4:251; S 627)

On the same theme Jennifer Robertson wrote: "Before and even after the Meiji period, published writers and critics—the vast majority of whom were male—relegated sexual desire in females to courtesans and prostitutes" (Robertson 1998, p. 62). This attitude is by no means peculiar to Japan.

43. From the "Akashi" chapter, NKBZ 2:262; S 269. The passages quoted below, interspersed with commentary, are continuous text in the original. In this one Murasaki alludes to *Shuishu* 870: "I care not for myself, who am forgotten, but grieve for the life of him who made me those vows".

44. NKBZ 2:281–82; S 276.

45. He foresees his daughter becoming empress.

46. NKBZ 2:282; S 276–77.

47. NKBZ 1:171; S 40. The "bluebells" are *asagao*, which I translate this way rather than as "morning glory" because in Heian times *asagao* probably referred to the modern *kikyo* , a bluebell-like flower. "His Highness of Ceremonial" renders Shikibukyo no Miya, the title of Asagao's father.

48. NKBZ 2:51; S 176.

49. Saito 1975, pp. 32–42.

50. NKBZ 2:459; S 348.

51. Saitō 1975, p. 37.

52. Field 1987, p. 177.

53. In "Fujitsubo chinkonka", in Shimizu 1967, pp. 43–49.

54. NKBZ 2:484; S 359.

55. Imai 1971.

56. NKBZ 2:484; S 359.

57. Akiyama 1964, pp. 93–113.

58. NKBZ 2:480; S 357.

59. Suzuki 1997, pp. 140, 144. As proof Suzuki cited the way Murasaki keeps her peace even after Genji's marriage to Onna Sannomiya and the admiration her silence arouses in Genji. He concluded that Murasaki's suffering turns her definitively into Genji's ideal, and that this transformation takes place in "Asagao," under the winter moon.

60. Akiyama 1964, p. 112; Suzuki 1997, p. 144.

61. NKBZ 3:12–14; S 360–61.

62. NKBZ 4:22; S 541. I will return to this matter in connection with Genji's marriage to Onna Sannomiya.

63. NKBZ 2:468; S 352.

64 NKBZ 3:12–13; S 361.

65. Could it be that Asagao's appointment as Kamo priestess was engineered by Aoi's father in order to remove this threat, and that the reason given in the text (no other suitable princess was available) is only an excuse?

66. Only Tanabe Seiko (Tanabe 1981, p. 145) attributed Genji's interest in Asagao to social pressure and observed that he is "a little bothered by not having a proper wife."

67. NKBZ 2:469–70; S 352. "The same old salt-burner's robe" (a poetic allusion) means, roughly, "the same old me."

68. NKBZ 2:479; S 356–57.

69. NKBZ 2:480; S 357.

70. "Who are so much like her."

71. NKBZ 2:482; S 357–58.

72. NKBZ 2:485; S 359.

73. NKBZ 4:21; S 541.

74. NKBZ 4:19; S 540–41. This sort of thing could probably be said of many men of exceptional power. Of Napoleon, for example, one observer remarked, "When I saw him go by my heart beat, and although it was very cold my forehead broke out in perspiration"; while another reported, "Nothing could equal Napoleon's grace and charm. Endowed as he was with ample wit, superior intelligence, and extraordinary tact, it was in his moments of relaxation and casual conversation that he was most astonishing and most enchanting." Castelot 1997, pp. 195–96. Like Genji (as noted below), Napoleon could annihilate a man with his glance.

75. NKBZ 4:270–71; S 634.

76 *Mumyozoshi*, p. 36. For this the text calls Genji "despicable" (*muge ni keshikaranu onkokoro*).

77. NKBZ 4:285; S 638.

78. Only Ko Shubin, a graduate student at the time, observed in passing that Genji marries Onna Sannomiya because he knows Murasaki is no longer good enough for him (Ko 1988, p. 32).

79. Oasa 1981, pp. 85, 88; Fukasawa 1965, p. 20.

80. NKBZ 2:468–69; S 352.

81. Shirane 1987, p. 113.

82. Nagai 1993, pp. 168, 170. See also Yokoi 1993, p. 282. Yokoi wrote that Onna Sannomiya gives Murasaki a new "identity as an individual."

83. Oasa 1981, p. 75; Akiyama 1964, pp. 150 f.

84. NKBZ 3:175–76; S 427–28.

85. *Mumyōzōshi*, p. 35.

86. Oasa 1981, p. 87.

87. NKBZ 2:478; S 356.

88. Elias 1983, especially chapter 5, "Etiquette and ceremony," pp. 78–116.

89. An exception is his night with Oborozukiyo in "Wakana 1." He then indeed resembles the old Genji, though he is not really the same man. The moment of calculated folly will not be repeated.

90. I discussed above, from another perspective, the narrator's discretion when evoking a great lady. This discretion convinced Matsuo Satoshi that Murasaki Shikibu had little knowledge of women like Murasaki no Ue, who were above her in class, hence little feeling for them and little interest in them (Matsuo 1968, p. 154). Later on, Ko Shūbin echoed Matsuo, but backwards, when he suggested that since Murasaki Shikibu clearly had little interest in high-ranking women such as Aoi, Oborozukiyo, or Onna Sannomiya, her more sympathetic treatment of Murasaki no Ue shows that the latter belongs after all only to the middle level (Ko 1988, p. 33). Confusion like this arises from the failure to recognize the constraints under which the author wrote.

91. Even when Genji lies outright, as when he tells Murasaki that Asagao means nothing serious to him, claims to be Tamakazura's father, or assures Yugiri (at the end of "Yokobue", The Flute) that he does not understand Yugiri's dream of Kashiwagi, the narrator never steps outside the narration to point it out.

92. NKBZ 2:247; S 263.

93. The Akashi Lady could not have opened it herself, for the reasons discussed above in connection with Genji's consummation of his marriage with Murasaki. It would have been shameless of her to so do.

94. NKBZ 4:21; S 540–41.

95. Oasa 1981, p. 76.

96. NKBZ 4:24–25; S 542.

97. Akiyama 1964, p. 165 and p. 183, note 4.

98. Mitoma 1995, pp. 64–65.

99. NKBZ 4:34–35; S 545.

100. NKBZ 4:42–43; S 548–49.

101. NKBZ 4:44; S 549.

102. NKBZ 4:45; S 549.

103. NKBZ 4:47; S 550.

104. NKBZ 4:47–48; S 550.

105. NKBZ 4:57; S 554.

106. NKBZ 4:60; S 555.

107. NKBZ 4:78; S 562.

108. NKBZ 4:159; S 592.

109. Fukasawa 1965, p. 25.

110. NKBZ 4:169; S 597.

111. NKBZ 4:169; S 597.

112. NKBZ 4:195; S 606.

113. NKBZ 4:196–97; S 607.

114. Fujitsubo died in her thirty-seventh year.

115. NKBZ 4:198; S 607.

116. NKBZ 4:199; S 607–608.

117. NKBZ 4:200–201; S 608.

118. Tanabe 1981, p. 165; Field 1987, p. 59.

119. Imai 1971, p. 351.

120. NKBZ 2:12; S 158.

121. Fujii 1990, pp. 157–60; Shirane 1987, p. 116; Bargen 1997, p. 120.

122. NKBZ 1:235; S 69.

123. NKBZ 4:202; S 608–609.

124. Although the passage on tales in "Hotaru" (Fireflies) deserves its fame, the way Murasaki turns to tales here, in despair, is particularly moving. Tales are her only resource. She cannot seek solace and guidance from the histories of China and Japan, as Reizei did after learning that he was Genji's son.

125. NKBZ 4:203; S 609.

126. NKBZ 4:205–206; S 610.

127. NKBZ 4:226; S 617. The influence of this spirit has been assumed from the start, since it begins its speech to Genji by saying, "For months you have cruelly confined me and inflicted on me such pain that I had thought I might teach you a proper lesson ..." (NKBZ 4:225; S 617).

128. Tanabe 1981, p. 130; Kojima 1991, p. 68.

129. Bargen 1997, pp. 124–44.

130. Bargen 1997, pp. 124, 27.

131. Bargen 1997, p. 26.

132. For me, Bargen's reading requires a strange understanding of Rokujo. Despite my admiration and sympathy for Rokujo, I cannot imagine why Murasaki or any other woman in the tale, however desperate, would seek the authority of someone so ill-used by Genji. Bargen described Rokujō as "a proud, dissatisfied, and demanding woman who knew how to gain control over a man" (Bargen 1997, p. 136), but Rokujo never gained control over Genji. If she had, he would have recognized his relationship with her publicly, as she wished. His failure to do so brought her years of intense suffering. To propose Rokujo as an inspiration to Murasaki is cruel to Rokujo and denies Murasaki any sense.

133. NKBT 4:226–27; S 618–19.

134. Bargen 1997, p. 142.

135. NKBZ 4:232; S 620.

136. Komashaku 1991, p. 152.

137. NKBZ 4:479–80; S 712–13.

138. NKBZ 4:481; S 713. She had probably had these copies made to pray for permission to leave the world.

139. Kurata 1993, p. 331.

140. Shigematsu 1978, pp. 22–23; Maruyama 1982, p. 50.

141. NKBZ 4:487–88; S 716.

142. NKBZ 4:490; S 717.

143. Shirane 1987, p. 30.

144. Shirane 1987, p. 30.

145. Oasa 1975, p. 352.

146. This is a manner of speaking. The text read now is unlikely to be exactly what Murasaki Shikibu wrote.

147. Wakashiro 1979, p. 223.

148. NKBZ 4:157–58; S 592.

REFERENCES

Akiyama 1964
    Akiyama Ken Genji *monogatari no sekai*. Tōkyō Daigaku Shuppankai, 1964.
Baba 1990
    Baba Taeko. "Jiga no ishiki o motsu Murasaki no ue". *Tōyoko kokubungaku* 22 (March 1990), pp. 249–259.

Bargen 1997
　　Doris Bargen. *A Woman's Weapon: Spirit Possession in The Tale of Genji*. University of Hawaii Press, 1997.
Castelot 1997
　　André Castelot. *Napoleon Bonaparte*. Paris: Perrin, 1997.
Elias 1983
　　Norbert Elias. *The Court Society*, tr. Edmund Jephcott. Oxford: Blackwell, 1983.
Enchi 1974
　　Enchi Fumiko. *Genji monogatari shiken*. Shinchosha, 1974.
Field 1987
　　Norma Field. *The Splendor of Longing in the Tale of Genji*. Princeton University Press, 1987.
Fujii 1990
　　Fujii Sadakazu. *Genji monogatari: Shigen to genzai*. Isagoya Shobō, 1990.
Fukasawa 1965
　　Fukasawa Michio. "Murasaki no ue: Higekiteki risōzōno keisei. *Kokugo kokubun* 368 (April 1965), pp. 18–33.
Genji monogatari
　　Genji monogatari. 6 vols. NKBZ 12–17.
Iijima 1981
　　Iijima Hisako. "Murasaki no ue no shitto". *Monogatari bungaku ronkyu* 6 (Dec. 1981), pp. 117–128.
Imai 1971
　　Imai Gen'e. "Murasaki no ue: Asagao no maki ni okeru. In *Kaku makimaki no jinbutsu* 1, vol. 3 of *Genji monogatari kōza*, ed. Yamagishi Tokuhei et al. Yūseidō, 1971.
Ko 1988
　　Ko Shubin. "Murasaki no ue no ron: Naka no shina no josei toshite". *Shirin* 4 (October 1988), pp. 25–33.
Kojima 1991
　　Kojima Yukiko. "Murasaki no ue". In *Genji monogatari o orinasu hitobito*, vol. 2 of *Genji monogatari kōza*, ed. Imai Takuji et al. Benseisha, 1991.
Komashaku 1991
　　Komashaku Kimi. *Murasaki shikibu no messeji*. Asahi Shuppan (Asahi Sensho 422), 1991.
Kurata 1993
　　Kurata Minoru. "Murasaki no ue no shi to Hikaru Genji: Wakamurasaki to igo no makimaki". In *Hikaru kimi no monogatari*, vol. 3 of *Genji monogatari koza*, ed. Imai Takuji et al. Benseisha, 1993.
Maruyama 1982
　　Maruyama Kiyoko. "Murasaki no ue shorōn: Murasaki no ue rikai ni kakawaru sankasho no kaishaku o chūshin ni". *Kashiigata* (April 1982), pp. 35–52.
Matsuo 1968
　　Matsuo Satoshi. "Murasaki no ue: Hitotsu no yaya kikyō naru shiron". Orig. pub. 1949, repr. in *Heian jidai monogatari ronko* . Kasama Shoin, 1968.
Mitoma 1995
　　Mitoma Kosuke. *Genji monogatari no densho to sozo*, 1995.
Morita 1989
　　Morita Yuka. "Murasaki no ue no miryoku: Shitto, jiritsu". *Otani Joshidai kokubun* (March 1989), pp. 60–64.

Mumyōzoshi
 Mumyōzoshi. Ed. Kuwabara Hiroshi . Shinchōsha, 1976.
Nagai 1993
 Nagai Kazuko "Murasaki no ue: 'Onna shujinkō' no teigiron". In *Genji monogatari sakuchu jinbutsu ronshu*, ed. Mori Ichirō. Benseisha, 1993.
Ōasa 1975
 Ōasa Yūji *Genji monogatari seihen no kenkyu*. Ofusha, 1975.
Ōasa 1981
 Ōasa Yūji. "Onna sannomiya no kōka". In vol. 6 of *Kōza Genji monogatari no sekai* , ed. Akiyama Ken et al. Yuhikaku, 1981.
Ōba 1996
 Ōba Minako. "Special Address: Without Beginning, Without End." In *The Woman's Hand: Gender and Theory in Japanese Women's Writing*, ed. Paul Gordon Schalow and Janet A. Walker. Stanford University Press, 1996.
Robertson 1998
 Jennifer Robertson. *Takarazuka: Sexual Politics and Popular Culture in Modern Japan*. University of California Press, 1998.
Saitō 1973a
 Saitō Akiko. "Murasaki no ue no shitto: Tai Akashi no baai (1)" (–). *Kaishaku* (February 1973), pp. 26–31.
Saitō 1973b
 Saito Akiko. "Murasaki no ue no shitto: Tai Akashi no baai (2)." *Kaishaku* (June 1973), pp. 54–59.
Saitō 1975
 Saitō Akiko. "Murasaki no ue no shitto: Akashi oyobi Asagao no saiin". *Murasaki* 13 (June 1975), pp. 32–42.
Seidensticker 1976
 Edward Seidensticker, trans. *The Tale of Genji*. Knopf, 1976.
Setouchi 1997
 Setouchi Jakuchō. *Genji monogatari no joseitachi*. NHK Ningen Daigaku NHK, April–June 1997.
Shigematsu 1978
 Shigematsu Nobuhiro. "Murasaki no ue no ningenzo" *Geibun* 10 (Nov. 1978), pp. 5–22.
Shimizu 1967
 Shimizu Yoshiko. *Genji no onnagimi*. Hanawa Shobo, 1967.
Shirane 1987
 Haruo Shirane. *The Bridge of Dreams: A Poetics of "The Tale of Genji."* Stanford University Press, 1987.
Suzuki 1997
 Suzuki Hideo. "Fujitsubo kara Murasaki no ue e: Asagao no maki ron". In *Genji monogatari shiron shū*, vol. 4 of *Ronshū Heian bungaku*, ed. Gotō Shōko et al. Benseisha, 1997.
Tamagami 1968
 Tamagami Takuya, ed. *Shimeishō, Kakaishō*. Kadokawa Shoten, 1968.
Tanabe 1981
 Tanabe Seiko. *Genji monogatari kami fusen*. Shinchōsha, 1981.
Wakashiro 1979
 Wakashiro Kiiko. *Genji monogatari no onna*. Nippon Hōsō Shuppan Kyokai, 1979.
Yokoi 1993
 Yokoi Takashi. "Murasaki no ue to Onna sannomiya: Wakana jō, ge to igo no makimaki". In *Hikaru kimi no monogatari*, vol. 3 of *Genji monogatari kōza*, ed. Imai Takuji et al. Benseisha, 1993.

HARUO SHIRANE

Kingship and Transgression

THE "EXILE OF THE YOUNG NOBLE"

In an essay on Herman Melville, R. P. Blackmur once wrote that "the artist must dramatize his themes, his vision, his observations, his 'mere' story, in terms of the existing conventions however adverse those conventions may seem to his intentions, or however hollow or vain they ring when struck."[1] To the reader unfamiliar with the narrative tradition, the *Genji monogatari* may appear to be the product of Murasaki Shikibu's imagination or the result of a realistic impulse to record her observations and experiences, but the author employed plot conventions which were already known to her audience and which they no doubt expected her to use. The youth, exile, and triumphant return of the shining hero derive from a familiar plot convention which Origuchi Shinobu has called the *kishu-ryūri-tan*, or the "exile of the young noble," in which a young god or aristocrat undergoes a severe trial in a distant and hostile land.[2] In the process, the young man proves his mettle, comes of age, and acquires the power and respect necessary to become a true leader and hero. This pattern of exile and triumph applies not only to a number of mythic and legendary figures of the ancient period (Ōkuninushi, Susanoo, Yamasachi-hiko, and Emperor Jimmu), but to the protagonists of the early Heian *monogatari*. In the *Utsubo monogatari* (983), for example, Toshikage, the hero of the opening chapter, wanders to a distant island where

From *The Bridge of Dreams: A Poetics of 'The Tale of Genji.'* © 1987 by the Board of Trustees of the Leland Stanford Junior University.

he undergoes an ordeal, is saved and blessed by heavenly spirits, and returns home with a divine secret that eventually brings glory to his descendants.

In Heian *monogatari*, which were aimed at a female audience, the "exile of the young noble" sometimes takes the form of the *mamako-tan*,[3] or the stepdaughter tale, in which a hostile stepmother favors her own children over the disadvantaged heroine. The young woman manages to survive the trial, which usually occurs indoors, and is eventually rewarded by a handsome and highborn noble who marries her and brings her unexpected prominence. When the protagonist is a stepson instead of a stepdaughter, as in the *Genji*, the trial occurs outside the household, in a hostile country. Here the evil stepmother takes the form of the reigning emperor's chief consort, the Kokiden lady, who favors her own child (the future Suzaku emperor) over her new stepson (Genji), whom she persecutes and eventually drives into exile. In the pattern of the *mamako-tan*, the motherless protagonist manages to overcome the extended ordeal. With the aid of external forces, Genji eventually returns to the capital; the stepmother dies; and the hero goes on to achieve unparalleled glory.

The interest of the "exile of the young noble" and "stepdaughter" paradigms, both of which can be found throughout world literature,[4] lies not in their appearance so much as in the manner in which Murasaki Shikibu transforms these archetypal configurations. The author not only endows these familiar plot types with a specific historical and political context, she transposes the ideal of kingship, a notion implicit in the mythic versions of the "exile of the young noble," to a distinctly Heian context.

KINGSHIP

The early chapters of the *Genji* resemble what Northrop Frye defines as a quest-romance: the "search of the libido or desiring self for a fulfillment that will deliver it from the anxieties of reality but will still contain that reality."[5] As noted earlier, this type of romance is not simply the substitution of some more ideal realm for ordinary reality but rather a process of transforming contemporary circumstances and implicitly criticizing them.[6] "What is" often yields to "what ought to be" or "might be," the "ought" and "might" implying what "is" by their particular distortion of it. The relationship of the *Genji* to socio-historical reality is not simply one of reflected content but one of complex interplay and inversion.

In Murasaki Shikibu's day the most powerful aristocratic families competed to marry their daughters to the emperor, for it was by maternal control of the throne that power was ultimately obtained. Normally, a minister who was the emperor's maternal grandfather or uncle was chosen to assist the sovereign or govern in his place. (When the emperor was still in his infancy, this position was called *sesshō*, or regent, and when he came of age it was called *kanpaku*, or civil dictator—thus the modern term *sekkan*, an abbreviation of *sesshō–kanpaku*.) The ideal route to power for an aspiring minister was to place his daughter in the imperial harem as a high-ranking consort in the hope that she would bear a son for the emperor. If the boy was designated crown prince, the minister could eventually become the grandfather of the emperor and, more often than not, the *sesshō*, the most influential figure behind the throne. Historians generally trace this form of *sekkan* rule back to Fujiwara no Yoshifusa (804–872), who, through a process of careful intrigue, placed his nephew on the throne and married his daughter (Empress Akirakeiko) to him. In 858 Yoshifusa succeeded in replacing his nephew, Emperor Montoku, with his daughter's son, who became Emperor Seiwa (r. 858–76). As the maternal grandfather and *sesshō* of a child emperor, Yoshifusa monopolized court politics. Over the next century and a half this particular family line within the Northern Branch of the Fujiwara clan consolidated its power, and by the beginning of the eleventh century Fujiwara no Michinaga (966–1027) had gained almost absolute control of the throne through a series of carefully arranged and fortuitous marriages.

No *sesshō* presides in the opening chapter of the *Genji*. The emperor is not a child fettered by his maternal relatives but a mature adult who flagrantly ignores his ministers. Instead of paying obeisance to the Kokiden lady, the daughter of the powerful Minister of the Right, he dotes on the Kiritsubo lady, a low-ranking consort whose father is dead. If Genji, the emperor's son by the Kiritsubo lady, is placed on the throne, as the emperor privately hopes, the next reign will also be free of *sekkan* rule. But should the First Prince, the son of the Kokiden lady, assume the crown, as is publicly expected, the next emperor will probably be manipulated by his mother and maternal grandfather, the Minister of the Right (*Udaijin*), who would be in a position to become *sesshō* or *kanpaku*. The political configuration echoes the dawn of the *sekkan* era when the emperor was constrained but not yet overwhelmed by the Fujiwara.

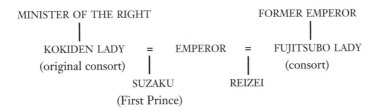

Subsequent events reveal that the emperor cannot determine the imperial succession, which passes to the son of the Kokiden lady. His implicit defeat at the hands of the Kokiden faction, however, does not dampen his desire to control the throne. As the following passage from "Momiji no ga" ("An Autumn Excursion") reveals, the birth of a prince to his new consort, the Fujitsubo lady, rekindles the emperor's hopes for imperial power.

> The boy bore a stunning resemblance to Genji, but the emperor, unaware of the child's true parentage, concluded that those of great beauty had a tendency to look alike. He doted on the baby, lavishing upon him the utmost care. The emperor had viewed Genji as superior to all the others, but the opposition of the court had, to his unending regret, prevented him from installing Genji as crown prince. He felt sorry for Genji, whose maturing appearance and manner were worthy of far more than commoner status. But now the same shining light had been born to a lady of high rank, and he looked upon the child as a flawless jewel. ("Momiji no ga" I: 400–401; S: 139–40.)

In the *Genji* what cannot be attained through one figure is often gained by or through another person of similar countenance, the second figure becoming an extension of the first. This principle applies to the Fujitsubo lady, the mirror image of the Kiritsubo lady, as well as to the new prince, who becomes, at least in the eyes of the emperor, a reincarnation of the hero and who eventually accedes to the position that was privately intended for Genji.[7]

To prevent Fujitsubo's new child from succumbing to the pressures that defeated Genji, the emperor promotes his mother to *chūgū*, or empress, at the end of "Momiji no ga" and then prepares to leave the throne. Two chapters later, in "Aoi" ("Heartvine"), a change of reign has occurred: the emperor has retired; Kokiden's son has come to the throne; and the Fujitsubo lady's son (the future Reizei emperor) has been designated crown prince. If the new crown prince can ascend the throne, the emperor's private ambitions will be realized. But from this point onward the Kokiden lady and the Minister of the Right assume control in the manner of the Fujiwara and threaten to crush both Genji and the new crown prince.

Genji's gradual political decline from "Aoi" is, to a large degree, a reflection of contemporary sekkan politics.[8] Shortly before his death in "Sakaki" ("The Sacred Tree"), the retired emperor asks his son, the new Suzaku emperor, to regard Genji as his friend. The last words of a dying person take on particular significance in the *Genji*, for they reveal the unfulfilled desires of the dying and the burden and responsibility that must be borne by the survivors. But the Suzaku emperor, now a puppet of his maternal relatives, is unable to honor his father's wishes.

> The Suzaku emperor did not want to violate his father's last wishes and was sympathetic toward Genji, but he was young and docile and lacked the ability to impose his will. His mother, the Empress Dowager, and his grandfather, the Minister of the Right, each had their way, and his administration was not, it seemed, what he wished it to be. ("Sakaki" II: 96-97; S: 194.)

By the end of "Sakaki" the open hostility of the opposition, the death of the retired emperor, the Fujitsubo lady's retreat from secular life, and Genji's scandalous affair with Oborozukiyo have placed supporters of the crown prince in precarious circumstances. Instead of protecting his younger brother, the Suzaku emperor is eventually forced to turn against Genji, now the crown prince's principal ally. By the beginning of "Suma," the hero has been stripped of his post and has little alternative but to leave the capital.

If the decline of the hero reflects the realities of the *sekkan* system, his return to power does not. A number of prominent leaders, Sugawara no Michizane (845–903), Minamoto no Takaakira (914–82), and Fujiwara no Korechika (973–1010), were banished from the capital by the Fujiwara in power struggles to control the throne, but none of these men returned to the capital in triumph or regained their former status. Genji's exile and recovery do, however, follow the pattern of the "exile of the young noble," in which a young god or noble is aided by animals, divine forces, or some treasure that enables him to survive his ordeal and return home successfully. At the end of "Suma" supernatural forces come to Genji's rescue and make possible the improbable: the hero's restoration to power. At the beginning of "Akashi" the spirit of the deceased emperor appears to Genji in a dream and instructs him to leave Suma and follow the Sumiyoshi god, who in turn leads him to the Akashi family and the beginning of a new public tie to the throne. The same spirit appears to the Suzaku emperor and angrily rebukes him for disobeying his last instructions. A series of disasters then strike the opposition: the Minister of the Right dies, the Kokiden lady falls ill, the Suzaku emperor has eye trouble, and a series of natural disturbances reveal the displeasure of the heavens. Taking these signs as a warning, the Suzaku emperor turns against his maternal relatives and pardons Genji, who returns to the capital in triumph. Shortly afterwards, the Fujitsubo lady's son, whose position has long been in jeopardy, ascends the throne as the Reizei emperor.

One of the continuing narrative threads from "Kiritsubo" through "Miotsukushi" ("Channel Buoys") is thus the gradual fulfillment, even after death, of the emperor's desire for imperial authority.[9] By leading Genji to Akashi and reprimanding the Suzaku emperor, the spirit of the emperor opens the way for the hero's return to the capital and for the accession of the son of the Fujitsubo lady. The emperor finally attains what he was unable to while alive and what no mid-Heian emperor ever achieved: control of the imperial succession.

THE GOLDEN AGE

The ideal of kingship is more than a matter of plot. Details in the first chapter suggest that the present imperial reign is that of Emperor Daigo (r. 897–930) and that the setting is the Engi Era (901–23), which came almost a hundred years before the appearance of the *Genji*. Murasaki Shikibu establishes a tacit correspondence between the emperor and Daigo through a number of allusions, of which the most obvious are two direct references to Emperor Uda (r. 887–97), Daigo's father and immediate imperial predecessor. In the first, the emperor, following the death of the Kiritsubo lady, gazes at a painting which was "painted (or commissioned) by the Retired Emperor Uda" (*Teiji-no-in no kakasetamaite*).[10] In the second, the emperor consults with a Korean fortune-teller in secret "since Emperor Uda had issued an injunction (against summoning foreigners) to the imperial court" (*miya no uchi ni mesamu koto wa Uda no on-imashime areba*).[11] Both passages suggest that the emperor's immediate predecessor is the historical Emperor Uda and that the emperor is Uda's son Daigo.[12]

By setting her work in the past, or at least by evoking it, Murasaki Shikibu released herself from the constraints imposed by the present and avoided offending her patron, Fujiwara no Michinaga. But the choice of Emperor Daigo and the Engi–Tenryaku period (901–57) had a more specific and immediate literary effect: it summoned up the image of a sage emperor and a golden age of direct imperial rule. In the opening scene of "Hana no en" ("The Festival of the Cherry Blossoms"), for example, the emperor sponsors a lavish festival at the Southern Pavilion. The festival shows the emperor presiding over a glorious reign, a time when all high courtiers, including the emperor and the crown prince, freely composed Chinese poetry-an unlikely happening by Murasaki Shikibu's day. As the Minister of Right later tells Genji:

> I have lived a long time and witnessed four illustrious reigns, but I have never seen such superb Chinese poetry and prose, nor has the dance and music ever been in such harmony. Never has an occasion added so many years to my life. Thanks to your

guidance and extensive knowledge, each of the different fields
now has many outstanding performers. ("Hana no en" I: 432; S:
155.)

As the *Genji* commentary the *Kakaishō* (1364) points out, the Cherry Blossom
Festival, which was frequently held during the reign of Emperor Daigo, is a
reminder of the Engi–Tenryaku era.[13] The imperial excursion to the Suzaku-
in, which provides the setting and the title for the previous chapter, "Momiji
no ga," is also a symbol of the past. During the Engi–Tenryaku period the
emperor often journeyed to the Suzaku Villa, especially on two notable
occasions, in Engi 6 (906) and Engi 16 (916), when Emperor Daigo visited
the famous villa to honor the fortieth and fiftieth birthdays of his father, the
retired Emperor Uda.[14]

    The eleventh-century chronicle *Ōkagami* (*The Great Mirror*, ca. 1093)
compares the imperial rulers of the Engi–Tenryaku era, Emperors Daigo and
Murakami, to the legendary Chinese emperors Yao and Shun.[15] Even today
the Engi–Tenryaku period is regarded as a memorable age of cultural and
literary efflorescence. Music, painting, dance, calligraphy, and poetry
flourished, particularly under the patronage of Emperors Uda and Daigo.
The first imperial anthology of native poetry, the *Kokinshū* (ca. 905), was
edited; the *Engi shiki* (905–27) was compiled; and the last of the Six National
Histories (*Rik-kokushi*) was completed (901). As the writings of such literati
as Minamoto no Shitagō (d. 983) and Ōe no Masahira (952–1012) reveal, the
Engi–Tenryaku period also represented a time of benevolent and direct
imperial rule, one that stood in contrast to their own age of *sekkan* politics.[16]
Here the Confucian ideal of the sage emperor is fused with a historical ideal
derived from the example of earlier Japanese emperors. To many of these
Confucian-trained scholars and poets, whose political influence had rapidly
deteriorated in the course of the tenth century, the Engi–Tenryaku era
represented not only an imperial golden age but a time when, in accordance
with Confucian ideals, arts and letters directly contributed to harmonious
government.

    Murasaki Shikibu's family also enjoyed its peak of glory during the
Engi–Tenryaku period. The author's great-grandfather, Fujiwara no
Kanesuke (d. 933), had been patronized by Emperor Daigo and was one of
the prominent men of letters of his time. By Murasaki Shikibu's time,
however, her father, like many other scholar-poets and graduates of the
university, had considerable difficulty obtaining even an appointment as a
provincial governor. Murasaki Shikibu no doubt looked back on the
Engi–Tenryaku period with considerable nostalgia, as did many educated
members of the middle aristocracy.

Modern historians point out that the Fujiwara *sekkan* had already exerted considerable influence by Emperor Daigo's reign and that the Engi–Tenryaku period was by no means a trouble-free era of imperial rule.[17] In 901, for example, the Fujiwara banished Sugawara no Michizane, Emperor Uda's loyal minister and ally. The Engi–Tenryaku age had, in other words, become an ideal by the end of the tenth century, and it is this vision that is reflected in the early chapters rather than history as it actually was. Murasaki Shikibu paid great attention to contemporary detail, but she was also depicting a romantic world, and the allusions to the Engi–Tenryaku era were meant to underscore, within the context of the *sekkan* system, those political ideals.

THE GENJI

The nostalgic nature of the *Genji* extends to the hero himself. The title of Murasaki Shikibu's great narrative—which could also be rendered as *The Tale of a Genji*—suggests that the hero will achieve imperial glory not as a prince but as a commoner. After considering the weak position of Genji's maternal relatives and weighing the advice of the fortune-tellers, the emperor lowers his son to commoner status and makes him a first-generation Genji. The Genji, or the clan of the Minamoto, emerged almost two centuries prior to Murasaki Shikibu's time, during the reign of Emperor Saga (r. 899–930), when an attempt was made to reduce the expenses of the shrinking imperial treasury by lowering over thirty princes and princesses to commoner status.[18] This practice of conferring the surname of Genji upon princes lasted until the reign of Emperor Daigo (r. 897–930).[19] Of these first-generation Genji, perhaps the most distinguished was Minamoto no Takaakira (914–82), the son of Emperor Daigo and the person most often cited as a historical model for Genji. Takaakira, who was politically active during the Engi–Tenryaku period, gradually rose to the position of Minister of the Left and managed to marry his daughter to Prince Tamehira, the son of Emperor Murakami (r. 946–67) and a likely successor to the throne. The Fujiwara, fearful that a Genji would become a maternal relative of a future emperor, managed to have Tamehira's younger brother designated as crown prince. This crushing defeat was followed by an even greater blow. In 969 Takaakira was implicated in a plot against the government, stripped of his post, and exiled in a manner that anticipates the hero of the Genji. The Fujiwara *sekkan* family subsequently monopolized palace politics, and almost all major struggles occurred within that family line.[20] When the *Genji* first appeared in the early ninth century, they occupied high positions (the Saga Genji started at the Fourth Rank),[21] but they were gradually pushed out of power by the Fujiwara. By the beginning of the eleventh century, there were few upper-rank Genji, and no first-generation Genji. The notion of a first-generation Minamoto hero gaining imperial power in the face of the Fujiwara thus provided excellent material for romance, particularly when the hero, as medieval commentaries point out, bore the shadow of Minamoto no Takaakira.[22]

Genji heroes such as Minamoto no Masayori and Minamoto no Suzushi appear in the *Utsubo monogatari*, but none of them are, like the protagonist of the *Genji*, directly related to imperial succession and power. The historical emperors Kōnin (r. 770–81), Kammu (r. 781–806), Kōkō (r. 884–87), and Uda (r. 887–97) had been lowered to commoner status but were able, owing to good fortune and the lack of an appropriate successor, to return to royal status and ascend the throne.[23] This type of plot, which is found in the *Sagoromo monogatari* (1027), lacks the interest of the *Genji* since it differs little from the notion of a crown prince becoming an emperor. In Murasaki Shikibu's narrative the hero not only must become a commoner, he must remain one. As the Korean fortune-teller observes in the opening chapter, Genji has the appearance of an emperor, will attain a position equivalent to one, but cannot ascend the throne without causing disaster.[24]

Though the shining Genji must be relegated to commoner status, the aura of light suggests that the throne belongs to him. From as early as Amaterasu, the sun deity and ancestral goddess of the imperial family, radiance has been associated with divine origin and heavenly descent. Closer in time is the heroine of the *Taketori monogatari*, the Shining Princess (Kaguyahime), who temporarily descends to earth to atone for certain unspecified sins. In the opening chapter of the *Utsubo monogatari* seven heavenly spirits inform the hero Toshikage that his descendant will be a reincarnation of the seven deities.[25] Nakatada, Toshikage's grandchild, proves to be "a beautiful, dazzling boy" (*tama hikari kagayaku onoko*)[26] whose brilliance reflects his divine origins.

In the *Genji* the mythic power of the divine is displaced. Instead of a heavenly being, Murasaki Shikibu presents the aura of the imperial line, thought to be of divine origin. Both Genji and the First Prince are the sons of the same emperor, but only Genji is blessed with the shining light, which suggests that the right of succession should lie with the hero rather than his elder brother, to whom the secular powers have consigned the crown. The association of radiance and royal mystique is further reinforced by the emergence of the Fujitsubo lady, referred to as the "Princess of the Dazzling Sun" (*Kagayakuhi no miya*).[27]

The luminous affinity between Genji and the emperor's new consort implies that imperial power belongs to them and their child, the future

Emperor Reizei. It is thus appropriate that "Momiji no ga" should end with
the remark that Genji and the little prince "were like the sun and the moon
shining side by side in the heavens" (*tsuki hi no hikari no sora ni kayoitaru yō ni
zo* [I: 420; S: 149]).

TRANSGRESSION AND RENEWAL

The full implications of transgression are not explored until the
"Wakana" ("New Herbs") chapters when Genji's wife, the Third Princess,
commits adultery with Kashiwagi. But even in the early chapters the
religious implications are evident. Like his historical counterpart, Genji not
only evokes the aura of royalty, he also recalls the Fujiwara, by whom the
Minamoto were suppressed. Genji's mother, a low-ranking consort, proves to
be no match for the Kokiden lady, the daughter of the Minister of the Right.
Furthermore, the hero must, like other mortal beings, live in a world of
impermanence and suffering and take moral responsibility for his actions.
Though the radiant image of Genji and the Fujitsubo lady makes their illicit
union in "Wakamurasaki" ("Lavender") seem almost inevitable, the author
does not overlook the fact that the hero has committed adultery with his
father's wife and violated an imperial consort.

Like his great literary predecessor, the hero of the *Ise monogatari* (*Tales
of Ise*, ca. 961), the young Genji is a passionate and subversive youth whose
transgressions eventually result in expulsion and exile. In the opening
episodes of the *Ise monogatari* the legendary Ariwara no Narihira has a brief
and painful affair with the future Empress of Nijō, known otherwise as
Takaiko (or Kōshi). Shortly afterward, Narihira, "finding himself beset by
troubles in the capital, sets out for the Eastern Provinces" (Episode 7).[28] The
exact cause of his difficulties remains ambiguous, but the order of the
episodes points to his illicit affair with Takaiko. The prophecy Genji receives
after his tryst with the Fujitsubo lady in "Wakamurasaki" suggests a similar
pattern of events.

> The Middle Captain (Genji) had a strange and frightening dream
> and summoned a soothsayer, who informed him that it foretold a
> future so extraordinary as to be almost unimaginable. "In the
> meantime you will meet with adversity. You must be
> circumspect," he added. ("Wakamurasaki" I: 308; S: 100.)

In the context of the Fujitsubo lady's pregnancy, the soothsayer's words
suggest that Genji will become the father of a future emperor. The nature of
the "adversity," though left unclear, anticipates the hero's political decline

and exile. The young hero, however, pays little heed to the warning and continues to pursue his father's consort. It is not until "Suma," when the hero has been stripped of his rank, that he begins to act with circumspection. Here Genji speaks to his father-in-law, the former Minister of the Left, shortly before his departure for Suma.

> They say that everything is retribution for acts in one's previous life. It seems that destiny has not been on my side. Even a person who has been charged with only a minor violation and who has not been stripped of his rank as I have must be on good behavior. To carry on as if nothing had happened would be a major offense. I understand this is true even in China. I hear that I am being considered for distant exile, which means that I have been accused of a particularly serious offense. Though I am completely innocent, I would be afraid to go on acting as if I were indifferent. I have decided that it would be better to leave the capital before I am humiliated yet further. ("Suma" II: 157–58; S: 220–21.)

The text does not reveal why Genji has been stripped of his rank and post, a severe penalty by Heian standards, but Genji's affair with Oborozukiyo, the Minister of the Right's daughter and the new *naishi no kami* (chief of the Palace Attendants Office) to the Suzaku emperor, suggests that this scandal has provided the opposition with the opportunity to bring serious punitive measures against Genji.[29] By voluntarily leaving the capital, Genji preempts any attempt by the Kokiden faction to take further legal measures— particularly distant and forced exile, a sentence that would end his political career. But though Genji's decision to go to Suma is politically motivated, he is, as the following conversation with the Fujitsubo lady suggests, well aware of having committed another offense.

> Now that I have been unexpectedly punished, I am reminded of that one deed and am afraid to face the heavens. As long as the reign of the crown prince is unhampered, I will have no regrets if this worthless body of mine fades away. ("Soma" II: 171; S: 226).

Though Genji claims to be innocent of the public charges brought against him, he privately associates his loss of office and present difficulties with that "one deed," his illicit affair with his father's consort.

Genji's self-exile echoes the Fujitsubo lady's earlier decision in "Sakaki" to take holy vows, a gesture with both religious and political implications. Though the Fujitsubo lady's motives for leaving the secular world are never directly stated, the larger context suggests her realization that Genji's support is necessary to guarantee the future of the crown prince, and her fear that his continued pursuit will result in a scandal that could destroy her son's political future. By renouncing the world she avoids Genji's advances while maintaining him as an ally. This strategy also enables her to lessen her burden of accumulated sin. Like the Fujitsubo lady's renunciation, the hero's self-exile to Suma is both a political maneuver (designed to protect the crown prince) and an act of penitence, a retreat from the opposition as well as from secular life.[30] In "Suma," we find Genji spending much of his time praying, chanting, and reading sutras. As the following passage reveals, Genji even forgoes women.

> ... [D]ay and night Murasaki's image floated up before his eyes. His longing became so intense that he once more considered bringing her in secret to Suma. But upon further reflection he dismissed the idea. The least he could do while in this sorrowful world was to lessen his sins, he thought, and immediately proceeded to fast and spend his days and nights in prayer and meditation. ("Sums" II: 184–85; S: 233.)

The question of sin and transgression is brought up again by the violent storm at the end of "Suma." Before the rainstorm Genji participates in a purification ceremony (*harae*) designed to wash away sins and pollutions. At the end of the seaside ritual the hero addresses the following poem to the gods ("Suma" II: 209; S: 246):

Yao yorozu	The multitude of gods
Kami mo aware to	Surely regard me with pity,
Omouramu	For I have committed
Okaseru tsumi no	No particular sins.
Sore to nakereba.	

Genji makes a claim here which he has repeated since the beginning of the chapter, that he is innocent of the charges brought against him. His poem, however, is immediately answered by a sudden wind, violent rain, and lightning that burns his dwelling and almost takes his life. The natural disturbance reflects the response of the heavens, but the unexplained significance of the storm—is it punishing or aiding the hero?—has given rise to a number of differing interpretations, including both Shintōistic and Buddhistic views. Hayashida Takakazu argues that, like the *harae* ceremony, which was traditionally performed at the water's edge, the sudden storm on the Suma shore is a purificatory act by which the hero is ritually cleansed by the gods.[31] Yanai Shigeshi contends that the lightning and storm are necessary to usher in the supernatural, particularly the Sumiyoshi god and the spirit of the deceased Emperor.[32] According to Fukasawa Michio, the tempest expresses the anger of the gods at Genji's claim to innocence. The hero may not be guilty of the accusations brought against him by the opposition, but he is still responsible for that great misdeed.[33] It must be added, however, that Genji does not feel repentant. Nor is he conscious of the storm as a form of retribution. Mitani Eiichi interprets the storm as a rite of passage from youth to adulthood,[34] the function that exile symbolically performs in the "exile of the young noble" mythic archetype. Northrop Frye's argument that the theme of descent to the romance involves some displaced form of death and resurrection also seems applicable here.[35] The storm almost kills Genji, but in the end the same force leads him—via the spirit of the deceased emperor, the Sumiyoshi god, and the dragon king—to Akashi, where Genji is saved and given new life.

In the Japanese narrative tradition exile is associated with purification (in the Shintōistic view) and the expiation of earlier transgressions (in the Buddhistic perspective). In the *Kojiki*, for example, Susanoo is cast out from the Plain of High Heaven (*Takama no hara*) after committing "sins of heaven" (*ama tsu tsumi*) and wanders through the world. After an ordeal in distant Izumo he reemerges as a new hero.[36] In the *Taketori monogatari* the Shining Princess descends to earth to atone for earlier violations and serves a term in the human world before returning to her home on the moon. Genji's retreat to Suma and Akashi likewise implies, at least in its larger outlines, both atonement and renewal. Having borne the tribulations of exile and survived a trial by lightning and fire, the hero now appears free to proceed on the path of glory and return to power via Reizei, his natural son. By the beginning of "Miotsukushi" Reizei has come to the throne, the Fujitsubo lady has returned to political life, and Genji is in the process of attaining imperial glory as a commoner and a Minamoto.

The storm, which simultaneously occurs in the capital, also echoes a pattern from Chinese literature. During a banquet in "Sakaki," Genji cites a passage from the *Shih chi* (*Records of the Grand Historian*): "I am the son of King Wen, the brother of King Wu" (I: 135; S: 210).[37] The phrase compares the recently deceased Emperor to King Wen, the reigning Suzaku emperor to King Wu, and Genji to the Duke of Chou, one of China's foremost cultural heroes. According to the *Shu ching* (*Book of Documents*),[38] the Duke of Chou faithfully served his father King Wen and then later his own elder brother King Wu, the founder of the Wu dynasty, but during the subsequent reign of King Ch'eng (Wu's son) the Duke was slandered and accused of treason by his own brothers. Rather than struggle against King Ch'eng, the Duke of Chou chose to retreat from the capital. Two years later, after a violent thunderstorm destroyed the harvest and awakened the young king to the Duke's innocence, Chou was pardoned and summoned back. Like this ancient Chinese hero, Genji is falsely accused, voluntarily leaves the capital, and is exonerated after storm and lightning reveal to the blinded ruler the anger of the heavens and the innocence of the persecuted.[39]

NOTES

1. Blackmur, *The Expense of Greatness*, p. 140. Cited by Horton, *Interpreting interpreting*, p. 139.

2. Origuchi Shinobu, "Shōsetsu gikyoku bungaku ni okeru monogatari yōso," pp. 243–46.

3. Mitani Eiichi, "*Genji monogatari* no minzokugakuteki hōhō," in his *Monogatari bungaku no sekai*, p. 131.

4. "There is no major epic in which the hero is not in some sense an exile. In the *Odyssey* the hero is kept away from Ithaca for more than half the work. Aeneas loses his homeland before the epic opens. Siegfried is seen at home only in the opening scenes of the *Nibelungenlied....*" Jackson, *The Hero and the King*, p. 5.

5. Frye, *Anatomy of Criticism*, p. 193.

6. Jameson, *The Political Unconscious*, pp. 17–18.

7. Fujii Sadakazu, "Shinwa no ronri to monogatari no ronri," in his *Genji monogatari no shigen to genxai*, p. 150.

8. Akiyama Ken, "Hikaru Genji ron," in his *Ōchō joryū bungaku no sekai*, p. 29.

9. Fukasawa Michio, "Hikaru Genji no unmei," in his *Genji monogatari no keisei*, p. 66. Hirota Osamu, "Rokujō-in no kōzō," p. 121.

10. "Kiritsubo,": 109; S: 11. The Teiji-no-in was a residence used by the retired Emperor Uda.

11. "Kiritsubo," I: 115; S: 14. Emperor Uda's injunction, usually referred to as the *Kanbyō no goyuikai*, was given by Uda to Emperor Daigo upon Daigo's accession to the throne.

12. Parallels also exist between this Suzaku emperor and the historical Emperor Suzaku (r. 930–46), who succeeded Emperor Daigo. The succession of the first three fictional emperors in the *Genji*, in other words, directly echoes the sequence of historical emperors: Uda, Daigo, and Suzaku. Correlations also exist between the Reizei emperor, the fictional successor to Emperor Suzaku, and Emperor Murakami (r. 946–67), who succeeded the historical Emperor Suzaku in 946. For more on this subject, see Shimizu Yoshiko, "*Genji monogatari* ni okeru junkyo," and "Tennōke no keifu to junkyo," in her *Genji monogatari no buntai to hōhō*, pp. 275–303.

13. Kakaishō, pp. 278–79. See also Shimizu Yoshiko, *Genji monogatari ron*, pp. 192–217, and Yamamoto Ritatsu, "Ga no en to Hana no en."

14. Shimizu Yoshiko, "Momiji no ga," in her *Genji monogatari ron*, pp. 166–77, and Yamamoto Ritatsu, "Ga no en to Hana no en."

15. Ōkagami, p. 93. Similar views of the Engi–Tenryaku period can be found in the late-eleventh-century *Eiga monogatari*, the thirteenth-century *Gukanshō*, and the early-fourteenth-century *Jinnō shōtōki*.

16. On the notion of the Engi–Tenryaku period as a golden era, see Fujiki Kunihiko,

"Engi Tenryaku no chi" and "Engi Tenryaku no chi sairon," and Ryō Susumu, "Engi no chi," in his *Heian jidai*, pp. 61–75.

17. Yamanaka Yutaka, *Heianchō no shiteki kenkyū*, pp. 54–55.

18. Emperor Saga had 21 sons, of whom 17 were lowered to Genji status. Most of the first-generation Genji appeared between the reigns of Emperors Saga (r. 809–23) and Kōkō (r. 884–87). Hirata Toshiharu, "Hō shinnō kō," in his *Heian jidai no kenkyū*, pp. 46–71.

19. Genji did continue to appear. The Murakami Genji, for example, emerged as a powerful clan in the late Heian period. Yet like the hero of the *Genji*, they were not first-generation Genji but rather imperial grandchildren or more distant descendants of the emperor when they were severed from the royalty.

20. Though the Fujiwara *sekkan* excluded the Genji from the political center, they maintained special respect for them. In contrast to other clans who were deprived of power, the Genji retained a royal aura. Michinaga's two principal wives were the daughters of Genji: Rinshi was the daughter of Minamoto no Masanobu, the grandson of Emperor Uda, and Meishi was the daughter of Minamoto no Takaakira, Emperor Daigo's son. Yamanaka Yutaka, *Heianchō no shiteki kenkyū*, pp. 123–36.

21. Hashimoto Yoshihiko, "Kizoku seiken no seiji kōzō," p. 33.

22. *Shimeishō*, pp. 10–11, and the *Kakaishō*, p. 186.

23. *Kakaishō*, p. 360.

24. "Kiritsubo," I: 116; S: 14.

25. "Toshikage," *Utsubo monogatari*, vol. I, p. 48.

26. *Utsubo monogatari*, vol. I, p. 71.

27. "Kiritsubo," I: 120; S: 16.

28. *Ise monogatari*, p. 139.

29. Many medieval commentaries, beginning with the *Kachō yosei* (1472), see Genji's scandalous relationship with Oborozukiyo as the primary cause of his exile.

30. Abe Akio, "Suma ryūri no keii."

31. Hayashida Takakazu, "Suma no arashi," cited by Hasegawa Masaharu, "Suma kara Akashi e," p. 104.

32. Yanai Shigeshi, "*Genji monogatari* to reigen-tan no kōshō."

33. Fukasawa Michio, p. 65.

34. Mitani Eiichi, "*Genji monogatari* no minzokugakuteki hōhō," in his *Monogatari-bungaku no sekai*, pp. 107–9.

35. Frye, *The Secular Scripture*, p. 4.

36. *Kojiki*, pp. 79–89.

37. The Hereditary House chapter on Chou-kung (Duke of Chou). Ssu-ma Ch'ien, *Shih chi*, Chap. 33, p. 1518.

38. The "Metal-bound Coffer" (C. "Jin teng," J. "Kintō") chapter of the *Shang shu* (J. "Shōsho"), or the *Book of History*, otherwise known as the *Shu thing* (*Book of Documents*), one of the Five Classics. See Legge, trans., *The Shoo king*, pp. 351–61.

39. Imai Gen'e argues that this episode—particularly the thunder, the lightning, and the Sumiyoshi god—echoes the legend of Sugawara no Michizane, whose spirit is said to have become a thunder god. "Kankō to *Genji monogatari*," in his *Shirin shōkei*, pp. 90–102.

JOHN R. WALLACE

Tarrying with the Negative: Aesthetic Vision in Murasaki and Mishima

$\mathbf{M}$urasaki shikibu, 973?–1014?, in writing *Genji Monogatari*, and Mishima Yukio, 1925–1970, in writing *Kinkakuji*, fashion elaborate narratives around the beautiful and the nature of desire as it relates to beauty. Each sees a disturbance in this relationship. A notion of the 'negative' is a critical mediating factor for both writers regarding this relationship, but differences in theory require of them different conclusions about the possibility of encountering beauty, and the potential of literary effort to that purpose.

The present article will argue that Murasaki and Mishima come close to one another in how they narrate desire and describe compelling beauty, even though they differ on the function of a 'negative' within their aesthetics.

In both cases, this 'negative' darkens the vision of beauty; both authors explore beauty's insubstantiality as well as links with anguish and death. But Murasaki's 'negative' is essentially Buddhist. In *Genji Monogatari*, she describes the destructiveness of Hikaru Genji (and others) in the pursuit of his objects of desire; that is, she set desire under the Buddhist rubric of that which is the source of suffering. This belief, together with a deep sense for the fleeting nature of beauty, contributes significantly to her sophisticated version of *mono no aware*. In her writings, the Buddhist teaching of the radical emptiness of material existence consistently threatens to subvert the

From *Monumenta Nipponica* 52, no. 2 (Summer 1997). © 1997 by Sophia University.

magnificence of the heart yearning for the material finery of the world in which her narratives are set. Hikaru Genji is magnificent, but he ages and his light inevitably vanishes altogether.

Mishima, on the other hand, constructs a world in *Kinkakuji* where violence is a compelling, if not root, component of desire and one's relationship to beauty. This 'negative' of Mishima formally resembles that of Hegel where death and destruction are, by dialectic logic (a structure within the realm of reason), a necessary part of truth. At a more sensual level, however, Mishima parts with Hegel's spiritual vision by making central to his discourse the transgression of taboos censoring an impulse to defile one's erotic object. In this sense his notion of eroticism and one's relationship to the beautiful is closer to that of Georges Bataille.[1] For Bataille the erotic object is an intersection of a complex set of archaic impulses that have taken the shape within human consciousness of a double bind where one both seeks and seeks to flee from 'death' (not biological death, but a psychological sense of individuated being—an existence cut off from others which we both desire and fear). Taboos and their transgression form a complementary economy that negotiates this double bind:

> The inner experience of eroticism demands from the subject a sensitiveness to the anguish at the heart of the taboo no less great than the desire which leads him to infringe it. This is religious sensibility, and it always links desire closely with terror, intense pleasure and anguish.[2]

It is from this philosophical basis that Bataille arrives at a concept of beauty where,

> Beauty is desired in order that it may be befouled; not for its own sake, but for the joy brought by the certainty of profaning it.
>
> Beauty has a cardinal importance, for ugliness cannot be spoiled, and to despoil is the essence of eroticism. Humanity implies the taboos, and in eroticism it and they are transgressed. Humanity is transgressed, profaned and besmirched. The greater the beauty, the more it is befouled.... The forms may alter but violence is constant, at once horrifying and fascinating.[3]

There is no direct link between Bataille and Mishima. Bataille's important work in this area, *L'Erotisme*, was not published until 1957, and *Kinkakuji* was completed in 1956. But Bataille was active on the French intellectual scene from the 1920s until his death in 1962, and his ideas were as influential as they were the extension of a certain philosophical and artistic proclivity in Europe to explore the links of death, eroticism, evil, and transgression. Reading Bataille does not delineate origins for Mishima's ideas, but it does provide a cross-light that makes certain features of Mishima's texts more apparent. Mishima might not have been attracted to Bataille's argument for the basis of eroticism (as briefly noted above), but such statements as 'Eroticism ... is assenting to life up to the point of death,'[4] does resonate well with Mishima's own views.

BEAUTY AS A PROBLEM

Let us begin with a few quotations describing the state of mind of men confronting their objects of desire:

> The [Akashi] lady was most aristocratic—tall and slender—and Genji felt humbled.[5]
>
> Then I felt that I had been turned into stone. My will, my desire-everything had become stone.[6]
>
> It is no exaggeration to say that the first real problem I faced in my life was that of beauty.[7]

The first of these quotations is from the 'Akashi' chapter of the *Genji*. Genji has chased Akashi no Kimi past her locked door, and now confronts her in private. But before her commanding elegance, he suddenly hesitates. Akashi radiates composure and beauty even at the very moment when she is most compromised. Genji is stalled (*kokoro hazukashiki kehai,*) by the grossness of his own desire. In the second quotation, Mizoguchi, the protagonist of *Kinkakuji*, has leaped out in front of the bicycle of Uiko, a neighborhood girl whom he secretly desires. But when he thus confronts her, his resolve, even his passion, falters. She rides wordlessly past. He later explains, 'It is no exaggeration to say that the first real problem I faced in my life was that of beauty.'

Genji will spend the night in Akashi's chambers, at which time they conceive a child. Their relationship does not end with this one night of love. Eventually Genji brings her and this daughter to his Rokujō mansion in the capital. Mizoguchi, on the other hand, will never again try to express his heart to Uiko. But he will watch enraptured as she betrays her lover. He will mourn and admire her, or, perhaps more precisely, her death at the hand of that lover.

The difference in these outcomes, that is, the success or failure to establish and maintain relationship with what one desires, is a result of how

Murasaki and Mishima define beauty (and beauty's context) and the capacity to encounter beauty. But the above quotations belong to narratives which both start with the notion that the presence of the beautiful, erotic object confronts or disturbs. For both writers, erotic beauty demands their artistic and philosophical attention.

MURASAKI: BEAUTY AND SUFFERING

In *Murasaki Shikibu Nikki*, Murasaki describes a time when she thinks over the meaning of her contemplating and writing about beauty:

> Seeing the water birds on the lake increase in numbers day by day, I thought to myself how nice it would be if it snowed before we got back to the Palace, the garden would look so beautiful; and then two days later, while I was away on a short visit, lo and behold it did snow. As I watched the rather drab scene at home, I felt depressed and confused. For some years I had existed from day to day in listless fashion, taking note of the flowers, the birds in song, the way the skies changed from season to season, the moon, the frost, and the snow, doing little more than registering the passage of time. How would it all turn out? The thought of my continuing loneliness was quite unbearable, and yet there had been those friends who would discuss trifling matters with me, and others of like mind with whom I could exchange my innermost thoughts.[8]

In *Kinkakuji*, Mizoguchi says:

> When people concentrate on the idea of beauty, they are, without realizing it, confronted with the darkest thoughts that exist in this world. That, I suppose, is how human beings are made.[9]

The forces that bind the *Genji* narrative are those of bright silver and gold *miyabi* as Heian aesthetic and ethic. But in the *Genji*, Murasaki expands the scope of the ethics of this *miyabi*. She adds significantly to that cultural formula by testing and deploying at a new or deep level Buddhist concepts of insubstantiality. The brightness of *miyabi* achieves something close to a sacred quality (that is, a uniquely moving quality that derives its bewitching presence by gesturing to another, unknown world) by being set within the structure of *yūgen* with its contrast of light and dark. The structure of *yūgen*, although not yet clearly defined in Murasaki's time (indeed, I would suggest that *Genji Monogatari* significantly contributed to the developing formula), is the fleeting moment of a beautiful object that embraces a sense of another, dark or infinite world. The manifestation of a specific, well-defined beautiful object is enhanced by sensing through it a mysterious and nearly formless 'world'.

Murasaki follows this aesthetic link from the bright attractiveness of beauty into the dark mystery of beauty, making then a further and important extension, an associative link into the destructive power of human desire. For Murasaki, that which is most beautiful has the quality of *yūgen*—the meeting of light and dark—but for her this meeting point exists at the border of life and death, pleasure and suffering, this world and the other. Superior beauty is tightly bound to brevity of existence. That which is exceptionally beautiful is short-lived. As Aileen Gatten has pointed out, the visitation of death in the *Genji* enhances the person's beauty rather than detracting from it:

> Characters in *Genji* who die a good death always become more beautiful as their lives end. As we shall see with Murasaki, death can give a character far more beauty than she ever possessed in life.[10]

Indeed, Gatten suggests that this link of death with beauty may originate with Murasaki (although she speaks, I am sure, of the case of literary prose).[11] The death scene of Murasaki no Ue is, as Gatten notes, the example par excellence of this:

> Though her hair had been left untended through her illness, it was smooth and lustrous and not a strand was out of place. In the bright lamplight the skin was a purer, more radiant white than the living lady, seated at her mirror, could have made it. Her beauty, as if in untroubled sleep, emptied words like 'peerless' of all content.[12]

Murasaki takes up a discussion of the gross or vulgar aspect of human desire—whether these are Mizoguchi's 'darkest thoughts' is precisely the topic of the present article—from the perspective of *miyabi*'s high culture and elegance. She introduces and examines, approaches, human baseness from a removed or protected, perhaps some might say transcendental, perspective. Elegance is the critical mediating factor, the code or license that she uses to move through an erotic, intimate world of sexual events. Her management of this discourse is most keen. She seeks not to repress the presence of various erotic impulses in her narratives. Rather, she manages to make a debasing aspect of desire both distant and close depending on whether one leaves in place the mediating code of *miyabi*, or translates past it and reads her story as one of rape, abduction, confinement, erotic competition at the expense of another, and so forth. An additional reading that, I believe, she welcomed.

At the sublime level, that is, in the elegant, Buddhism-infused world of Murasaki's *mono no aware*, beauty is moving because it is insubstantial, part of the ever-changing working out of fate. However, through its constant repetitions, variations, and reformulations that are the very texture of the *Genji* narrative, the inexorable, karmic forward momentum of desire is also made out as that which can disclose our own emptiness and insubstantiality, as we are in and constituted of that false world where desire arises and suffering unfolds. Here is a slippage from the appreciation of love and amorous fate in the beautiful terms of *mono no aware* to a more disturbing, and less beautiful, view of desire's intentions and results as indicated by Buddhism. As one of the *Genji*'s extreme narrative effects, desire is karmically linked to death. Murasaki makes this clear early in the narrative when Yūgao dies in the arms of a Hikaru Genji who has just proclaimed his love for her. But Yūgao is far from an abject object that, in Buddhist tracts such as *Ōjōyōshū*, would serve as an example of the world of suffering and the reason why one should flee from it. Rather, Murasaki places the secret of Yūgao's beauty on the other side of death.

This is precisely where Murasaki exceeds the discursive space of Buddhism. She determinedly links to a traditional notion (that is, a formula prior to the importation of Buddhism) of the truly beautiful as brief-lived a structure of suffering or loss that co-arises with the passionate response to the ephemerally beautiful. But she does not effect a closure at that point. Instead, she develops a path that loops anguish back into notions of suffering as beautiful. In this way she creates a unique and surprisingly functional mobility between a sublime ethics of *miyabi* that regards romance as refined human expression and Buddhist teaching that reproves amorous desire. She imports into *miyabi* some of the disturbing qualities of the erotic impulse while refusing to teach against it.

The figures of the *Genji* narrative achieve supreme moments of elegant beauty. Their power to transport the reader into the sublime field of *miyabi* is fairly undiminished with the passage of nearly a thousand years. Murasaki mastered Heian literary expressive potential by producing a breath-taking discourse superior to any other prose working within or upon the values of *miyabi*. But her writing agenda is not to lift us 'up' into a world of courtly beauty that is successfully blind to suffering. The long, bleak road of unwelcome fate that stretches out over endless days of longing with little hope, of separation from one's beloved, and the anxiety surrounding the risks of transgression are also an important part of the text's mood and the narrative turns. *Miyabi* and suffering are dynamically at odds even while producing a surface effect of harmony. How can the magnificent Hikaru Genji be such an emotional wreck inside? Yet how can he not? To love is to suffer gloriously, to make others suffer similarly. Yet, as mentioned above, the redundancy of the plots of desire begins to question the 'gloriously' portion of that appraisal.

While Murasaki's text might delineate the suffering of love, indicate the fragility of elegant self-assurance, and even explore the eroticism of vulnerability, her works cannot be usefully taken down the path articulated by Bataille, where, as suggested at the beginning of this article, the formative force of eroticism and erotic literature itself is the ecstasy of a violence that threatens the logic of community and personal psychic integrity. While this may be so with Mishima, in the case of Murasaki this would be to misread her pact with her society. Murasaki is not first and foremost subversive to her world. Bataille's position despite the subject matter is essentially an early Christian moral stance: truth will be found in opposition to current social values that are widespread and widely corrupt. Opposition to a corrupt social norm, plus sacrificing all interest in material success within this corrupt context, is the first step toward godliness. Murasaki's position is classical Chinese and *uji*-oriented Japanese: truth will be found within a genuine reading of and contribution to the social order. Her narrative relies upon the Buddhist tenet of non-materiality that operates beyond issues of individual suffering (a sacred image in Christianity) and that leaves aside rather than subverts the norms of her social world.

Genji, exquisite figure of male desire, simply disappears with the first words of Chapter 42: 'After the Shining One had withdrawn it seemed unlikely there to be any descendants of the same brilliance.'[13] The ideal that was invoked through the complex figure of Genji and marked by the metaphor of his light simply goes out. This is the phenomenology of desire in its vicissitude as seen by Buddhism. Genji must die before the end of the narrative because desire itself is, for Murasaki, the secondary knowledge of insubstantiality. Death in this context does not mark a Wagnerian idealistic and dramatic union on a higher plane (a transcendence of a corrupt social order) which is presented as a glorious event; instead, it is the pedestrian, if sad, turning of the dharmic wheel, which is the same on all planes. Desire occurs in the presence of fate that portends the certainty of loss. It can embrace only frangible hopes. Its flight is limited.

MISHIMA: BEAUTY AND THE ABJECT

Mishima places greater emphasis, or at least speaks more directly, than Murasaki on the sensual origins of his aesthetics, and understands sensuality itself differently. No doubt there is here a significance in gender difference, if not in terms of how Mishima's 'body' is present in his writings and Murasaki's in hers, then at least certainly in a difference of discursive restraints and possibilities afforded to the social interface of the two writers in terms of their gender. But I do not seek here to explore the origins of their differences but only to describe in broad terms the character, and something of the implication, of those differences.

Despite a running discourse in *Kinkakuji* regarding Buddhist metaphysics (one that sharply critiques physical pleasure and beauty itself), sensuality for Mizoguchi remains a present negative force, stubbornly resisting Buddhist authoritative assertions of insubstantiality. Mishima retains a concern over ecstasy and its origins in 'the darkest thoughts that exist in this world' that Murasaki viewed with Buddhist poise (or hesitation) as well as through the mediation of a discourse of *miyabi*. The Golden Pavilion is an obtrusive presence that Mizoguchi believes needs to be either thoroughly understood or thoroughly destroyed if he is to preserve his very right to self-existence, where self-existence is defined as the capacity to be enveloped in ecstasy. Beauty is a puzzle that demands action from Mizoguchi. No doubt in this area of response to beauty as well we are confronting differing imperatives embedded in cultural notions of gender.

Yet despite what amounts to the confession of a tenacious faith in beauty (since as a hindrance to pleasure beauty is taken as presenting a significant challenge), Mishima is acutely aware of a subjective (not metaphysical as with Murasaki) phenomenon of insubstantiality. Mishima's beautiful object includes within it a destabilizing immanence just as did Murasaki's, that is, the structure of *yūgen* that suggests a darkness within its very brightness. For example:

> I recalled the night of the typhoon at the beginning of autumn when I had stood watch in the temple. Much as the building may have been exposed to the moonlight, a heavy, luxuriant darkness [*gōsha na yami*] had settled over it and this darkness had penetrated into the nocturnal temple, into the shutters, into the wooden doors, under the roof with its peeling gold-foil. And this was only natural. For the Golden Temple itself was simply a nihility that had been designed and constructed with the most exquisite care. Just so, although the outside of this breast gave

forth the bright radiance of flesh, the inside was filled with darkness. Its true substance consisted of the same heavy, luxuriant darkness.[14]

This darkness for Mishima, however, is not suggesting a mysteriousness that gestures toward a dharmic universe that transcends the pleasure and pain of the human condition. Instead, this darkness is fecund with abject images, even evil in something close to a pure essence. The beautiful and the abject are near to one another and in active relationship. Thus the sleeping and desirable Mariko appears to be a corpse, while she herself finds a harmonious unity with the abject image of a fly (an image that surely parodies the Buddhist image of the butterfly sleeping on the temple bell, meant to represent the illusory nature of the world):

> Then I noticed that all of a sudden Mariko had fallen asleep. She lay there like a corpse and on the roundness of her bosom, which was illuminated by the bed lamp, the fly, too, was motionless and had evidently dozed off.[15]

Throughout *Kinkakuji*, there are reversals between an oppressive, enormous Golden Pavilion and the ordinary-sized, disappointing Golden Pavilion. Their displacement of one another is clearly taken up as a central problem of the work. Not at all unlike Murasaki's narrative, in *Kinkakuji* beauty is unstable. In Murasaki's vision, magnificence is subverted by fate (the formative theme of the other great classical narrative, *Heike Monogatari*) and beauty is related to suffering both as its cause and even with suffering as an aspect of beauty itself. For Mishima, the abject, defilement, transgression, and evil present themselves together with beauty as part of its essence. In *Kinkakuji*, it is Kashiwagi Mizoguchi's club-footed, cynical friend, who functions as the informant about this strange intersection of the beautiful and the repulsive:

> 'How shall I put it? Beauty—yes, beauty is like a decayed tooth. It rubs against one's tongue, it hangs there, hurting one, insisting on its own existence. Finally it gets so that one cannot stand the pain and one goes to the dentist to have the tooth extracted. Then, as one looks at the small, dirty, brown, blood-stained tooth lying in one's hand, one's thoughts are likely to be as follows: "Is this it? Is this all it was? That thing which caused me so much pain, which made me constantly fret about its existence, which was stubbornly rooted within me, is now merely a dead object...."'[16]

When sensuality is understood as an important component of beauty, as it is with Mishima and Murasaki, it is linked to an unstable, organic, vicissitudinous complex of representations. The instability of making the human body a reference point is precisely what Plato wished to sublimate in his 'ascending ladder' of the pursuit of eternal truth through philosophical inquiry. Sexual desire is transformed, stabilized, and purified by being reset into an entirely discursive universe disassociated from sensuality, into the love of philosophy. In *Symposium*, where most of Plato's ideas about Eros are developed, the goddess Diotima explains to Socrates the path to the highest truth:

> First of all ... he will fall in love with the beauty of one individual body.... Next he must consider how nearly related the beauty of any one body is to the beauty of any other, when he will see that if he is to devote himself to loneliness of form it will be absurd to deny that the beauty of each and every body is the same.
>
> Next he must grasp that the beauties of the body are as nothing to the beauties of the soul.... And from this he will be led to contemplate the beauty of laws and institutions....
>
> And next, his attention should be diverted from institutions to the sciences, so that he may know the beauty of every kind of knowledge.... And, turning his eyes toward the open sea of beauty, he will find in such contemplation the seed of the most fruitful discourse and the loftiest thought, and reap a golden harvest of philosophy.[17]

Freud, however, returned the body to the discourse that searched for truth or understanding. Thus post-Freudian critics, from Marxists to feminists to psychoanalytic philosophers, have all had to reconfront the problem of the body's place in language. Julia Kristeva has explored this contact point between biology and language with her theory of semiotic and symbolic representation, where the pre-linguistic, semiotic 'chora' ('the *chora*, as rupture and articulations [rhythm] precedes evidence, verisimilitude, spatiality, and temporality')[18] impute important affective meaning into language's discursive grammar of representation. Meaningful language, for Kristeva, always has its semiotic and symbolic portions.[19]

Kristeva's claim, one that seeks to capture something of how language becomes artistic language, that is, how literature moves us, is a large one. Language in all cultures and times would have this two-part structure. The present article operates under her thesis. It is from this position that I suggested above that sensuality, when taken as an important component of beauty, links the effort to represent beauty discursively to an unstable, organic, vissitudinous complex of not necessarily grammatical, or even fully understandable, formations. In taking this position, I set aside space within this critical analysis for the possibility of signification that exceeds or refuses discursive logic, that makes its claims from affective ('semiotic') movements, not metonymic ('symbolic') argument. This is, I believe, useful when talking of Murasaki, but essential when trying to discuss Mishima's associative leaps from ideal beauty to self-destructive evil. Murasaki obviously accomplished her work outside the Platonic tradition. But her articulate expansion of *miyabi* to include suffering as a beautifying element, or her exploration of the role of separation and death in the beauty of romance, produced a sublimating movement that reset sexual activity within a code of regulated manner and the outlines of appropriate emotions. It was with mediation and sublimation, and in the realm of an aesthetics that borders on ethics, that she negotiated the body–language interchange—a strategy not so distant from that of Plato.

Mishima also confronted this problem of representation, of trying to place within discourse something essentially pre-linguistic. He tried in his own way to order, outline or stabilize this body–language interchange, to encode in his/our language the signifiers of sensuality. But his method is not Murasaki's socializing, as it were, loop of romance and suffering (by taking sexual desire and the anxiety of loss, and placing it into a discourse of courtly elegance that is designed to manage or moderate the disruptive potential of these states of mind/body). Rather, Mishima follows a model of transgressive behavior, where the eruption of anti-social acts (betrayal, arson, rape, and so on) articulates or at least outlines the nature of erotic demand as he 'understands', perhaps we should say 'feels', it. Beauty is the target and receptacle of this eruption which is a response to that very beauty. Again, while we are certainly walking a line close to gender issues, we are also working within two different worlds of discourse—a classical tradition where artistic activity was meant to essentially uphold social norms, to participate in a society where the producers and consumers of art were of the same group, as Konishi has rightly described it,[20] and a Western modern tradition (in which Mishima by choice participated) where social norm lies as a hindrance between the subject and truth, and must be transcended or violated in order to reach a deep understanding of things. The philosopher/artist must travel alone to know life.

'Tarrying with the Negative'

The title of the present article is based on a passage in Hegel's *Phenomenology of Spirit* that describes the necessary, dialectic structure of true 'Spirit' (the thinking soul that has the courage and strength to embark on pure scientific analysis). In the following quotation, he is talking about Beauty associated with a positive force which resists intellectual analysis that would reduce something to its parts, which is regarded as a type of 'death'.

> Lacking strength, Beauty hates the Understanding for asking of her what it cannot do. But the life of Spirit is not the life that shrinks from death and keeps itself untouched by devastation, but rather the life that endures it and maintains itself in it. It wins its truth only when, in utter dismemberment, it finds itself .... Spirit is this power only by looking the negative in the face, and tarrying with it. This tarrying with the negative is the magical power that converts it [Spirit] into being.[21]

I chose this title because Murasaki's beautification of bad fate and Mishima's interest in abject images and how they relate to the beautiful seem to share something with the upward spiral of the Hegelian dialectic where the 'negative' is both a stimulant and embedded remainder of a higher consciousness. I am interested in how Murasaki and Mishima have included to useful effect 'negative' aspects that would mediate between a desiring subject and a desirable object. Hegel, Murasaki, and Mishima all explore how one object (or subject) relates to another (person or concept), and what makes possible or enhances this encounter. This 'negative', this dismemberment of the familiar through the 'tremendous power of the negative'[22] that Hegel says can be called death—and the tarrying there— becomes famously in Freud the forbidden wellspring of culture. Hegel's dualistic structure of a dialectic of conflict that produces a higher unity undergoes a significant and irreversible alteration in Freud's model of *id-(super)* ego that produces culture.

Freud's commitment to medicine and biology made him set aside some of Hegel's idealism, but the notion that the human soul necessarily engages and is reformulated by a darkness, an unknown, an Other or death (as a biological impulse) is a linchpin of his theory of self and culture. But he locates in these archaic layers of the human psyche impulses of violence that make a new interpretation of Hegel's metaphysics by claiming a biological content for such forces. Hegel's death 'dismembers', but is also the necessary occasion for a unitary reformulation. Freud's *Thanatos* is no less grand in scope, but it has a dense, material content of violent, destructive forces that play out their destructiveness at both the level of the individual's inner life and in social phenomena such as war.

Thus the significance of death, evil, and the abject were important themes in Europe and European writers of interest to Mishima, such as Marquis de Sade (1740–1814) and *Justine*, Charles Baudelaire (1821–1867) and *The Flower of Evil*, and Raymond Radiguet (1903–1923) and *The Devil in the Flesh*.[23] All of these philosophers and writers retain something of Plato's view of Eros, that is, they conceive of the sexual drive (with its intrusions, as eroticism, at the borders of social norms) as a disruptive force that threatens individual (and community) stability. In *Phaedrus*, Plato, using the metaphor of the white and dark horse that together pull a single chariot, describes man's nature as dual. The white horse wishes to soar up toward ideals, but the dark horse (which must be beaten into submission, as the charioteer 'covers his scurrilous tongue and jaws with blood, and forces his legs and haunches to the ground, causing him much pain')[24] seeks only bodily pleasures.[25] Further, if we provisionally follow Foucault's rereading of the history and production of sexuality in the West, from about the time of Freud, and owing to his works (but only in part), eroticism also begins to be viewed as hiding secrets regarding self and being.[26] It is within this philosophical context that Mishima finds the legitimacy and stimulation to embark on his expedition into the mysteriousness of eroticism that he, too, associates with disruptive, violent, even evil impulses. Mizoguchi's 'dark thoughts' include ruminations of this sort.

Murasaki works with a less problematized or valorized view of the erotic. Sexual intercourse was constituted as a healthy act (at least for the men) within Chinese medical theory as propounded by Heian physicians, indigenous ('Shinto') notions, and Shingon Buddhist tantric teaching. For example, in the case of Chinese medical teachings imported to Japan and used by the Ministry of Medicine during Murasaki's time, sexual intercourse was considered both preventative medicine and a supplement to the administration of drugs for the recovery from illness. It drew into the man yin forces to balance his yang; further, once sexual intercourse was complete with one woman, she was no longer beneficial to the man as her yin, once transferred to him, was temporarily gone. Thus the man should sleep with several different women in the course of one night. The number of women recommended differed, but one text, *Gyokubō Hiketsu*, recommended three, nine or eleven women in one night, a count corresponding to the number of brush strokes in the character for *yang*.[27]

Thus, from several points of view, sexual relations and sexual desire were not articulated as a moment drawing one close to inner psychic violence as they were an occasion for health, hope, and felicity in terms of sexual politics. Suffering that results from loss and longing owing to the conditions of fate are the primary motifs of Murasaki's texts, not an inner struggle with violence or evil seeking expression. Her 'negative' is not associated with Plato's dark horse that required violent, one might say, virile control.[28] Her 'negative' was refined within the descriptive discourse of Buddhism that posits radical material insubstantiality. Murasaki thus places the possibility of 'truth' outside the vagaries of desire. But she does not vigorously pursue this truth; rather, she lingers with the compelling narratives generated by movements of desire, finding there the source for the richness of her stories and the beauty of her diction itself.

Genji Monogatari is, then, not by any true measure a religious text in either the Western or Buddhist sense, where 'religious text' means discursive indications of a determined intent to forsake or surpass sexual interest. In this sense Murasaki's narrative shares with Mishima a non-Buddhist interest in and interpretation of sensuality. The difference is how the content of the 'negative' is conceived, and how it is invited into their understanding of aesthetics and texts articulating those aesthetics. In other words, the issue is the characteristics of the mediating function of that 'negative', what relationship it sets up between the subject and the desirable object considered beautiful (or, in Mishima's case, sometimes directly with an abstract figure called 'beauty' itself). In this regard, Murasaki and Mishima part ways.

For Murasaki, *miyabi* mediates between the desiring subject and its object, not only to enhance the beauty of the object, but to place it in reach, to create the possibility of subjectively meaningful contact with what is beautiful through the discipline of sensitivity and the capacity to understand the nature of a situation, whether it be a natural scene, an artistic occasion, or the words and heart of one's lover. One 'touches' the beautiful through understanding—where understanding is a sort of selfless, harmonious appreciation of and adjustment to the object. In a sense, the object itself is left undisturbed. This capacity to understand is the result of refined sensitivity, which is itself the result of training in the arts and disciplined nurturing of the emotions.

But Murasaki's *miyabi* is more than courtly refinement. By placing *mono no aware* at the center of one's capacity to be sensitive, its refined spirit is linked to broader issues of karmic fate and the Buddhist assertion of the illusory nature of the world. Beauty is framed with both the sensuality of the courtly arts and the unreliability of the human bond, the inevitability of the cycle of suffering, or simply the essential transitory nature of the object that one finds beautiful or desirable. Under the sign of a Buddhist negative that asserts the insubstantiality of the desiring mind, Murasaki subjugates desire, but precisely in so doing keeps it at hand. The Buddhist negative is put to work to deepen one's sensitivity, not to thwart it. Surface beauty is linked to an unseen world through the aesthetic structure of the mysterious immanent in the concrete, that is, *yūgen*, making the beautiful object not less convincing but on the contrary more compelling in its mystery. Beauty in the *Genji* is never the towering Golden Pavilion of Mishima's *Kinkakuji*, not because Murasaki's estimation of the significance of the beautiful was any less, but because the enormous part of beauty is kept, with most definite intention, invisible. Murasaki's beauty has the vibrancy of that which embraces a contradiction, namely, *miyabi*'s limited optimism that one can have a significant encounter with or understanding of the beautiful with Buddhist admonition that desire arising around a beautiful object is the first step in the cycle of suffering (a teaching that Murasaki shows she can read backward as the beauty of suffering). *Miyabi* is supported by a belief that beauty and harmony are possible through proper, hard work, but to touch the beautiful nevertheless does not alter the truth of insubstantiality and of fate that will find its path into misfortune.

Mishima sees the problem in more imperative terms, with a more active posture, and with a radical pessimism that Murasaki might find not entirely unintelligible in the language of her own aesthetics of fate (Buddhist notions of salvation through *tariki* , 'grace'). For Mishima, the beautiful must be engaged, but this achievement is from the outset impossible. Only inverted contact is possible: the mediating act that can bring together the desiring subject and its object is an invasion of rights via transgression, especially betrayal. Here the 'negative' with which Mishima productively tarries is not a categorically different type of thing (no-thing) as it is in Buddhism that adds a qualitatively different, if mysterious and formless though affectively downbeat, facet to the experience of beauty. Rather, like Freud's *Thanatos*, it is a force of the same presence as other forces. Murasaki regulates, transforms, and enhances—socializes—the psychic energy of eroticism by translating it into the controlled discourse of *miyabi* that can comfortably mix with, even support, other public discourses, especially those of politics and the arts.

Mishima, in *Kinkakuji* at least, envisions eroticism as having a violent and amoral, if not immoral, essence that provides a channel to the beautiful only through the inverted terms of transgression. Mizoguchi's excessive passion moves in two directions, but both are violent. He either wishes to submit entirely to beauty (where it will engulf him—he is at the receiving end of a transgression of his rights), or to establish rights of possession through mastery over it, defined in terms of the violation or defilement of 'rights' proper to beauty through acts of betrayal. Mishima has Mizoguchi seek to encounter beauty by making it an object of defilement and betrayal. Calling this the 'logic of profanation', Julia Kristeva puts it succinctly when she writes of Proust's placing his family furniture and photographs on display at a brothel: 'Desire debases its object in order to get to it more effectively.'[29] Kristeva argues that in order to narrate the unsettling significance of the sexual act, the narrative must first become obscene, then treat its beloved 'like an ancient God'.[30] Mizoguchi's view of relationship pivots on the hierarchical that is close to this double movement of debasement and over-estimation: either one possesses an object or is possessed by it through subjugation or extreme submission.

As mentioned above, in addition to the theoretical room in Murasaki's Buddhist referenced aesthetics to entertain Mishima's radical pessimism, there is other common ground. Despite Murasaki's interest in the appreciation and production of beauty through the socializing intent of the discipline of *miyabi*, transgressive moments are often found in her narratives. Murasaki incorporates such ambiguities within her aesthetic (and in a way that enhances her works). The following is from her diary.

> On the way back to my quarters I looked in at Lady Saishō's room, only to find that she was asleep. She lay with her head pillowed on a writing box, her face all but hidden by a series of robes, dark red lined with green, purple lined with dark red, over which she had thrown a deep crimson gown of unusually glossy silk; she made an entrancing scene. Almost convinced that she had stepped right out of a painting I pulled back the sleeve that covered her face. 'You look just like a fairy-tale princess!' I said.
>
> She awoke with a start.
>
> 'Are you out of your mind?' she said, propping herself up. 'Waking people up like that. It's scandalous!'
>
> I was charmed by the delicate flush on her features. A good example of someone looking even more attractive than usual.[31]

Drawn into a friend's room by her languorous repose, Murasaki seats herself aside the woman's head and gently pulls down her silk coverlet to peak at her mouth. She then teases, 'You look just like a fairy-tale princess.' This is a delicate passage of violation that embodies in the figure of a self-written Murasaki Shikibu the function of gazing and the pleasure of transgression. Although reprimanded by Saishō no Kimi, who is angry at being awakened or awakened in such a fashion, Murasaki does not retreat at her friend's words but rather is taken by the pleasure of the woman's flush.

This little episode is small in scale, but it provides a good model for reading Murasaki's type of transgressive event.

In *Genji Monogatari*, we cannot progress far without this shadow of transgression crossing our path. The prime energy of the narrative for its first forty or so chapters is the forbidden relationship between Genji and his surrogate mother Fujitsubo no Chūgū , consort to his father. The *Genji* can be and has been read as the story of a boy's efforts to recover his mother erotically by romancing women who remind him of her (or perhaps her first representative, Fujitsubo). But this act of recovery is put to us precisely as an act of transgression by Genji toward his father specifically and social mores in general. This first relationship is the beginning of a series of transgressions where it is the act of transgression that provides the liveliness of the passage. What repeats in the *Genji* narrative is not just a number of love affairs that each point back to a founding first and lost love, but a series of present-time transgressions that gesture at covering, while keeping vital, the narrative's erotic, open secret; these are transgressions that mean to establish certain bonds.

On the one hand, Hikaru Genji expresses his love for Fujitsubo:

> Now that Genji had come of age, the emperor no longer allowed him inside the [consort] Fujitsubo lady's blinds as he had done in the past. The boy expressed his feelings by playing his flute in harmony with the consort's koto when there was music, or sought consolation in the faint sound of her voice.[32]

On the other hand, Mizoguchi expresses his fascination for a graduate from his school who has entered naval engineering academy and who has returned, in uniform, to visit his old school. The handsome soldier-student has removed his jacket and sword, and is in another corner of the school grounds, wrestling:

> From my pocket I took out the rusty knife that I used for sharpening my pencils; then I crept up to the fence, and on the back of the beautiful black scabbard of the sword I engraved several ugly cuts....[33]

Mishima makes his point with precision: Mizoguchi willfully defiles the beautiful sword that is the object of his admiration. Murasaki's passage is more convoluted, but arrives at the same point: Genji challenges his father for his most prized possession. Here Genji 'draws a cut' across the relationship between himself and his father by playing his flute in harmony to that of his father's young and beautiful lover.

These acts of transgression are inverted acknowledgments of the importance of certain relationships: Mizoguchi admires the young soldier whose sword he damages, while Genji acknowledges his relationship, complicated and deep, with his father by sharing desire for Fujitsubo, just as Genji and Tō no Chūjō will confirm their friendship by directing their passions (significant and frivolous) at times toward the same women. The transgression of Murasaki, although disruptive, proposes, however provisionally, to honor the rule of discretion. That is, it will make a gesture of regulating itself to the needs of social stability. The damage of Hikaru Genji's transgressions are slow to appear, but make their appearance in due time. No one could set fire to Fujiwara Michinaga's Tsuchimikado mansion and expect Murasaki to narrate it as a sincere search for beauty. Her fires are more coded in their narrative representations. Transgression for Mishima is, on the other hand, articulated as a participation in the disruptive 'pre-social' violence found at the deepest levels of the erotic impulse. His perspective is an inner and absolute one, not—intentionally not—socially moderated.

How to Encounter Beauty Substantively?

In seeking confirmation of human relationship, Mishima and Murasaki both explore questions such as: How do we encounter something or someone substantively? How can we look directly into the face of beauty? How do we possess our object of desire? How do we gain satisfaction? Both writers forge their answering narratives in terms of hierarchical power, that is, in order to establish contact with the other, we either submit to the other or overcome the other. Yūgao expires in the arms of a passionate Genji; Akashi is plucked from the provinces; Ukifune becomes Niou Miya's sexual captive for several days in his boat. Murasaki stays, enduring, at Genji's side for all her adult life, submitting most of the time, prevailing on occasion. We might even interpret the relationship between Rokujō no Miyasudokoro and Aoi no Ue (unwitting murderer and victim) as a type of violent, hierarchical intimacy.

In the case of Mishima's *Kinkakuji*, Mizoguchi describes Uiko's betrayal to the authorities of the location of her lover who has defected from the army:

> ... I was intoxicated by the pellucid beauty of Uiko's treachery. This girl was qualified to walk alone up those white stairs, proudly throwing out her chest. Her treachery was the same as the stars and the moon and the pointed cedars. In other words, she was living in the same world as we, the witnesses; and she was accepting the nature that surrounded us all. She was walking up

those steps as our representative. And I could not help thinking breathlessly: 'By her betrayal she has at last accepted me too. Now she belongs to me!'[34]

This passage—indeed the entire *Kinkakuji* does no differently—describes the mundane (common and commonly accessible) act of betrayal that by its reversal of loyalties is perhaps the human act most centrally tied to both submission and subjugation. Betrayal for Mishima, it seems to me, is a reversed circuit where the intimate energies of 'Master/Slave' are exchanged; that is, one human can commune with another through an inverted economy where betrayal exactly replaces loyalty, while carrying the same recognition of the importance of the relationship.

Through the ethic of *miyabi*, Murasaki subscribes to the belief that meaningful human bands are forged through the effort of understanding one's lover. For her, we live intensely—that is, we find love, beauty, and brief moments of satisfaction—by faith in the graces of sensitivity. The extent that we notice the minute and can be moved by *mono no aware* is an important measure of our humanity. *Mono no aware* is the mind/heart in transcendental flight—a spiritual state that Murasaki would place as prior to the narrow labyrinths of transgressive acts. For Murasaki, transgression causes a step-by-step karmic constricting of our fate (*sukuse*), whereas for Mishima transgression is a liberating moment that negates barriers. For Murasaki, the life of *miyabi* provides for attaining the most stable understanding. The training, restraint, and meticulous care necessary for this aesthetic discipline the heart even while making it more sensitive. We should note, however, that understanding and behavior according to the constrictions of *miyabi* fully incorporate hierarchy in human relationships in ways not all that dissimilar from Mishima's subjugation and submission; in other words, *miyabi* also organizes eroticism to make sense with the hierarchical lines of her society's network of relationships.

Mishima admired training and meticulousness in his art as much as Murasaki; his metaphors are stunningly crisp, his narratives paced and controlled. But he is not committed to the agenda of *miyabi* where symbols help to harmonize troubling psyche impulses. The difference between the two writers is what they demand of their words, based on what they believed words could do. Murasaki never doubts the power of words and other symbols that point to beauty. For her, clothing, fashion, poetry, perfume, a fingertip, the way of seating—all these are symbols that uphold her belief in the possibility of encountering beauty face to face. Beauty's face is not dauntingly abject. Murasaki does not claim that we cannot encounter beauty (in other words, that we cannot successfully desire), just that it has no lasting presence and that, from the point of Buddhism as she interprets it, it is ultimately not a felicitous event.

While Murasaki asks us to suspend our wisdom for the flavor of the moment and anticipate hopefully that the distance between the one who desires and the desirable object can be satisfyingly collapsed, Mishima asserts the necessity of distance between the desiring subject and its object. Thus he insists on a gap between the hope for a meaningful encounter and the actual possibility for that encounter. Mizoguchi says, 'I realized that the problem lay not in trying to shorten the distance between myself and the object, but in maintaining this distance so that the object might remain an object.'[35] This, again, is squarely within Hegelian dialectic, where desire and self-consciousness require that the other remain fully separate in order for each to exist.[36] Mishima comes to this position, I would suggest, because he over-considers the capacity of symbols:

> Still, I do not want to say anything untrue, and there is no doubt that at the sight of her [Kashiwagi's lover's] white breast I was overcome by dizziness. The trouble was that I looked too carefully and too completely, so that what I saw went beyond the stage of being a woman's breast and was gradually transformed into a meaningless fragment.[37]

Mishima, as 'understanding', has tried 'asking of her [Beauty] what [he himself] cannot do,' namely, provide an authentic moment of encounter with one's object of desire. He wishes to put the significance of beauty and one's relationship to it entirely within the discursive field of 'Understanding'. In attempting this immoderate demand, he concludes that such a project loses the capacity to suspend logic (accept the limits of discursive language) when confronting a symbol, a suspension that would allow a representation to feel authentic. It is, in short, a problem (more precisely a critical doubt) of how metaphor works, and how much meaning it can bear. This was something that troubled him from an early age, and is eloquently considered in *Shi o Kaku Shōnen*, 1954.[38] Desirable objects appear to promise something, but Mishima felt that desire could not be satisfied within the universe of words. He looks elsewhere, namely, in the cultivation of physical action, to build his meaning for living. Murasaki's texts, on the other hand, suggest an alternation between the enjoyment of writing and wondering whether it is ultimately meaningful. With Murasaki, her doubts serve to make her language more beautiful, not less credible. Beauty is nurtured by leaving it its secrets. Mishima, on the other hand, seeks to expose its most living sinews, but ends up with a text that is as mysterious as the *Genji*.

SUMMARY REMARKS

Murasaki and Mishima approach beauty as a disturbance to which they respond, and the two authors draw close to one another as they descend the vortex of discourse on desire. Both writers place into their discourse mediations that refer to a 'negative' of some type, and that organize and enhance the presence of eroticism in their texts: an ethics of *miyabi* in the case of Murasaki, while Mishima posits the powerful but unsettling act of betrayal as the relay between insignificant, self-existence, and the potency of beauty. Murasaki's Buddhist 'negative' within her aesthetics both moderates the reach and significance of desire, and expands its meaning on another level to incorporate a notion of suffering. Mishima's 'negative' is more closely allied to the erotic as a fundamental and fundamentally violent force, an interpretation that probably has more to do with European interpretations of eroticism than traditional Japanese ones. His language of eroticism tries to bridge the gap between the sexual body and language by taking squarely as a narrative issue the paradox of the desiring subject's violent reaction to beauty, then mediating this reaction through the structure of transgression and betrayal.

NOTES

The author is an assistant professor in the Department of East Asian Languages and Literature, University of Wisconsin. An earlier version of this article was presented in honor of the retirement of Professor Sidney D. Brown at the Midwest Conference on Asian Affairs held at the University of Western Illinois, Macomb, on 24 September 1994. He wishes to thank the two anonymous readers for their helpful suggestions.

1. Roy Starrs traces this inclination toward taking a destructive relationship with one's object of desire to German nihilism, specifically Nietzsche. See Roy Starrs, *Deadly Dialectics: Sex, Violence and Nihilism in the World of Yukio Mishima*, University of Hawaii Press & Japan Library, Curzon Press, 1994. In the present article I will instead privilege the influence of French literaries in the Baudelaire tradition on Mishima. For an interesting consideration of sexuality in Mishima, see also Susan I. Napier, *Escape from the Wasteland: Romanticism and Realism in the Fiction of Mishima Yukio and Ōe Kenzaburō*, Council on East Asian Studies, Harvard University, 1991.

2. Georges Bataille, *Erotism: Death and Sensuality*, City Lights Books, San Francisco, 1986, pp. 38–39.

3. Bataille, pp. 144–45.

4. Bataille, p. 11.

5. Abe Akio, Akiyama Ken & Imai Gen'e, ed., *Genji Monogatari*, NKBZ 13, Shōgakukan, 1972, p. 247. The translation is slightly modified from Helen Craig McCullough, tr., *Genji & Heike: Selections from The Tale of Genji and The Tale of the Heike*, Stanford U.P., 1994, p. 206.

6. Mishima Yukio, *The Temple of the Golden Pavilion*, Knopf, New York, 1977, p. 11; *Kinkakuji*, in *Mishima Yukio Zenshū*, 10, Shinchōsha, 1973, p. 17.

7. *Golden Pavilion*, p. 21; *Kinkakuji*, p. 27.

8. Richard Bowring, tr., *Murasaki Shikibu: Her Diary and Poetic Memoirs*, Princeton U.P., 1982, p. 95; Fujioka Tadaharu et al., ed., *Izumi Shikibu Nikki, Murasaki Shikibu Nikki,*

Sarashina Nikki, Sanuki no Suke Nikki , NKBZ 18, Shōgakukan, 1971, pp. 205–06.

9. *Golden Pavilion*, p. 48; *Kinkakuji*, p. 55.

10. Aileen Gatten, 'Death and Salvation in *Genji Monogatari*', in Aileen Gatten & Anthony Hood Chambers, ed., *New Leaves: Studies and Translations of Japanese Literature in Honor of Edward Seidensticker*, Center for Japanese Studies, University of Michigan, 1993, p. 8.

11. Gatten, p. 9.

12. Edward Seidensticker, tr., *The Tale of Genji*, Knopf, New York, 1976, p. 719; Abe, NKBZ 15, 1974, pp. 495–96.

13. Abe, NKBZ 16, 1975, p. 11.

14. *Golden Pavilion*, p. 152; *Kinkakuji*, pp. 162–63.

15. *Golden Pavilion*, p. 233; *Kinkakuji*, p. 245.

16. *Golden Pavilion*, p. 144; *Kinkakuji*, p. 154.

17. *Symposium*, 210a–d, quoted in Henry Staten, *Eros in Mourning; Homer to Lacan*, Johns Hopkins U.P., 1995. p. 3.

18. Julia Kristeva, *Revolution in Poetic Language*, Columbia U.P., 1984, p. 26.

19. Kristeva, p. 24.

20. Jin'ichi Konishi, *A History of Japanese Literature: Volume One. The Archaic and Ancient Ages*, Princeton U.P., 1984, pp. 15–16.

21. G. W. F. Hegel, *Phenomenology of Spirit*, Oxford U.P., 1977, p, 19.

22. Hegel, p. 19.

23. See, for example, Mishima Yukio, 'Reimon Radige', 'Raymond Radiguet', in *Zenshū*, 26, 1976, pp. 215–17.

24. Plato, *Phaedrus*, in *Plato I: Euthyphro, Apology, Crito, Phaedo, Phaedrus*, Loeb Classical Library 36, Harvard U.P., 1914, pp. 497 & 499.

25. Irving Singer, *The Nature of Love: I, Plato to Luther*, 2nd ed., University of Chicago Press, 1966, p. 60. See also Plato, *Phaedrus*, pp. 471–505.

26. 'The essential point is that sex was not only a matter of sensation and pleasure, of law and taboo, but also of truth and falsehood, that the truth of sex became something fundamental, useful, or dangerous, precious or formidable: in short, that sex was constituted as a problem of truth.' Michel Foucault, *The History of Sexuality, I, An Introduction*, Vintage Books, Random House, New York, 1990, p. 56.

27. Nakamura Shin'ichirō, *Irogonomi no Kōzō*, Iwanami Shinsho 319, 1985, pp. 112–13.

28. Although we could say that Confucian interest in discipline, and the tension within Confucianism about man's original nature are not so distant from Plato's interest in subduing wayward, base desires.

29. Julia Kristeva, *Proust and the Sense of Time*, Columbia U.P., 1993, p. 41.

30. The comment is made with regard to Georges Bataille's *My Mother*, in Julia Kristeva, *Tales of Love*, Columbia U.P., 1987, p. 366. Kristeva's view derives its theoretical bases from Freud's essay 'On the Universal Tendency to Debasement in the Sphere of Love', in *The Standard Edition of the Complete Psychological Works of Sigmund Freud*, 11, Hogarth Press, London, 1957.

31. Bowring, p. 49; NKBZ 18, pp. 165–66.

32. *Genji & Heike*, pp. 39–40; Abe, NKBZ 12, 1970, p. 125.

33. *Golden Pavilion*, p. 9; *Kinkakuji*, p. 15.

34. *Golden Pavilion*, p. 17; *Kinkakuji*, pp. 23–24.

35. *Golden Pavilion*, p. 102; *Kinkakuji*, p. 110.

36. Hans-Georg Gadamer, 'Hegel's Dialectic of Self-consciousness', in *Hegel's Dialectic: Five Hermeneutical Studies*, Yale U.P., 1976, p. 64.

37. *Golden Pavilion*, pp. 151–52; *Kinkakuji*, p. 162.

38. *Zenshū*, 9, pp. 257–74.

Chronology

Note: Dates are necessarily approximate.

973　　　　　Murasaki Shikibu is born to Fujiwara no Tametoki and his wife, both descendents of the highly distinguished Fujiwara no Fuyutsuga family. Tametoki enjoys only a mediocre career as a provincial governor, but he is also an accomplished poet. Murasaki's great-grandfather, Fujiwara no Kanesuke, was one of the chief *Gosenshō* poets.

　　　　　　Murasaki's mother dies when she is a small child.

　　　　　　Murasaki studies Chinese literature at home, probably taught to her by her father.

996　　　　　Accompanies her father to his government post in Echizen.

998　　　　　Returns to the capital to marry Fujiwara no Nobutaka, her second cousin.

999　　　　　Gives birth to daughter, Kenshi (Kataiko).

1001　　　　Murasaki's husband Nobutaka dies, probably of a plague.

1002–1003　Begins to write *The Tale of Genji*.

1005　　　　Appointed lady-in-waiting to Empress Shōshi, the consort of the Emperor Ichijō. Continues writing *The Tale of Genji*. Parts of the book are circulated and admired by the Court Ladies.

1010   Finishes the *Murasaki Shikibu Diary*.

1011   Emperor Ichijō retires from the throne and dies
              immediately afterward. Empress Shōshi leaves the imperial
              residence, and Murasaki Shikibu moves with her to the
              Biwa Mansion.

1009–1014   Somewhere between these dates Murasaki completes *The
              Tale of Genji*.

1014   Dies on this date or sometime shortly after.

Contributors

HAROLD BLOOM is Sterling Professor of the Humanities at Yale University and Henry W. and Albert A. Berg Professor of English at the New York University Graduate School. He is the author of over 20 books, including *Shelley's Mythmaking* (1959), *The Visionary Company* (1961), *Blake's Apocalypse* (1963), *Yeats* (1970), *A Map of Misreading* (1975), *Kabbalah and Criticism* (1975), *Agon: Toward a Theory of Revisionism* (1982), *The American Religion* (1992), *The Western Canon* (1994), and *Omens of Millennium: The Gnosis of Angels, Dreams, and Resurrection* (1996). *The Anxiety of Influence* (1973) sets forth Professor Bloom's provocative theory of the literary relationships between the great writers and their predecessors. His most recent books include *Shakespeare: The Invention of the Human* (1998), a 1998 National Book Award finalist, *How to Read and Why* (2000), *Genius: A Mosaic of One Hundred Exemplary Creative Minds* (2002), and *Hamlet: Poem Unlimited* (2003). In 1999, Professor Bloom received the prestigious American Academy of Arts and Letters Gold Medal for Criticism, and in 2002 he received the Catalonia International Prize.

DONALD KEENE is Shincho Professor of Japanese Literature and University Professor Emeritus at Columbia University. He is the author of a multivolume history of Japanese literature, of which *Seeds in the Heart* is the first part, and more than thirty other books, including many translations from Japanese literature. He has received numerous honors in both the United States and Japan, and is a member of the American Academy and Institute of Arts and Letters.

DORIS G. BARGEN is an Associate Professor of Japanese at University of Massachusetts at Amherst. She received her Ph.D. in American Studies from Tübingen University (Germany) in 1978. She is the author of *A Woman's Weapon: Spirit Possession in the Tale of Genji* (1997).

RICHARD BOWRING is Professor of Japanese Studies at the University of Cambridge and a Fellow of Downing College.

NORMA FIELD is Professor of East Asian Languages at the University of Chicago. She is also the author of *In the Realm of a Dying Emperor* (1991) and *From My Grandmother's Bedside: Sketches of Postwar Tokyo* (1997).

AMY VLADECK HEINRICH is Director of the C.V. Starr East Asian Library at Columbia University, where she received her Ph.D. She is the author of *Fragments of Rainbows: The Life and Poetry of Saito Mokichi, 1882–1953* (1983) and is the editor of *Currents in Japanese Culture: Translations and Transformations* (1997).

AMANDA MAYER STINCHECUM is a textile historian with a specialty in Japanese and Ryukyuan textiles. She teaches at Long Island University and is a research fellow at the Institute of Okinawan Studies, Hosei University, Tokyo. In addition to writing scholarly articles, she also writes about Asian culture, food, and travel for *Natural History, The New York Times*, and other publications.

IVAN MORRIS received his Ph.D. from the University of London in 1951, and in 1960 he joined Colombia University. He was department chair of the Department of East Asian Languages and Cultures, and he taught at Columbia until his death in 1976. Morris published numerous books on Japanese history, literature, and politics, and produced translations of classical and contemporary Japanese works. He also served as chair of the U.S. section of Amnesty International.

H. RICHARD OKADA is Assistant Professor in the East Asian Studies Department at Princeton University. He is the author of *Figures of Resistance: Language, Poetry, and Narrating in The Tale of Genji and Other Mid-Heian Texts* (1991).

ESPERANZA RAMIREZ-CHRISTENSEN teaches at the University of Michigan in the Department of Asian Languages and Cultures. She is the author of *Heart's Flower: The Life and Poetry of Shinkei* (1994) and is co-editor, with Rebecca L. Copeland, of *The Father-Daughter Plot: Japanese Literary Women and the Law of the Father* (2001).

ROYALL TYLER taught Japanese language and literature for many years at Australia National University. In addition to his translation of *The Tale of Genji* (2001), he is the author of *Japanese Tales* (1987), *The Miracles of the Kasuga Diary*, and *Japanese No Dramas* (1992).

HARUO SHIRANE is Shincho Professor of Japanese Literature at Columbia University. He co-edited the book *Inventing the Classics: Modernity, National Identity, and Japanese Literature* (2000) with Tomi Suzuki. He is also the author of *Traces of Dreams: Landscape, Cultural Memory, and the Poetry of Basho* (1998).

JOHN R. WALLACE is currently a visiting assistant professor at Stanford University. His book *Objects of Discourse: Memoirs of Heian Period Japanese Women Writers* is forthcoming with the Center for Japanese Studies, the University of Michigan.

Bibliography

Bargen, Doris. *A Woman's Weapon: Spirit Possession in the Tale of Genji.* Honolulu: University of Hawai'i Press, 1997.

———."The Search for Things Past in the *Genji monogatari.*" *Harvard Journal of Asiatic Studies* 51, no. 1 (June 1991): 199–232.

Bowring, Richard. *Murasaki Shikibu: "The Tale of Genji."* Cambridge, UK: Cambridge University Press, 1988.

———. *The Diary of Lady Murasaki* London: Penguin Books, 1996.

Childs, Margaret H. "The Voice of Vulnerability: Sexual Coercion and the Nature of Love in Japanese Court Literature." *Journal of Asian Studies* 58, no. 4 (November 1999): 1059–79.

Cramston, Edwin. "Murasaki's Art of Fiction." *Japan Quarterly,* 27 (1971): 207–223.

Dodson, Charles B. "A Different Kind of Hero: *The Tale of Genji* and the American Reader." *No Small World: Visions and Revisions of World Literature.* Ed, Michael Thomas Carroll. Urbana, IL: National Council of Teachers of English, 1996: 179–88.

Field, Norma. *The Splendor of Longing in 'The Tale of Genji.'* Princeton: Princeton University Press, 1987.

Gatten, Aileen. "The Order of the Early Chapters in the *Genji monogatari.*" *Harvard Journal of Asiatic Studies* 41, no.1 (June 1981): 5–46.

————. "Death and Salvation in *Genji Monogatari.*" *New Leaves: Studies and Translations of Japanese Literature in Honor of Edward Seidensticker.* Eds. Aileen Gatten and Anthony Hood Chambers. Ann Arbor: University of Michigan Press, 1993. 5–27.

Goff, Janet. *Noh Drama and "The Tale of Genji."* Princeton: Princeton University Press, 1991.

Keene, Donald. *Seeds in the Heart.* New York: Columbia University Press, 1999.

Hirota, Akiko. "*The Tale of Genji*: From Heian Classic to Heisei Comic." *Journal of Popular Culture* 31, no. 2 (Fall 1997): 29–68.

Inge, M. Thomas. "Lady Murasaki and the Craft of Fiction." *South Atlantic Review* 55, no. 2 (May 1990): 7–14.

Kamens, Edward, ed. *Approaches to Teaching Murasaki Shikibu's "The Tale of Genji."* New York: Modern Language Association, 1993.

Konishi, Jin'ichi. *A History of Japanese Literature, Vol 2, The Early Middle Ages.* Trans. by Aileen Gatten. Princeton: Princeton University Press, 1984.

Mikals-Adachi, Eileen B. "Echoes of the Past: *The Tale of Genji* and Modern Japanese Literature." *South Asian Review* 19, no. 16 (December 1995): 115–21.

Miner, Earl. "Some Thematic and Structural Features of the *Genji Monogatari.*" *Monumenta Nipponica* 24, no. 1 (1969): 1–19.

Morris, Ivan. *The World of the Shining Prince: Court Life in Ancient Japan.* Introduction Barbara Ruch. New York: Kodansha International, 1994.

Nickerson, Peter. "The Meaning of Matrilocality: Kinship, Property, and Politics in Mid-Heian" *Monumenta Nipponica* 48, no. 4 (Winter 1993): 429–67.

Okada, Richard H. *Figures of Resistance: Language, Poetry, and Narrating in "The Tale of Genji" and Other Mid-Heian Texts.* Durham, NC: Duke University Press, 1992.

Pekarik, Andrew, ed. *Ukifune: Love in the Tale of Genji.* New York: Columbia University Press, 1982.

Puette, William J. *Guide to 'The Tale of Genji.'* Rutland, Vermont and Tokyo, Japan: Charles E. Tuttle Co., 1983.

Rowley, G.C. *Yosano Akiko and 'The Tale of Genji.'* Ann Arbor: Center for Japanese Studies, University of Michigan, 2000.

———. "Literary Cannon and National Identity: *The Tale of Genji* in Meiji Japan." *Japan Forum* 9, no.1 (1997): 1–15.

Shirane, Haruo. *Bridge of Dreams: A Poetics of 'The Tale of Genji.'* Stanford, CA: Stanford University Press, 1987.

Stevenson, Barbara and Cynthia Ho, eds. *Crossing the Bridge: Comparative Essays on Medieval and Heian Japanese Women Writers*. New York: Palgrave, 2000.

Stinchecum, Amanda Mayer. "Who Tells the Tale? 'Ukifune': A Study in Narrative Voice." *Monumenta Nipponica* 35, no. 4 (Winter 1980): 375–403.

Tomiko, Yoda. "Fractured Dialogues: *Mono no aware* and Poetic Communication in *The Tale of Genji*." *Harvard Journal of Asiatic Studies* 39, no. 2 (December 1999): 523–57.

Tyler, Royall. "'I am I': Genji and Murasaki." *Monumenta Nipponica*, 54, no. 4 (Winter 1999): 435–80.

———. "Marriage, Rank and Rape in *The Tale of Genji*." *Intersections: Gender, History, and Culture in the Asian Context* (March 2002): 7: 35 paragraphs.

Waithe, Mary Ellen, ed. "Murasaki Shikibu." *A History of Women Philosophers: Medieval, Renaissance and Enlightenment Women Philosophers*, A.D. 500–1600, II. Boston: Kluwer Academic Press, 1989.

Wallace, John R. "Tarrying with the Negative: Aesthetic Vision in Murasaki and Mishima." *Monumenta Nipponica* 52, no. 2 (Summer 1997): 181–99.

Acknowledgements

"*The Tale of Genji*" by Donald Keene. From *Seeds in the Heart.* © 1999 by Donald Keene. Reprinted by permission.

"The Search for Things Past in the *Genji monogatari*" by Doris Bargen. From *Harvard Journal of Asiatic Studies* 51, no. 1 (June 1991): 199-232. © 1991 by Harvard Journal of Asiatic Studies. Reprinted by permission.

"Language and Style" by Richard Bowring. From *Murasaki Shikibu: "The Tale of Genji."* © 1988 by Cambridge University Press. Reprinted with the permission of Cambridge University Press.

"Three Heroines and the Making of the Hero" by Norma Field. From *The Splendor of Longing in 'The Tale of Genji.'* © 1987 by Princeton University Press. Reprinted by permission of Princeton University Press.

"*Blown in Flurries:* The Role of the Poetry in 'Ukifune'" by Amy Vladeck Heinrich. From *Ukifune: Love in the Tale of Genji.* © 1982 by Columbia University Press. Reprinted by permission.

"Who Tells the Tale? 'Ukifune': A Study in Narrative Voice" by Amanda Mayer Stinchecum. From *Monumenta Nipponica* 35, no. 4 (Winter, 1980): 375–403. © 1980 by Sophia University. Reprinted by permission.

"Aspects of 'The Tale of Genji'" by Ivan Morris. From *The World of the Shining Prince: Court Life in Ancient Japan.* © 1964 by Ivan Morris. Used by permission of Alfred A. Knopf, a divison of Random House, Inc.

"Speaking For: Surrogates and *The Tale of Genji*" by H. Richard Okada. From *Crossing the Bridge: Comparative Essays on Medieval and Heian Japanese Women Writers.* © 2000 by Barbara Stevenson and Cynthia Ho. Reprinted by permission of Palgrave Macmillan.

"*The Operation of the Lyrical Mode in the Genji Monogatari*" by Esperanza Ramirez-Christensen. From *Ukifune: Love in the Tale of Genji.* © 1982 by Columbia University Press. Reprinted by permission.

"I am I": Genji and Murasaki by Royall Tyler. From *Monumenta Nipponica,* 54, no. 4 (Winter 1999): 435–80. © 1999 by Sophia University. Reprinted by permission.

"Kingship and Transgression" by Haruo Shirane. From *Bridge of Dreams: A Poetics of 'The Tale of Genji.'* © 1987 by the Board of Trustees of the Leland Stanford Junior University. Reprinted by permission.

"Tarrying with the Negative: Aesthetic Vision in Murasaki and Mishima" by John R. Wallace. From *Monumenta Nipponica* 52, no. 2 (Summer 1997): 181–99. © 1997 by Sophia University. Reprinted by permission.

Index